MANDERLEY
FOREVER

Tatiana de Rosnay

MANDERLEY FOREVER

THE LIFE OF
DAPHNE DU MAURIER

TRANSLATED FROM THE FRENCH BY SAM TAYLOR

ALLEN&UNWIN

First published in Great Britain in 2017 by Allen & Unwin
First published in the United States in 2017 by St Martin's Press
First published in France in 2015 by Édition Albin Michel/Édition Héloïse d'Ormesson
under the title *Manderley for ever*

Allen & Unwin
c/o Atlantic Books
Ormond House
26–27 Boswell Street
London WC1N 3JZ

Phone: 020 7269 1610
Fax: 020 7430 0916

Email: UK@allenandunwin.com
Web: www.allenandunwin.com/uk

A CIP catalogue record for this book is available from the British Library.

Hardback ISBN 978 1 76063 203 8
E-Book ISBN 978 1 76063 880 1

Printed and bound by CPI Group (UK) Ltd, Croydon, CR0 4YY

10 9 8 7 6 5 4 3 2 1

For NJ, LJR, CJR

Contents

❦ *Preface* ❧

When, at the age of eleven, I first opened a copy of *Rebecca,* I had no idea how important that novel would become in my life. Like so many other readers before me, I was transfixed from the first, mythical sentence: *Last night I dreamt I went to Manderley again.* That book had such an effect on me that barely had I finished it before I started reading it again. I was under the spell of the "du Maurier magic," her singular style, that famous psychological suspense. Before *Rebecca* I had already written several short stories—in English, my first language—in my school exercise books. Later, when I wrote other stories, I signed them *Tatiana du Maurier.* It was Daphne du Maurier who bequeathed me my taste (or obsession) for houses, for family secrets, for the memories held by walls. Each and every one of my novels bears her influence.

When, several years ago, Gérard de Cortanze suggested I write the first French biography of my favourite novelist, I felt simultaneously honoured and nervous, but I accepted the challenge. I decided to follow in her foot-steps, as if I were leading an investigation, travelling from London to Cornwall, by way of Montparnasse—because she adored Paris. This liter-ary pilgrimage allowed me to discover how Daphne du Maurier wrote, the secrets of her life, her inspiration, her work.

I described her as if I were filming her, camera on my shoulder, so that my readers could instantly understand who she was. I studied her books, her voice, the look in her eyes, the way she walked, the sound of her laugh-ter. I met and spoke with her children and grandchildren. Around the houses that she loved so passionately I constructed the portrayal of an unusual and enchanting novelist, scorned by critics because she sold mil-lions of books. Her macabre and fascinating world produced a complex, surprisingly dark oeuvre, far removed from the "romantic novelist" she was unfairly labelled as.

This book reads like a novel, but I did not invent any of it. Everything here is true.

It is the novel of a life.

People and things pass away, not places.

—DAPHNE DU MAURIER[1]

PART ONE

LONDON, 1907–25

The child destined to be a writer is vulnerable to every wind that blows.

—Daphne du Maurier[1]

Mayfair, City of Westminster, London
November 2013

There are usually crowds of people in Regent's Park. Visitors come here to walk around and admire the flower beds, see Queen Mary's rose garden, take boat trips on the lake. But on this very British grey and drizzly November morning, the park is deserted.

The Queen was born here; Oscar Wilde lived here, as did Handel, Somerset Maugham, and Nancy Mitford. In place of the previous century's patrician families, the elegant Georgian buildings are now home to luxury stores and fashionable restaurants, embassies, and five-star hotels. Impossible not to notice that the people who live here or frequent these places have money. There are fur coats on display everywhere, while only the priciest, flashiest cars are parked by the side of the road. In Monopoly, Mayfair has been the most desired space on the board for more than eighty years.

To the east of the park are the Terraces, quiet residential streets where rows of identical terraced houses stretch out towards the horizon, perfectly symmetrical. Chester Terrace is the longest, Clarence Terrace the shortest; Park Crescent is formed in a graceful semi-circle. The one I have come to see this morning is the most imposing of all: Cumberland

Terrace. I read that it dates from 1826 and comprises about thirty houses. It is located between the Outer Circle, the street that borders the park, and Albany Street.

It's not especially easy to find. Despite my map, I get lost several times before spotting its neoclassical façade from a distance. I walk through the rain towards it, impressed by its immense size and its famous Wedgwood blue pediment. I daren't move any closer; I feel as if I am being watched. What could I say to one of the building's inhabitants if they came out to ask me why I was taking photographs?

I could say, quite simply, that I am here for her, that I am following the footsteps of her life, and this is where my journey begins. Because it was here, at number 24, under these huge ivory columns, behind that white door, that Daphne du Maurier was born on May 13, 1907.

❧

Leaving the park after going for a walk, the little girl has to pass under that gigantic-seeming arch, then climb the steps that lead to the house, on the right. The white front door matches the cumbersome pram, which Nanny cannot lift up on her own. They have to ring the doorbell so someone will come to help them. The little girl bickers with her sister Angela over who gets to press the copper-coloured button first, and she has to stand on tiptoes in her Start Rite shoes in order to reach it.

Their childminder wears the same uniform, day after day. The little girl likes to look at it: the grey coat, the black hat, the veil covering her face. It is one of the maids who comes out to help Nanny with the baby carriage. She is wearing an apron and a white bonnet. They struggle to lift the pushchair with the baby inside it. From inside the carriage, Jeanne smiles, and the little girl notices the way everyone melts at her pink-cheeked sister's smile.

Inside the long entrance hall, the little girl sees coats, stoles, and capes hung on pegs; she hears the hubbub of a conversation, peals of laughter coming from the living room, to her left; she sniffs out the whiff of an unfamiliar perfume. Her heart contracts. That means there are ladies invited to lunch, that she'll have to go downstairs, later, after the meal in the nursery, to say hello. This does not bother Angela; in fact, she's excited, already asking who is there with their mother. The little girl rushes upstairs, taking the steps two at a time, escaping while she can, and taking refuge in the large nursery on the top floor of the house, in that comforting warmth, near the doll's house, of the toy cupboard with two shelves (one for Angela, one for her), of the treasure chest lined with cotton cloth, of the old armchair that transforms so easily into a shipwreck run aground on a beach. She moves towards the fireplace, where flames crackle behind the fire screen. The table is set for three—Nanny, Angela, and her—because the baby still sits in her high chair to eat. She looks out on Albany Street, towards the army barracks. Nanny's voice is raised and it pursues her, repeating her name several times over. It is telling her to wash her hands before lunch. Daphne doesn't want to wash her hands, she doesn't want to eat lunch. She wants to continue looking out of the window, watching the troop of Life Guards officers as they return from their morning patrol. Her father has explained that this is the oldest regiment in the British Army, its mission to protect the king and the royal buildings. There is no way she is going to miss seeing the glint of their shining armour, the plume of feathers on their helmets, the red lightning flash of uniforms. Since she stopped sleeping with Jeanne and joined her older sister on the other side of the nursery, she is woken at dawn every day by the bugle call, but this doesn't bother her at all.

During the meal, Nanny lectures Daphne about the need to finish her vegetables, and at dessert she orders her to eat every last morsel of her rice pudding. Daphne does not like rice pudding. Why must she always do what Nanny tells her? Because she's only a four-year-old girl? And yet she likes Nanny; she sees her more often than she sees her own mother.

After lunch, the dreaded moment arrives. Nanny rubs Daphne's face clean, brushes her hair. Angela admires herself in the mirror. The sisters wear identical embroidered mauve velvet dresses and pale pink pelisses; even the baby is dressed to match. They must walk downstairs, open the door of the dining room, and they must smile, in front of that sea of strange faces. Why doesn't Angela suffer during this ordeal? Murmurs of approval. The ladies are elegant, they wear large hats. Mummy too. Daphne finds this odd: How can anyone eat lunch while wearing such a big hat? Nanny hands the baby to their mother; the baby gurgles, and everyone coos over her. Daphne wants to run away, back to the nursery; she hides behind Angela, who is prancing around in her velvet dress in front of the ladies. Their mother gives the baby lumps of sugar. When the ladies all stand up to move through into the living room, Daphne finds them too tall, too fat; they laugh too loud, cackling like hens, and not only that, but they all want to kiss her. It's horrible. She hates it. Angela puts up with the kissing gracefully (how can she?), but not her, no way, no kissing. She scowls, bites her fingernails. The ladies laugh—they think she's shy and sweet—but they notice the nail chewing, the naughty little thing. Her mother shoots her a reproachful look. *We've tried everything with Daphne's fingernails.* . . . Thankfully, no one is paying any attention to her now; she is free to go back upstairs at last. It's over. Until the next time.

She loves this view over the roofs of the city. Look, down there, that house painted red: Why is it red? Who lives there? How can she find out? It looks like that house is not friends with the house next to it; it's different, separate. Daphne imagines living there, all alone. In that red house, no one would force her to finish her vegetables or her rice pudding, no one would order her to put on embroidered velvet dresses, no one would make her go downstairs to say hello to the guests. She would have a sword, like Peter Pan, whom she admires so much. She would love to be able to fly like him, over the chimneys.

It's already time for lessons with Mrs. Torrance, the governess. Angela, who is three years older than Daphne, is far ahead of her. Daphne struggles with her capital letters. Why isn't she able to master her Ss? She tries as hard as she can, leaning over the table, tongue between her teeth. *You're making lots of progress, Daphne; that's very good. Have you written before?* Daphne sits up proudly and gives the governess a haughty look. Yes, she has already written a book. Angela bursts out laughing, and says that Daphne can hardly write at all, she's talking nonsense, she's only four. Mrs. Torrance asks her, in a serious voice, what the title of her book is. Daphne replies, "*John in the Wood of the World.*" Deep down inside, Daphne knows that she is not telling the truth, that she has not written a book, that she just made up that strange-sounding title. The governess understands; kindly, good-naturedly, she smiles at the little girl. Daphne starts work on her capital letters again. Silence falls in the nursery. There is no sound but the crackling of flames in the hearth. Time passes slowly. She looks up at the window and starts to daydream.

Peter Pan is there, hidden behind the shutter. He's come to fetch her, to take her to Neverland. Her, and no one else.

❧

One day, Nanny leaves. The little girl asks her mother why. It's because Jeanne is no longer a little baby, Angela is nearly nine, and Daphne will be six. They're big girls now; they don't need Nanny anymore. Daphne looks at Nanny, who is going away forever. Why are her eyes red? What is she doing with her handkerchief? She looks like she's crying. Daphne is surprised: she didn't know grown-ups cried, too. After Nanny, there is a succession of nurses that Daphne doesn't like: a fat one who spends all her time eating snacks, another who hums annoying tunes, and yet another who scolds them constantly from morning till night. The walks in Regent's Park last longer nowadays: they are no longer simple strolls along Broad Walk to the zoo, where little Jeanne gets excited at seeing the wild animals. Sometimes, they go around the lake. Daphne's father tells her that a long time ago, before he was born, a tragic accident occurred here during one exceptionally severe winter. Back then, he explains, Londoners adored ice-skating. Despite being warned, hundreds of skaters went out onto the frozen lake. But the ice was too thin, and it cracked. Horrified, Daphne sees the tragic scene unfold as she listens to her father. She seems to hear the fatal creak and snap of the ice, the screams of fear. The skaters were wearing heavy Victorian clothes (wide, frilly skirts and thick, elegant fur coats, her father specifies) and it was difficult to fish the victims' corpses out. About forty people drowned. Daphne can't help thinking about this every time they walk around the lake, one hand resting on Jeanne's pushchair.

One of the nurses prefers a large, private garden surrounded by a fence. They have to use a key to get in. The nurse meets up with her friends there, and they sit under cover with a Thermos of hot chocolate and some cakes and talk in low voices. The children are urged to play elsewhere, except for Jeanne, who stays close to them in her pushchair. Daphne thinks this unfair. She wants to stay under the roof and eat cakes, too. The nurse orders her to go farther off and enjoy herself. Daphne sulks, walking slowly down a path. There's no one here to play with, and Angela's having a lesson with Mrs. Torrance. Where have the other children gone? Suddenly Daphne sees that boy. Older than her, at least seven, maybe eight, blond hair cut very short, light-coloured eyes, looking like a bit of a thug. She doesn't like him at all; she's seen him before at the park. He goes up to her and kicks her. She doesn't say a word. She's not going to cry in front of him. *You're the little Frenchy, aren't you? Little French idiot.* She doesn't flinch. *Go on; tell me your name. What's your name, Frenchy?* Another kick. She mumbles her first name. *Your surname, you stupid girl!* She stands up straight, looks him in the eye, and pronounces her full name. *What did I tell you? That's French, that is, du Maurier. Stupid Frenchy!* Another boy appears, smaller, but looking just as mean. *You're going to listen to us now, Frenchy. We're going to leave and you're going to stay here. If you move, you'll regret it.* They walk away, sniggering. Daphne stands motionless, like a statue. How can she escape? Who could help her? The nurses are far off, at the other end of the garden. She doesn't dare move a muscle, staying exactly where she is, numb, freezing, trembling with fear. After an eternity, the boys return. *You moved, Frenchy. We were watching. We saw you.* She denies this, but they start laughing, nastily, and the kicks rain down on her again. This time she doesn't just take it; she kicks back at them. Her bonnet is askew, she's out of breath, her cheeks are red, she's hot. How stupid it is to wear a dress, to be a girl, not to be able to lift her leg up like a boy in trousers.

Back at Cumberland Terrace, she is still trembling. That night, at bedtime, the nurse gasps when she sees Daphne's bruises. Daphne says nothing. She doesn't want to talk about those boys. The blond-haired one is her enemy, her worst enemy. She has to watch out for him, always be on her guard. But there is one thing she doesn't understand. Why did he call her Frenchy? Is du Maurier really a French name? She decides to talk to Daddy about it. She asks him the question later, in the living room, when she's sitting on his lap in front of the fireplace. Her father always smells nice; he is elegant, his blue eyes sparkle. He tells her that du Maurier is indeed a French name. His father, Daphne's grandfather, was born in Paris. He was a great artist and a great writer, but he died before she could get to know him, alas. Daddy will show her his father's drawings and his books. The look in Daddy's eyes turns thoughtful. Paris is one of the most beautiful cities in the world, she'll see. Daphne must never forget that she is one-fourth French and she should be proud of it. She feels reassured. She trusts Daddy; he's always right. She doesn't care about her enemy. *He* doesn't have a famous grandfather.

Her father teaches her to pronounce their name correctly: she must say *du Maurier,* not *dou Maurier.* A sharp *u,* very French. As he strokes her hair, her father whispers that one day Daphne will learn to speak French fluently like her grandfather. He himself speaks it with an awful English accent. But he is certain, he knows for sure, that Daphne will speak it perfectly; she will be the most French of all his daughters. Sitting on her father's lap, Daphne starts daydreaming about this grandfather she never knew, a writer, an artist, born in the most beautiful city in the world.

~❧~

One winter morning, in the nursery, the black letters on the white page soar up and come to life. Amazed, Daphne starts deciphering word after word: she can read on her own, in her head. She devours the books of Beatrix Potter, fascinated by the adventures of Peter Rabbit. What a bore to have to go and eat dinner when she is dying to find out what the terrifying Mr. McGregor will do! How can she leave Tom Kitten and Mrs. Tiggy-Winkle? Daphne has to explain to the nurse that what happens next in the story of Jeremy Fisher is far more important than taking her bath.

One story frightens her, even more than her blond enemy from the park. *The Snow Queen.* She is paralyzed with fear by the evil monarch who takes little Kay in her sleigh of ice, and by that shattered mirror, whose tiny splinters get stuck in the little boy's heart and eyes. Thankfully, brave Gerda goes off to save him. Daphne is so frightened by this tale that one night, when she sees her mother climbing the staircase, she seems to have the beautiful and terrifying face of the evil queen. And yet Mummy is gentle and kind. Why is it only with her father that Daphne feels such a strong attachment? Why does she want to be with him all the time? He often watches her, proudly. He watches his two other daughters as well, but there is a special relationship between Daddy and her, a connection she could never describe, a strong and almost secret connection, and she knows that Mummy has noticed it.

In the mornings, Daphne and her sisters have to be careful not to make noise in the nursery, as their parents' bedroom is just below. Daddy gets back late from the theatre, never before midnight. And then he has to eat supper, so he doesn't go to bed until two in the morning at the earliest. Daddy can't bear noise, especially not the racket made by children laughing and jumping about. He doesn't like the sound of a dog's bark either, or a car engine backfiring, or a bird singing too loudly in the park. While she waits, Daphne reads. When she gets up, she walks on tiptoes, and so does Angela. They have to wait for the maid to take Daddy's breakfast to him in

LIBRARY IRELAND WEEK

2018

november 26th - December 2nd

Librarians Transforming Lives

ww.libraryassociation.ie

#LIW2018

 The LIBRARY ASSOCIATION of IRELAND
Cumann Leabharlann na hÉireann | Representing
librarians and libraries
in Ireland

A trained Librarian is a powerful search engine with a heart.

bed. Her footstep on the stairs, her cheerful *Good morning, sir*: these are the signals that the girls can go and say hello to their father. He wears a green bathrobe over his silk pyjamas, and Daphne loves the pleasant scent that floats around him. Daddy is never in a bad mood. She once got her bottom spanked, when she stuck her tongue out at Nanny, but that was a long time ago.

Daphne's father is an actor. Every evening, he plays at being someone else, at the theatre. To begin with, she doesn't understand what this means: How can Daddy transform himself? It is only when she sees him onstage for the first time, in makeup and costume, that she grasps his mystery: Daddy is capable of being pompous Mr. Darling one moment and becoming scary Captain Hook the next. How does he manage to change his voice, his expressions, his mannerisms, even the way he walks, to such an extent? She is fond of the dusty smell of the theatre, the bar she must push on the heavy door that leads backstage, the kindly stage manager, Bob, with his friendly winks. She enjoys watching these shadowy figures at work in the wings, the light show, the shifting backdrops, the last-minute details, the concentration in the eyes of Poole, the red-faced costumer who helps her father change his clothes. She never misses the chance to watch her father removing his makeup after the play is over. Daddy's work is not like other people's work. Her friends have daddies who go to the office each morning. Hers goes to the theatre each evening. The theatre is his life.

Mummy tells her daughters that she too, was an actress when she was younger. That was how she met Gerald, in 1902, when they were acting in the same play, *The Admirable Crichton*. Daddy was playing the role of Ernest Woolley, while Mummy was Lady Agatha. The man who wrote it would become a very close friend of theirs: James Matthew Barrie, known as Uncle Jim, the author of *Peter Pan*. Daphne has seen a photograph of Mummy in that role: she was a beauty back then, with her thick dark hair in a bun and her eyes accentuated by eye shadow and mascara. In the play, they fell in love, and in real life, too. Mummy's name was Muriel Beaumont, her maiden name and her stage name. She took to the stage very young, but she decided to stop acting after her wedding. Angela asked her why, and Daphne could guess what her response would be. She had already understood that there was only a place for one actor in the du Maurier clan, one person only who would shine, one person only who would call the shots at Cumberland Terrace.

Gerald gets bored easily. He needs to be entertained; he needs a court. He likes to be applauded, admired, and Muriel knows exactly how to look after him, his house, his well-being, how to ensure he gets enough rest, the right meals, his afternoon nap. She invites lots of people, organizes outings, parties. She is the one who prepares his supper, in her bathrobe, late at night, when he comes home from the theatre, starving; what he likes best is bacon and eggs, even at one in the morning. Everything revolves around Daphne's father, and apparently it has been this way since he was born. When Daddy was a little boy, he was the favourite son of the du Maurier family, the last of five siblings, and his mother called him "ewee lamb." Daphne finds it hard to imagine "Big Granny"—serious-faced, imposing, always dressed in black—whispering "ewee lamb" to Daddy.

Every day, Daphne's father gets up late, in no rush, and the household waits on him hand and foot. He takes his time choosing his shoes, his suit, and then goes off to the theatre for rehearsals. He has lunch at the Garrick Club, not far from Leicester Square, and in late afternoon—before taking his quick nap, before the curtain rises—he returns to the house and always gives his daughters a hug in the nursery, a cigarette perpetually between his lips. Daphne looks forward impatiently to Daddy's arrival. This is the hour of games and tales, and her father is funny, sparkling: he makes them howl with laughter when he imitates the next-door neighbour with her stiff-backed gait, her pouty fish lips, the way she holds her umbrella. He adores making fun of other people behind their backs, while being perfectly polite to their faces. Daddy is skilful, creative; with his help, the girls start to invent a personal jargon, a sort of code that they add to little by little, and which enables them to communicate without anyone else being able to guess what they're really talking about. Sitting on a "hard chair,"* "see-me,"* "tell-him,"* all have other meanings. Daddy encourages them to put on plays at home. He watches enthusiastically, applauds them, calls Muriel over so she can encourage them, too. Daphne always insists on being given the role of a boy. No way will she play a girl. Angela prefers to remain a girl. Besides, with her curves, it would be difficult for Angela to pass for a boy. How boring, to be a girl. Wouldn't Daddy have preferred a boy? Daphne is sure of one thing: she would have made an excellent son.

One summer evening, Daddy turns up at the nursery along with a small man with intense eyes, a high forehead, and a big black moustache: the famous J. M. Barrie, the man who created *Peter Pan,* the author of several plays starring their father. Uncle Jim speaks with a rough Scottish accent. He is the legal guardian of their five cousins, the Llewelyn Davies boys, the sons of their aunt Sylvia, Daddy's favourite sister. Daphne does not remember Aunt Sylvia, who died tragically of cancer when Daphne was only three. She doesn't remember her uncle Arthur either, Sylvia's husband, who also died of cancer, a few years before his wife. All Daphne knows is that Barrie adopted the five orphans and he is now raising them himself. It was for them that Uncle Jim invented *Peter Pan,* the adventure of a boy who didn't want to grow up. The handsome and charming George, Jack, Peter, Michael, and Nico were his inspiration for the Lost Boys.

Sitting by the fire in the nursery, Uncle Jim asks the girls to perform his own play, *Peter Pan.* They know it by heart, performing it almost every night for their own pleasure, but they never tire of it. They are even capable of singing him the musical opening. Of course, Daddy will play both Captain Hook and Mr. Darling, as he's done so brilliantly onstage many times. Angela plays Wendy and Mrs. Darling. Jeanne takes the roles of Tinker Bell and Tiger Lily. Daphne does all she can to make sure she plays Peter Pan; no way is she letting either of her sisters take "her" Peter! They leap from chair to chair, pretend to fly, wriggle on the floor in imitation of swimming mermaids, mimic perfectly the tick-tock of the crocodile that frightens Captain Hook so badly. It's such a success that Gerald insists his daughters put on their plays for guests downstairs, in the living room. Daphne understands why her father loves becoming someone else: it's true, she thinks, how intoxicating it is to put on a costume and change one's appearance. She no longer feels shy at all when she acts in front of her parents' friends. Mrs. Torrance, the governess, helps the sisters to rehearse. The guests clap and cheer. And what if life was, ultimately, about pretending? For Daphne's father, this seems to be exactly the case, and he does it with such ease that she wonders if she might not manage it, too. As well as ridding herself of her shyness, she could, at last, be something more than a mere girl. She could become a boy.

Gerald looks so handsome in his makeup; she loves to watch him on-stage in his various roles, season after season: Arsène Lupin, elegant and cunning, the audacious Raffles, Hubert Ware, sinisterly attractive, and Jimmy Valentine, the safecracker with the eventful life. Daphne notices the way the girls in the audience devour her father with their eyes. They seem to be in a trance from the moment he appears; they breathe differently, faster, as if they are in love with him.

One day, Daphne gets some sense of Daddy's aura. It is Angela's tenth birthday, and Gerald takes the family to lunch at the Piccadilly Hotel. On the pavement in front of the building, two passersby turn around. They look excited, thrilled. Inside the restaurant, it's the same story: the insistent stares, the complicit smiles. Daphne reads their surname on everyone's lips. *Du Maurier. Du Maurier.* She watches her father while he chooses his meal, the wine, while he leans down to reply to little Jeanne. Gerald is not really handsome, with his long, thin face and his large ears, but he has a godlike radiance that attracts the gaze of everyone near him. She observes the waiters' obsequiousness, the bowing and scraping of the hotel manager who comes out to greet them, and, all the way through their lunch, the eyes of the other customers turned towards her father. Daphne is only seven, but for the first time she realizes how famous her father is, and how famous, too, is her French-sounding surname.

❦

There is a word that sounds constantly in the mouths of the grown-ups, a word that Daphne dislikes. It is short and hard. It is the word "war." They say it every day. Since when? She can't remember, but she understands that something serious is happening in the outside world, far from Regent's Park, far from this city where she was born. This word is like a cloud moving towards her, casting a shadow over her tranquil life. On the face of it, nothing changes: the walks in the park, the games, the reading, the meals, the lessons with Mrs. Torrance. What changes is the expression on the adults' faces. It looks like fear. But why are they afraid? And why do people hate the Germans so much? What have they done? Around the table, during meals, with cousins, uncles, and aunts, everyone vehemently criticizes the Germans. She has to come to their defence. One evening, Daphne takes advantage of a pause in the lively conversation to proclaim in a loud, clear voice that she, personally, likes the Germans and that it would be wonderful if a German could come to tea at their house. All eyes turn to her. Icy silence. Muriel's face is red as a brick. *You stupid little girl, how dare you talk about things you don't understand?* Daphne falls silent, stares at her plate. The conversation resumes, the subject changes. She feels ashamed. But behind her embarrassment, she feels a new sense of pride. Because she has made the grown-ups notice her.

Soldiers appear all over the neighbourhood. Daphne sees them each time she goes for a walk with the nurse. They are dressed in khaki uniforms, marching proudly along Albany Street, across Regent's Park. The passersby applaud them, wave at them. One morning, the family accompanies Uncle Guy—Gerald's older brother—to Waterloo train station. The platform is crowded with people. Uncle Guy is going off to war. She doesn't know where the war is, but she notices the sadness in her father's eyes, the sorrow and the fear, too. Big Granny's face crumples when she embraces her son the soldier for the last time. When the train has left the station, when Uncle Guy's waving hand can no longer be seen, Big Granny suddenly collapses on the ground. Daphne sees her dress and her cape spreading out beneath her like a huge black flower, her hat tipped sideways to reveal her white hair. Gerald and Muriel rush over, they fetch her a glass of water, and Big Granny regains consciousness, but the tears roll ceaselessly over her wrinkled cheeks.

The sadness stains each passing day. Big Granny falls sick and dies a few months later. Daphne's cousin George, the eldest of the Llewelyn Davies boys, dies at the front. He was only twenty-one. And then there is that day in March, even darker, when, climbing the staircase in Cumberland Terrace, Daphne sees her sister standing outside her parents' room, her eyes swollen and full of tears. Between sobs, Angela whispers that Uncle Guy has been killed, Daddy is inconsolable.

Daphne has to wear a black armband around her left arm. In the park, she is not the only child with an armband, but she is one of the few to have lost two members of her family; three, if you count her grandmother. The only thing that brightens up her days is the arrival of Jock, their first dog, a Westie. Jock likes Daphne more than her sisters—she is his mistress—and this makes her very proud. When she runs with him in the park, she becomes once again the carefree little girl she used to be; she forgets the war, the dead, the sadness of adults. She forgets her black armband.

The conflict rages, but in a family of actors the show must go on. Gerald performs to packed houses. The sisters' allegorical plays in the nursery take on more importance. Daphne deigns to play a girl only if she is heroic and wears armour, like Joan of Arc. For *The Three Musketeers* Angela is Athos, Jeanne is Aramis, and Daphne takes the role of the bold d'Artagnan. Nobody wants to get stuck with gormless Porthos. *Treasure Island* becomes a favourite, with Daphne as Long John Silver or Jim Hawkins. They are inspired by William Harrison Ainsworth's historical novels for children, gripping and stuffed full of fascinating details. It is Daphne who leads her sisters into her imaginary world, Daphne who hands out roles and directs scenes. Angela and Jeanne submit to her initiatives, but when Angela grows older and becomes more interested in her friends and in birthday parties Jeanne proves herself willing to take on any role her sister assigns her, never complains, and dies divinely at the hands of Daphne, dressed as an executioner with a bloody axe.

One October morning, when Daphne returns from a walk in the park with her sisters, Daddy is waiting for them, a smile on his lips. He spins Jeanne around like a top and, in a singing voice, announces that he has a surprise for his daughters. Daphne wants to know what it is. She pulls at his sleeve. The family is going to move to a new house. The girls are not babies anymore—they are twelve, nine, and five years old—so farewell Cumberland Terrace, Albany Street, Regent's Park, farewell the nursery on the top floor. The girls are ecstatic, they jump up and down and applaud. But where is this house? Gerald looks dreamy, almost at peace. Their new house is large, beautiful, and it is located close to the place where he grew up. Its name is Cannon Hall.

Cannon Hall, Hampstead, London
November 2013

As I emerge from Hampstead tube station, in the north of London, the first thing that comes to my mind is that I have been here before: I came when I was a teenager, to visit the house of the poet John Keats, on Primrose Hill. Hampstead hasn't changed at all; with its narrow, sloping, tree-lined streets it is identical to the place in my memory. It feels like being in a small village, in spite of the signs for hip stores and restaurants that have opened up along Heath Street. There are few apartment buildings here; it's mostly houses with gardens. I have read that it was in Hampstead, in the nineteenth century, that a community of avant-garde intellectuals was formed. The area still retains that bohemian-bourgeois atmosphere. Sigmund Freud, Agatha Christie, Liz Taylor, and Elton John all lived here. But Hampstead would not be so attractive, so sought-after, were it not for its park, known as the Heath, one of the largest in London, with a magnificent view of the capital. There are three open-air swimming pools, former drinking-water reservoirs, one of them a ladies' pond. Marx liked to walk these rolling paths with Engels. A scene from the film *Notting Hill*, starring Hugh Grant and Julia Roberts, was shot on the Heath.

Hampstead is built on a hill. The streets are calm, silent, the houses charming in their elegant gardens. One must climb and climb to reach the edge of the Heath. I have no trouble locating Cannon Place: it is accessible via the long, steep street of Christchurch Hill. I feel a strange emotion as I look at Cannon Hall for the first time. Situated at number 14 Cannon Place, it is a large, austere redbrick house in a Georgian style, purchased by Daphne's father in 1916. It was constructed in 1710; George III's personal physician lived here. Set back from a cobblestone courtyard with a fountain, it seems to hide behind its black gates and is surrounded by a high wall made of the same brick , encircling a vast garden. A round blue plaque is attached to the façade, announcing that the actor Gerald du Maurier, who was born in 1873 and died in 1934, lived in Cannon Hall from 1916 until his death. I approach the house and the wall to take photos. A woman watches me from a second-floor window. How many of us are there, I wonder, who come to Hampstead on a pilgrimage, following in the footsteps of a famous and enigmatic novelist?

❦

Daphne already loves her new abode, much more spacious than Cumberland Terrace. The entrance hall is impressive, with its black-and-white checkerboard tiles, its marble fireplace, and the stately staircase covered with a red-and-gold carpet. The furniture and paintings bought by her parents are more spectacular than any she has seen before. On the wall above the staircase is a beautiful but sad profile of King Charles, a portrait of Elizabeth I, and a battle scene, fascinating when studied up close, with all sorts of gory details. Daphne counts four reception areas, eight bedrooms, four bathrooms, not forgetting an entire floor for the servants. There is space for three cars in the garage. And then there is the garden—a garden just for them, with a veranda, two greenhouses, an immense lawn, an orchard, and a tennis court. No need to put on her coat and hat to go and play outside anymore. The girls are intrigued by a rusty old locked gate on the other side of the brick wall, on Cannon Lane. Behind this, Gerald tells them, is an old cell constructed inside the wall itself, and it was here, in the previous century, that prisoners were locked up on a straw bed before being taken to court. Often, Daphne thinks about the sleepless nights those prisoners must have spent in this secret dungeon with its barred windows, hidden inside the thickness of the wall.

There are three different ways of getting into the games room. Daphne and Jeanne have fun running like mad through the long hallways, rushing up the main stairway, then hurtling down the other stairways, until the shouts of their parents put an end to their stampede. But they always start up again, to the despair of Dorothy, the young maid tasked with looking after them; there is no longer a nurse to watch over the three sisters. The new house provides the ideal stage to continue their theatrical performances. This time, it's Shakespeare. Daphne plays Prince Hal, who tramples on poor Hotspur, acted by Jeanne, incapable of saying no to her sister. Daphne is Macbeth, Daphne is Othello, while Jeanne is Desdemona, suffocated by her jealous husband. Angela condescends to take the role of Titania, queen of the fairies. Gerald takes part in these Shakespearian plays. He is capable of quoting interminable monologues. Well, he is an actor, after all! After a while, Daddy gives up on Shakespeare, takes his daughters out to the garden, and teaches them to play cricket. Muriel is worried that this might damage the beautiful lawn. Frowning, she watches them through the window. Gerald gives his daughters boxing gloves. Angela pouts at this. What a strange present; boxing is for boys! Daddy ignores his eldest daughter and explains to the two younger ones how to box without getting hurt. Daphne is in seventh heaven and shows her father what a perfect boy she can be in spite of the girlish appearance that annoys her so much. Why is she so delicate, slender, blonde? Why are her eyes so blue (lavender blue, apparently) with such long lashes?

Since the family moved to Cannon Hall in that spring of 1916, Gerald has grown nostalgic. He wanted his children to live in the place where he spent his idyllic, pampered childhood with his parents, and in particular with his father. Daddy talks about him all the time: George du Maurier. Daphne gets the impression that the history of Muriel's family, the Beaumonts, is of no—or certainly less—interest to Daddy. Why? In the Beaumont family, Daphne knows, her uncle Willie runs a famous magazine, *The Bystander*, read by the most elegant ladies. Perhaps Daddy is less interested in his in-laws because there are no actors in their family? The girls' other grandfather, who came from East Anglia, was a notary in his youth, but his company went bankrupt and he lost almost his entire fortune. The Beaumonts are not as rich as the du Mauriers, as Daphne is quick to realize. The Beaumont grandparents' modest house on Woodstock Avenue has none of the grandeur of Cannon Hall, and when she stays there Daphne has to share a room with her aunt Billy, Mummy's sister. Not that this bothers Daphne; on the contrary, she enjoys the cozy atmosphere of this house. Her "Little Granny" does the cooking herself. There are no servants, as there are at Cannon Hall, and on Saturday mornings Daphne accompanies her grandmother when she goes grocery shopping in Golders Green, near Hampstead, then helps her knead the dough before the house is filled with the wonderful smell of freshly baked bread.

Every month, come rain or shine, Gerald takes his daughters on a pilgrimage to New Grove House, where he grew up. The house is occupied by other people now, so they can't go inside, but Daddy insists on telling them all about the façade. *That downstairs window is where your grandfather had his studio. He would draw there every day, and he didn't mind if we played while he worked.* Through Gerald's words, Daphne builds a strong impression of her grandfather: a good, gentle man, a man who loved his family, and whose family loved him. Once, Gerald tells them, when a dog was drowning in a pond on the Heath, their grandfather jumped right in to rescue it. The next stage of the pilgrimage takes place on the Heath, at the base of a tall tree. Gerald always sits in the same spot, in the hollow of a branch. *This is where I used to come with my father when I was your age, and the two of us would sit up here.* Afterwards, he goes to the cemetery at the bottom of the hill, next to the church, where his parents and his sister Sylvia are buried, and where there is a memorial for Uncle Guy. Daphne likes the peacefulness of this place, but she thinks her father spends too much time here, and his face takes on a melancholic expression that pains her. She prefers sitting in Daddy's study to look at the photographs of her grandfather, at all his drawings and books. She is now able to recognize the face of that relative she never knew, his fine features, his straight nose, his little goatee. Daddy shows her a very old glass tumbler, the family's lucky charm, which he guards jealously in his desk, inside a worn leather case, and removes only at Christmas. He touches the glass ritually before every premiere in order to ward off bad luck. It was given to him by Kicky, his father. Gerald tells his daughters the story of his paternal family, the Bussons du Maurier, and when he speaks about this his eyes seem to shine with satisfaction at belonging to this clan; and he makes them, too, feel proud to bear the family name. Their grandfather's father was named Louis-Mathurin. He was part-French, the son of émigrés from the French Revolution, from a great aristocratic family of glassblowers, originally from Sarthe, who had a château, lands, a factory. But it all burned down during the revolution, and the family lost everything.

Listening to her father, Daphne finds this tale almost too novel-like. Is it possible Daddy is embroidering the facts, exaggerating? Quite possibly: he's an actor after all, and actors exaggerate everything, as she is beginning to understand. What is true, however, what cannot be denied, is that French blood flows through her veins. Her grandfather was born in Paris, in a second-floor apartment on the Avenue des Champs-Élysées, at number 80. His mother was Ellen Clarke, an Englishwoman. Louis-Mathurin and Ellen were married at the British embassy, a handsome building on Rue du

Faubourg–Saint-Honoré with a private garden. Her ancestor's full name stirs something in Daphne: George Louis Palmella Busson du Maurier, although he was known simply as Kicky. Why Kicky? she asks. Because he was given that nickname by a Flemish nurse, inspired by the *Manneken-Pis,* the statue in Brussels of a little boy peeing, and the name stuck. His younger brother, Alexandre Eugène, born two years after him, was nicknamed Gygy. The du Maurier family lived in Paris, on Rue de Passy, at the corner of Rue de la Pompe, in the 16th arrondissement. Kicky and Gygy would play near the Auteuil pond, catching tadpoles, and in winter they would skate on the lake in the Bois de Boulogne and eat roasted chestnuts. It was a radiant Parisian childhood, despite the family's financial difficulties. The father of Kicky, Gygy, and their little sister, Isobel, was an inventor of genius, according to Daddy. Louis-Mathurin had a superb voice—and Kicky inherited that extraordinary musical range—but he was also a man of ideas. He invented portable lamps, and he attempted all sorts of scientific experiments in his laboratory in the Poissonnière neighbourhood, but alas, no one believed in him, no one wanted to invest in his inventions, and he never had enough money to bring them to fruition.

Daphne always looks forward to these privileged moments on the second floor of Cannon Hall, when Gerald—sitting by the fire with a cup of tea and a cigarette—would tell stories about his father's childhood. At the age of seventeen, Kicky failed his exams, the famous baccalaureat. All he enjoyed was reading and drawing. His specialty was sketching caustic, funny family portraits, executed in three pencil strokes. Under pressure from his parents, Kicky moved to London to study science in a laboratory. Daphne feels the pain Kicky must have felt at being torn away from his beloved Paris; she feels his homesickness, exiled in London with its grey skies and thick fogs. Listening, captivated, Daphne falls under the charm of a city she has not yet seen; just like her grandfather, she yearns to devour a piece of cheese with a still-warm baguette, to taste a cup of chicory, to stroll along the embankment near Notre-Dame. Like Kicky, she dreams of Paris at night, understands why he feels more French than English: after all, wasn't he born in the City of Light? Weren't his ancestors French aristocrats of a noble lineage? His parents became alarmed: What is Kicky doing, daydreaming all day long instead of concentrating on his scientific studies? The girl guesses the reason: Kicky wants to return to Paris! After the death of his father, a few years later, the young man goes back to the city he loves so much. He is twenty-two. In the meantime, Gerald explains, Paris has changed: the prefect Haussmann has left his mark, the man nicknamed the Attila of the Straight Line or the Ripper Baron, the man who modernized Paris with the construction of long, rectilinear boulevards. Kicky no longer recognizes his medieval Paris with its damp, twisting alleys. But who cares? He makes friends; he feels happy; he takes art classes in Montparnasse, on Rue Notre-Dame-des-Champs. Life is beautiful.

One day, Daphne will go to Paris. She makes this promise to herself. She will see all those places with her own eyes; she will be the first du Maurier to follow in the footsteps of her grandfather.

❦

One new element in Angela's and Daphne's lives is the school where they go each day, in Oak Hill Park. Gerald has very specific ideas about his daughters' education. For him, the most important subjects are art, music, French, and literature. To this must be added algebra, alas, a subject loved by no one in the du Maurier family. To reach the school, the girls must walk, alone, down a deserted path. They are big girls now—thirteen and ten—and their parents have decided they no longer need to be chaperoned. One morning, a soldier in his blue uniform is lurking on the path. He is wounded: his leg is in plaster. Daphne pays no attention to him, but her sister, more fearful, thinks him suspicious. As the two girls pass, the soldier unbuttons his trousers and exposes himself. Angela runs off at top speed, and Daphne follows her, though she doesn't understand why, and her elder sister is too shocked to explain.

Angela works harder than her sister, receives better grades. In the end, Daphne starts imitating Muriel's signature on the weekly report in her notebook, which she is supposed to show to her parents. Miss Druce, her teacher, eventually notices that Mrs. du Maurier's signature never looks the same. She hands the notebook to her student and asks, *Daphne, did your mother sign this?* Daphne replies, without batting an eyelid, that it wasn't her mother, but her. *But don't you realize, my child, how dishonest that is?*

It's forgery! Did you know that people go to prison for that? No, Daphne didn't know. She won't do it again. It's not really so important, after all. The most important thing is to make friends at Oak Hill Park, to have fun, to forget the war.

One morning, Miss Druce makes a solemn announcement to her students: Daphne du Maurier has written an excellent essay, by far the best. Unfortunately, her handwriting and spelling are atrocious. Consequently, Daphne is not top of the class; she is beaten by another girl. Daphne smiles to herself: Who cares about being top of the class? She was the one who wrote the best essay. She is so proud! Later, Daddy congratulates her warmly, while Mummy seems slightly disappointed. Why is there always this invisible barrier between Daphne's mother and her, like a sort of strange shyness, a mutual reserve? The barrier seems as high as the redbrick wall that encircles Cannon Hall. Is it possible that Mummy is a bit jealous of the obvious complicity between Daddy and his middle daughter?

One night, before Gerald has returned from the theatre, the household is woken by the screaming of a siren. The deafening sound of cannon fire, close by, makes everyone jump. The maid, young Dorothy, cowers under her bed in terror. Muriel, wearing a bathrobe, makes hot chocolate and attempts to reassure her daughters. Daphne can see clearly that her mother is worried: she keeps looking out of the window. Where is her husband? She appears to pray silently that nothing has happened to him. Daphne prays, too, in her head. She feels suddenly afraid, sensing the vulnerability of her family, of this whole city. At last, the headlights of Daddy's car sweep the façade of Cannon Hall. So he has come home. The little girl breathes easily again. During another air-raid warning—this one in mid-morning—the sirens strike up their familiar howl, and the cannon booms so loudly that they decide to take shelter in the dusty cupboard under the stairs. Gerald, in pyjamas, announces from the top of the stairs, with a hint of provocation, that he is going up to the attic. Perhaps he will see a zeppelin from up there: wouldn't that be splendid? He's never seen one: it must be an impressive sight. Although Muriel continues smiling, Daphne can tell that her mother does not find this at all amusing. Daphne feels faint at the thought of her father going up to the roof—he might die; she would never see him again—and an unbearable pain bores into her stomach. She has never felt so frightened, so sick, in her life. She reaches out her arms to him, crying at the top of her voice, *Daddy, don't go, don't go, don't ever leave me!* Her father stares at her in silence, then looks at his wife's pale face. Slowly, he walks downstairs and joins them in the cupboard. Finally, the sirens stop screaming. The air-raid warning is over.

Despite their country being at war, Londoners continue going to the theatre. Gerald has never been in such demand. He triumphs in *Dear Brutus,* a hit play penned by Uncle Jim. Gerald plays Will Dearth, a failed artist and alcoholic. During one magical night, Will, who has no children, finds himself the father of a ten-year-old girl and his existence is transformed. At dawn, this chimerical child vanishes. At the premiere, Daphne is overwhelmed by emotion: the relationship between father and daughter onstage is so like the real-life complicity between Gerald and Daphne. She has to leave the box, in tears. Once again, she feels her mother's disapproving stare trained on her.

~❧~

Milton Hall . . . Daphne looks up at the sand-coloured cut-stone façade. The huge house rears up amid green fields. It is impossible to imagine anything altering its age-old beauty. Daphne, with her mother and sisters, travelled to Peterborough by train, and there was a chauffeur waiting for them at the station. It is September 1917 and they have been invited for a short stay by friends of the family. As the car entered the driveway, Muriel whispered proudly that the Fitzwilliam family had lived at Milton for four hundred years. Muriel and the girls are inside the mansion now, but Daphne lingers outside, admiring the porch with its pillars, the clock at the top of a turret, the rows of lattice windows. In the entrance hall, the mistress of the house, Lady Fitzwilliam, welcomes them, her white hair in a bun. Next to her are a lady's companion with a chow chow, and a shy adolescent boy who hops up and down. Behind them are two lines of servants, from the little chambermaid, whose task it is to light fires, to the self-important butler. Daphne sees only the splendour of the setting, the high ceilings, the wood-panelled walls, the portraits of gentlemen in frock coats and jabots. Why does she feel so at ease in Milton Hall? What a strange sensation. . . . Usually she hates visiting her parents' friends, all those strangers whom she has no desire to know, those hands to be shaken, those forced smiles, when all she wants to do is disappear into a book.

For ten days, Daphne lives at Milton Hall as in a dream. She will remember the large bedroom in the north wing that she shares with Angela, and the even more spacious room in the south wing where Jeanne and her mother sleep. She will recall the breakfast served in the dining room by a dedicated servant, the silent ballet of silver platters, poached eggs and bacon, smoked herring, the white napkins, and their host's welcoming smile at the other end of the table. She will think about those hushed moments in the morning room with the mistress of the house, at teatime, leaning over a jigsaw puzzle.

On rainy days, Daphne plays with her sisters in the unused rooms of the north wing, where there are dustcovers on the beds and chairs, where the closed shutters keep out the light of day. During these games, as her sisters are used to by now, she always plays a boy. He has a name, this boy. Eric Avon. He is ten years old, like her. Her little sister plays one of his friends, whom they name David Dampier. What could be easier than becoming a boy in these dark rooms where no one can see her? Her skirt, pulled up and slipped inside her tights, becomes a pageboy's puffed pants, the jumper draped over her shoulders is transformed into a cape, and the stick in her hand is brandished as a sword. Eric Avon is afraid of nothing, of no one. He is radiant, glorious, pure hearted. He roams the hallways of Milton, a scout, protecting his family.

At a bend in the hallway, Eric Avon hears a whisper of clothes rustling along the parquet floor, the clinking of a bunch of keys. He flattens himself against the wall and signals to those following him. Watch out, danger, enemy. Hide behind the curtains. It's the housekeeper of Milton Hall, a tall, thin woman in a black dress. She wears her keys on a belt and never smiles. Her face is scarily white. Her name is Mrs. Parker. Everyone is afraid of her, but apparently Mrs. Parker is a remarkable housekeeper and Milton would not be Milton without her. From his hiding place, holding his breath, Eric Avon watches her pass. His eyes follow the train of her dress as it skims over the floorboards.

At the end of their stay, when the time comes to leave Milton, Daphne feels distraught. She turns around to admire the immensity of the house one last time. Why does she feel she is leaving behind a friend? She will never forget Milton Hall, nor Mrs. Parker's long black dress.

❧

Every Saturday, for a month, the sisters pose in an icy cold studio for an artist friend of their parents, Frederic Whiting, who paints a portrait of the three du Maurier girls. The only amusing aspect of the picture is that it features Brutus, their new dog, a little fox terrier. Other than that, posing is deadly dull. Not only do they have to take the tube from Hampstead all the way to Kensington, but they then have to remain utterly still for hours on end. The huge portrait, when it is finally completed, is a source of pride and pleasure for the family and their friends, but Angela, on the right of the image, continues to think she looks ugly, with a red nose and a behind that she considers too plump. Jeanne, cuddling Brutus, is adorable. But Daphne, on the left of the picture, with her blue dress and slender figure, is the one who catches the eye. Daphne hears the whispered compliments; she doesn't know what to do with them, but she understands—how could she not?—that she is prettier than her sisters. Not that she thinks so. The idea is meaningless to her anyway. In her mind, she is a boy, she is Eric Avon, who couldn't care less what anyone says about him, because there's a damsel in distress to be rescued, a villain to arrest, a cricket match to play.

The war is over, and the heavy atmosphere is transformed into floating bubbles: the champagne flows once again in Cannon Hall. Daphne hears the guests all uttering the same phrases: The war changed everything, Nothing is like it was before, We've lost our points of reference. She wonders what has changed exactly: The dead who will never return? The sadness that has left its stain forever? Whatever! Gerald and Muriel have decided to travel, and there is nothing too wonderful for the du Maurier family: Monte Carlo, Beaulieu, Cannes, the Hotel Saint-Georges in Algiers, Lake Como in Italy.

In the days leading up to their departure, 14 Cannon Place is in a state of feverish excitement. Why do their parents need so many suitcases? The two taxis are weighed down under mountains of bags stuffed with tweed coats, blankets, pillows, stacks of novels that no one will ever read, Gerald's precious pair of binoculars for bird-watching . . . and now here come other servants, bravely carrying hatboxes and walking sticks, newspapers and packets of playing cards, tennis rackets and golf clubs, Fortnum & Mason picnic baskets filled with delicious snacks for the journey.

Gerald's personal assistant becomes agitated. She is the person responsible for looking after passports, tickets, and customs declarations. Good God, Gerald has forgotten something at the house; quick, they must send a taxi back to Cannon Hall; they're going to miss the train. Gerald sulks. Really, what is the point of insisting on going on a trip? It's complicated and exhausting, and besides, they're perfectly happy at home. Muriel sighs, patiently asks him to stop bellyaching. Daphne knows her father will calm down once he's on the boat, crossing the English Channel. He loves walking along the deck, in a raincoat, face whipped by the wind. Muriel locks herself in her cabin, curtains drawn, and lies down on the bed, moaning softly. The sisters are horribly seasick, throwing up and generally wishing they were dead. Only Gerald holds up in the face of the elements, like a stoical captain.

When they reach French soil, Gerald and his assistant take care of the customs process, which always takes ages. Gerald has hidden bottles of wine and cartons of cigarettes in one of the bags, but he can't remember which one. The French customs officers are suspicious of this elegant English family with their French-sounding name and their heaps of luggage. The officers are methodical, opening every bag, every suitcase. Sometimes the keys to the padlocks have gone missing and Muriel grows impatient while Gerald distributes generous tips (which will prove very useful when the cigarettes and wine are discovered) and remains curiously calm.

The long trek is far from over. Now they must find their seats on the train, but there are problems with their reservations. Daphne watches Muriel busying herself again, the assistant brandishes the tickets, Gerald repeats his routine with the tips and his hesitant French (which makes the girls giggle), and in the end everything is settled. Daphne's father turns his sleeper carriage into an exact replica of his bedroom in Cannon Hall: the same lotions, toothpaste, powders, little sponges, cologne, pyjamas, and bathrobe are neatly laid out, while in the neighbouring compartment he keeps his books, his newspapers, fruit, cigarettes, cushions. What Daphne likes best about these long journeys to sunnier climes is the meals in the restaurant carriage, because Gerald very skilfully ridicules the other travellers behind their backs, giving perfect imitations of their snobbish airs, the way they chew their food or wipe their lips on their napkins, and the girls choke with laughter under the affable but somewhat irritated gaze of their mother.

It is only when they arrive at the hotel that things turn sour. Gerald's hopes are dashed: his room does not have an attractive view, overlooking some boring road rather than the sea; what's worse, it faces northeast, not southwest, and he came here for the sunlight! The hotel manager is hastily summoned, and Gerald puts on a distressed face as he expresses his disappointment. The manager listens and offers him a south-facing room with a prettier view.

So they have to pack everything up again, the clothes, the books, the cards, the binoculars, the cushions, the newspapers, Muriel's knitting. But, as Daphne suspects, Gerald will, the next morning, continue his litany of complaints: this cold wind on the terrace, this over-salted food; the place is "shilling,"* there are too many people, and—what a bore!—all of them "Witherspoons."* And it's like that for the entire stay. Daphne is used to it by now. The local cuisine holds no interest for Gerald, who makes do with a slice of roast beef, a romaine salad, but *absolutely no garlic*! He hates chicken, veal, coffee, figs, and grapes. Even the best vintage wines leave him cold; he would rather drink champagne any day. And he must have his big cups of Indian tea with six sugar lumps in each.

Why go on vacation, when their house is perfect? Gerald whines, and Muriel smiles at him, indefatigable, just a bit tense, comforting him, trying to keep him entertained. Each morning, Daphne watches her mother as she anxiously checks the weather, because if by any chance the day is overcast or, even worse, rainy, Gerald will be unbearable for the rest of the vacation.

༺❀༻

No more school. From now on, a private tutor will come every day to give lessons to the sisters at Cannon Hall. Her name is Maud Waddell. Behind the comforting, maternal appearance of this well-rounded, blue-eyed brunette, however, there lurks an iron will. She begins every sentence with *My dear,* but you mustn't be fooled: she always gets what she wants. The sisters come up with a nickname for this new governess with her opera-singer voice: Tod, from the verb "toddle," derived from Maud's surname, which sounds like "waddle," but also based on one of their favourite Beatrix Potter characters, Mr. Tod the fox. Tod is appalled by Daphne's substandard grammar and spelling, which must be dealt with, and quickly. There is a connection between them, despite Tod's authority—to which Daphne submits—because the two of them share an insatiable appetite for reading, which Angela and Jeanne do not possess. Tod is thrilled by Daphne's enthusiasm for literature and provides her with a succession of books. Daphne likes the kinds of poetry collections that adolescents usually don't appreciate—Shelley, Browning, Keats, Swinburne, and Donne—then she devours the novels by her grandfather George du Maurier. Daphne has been told by her father that Kicky wrote these books quite late in life, in his late fifties, after he had returned to England, after the loss of his left eye (which put an end to his career as a painter), after his marriage with Emma Wightwick (Big Granny) and the births of their five children, of whom Gerald was the youngest. Kicky began writing thanks to his friend the famous novelist Henry James, who advised him one day to tell his own stories using the written word rather than simply drawing them. Before the publication of his books, Kicky was known for his illustrations: he was a renowned caricaturist who worked for the Victorian satirical magazine *Punch.* Daphne drinks in every detail of her grandfather's drawings: the comical way he sketched the hassles of family life and society life, the subtleties of class distinctions, the bitter moments of everyday existence.

She begins with Kicky's first novel, *Peter Ibbetson.* From the raw material of his memories, her grandfather resuscitated the lost Paris of his youth, depicting its former splendours, its rose-coloured hues, the enclosure at the end of the fence on Rue de Passy, the Auteuil pond, the building with green shutters where he grew up. It is more a fable than a novel, Daphne notes, an autobiographical account soaked through with a touching nostalgia. Kicky expresses himself through his protagonist, Gogo, who has also not forgotten his childhood seasoned with the odours of cabbage soup and beef boiled in vinaigrette. Daphne has the impression of being transported to Paris in 1840, of finding herself on Rue de la Pompe and seeing Kicky's characters as they savour a glass of red wine on their doorstep, while Gogo plays and sings with Mimsey, the little girl next door. But upon the sudden death of his parents, Gogo is torn away from his enchanted garden to live with a cruel uncle under the grey skies of London. His name is no longer Gogo Pasquier, but Peter Ibbetson. After killing his horrible uncle, he ends up in a lunatic asylum. And it is there, to Daphne's stupefaction, that his real life begins, thanks to the magic of "dreaming true," the capacity that the book's two heroes—Peter and Mary (the Mimsey of his childhood)—have to use to find each other through daydreams. Despite their physical separation, they succeed in loving each other, joining together in their dreams, visiting the Paris of their youth, building an imaginary house, diving into the past of their ancestors, and discovering an aristocratic glassblowing forebear. "Dreaming true": Daphne is enraptured by this idea. Could she do the same thing? Her grandfather did it, after all, while her father pretends to be someone else every single evening, so why shouldn't she do it, too? That way, she could escape, she could dream up, imagine, truly become, Eric Avon.

She follows this book up with *Trilby*, Kicky's second novel, which was, she knows, an immense success, even in the United States. It is the story of Trilby O'Farrell, a half-Irish girl working as a laundress and artist's model, who falls under the magnetic spell of Svengali, the darkly seductive pianist and hypnotist. The action takes place in Paris, where Kicky took his art classes, on Rue Notre-Dame-des-Champs in Montparnasse. Under hypnosis, Trilby becomes a famous opera singer. Svengali turns her into his puppet and manipulates her as he pleases in order to obtain fame and fortune. The fall of poor Trilby will thus be all the harder. Unlike *Peter Ibbetson,* this is no sweet tale of family and childhood memories; Svengali casts his evil shadow over everything. But while Daphne prefers the first novel for its gentle nostalgia and its invitation to dreaming, she is nevertheless marked by the captivating darkness of Svengali, who attracts her despite herself.

The months pass, and Daphne's craving for books still isn't sated. Tod suggests other novels: Dickens, Thackeray, Scott, Stevenson, Wilde and his *Portrait of Dorian Gray,* Sheridan's plays, the complete works of the Brontë sisters, particularly *Jane Eyre* and *Wuthering Heights.* The magic of books is a drug, an enchantment, an escape route, as powerful and bewitching as Peter Pan's Neverland. While her sisters go on with their lives (tea dances for Angela, tennis and cricket for Jeanne), while Muriel reigns supreme as the exemplary mistress of Cannon Hall, while Gerald makes his fans swoon on the boards of the theatre, Daphne reads.

One spring morning is engraved into her memory for the rest of her life. Her mother had asked her to come to her morning room on the first floor, next to Gerald's study, a sunny room with a brick and ceramic fireplace and a view of the rose plants and greenhouses. Muriel is sitting in her bergère chair, concentrated on her knitting. *Daphne darling, I have to talk to you.* It is never a good sign when her mother uses that voice. She thinks quickly, as she admires the knitting needles continuing their metronomic ballet: What could she have done or said to earn Mummy's wrath? Did she make a blunder? Behave rudely? Forget something? *Now that you are twelve, you mustn't be surprised if something not very nice happens to you in a few weeks. You have had backaches recently, and this may be a sign.* Daphne replies that her back does not hurt at the moment and feels relieved: A backache, is that all this is about? But her mother goes on in the same serious voice, *No, perhaps not, but what I have to tell you is this. All girls, when they turn twelve, begin to bleed for a few days every month. It can't be stopped. It's just something that happens. And it goes on happening, every month, until they are middle-aged, and then it stops.* Daphne, speechless, stares at her mother. What on earth is she talking about? Bleeding, every month, for forty years? Muriel attempts to reassure her, *It's all right, it's not an illness, and it's not even like a cut. It doesn't hurt. But you can have tummy ache. I myself have bad headaches at the time. Angela bleeds, but I have told her never to talk to you about it and you must promise never to tell Jeanne.*

Closing the door of her mother's room, Daphne feels dazed. Perhaps, with a bit of luck, this dreadful thing will never happen to her? If she were a boy, she wouldn't have to put up with this humiliation. How lucky boys are! She does her best to forget the whole story, but one morning Alice, the young maid, whispers to her that "the thing" has arrived. Daphne has just finished eating breakfast and is feeling a little under the weather. What thing? Alice asks her to follow her to the bedroom, hands her a pair of pajama bottoms, and points out a strange stain. What a nightmare, being a girl, having to trouble yourself with these thick bands of cloth that must be changed every four hours, having to endure this painful heaviness in your lower abdomen, this stiff back, the compassionate and oddly tender looks of adults who, nonetheless, say nothing, not even a word of reassurance, because they must think of little Jeanne, the poor little girl, the innocent, utterly clueless about the horror that awaits her. Is this what it means—no longer wanting to play cricket, to kick a soccer ball, to run in the garden, being reduced to curling up on the sofa with a hot water bottle on your belly—is this what it is to be a woman? Because if it is, then Daphne wants none of it. She curses her feminine gender; she wants to continue playing the role of the glorious Eric Avon, the young man, the conqueror, the hero, who will never be reduced to bleeding into nappies. If only she had been the son her father wanted so much, the boy he dreamed of producing, who would pass on to his own son the French surname of which he was so proud, she would never have become stuck in this shameful, pathetic situation. Code name: "Robert."* That is how the du Maurier sisters jokingly rechristen menstruation.

In the mirror of the third-floor bathroom at Cannon Hall, Daphne has not changed in spite of this damned Robert: she has the same fine features, the same blonde hair that she refuses to curl, cut short like a boy. She persists in dressing like a schoolboy, in shorts, shirts, ties, jumpers, long wool socks, clumsy clodhoppers on her feet.

She is a boy in a girl's body. The only person who suspects this ambiguous situation is Tod. The two of them have been close for two years now. For two years, Tod has been reading, every night, the notes Daphne leaves in her homework, the letters stuffed with spelling mistakes that make her roll her eyes in despair, but how can she fail to be touched by these intimate confessions, by the trust that Daphne shows her? *I really don't know why I feel like this. You don't know how I long to have a good talk with you and pour everything out. I must be an awful rotter as we have a ripping time always, and no kids could be more indulged and made more a fuss of, yet I long for something so terribly and I don't know what it is. The feeling is always there and I don't think I shall ever find it. It's no good telling the others, they wouldn't understand, everyone thinks I'm moody and tiresome. People say I'm acid and bitter, it's terrible at my age to get bored with life.*[2]

Eric Avon is gradually erased from Daphne's days as she grows into a woman. And he fades away when Gerald proudly leaves a sealed envelope on Daphne's plate one lunchtime. A letter from her father? Delighted, she rushes up to her bedroom to read it. It is a longish poem, which she deciphers slowly.

> *My very slender one*
> *So brave of heart, but delicate of will,*
> *So careful not to wound, never kill,*
> *My tender one—*
> *Who seems to live in Kingdoms all her own*
> *In realms of joy*
> *Where heroes young and old*
> *In climates hot and cold*
> *Do deeds of daring and much fame*
> *And she knows she could do the same*
> *If only she'd been born a boy.*
> *And sometimes in the silence of the night*
> *I wake and think perhaps my darling's right*
> *And that she should have been,*
> *And, if I'd had my way,*
> *She would have been, a boy.*
> *My very slender one*
> *So feminine and fair, so fresh and sweet,*
> *So full of fun and womanly deceit.*
> *My tender one*
> *Who seems to dream her life away alone.*
> *A dainty girl*
> *But always well attired*
> *And loves to be admired*
> *Wherever she may be, and wants*
> *To be the being who enchants*

Because she has been born a girl.
And sometimes in the turmoil of the day
I pause, and think my darling may
Be one of those who will
For good or ill
Remain a girl for ever and be still
A Girl.

What did her father mean? That he wishes she weren't a girl? Or that he is, ultimately, happy about it? Daphne does not understand. She doesn't dare ask him. The other day, playing cricket with her in the garden, he whispered in her ear, *I wish I was your brother instead of your father, we'd have such fun.*[3] In Kicky's novels, his heroines Trilby and Mary are tall, robust, they look and act like lads, possessing the masculine grace of Peter Pan, his boyish agility. Peter Pan, her hero, who does not want to grow up. She would have liked so much to be like him, adventurous, magnificent, like her Llewelyn Davies cousins, all so remarkable, so full of vigour. Her father's poem, which she recognizes as being tactless and awkward in spite of the love that throbs beneath it, brings back her unease. Feeling disorientated, she puts it in a drawer of her bedside table and, later, thanks her father with a tense smile.

∾❦ঌ

What she dreads most are Sundays. Her father's day of rest. The lunches given by Muriel at Cannon Hall are unmissable events to which only the cream of the theatre world and London high society are invited. In summer, these gatherings can sometimes last the entire day, to Daphne's dismay. The garden is a profusion of multicoloured dresses and roses, the murmur of voices and laughter rise above the high brick wall, and the neighbours feel certain that, once again, a party is in full swing at the du Mauriers' house. Muriel welcomes everyone with grace and poise, but the king is Gerald, spontaneous, elegant, irresistible. Even the famous playwright Sacha Guitry and American composer Melville Gideon come one Sunday to tread the impeccable lawn of Cannon Hall, applaud the rallies on the tennis court, and taste the mountains of food served by a silent army of servants dressed in grey alpaca uniforms.

The endless lunch mutates into afternoon tea, with cucumber sandwiches, sweets and tiered cakes, frappé coffee, and Earl Grey tea, before blurring into aperitifs. Daphne withdraws, hiding behind a bush, book in hand, while her sisters mingle with the guests, Jeanne shining on the tennis court, Angela chatting loquaciously. Good God, why is she so different? Why can't she enjoy herself with the others? Why is it such torture for her to speak to people, to answer questions? She is shy, but so what? People seem to mistake her timidity for arrogance. It is true that she has a very determined chin. Daphne pretends not to listen to those never-ending comments about her beauty, those disparaging whispers about her two sisters; it's tiresome and unfair. And now Muriel is calling her, insisting that she put her book down and come over to talk to Madeline, Audrey, Gladys, Leslie . . .

In every season, there are crowds at Cannon Hall on Sundays, a parade of elegant men and women, actors and actresses, producers and directors. It is difficult to be alone so she can read, can daydream, even in such a big house. Dinner on Christmas Eve is a sumptuous affair, more festive than religious, with eighteen people seated at the table in the vast first-floor dining room, wrapped gifts left on every chair, a magician who performs after the meal, and games of chance—roulette, Ludo—to end the evening. There is a succession of dishes, each more delicious than the last, then Muriel, standing straight-backed in her pretty party dress, cuts the twenty-five-pound turkey with such speed and skill that the guests always feel obligated to applaud.

Amid the opulence of the presents, there is one for Daphne that will prove especially important. You wouldn't guess it, though, to look at it. It is a simple notebook, long and black, containing fifty or so pages. A private journal.

To write. To dream true. To escape into her own world, her own personal Neverland. Peter Pan holds out his hand. Kicky urges her on. A pencil. Silence. The table in her bedroom, on the third floor. The view over the Heath. The closed door. Begin with the date . . .

January 1, 1920. Her age: twelve and a half. *New Year's Day. I over-sleep myself. We go for a long walk in the morning and stay indoors in the afternoon. It's my teddy-bear's birthday. I give a party for her. Angela is very annoying. Jeanne and I box, and then I pretend I am a midshipman hunting slaves. Daddy says I have a stoop. I begin to read a book called* With Allenby in Palestine. *(very good).*[4]

She does not reread it. What's the point? No one will read it. It is a private journal, after all.

> January 7th. *We give a dance. It is from 7 to 11. We have great fun. There are lovely refreshments. I only have to dance with two girls, all the rest, I dance with boys. Marcus Stedall is very nice. I believe he is gone on me.*[5]

From now on, Daphne wanders around the house with a pencil behind her ear, the journal under her arm. If anyone asks her why she has that suspicious look on her face, she replies unblinkingly that she is writing. And what is she writing? That is none of their business. She writes that she is going to dance, that she adores the fox-trot, that she has a best friend, Doodie, that she plays cricket, that she is crazy about the theatre. She admits that Dr. Playfair (who spends his life at Cannon Hall, dedicating himself to eliminating even the slightest health concern for the du Maurier girls) has told her to stop biting her fingernails: she has hurt her thumb, and she must wear a sort of poultice. This makes it impossible for her to write. Well, almost impossible. She relates that one rainy day in November she went for a walk alone in Hampstead, and that when she got home she began to write something other than her journal, in a pretty Italian notebook edged with green ribbon.

After four years of service with the du Maurier family, Maud Waddell leaves to educate the children of a sultan in Istanbul. Her departure greatly saddens Daphne, who sends letter after letter to her one and only confidante—she announces proudly that she has finished writing a book and the name of her hero is Maurice—and Tod replies every week. Since the loss of her governess, writing has become her favourite pastime, along with reading, but despite the arrival of a new governess, she still feels lonely. Miss Vigo is a pleasant person and an excellent tutor, but she will never replace Tod in Daphne's heart. The title of her book is *The Searchers*. She describes the story in detail to Tod. Maurice's father is dead, and his mother is still in love with her first boyfriend, Tommy. Each day, Maurice walks alone, barefoot, by a lake, far from any city with its noisy traffic, he listens to the wind, observes the waves that break on the sand. The more desolate, windy, and rainy a landscape is, the more he likes it. One day, Maurice gets lost during a hike and he is taken in by a pipe-smoking man with brown, sparkling eyes, a strange, capricious character, at once a friend and an enemy, a storyteller with a fertile imagination, capable of great irony. Daphne considers him a cross between Uncle Jim and Gerald, and this makes Tod smile, because she thinks secretly that Maurice resembles Daphne. At the end of the story, we discover that this man is none other than the famous Tommy, the former lover of Maurice's mother.

Tod's letters are affectionate and encouraging. What would Daphne do without the support of this correspondence? Solitude grips her, gnaws at her. She mopes about, thinking how unfair it is: she has no reason to be sad; she is a young, funny girl. She likes to laugh, like her father, laugh about anything, stupid things, silly things, but it seems to her that other people know how to live better than she does: Angela takes acting and singing classes, while Jeanne is passionate about painting, piano, and tennis. What does Daphne have? Words, and that magical, enchanting world where she locks herself away, day after day.

❧

May 13, 1921. Today is Daphne's birthday. She is fourteen. Not yet a woman, but no longer a little girl. She is given a nice party, a celebratory meal in an upmarket London restaurant, lots of presents. And then, seven days later, seven days after the sweetness of these shared moments, while the sun shines down on Cannon Hall, tragedy strikes. Daphne has gone to greet her parents in their bedroom, as she does every morning. Her father looks appalled, her mother weeps softly. It's Michael, the fourth of the five Llewelyn Davies cousins. He is dead. He was only twenty. Daphne doesn't understand. Dead? How did he die? Uncle Jim came to see Gerald in his dressing room at Wyndham's Theatre late last night, to bring him this terrible news. Michael drowned. Drowned in a reservoir, in Sandford, near Oxford University, where he was a student. Twenty years old. To die at twenty. There's no war anymore. His older brother George was already killed in combat. How is it possible that a second Llewelyn Davies should die so young?

Of her adored, cherished, divinely handsome cousins, Michael was the most handsome of all, the one she had dreamed of kissing, Uncle Jim's favourite, a beautiful boy, with his oval face, his smooth black hair, his dark eyes. But how did he die? What happened? He was swimming with a friend, Rupert, who also drowned. One tried to save the other. Daphne does not understand. In a state of shock, she imagines the scene: she sees the wide expanse of water, the two young men in bathing suits, their lifeless bodies. Later, when she is going up to her room, she hears the discreet whispering of the servants and pricks up her ears. Apparently, they died in each other's arms, clasped together. She doesn't know what to make of this. Who can she talk to about it? The only thing she knows is that Michael has gone forever, he has gone to join Peter Pan in a magical lagoon peopled with mermaids, Indians, and pirates, he is flying with Peter and Tinker Bell, for eternity.

A few days after the funeral, during a walk in town with her sisters and Miss Vigo, Daphne gives them the slip and runs down Heath Street until she reaches the little green cemetery on Church Row where her cousin lies, alongside his brother George, his parents, Sylvia and Andrew, close to Uncle

Guy, to Kicky, to Big Granny. With her pocket money, she buys violets at the florist's nearby. She is alone, standing in front of the gravestones of her family. The sun is shining; the air is warm. Gently, she places a few flowers on her cousin's grave. Her voice rings out in the empty cemetery. *They're for you, Michael.*

It is difficult to get over such a tragedy. Apparently, Barrie, in despair, locks himself in his apartment on Adelphi Terrace and suffers nightmare after nightmare. When summer comes, Gerald takes his family to the seaside in Devon, southwest of London. It does them good to get away from the city, the world, their sadness, to recharge their batteries. They rent a large house with a sea view in Thurlestone for the month of August: From its bay windows, they can see the two huge rocks standing in the middle of the water, each leaning towards the other, as if they are embracing. Gerald invites his nephew Geoffrey (his sister Trixie's youngest son) and his wife, Meg. The three du Maurier sisters spend their days on the fine sand beach, paddling in a canoe, fishing for shrimp, building sand castles. Daphne can stay for hours in the sun, and her skin turns a lovely golden colour—to the dismay of her mother, who exhorts her to take shade under an umbrella. The combination of sunlight and iodine turns her hair blonde, and her eyes seem even bluer. She is gorgeous, and she knows it, tall and slender in that cumbersome one-piece bathing suit, which she dreams of stripping off so she can go swimming, naked, behind the rocks, savouring the caress of the water on her skin. She is so pretty that one day, coming out of the sea, she feels the eyes of her cousin Geoffrey upon her, a man's gaze that checks her out from head to toe, and a slow smile, only for her, a smile that says everything: she's a beautiful girl; she's not a child anymore.

Geoffrey is thirty-six. Old enough to be her father. Twice divorced, tall, sturdily built, dark haired, with harmonious features, a sensual mouth. An actor, like his uncle Gerald. A real "menace."* Daphne does not look away. Her heart pounds, but she is not afraid, she does not feel intimidated, she smiles back at him, a pact between them; no one else has seen, no one else knows, just her, just him, that day, on the beach, a shared moment of exclusive complicity. She has always liked Geoffrey, despite the twenty-two-year age difference, but that day, on the sand, there is something more than sympathy between them, a sensation she has never felt before, that heat running through her, a feeling of risk, of entering a danger zone.

The summer days pass, sun filled and languorous, and the secret understanding between Daphne and her cousin intensifies, without a word being spoken, purely through their eyes, which meet, draw each other, magnetized. On the golf course, he waves at her behind Gerald's back. After lunch, it is time for coffee on the terrace. Daphne and her sisters lie on the grass in bathing suits, half-covered by their beach towels, faces turned towards the sun like sunflowers eager for light. Geoffrey sits down on the grass between Daphne and Jeanne, while Meg, Muriel, and Gerald have a conversation higher up on the terrace. Daphne smells Geoffrey's aftershave—a moment of panic—she keeps her eyes closed: above all, don't say a word, don't move a muscle; her sisters are just there, next to her; her entire body tenses, she knows that something is going to happen, she waits for it, shivers, doing her best not to betray her feelings, then suddenly her cousin's hand is under the towel, that man's hand furtively searching for hers, the touch of warm skin seizing her, she almost cries out, moans, but she controls herself: above all, she must not let it show; she must act as if nothing is happening.

Her cousin's touch awakens hundreds of sensors inside her, tiny particles of emotion and desire with the power of an electric shock, but she manages to stay silent. Geoffrey's wife is sitting there, only a few feet away, drinking coffee with Daphne's oblivious parents. Now she knows that, every afternoon, for the rest of the vacation, Geoffrey will grab her hand beneath the towel, without a word, and she will stay silent, too, intoxicated, dazed, she will wait for this moment with a nameless delight. She knows instinctively that she must say nothing, must never breathe a word, and it is this that most excites her: the power of the secret, the forbidden.

I think Daphne is old enough now to come dancing this evening at the Links Hotel. It is cousin Geoffrey who says this, and everyone seems to agree. She chooses a pretty dress, blue, to match her eyes, and finds herself in his arms, against him—how tall and muscular he is—and all this under the eyes of Meg, his wife, who doesn't notice a thing. Geoffrey embraces Daphne as they dance to Paul Whiteman's lively fox-trot "Whispering," which seems almost to have been written for them: "When I'd like to lean in close . . . Gorgeous and dressed in blue . . ."

The final day of the vacation arrives. The summer hours have lost their golden aura; it is nearly September. On the morning of his departure, Geoffrey asks Daphne to come with him to the sea one last time. They stand facing the waves, the two rocks leaning in together, and they remain silent, untouching. *I'm going to miss you terribly, Daph.* She agrees, in a quiet voice. Suddenly he turns around. *Oh, look up there, on the cliff. Uncle Gerald is spying on us.* It really is her father standing there, hands on hips, seemingly watching them, with a scowl on his face. In her journal, Daphne notes: *It is a lovely day. Geoffrey goes. I feel terribly depressed. We bathe and play tennis. I read also.*[6]

Return to London. Something has changed inside her. That sensual— possibly even amorous—awakening? The sudden death of Michael? She doesn't know. As if to forget all this, she throws herself into a whirlwind of outings to the theatre, books to be read (Thackeray, Stevenson, Galsworthy, Swinburne), long bicycle rides or horse rides on the Heath with her sisters; she gorges herself on dances and travels. Gerald is knighted at Buckingham Palace, a moment of glory he takes very seriously. Muriel thus becomes Lady du Maurier, which she doesn't mind one bit. Gerald affectionately calls her Lady Mo. The award of this knighthood is fully deserved, Daphne knows. Gerald has altered the way actors perform on the stage; he is the first to break with the stiff, affected style of his predecessors, the first to dare light a cigarette while performing, to wear his own clothes. Now nothing can slow down Sir Gerald du Maurier's lavish lifestyle: he hands out gold coins as tips, obtains the best seats for the Ascot horse races, for the Wimbledon tennis tournament, for operas in Covent Garden. The life of the outside world does not pass over the high wall surrounding Cannon Hall; little mention is made of the massive upheaval left by the war, the uncertain times ahead, the financial difficulties that other, less privileged people must endure.

Angela leaves for Paris, where she will attend Miss Ozanne's finishing school near the Eiffel Tower. She is not happy there. Gerald, Muriel, Daphne, and Jeanne go to visit her in the spring; it is the first time Daphne has been to the French capital. She is there only a few days, and the time goes by too quickly. How she would have loved to walk alone in the streets, not to be accompanied by her parents, to shake them off and explore those avenues, those boulevards where part of her already belongs, a legacy of her grandfather.

✦

On Sunday evenings in the first-floor dining room, Gerald likes to have conversations alone with his older daughters. Angela is back from Paris after several sad terms, thrilled to recapture her social life of balls, galas, and dates. Gerald likes to confide in his daughters, while smoking and savouring his Cointreau, and the later it gets, the more animated, audacious, and irreverent the conversations become. In all seriousness, what did they think of the outfit worn by the Countess of T., who came to eat lunch earlier; that material makes her look fat, don't you think? Hysterical laughter. And that moron Charles P. with his idiotic smile (mimicked). Good God, did they know that Viscount B. has had a baby with Miss H.? Yes, truly! Unbelievable. What is it that makes James R. so attractive, do they think? *Ah, you're very like me* (a remark most often addressed to Daphne). Sometimes they argue, have tiffs, but they always kiss and make up afterwards.

The conversations go on long into the night, until Muriel, infuriated, bangs her foot on the floor of the living room above. So Gerald lowers his voice and asks Angela to pour him another glass of Cointreau. The subject matter becomes mischievous, risqué; it is a sort of farce between father and daughters. They joke about Gerald's imaginary "stable," a very special stable in which the young actresses who share billing with him are catalogued like "fillies," judged according to their physique, the length of their legs, their complexion, their teeth. It is comical to think of these young debut actresses, blissfully unaware of what the du Maurier sisters, in collusion with their devilish father, are capable of saying about them.

Aided by the alcohol, Gerald lets slip confidences that are very far from paternal, and which fascinate the girls, eager to know about the latest "filly" to have joined the stable and how Daddy will go about "breaking her in," but of course they must keep their voices down because if Mo, upstairs, hears any of this, there will be a drama. Little by little, Daphne understands that her father is in the habit of wooing his young partners, that something more goes on between them than mere hugging and kissing. "Cairo,"* "waxing"* . . . these things do not happen only in the conjugal bed with a spouse, but elsewhere, with others. This disgusts her, revolts her; she thinks it ugly.

In that case, why get married? Daphne vents in her letters to Tod. How can Mo close her eyes to all this, how can she display that same calm face day after day, when everyone knows that Gerald is cheating on her? One day, however, Mo does fly off the handle, outraged to see that Gerald's Sunbeam is parked for an entire afternoon outside the home of a pretty young supporting actress. All hell breaks loose. The thunder rumbles. Doors are slammed in Cannon Hall. As he is about to escape to the theatre that evening, a sheepish Gerald whispers into his daughter's ear, *Mummy's so angry with me, I don't know what to do.*[7] Daphne feels simultaneously embarrassed and touched by these manly confidences, which should not be entrusted to his own daughter.

And yet this is the same man who waits up for Angela when she comes home late from a dance, who traps her in the entrance hall and aggressively interrogates her. Has she seen what time it is? Who brought her home? Did he try to kiss her? She had better tell him the truth! Daddy the enchanter, the imp, the charmer, the clown, is transformed into an intransigent father figure who cannot bear the idea that his darling daughters are growing up, that they have a social life, that they are attractive, that they seduce, and Angela is the first of the three to suffer from this.

Why can't his beloved daughters remain children, like Peter Pan, the family hero? Angela sobs as she confides in Daphne: How can he change in a flash into this unpleasant stranger, this cutting, nervous authoritarian, when that very morning he was all smiles? Gerald has always done whatever he likes, with no regard for others: you only had to see him at the casino in Monte Carlo, during the previous Christmas vacation, when he feigned to forget that he'd won the pot, leaving the table with supreme nonchalance, cigarette dangling from his lips, jacket slung over his shoulder, purely to enrage the men who had lost to him.

Gerald has paraded through his whole life, executing pirouettes, slaloming between crowds of admirers, assured and light-footed. So many times, Daphne sees him laugh too loud, admire himself in a mirror, spend without counting, leave extravagant tips, mock other people behind their backs, grovel hypocritically. This is who Sir Gerald du Maurier is: the actor, the theatre director, the star, the idol. His detractors find him vain, full of himself, superficial; and the worst thing is, he knows this and couldn't care less.

In the tranquility of her room, Daphne confides in her journal, continues down the path of her writing. A radio set arrives at Cannon Hall: it is incredible, amazing, she writes, to discover these voices, this music, coming out of this strange little box. She listens to it so much that she soon gets a migraine. In a letter to her darling Tod, still abroad, she tells how Angela is playing the role of Wendy in *Peter Pan*, directed by their uncle Jim, at Wyndham's Theatre, with Gladys Cooper—a young actress and a great friend of the whole du Maurier family (and who bears a slight resemblance to Daphne)—in the role of Peter. Something disastrous yet funny happened during one of the shows: the harness that was supposed to make Wendy fly snapped, and Angela flew spectacularly straight into the orchestra pit, very luckily without serious injury.

Daphne also writes to her about the dance given at the Claridge Hotel for Angela, but what she fails to inform her former governess of is that it is she, Daphne, who is the belle of the ball in a pale blue velvet tunic, whereas her older sister, stuffed inside a white satin ball gown, looks more like a meringue; nor does she reveal that she is the girl whom most of the boys want to dance with and that she enjoys herself wholeheartedly while poor Angela remains a wallflower. However, she does not hold back from telling Tod about the feeling of permanent emptiness that continues to gnaw at her, and her increasing dissatisfaction at being born a girl: *Why wasn't I born a boy? They did all the brave things.*[8]

There is one positive note, though: her father read a few of her poems and he liked them. She has discovered two writers she admires: Somerset Maugham and Katherine Mansfield. To write like them, as well as them, is that possible? Because that is all that interests her, and Tod knows it: Daphne wants to write; Daphne does write; Daphne is a writer. Other young girls look for husbands, think about starting a family, but not her; she doesn't believe in marriage. Just look at her parents' relationship—what a farce.

Each evening, when she draws her curtains, Daphne glimpses a light, not far away, on the edge of the Heath, a window lit late at night that seems to twinkle benevolently. Contemplating its golden glimmer pacifies her, fills her with hope. The vexations of the day fade away, like this morning when she had to pose for a photograph with Gerald, who wanted a portrait of himself with his favourite daughter. She hates the result. Her father is sitting to her left, turned towards her, staring at her possessively, his hand on hers, as if to prevent her moving, going away, leaving him. He holds her back, like a cuckolded husband might shut away an unfaithful wife, imprisoning her, bringing her to heel, and she—a prey, a victim—appears sullen under her cloche hat, her features frozen in an expression of gloom, looking away from him and from the lens, without even the hint of a smile on her face.

For the first time, Daphne feels oppressed by the atmosphere in Cannon Hall. The excessive love her father feels for her has become overwhelming, as has her mother's coldness. She is only seventeen, but she feels as if she is suffocating. She watches the mysterious window shining in the night and thinks about her friend Doodie, who has already gone to France, to a finishing school near Meudon. For several weeks, every letter Daphne has received from Doodie has been eulogistic: the place, the teachers, the other students, it's all so wonderful, so marvellous, so close to Paris, Daphne must *absolutely* come and join her here, as soon as she possibly can.

Paris. The city that draws her like a magnet.

Yes, of course, Paris.

PART TWO

FRANCE, 1925

❧

I leave my heart behind in Paris.

—DAPHNE DU MAURIER[1]

Meudon, Hauts-de-Seine, France
November 2013

The biographies of Daphne du Maurier state that the finishing school she attended was "located in Camposena, a village near Meudon." Camposena . . . As a Frenchwoman, I can't help smiling at the Italian-sounding name. If there had been a village with that name anywhere near Meudon, I would know about it.

I find the answer in the Hauts-de-Seine departmental archives. The Villa Camposenea (not Camposena) was located at 25 Rue de l'Orphelinat (formerly the main street of the village of Fleury), now known as Rue du Père-Brottier, in Meudon. I also obtain a list from the 1926 population census providing me with the name of each person working at the finishing school at that date. Meudon's communal archives send me a precise description of the place and the land registers, as well as some photographs: the property was constructed in Fleury in the eighteenth century; it belonged to Armand-Gaston Camus, the founder of the national archives, and then to the famous printer Charles Panckoucke. The mayor of Clamart, Jules Hunebelle, took possession of the house in 1860 and had it extended.

The dancer Isadora Duncan, states the same document, lived there in 1902, and the finishing school, directed by Mrs. Hubbard, and then by

Mrs. Wicksteed, was situated there between 1921 and 1934. After that (and this greatly amuses me) it was taken over by a community of nudists. The lot, consisting of "a main residence, a large circular greenhouse, an orangery, a stable, a shed, a concierge's house, in very poor condition, surface area of three hectares 47 acres," was sold by the Hunebelle heirs in 1943 to the commune of Meudon. The entire place was razed to the ground in 1950 in order to construct the apartment buildings of the "Fleury park."

I walk past these unattractive, grey, cubic buildings and wonder if the wide driveway lined with lime trees was saved at the last minute before the demolition took place. A pair of stone angels decorates the gardens of Meudon's art and history museum. In the old days, the angels sat atop pillars at the entrance to the Panckoucke-Hunebelle property. Apart from them, nothing remains of the original residence. Daphne would not have liked what Camposonea has become, nine decades later.

❦

Here, they don't call her Daphne, but Mademoiselle du Maurier. She loves hearing her name pronounced this way, *à la française,* and she thinks that Kicky would have loved it, too. She arrived at the station in Bellevue on January 19, 1925. Meudon and Fleury reminded her oddly of Hampstead, with its steep slopes, its affluent houses, its well-kept gardens. What does she know about Meudon? Not much, except that her compatriot Alfred Sisley never tired of painting the changing reflections on the Seine and that Wagner composed his *Flying Dutchman* here. Obviously, it is not Paris, but the capital city and its wonders are only a half-hour train journey away.

Inside a wooded garden, the Villa Camposonea, situated at the end of a long driveway bordered by lime trees, is a tall, pale house with a small clock tower and a bartizan. Daphne instantly likes its Gothic appearance. Mrs. Wicksteed, the manager of the establishment—a cheerful, grey-haired lady in her fifties—welcomes her new student warmly. It is a beautiful day, not too cold, and Mrs. Wicksteed decides to make the most of this to show the young lady around the park. Mrs. Wicksteed tells her about one of the house's previous owners, Mrs. Panckoucke, first name Ernestine, a pretty brunette painted by Ingres who used to receive celebrities here such as Alfred de Musset and Berlioz. Daphne listens, blank faced. No doubt Mrs. Wicksteed guesses that, behind this new student's haughty, almost arrogant appearance (that determined chin raised like a shield!) lies a pathological shyness. This is the first time, she knows, that Daphne has left home. Mrs. Wicksteed embarks on a story, explaining that the Panckoucke household entertained their guests with "constructions" set up in the park, few of which remain. She describes the Tell chapel, the Polynesian hut, the grotto built with rocks from Fontainebleau, the Chinese pavilion with dragons and pagodas at the top of the hill, and she congratulates herself when Daphne finally smiles, charmed by this nostalgic description.

In the long room on the first floor, which must have witnessed the most glorious moments of Mrs. Panckoucke's era, and whose stained-glass windows are now faded, its tapestries tattered, its chandeliers covered with dust, Mrs. Wicksteed eagerly introduces her team: the servants, and the twenty-five young boarders, most of whom are English. The school's headmistress, Mlle Yvon, her right-hand woman (pretty green eyes); Mrs. Evans, the (rather stiff) governess; Miss Engler, the (somewhat strict-looking) music teacher; Mr. Baissac, the guard; Mr. and Mrs. Sassisson, the cooks; Miss Chassagniole, the tough laundrywoman; Marcel, the groom (watch out for him); then Yvonne, Adrienne, Lucienne, Marguerite, the maids, and other, more humble servants who are not named. Next come Daphne's new classmates, all so bland and nondescript, so lacking in panache and style. Thank goodness her dear Doodie is there, with her impish smile.

Daphne is disappointed to discover, during the first meal in the freezing-cold dining room, that the illustrious du Maurier name carries no weight at Camposonea—no one seems impressed by it—because there are a plethora of aristocratic young ladies here, princesses, countesses, heiresses, and she feels invisible. Not easy, either, to become accustomed to this communal life, particularly for a girl such as Daphne, who has known only the quiet comforts of her childhood homes and the occasional luxury hotel. She must get used to her noisy classmates with their jokes, their cliques, their barely interesting manners.

She is not bothered by sleeping with Doodie, but by the room itself, which is, she complains in a letter to Tod, as bare as a maid's quarters: no carpet, and the drawers in the chests all squeak. As for the temperature in the building here, she finds it icy cold, and they're not even allowed to light a fire. She has always been sensitive to the cold: How will she survive? As it is, she has to jump up and down every night before she goes to bed just to warm herself up a bit, watched by the giggling Doodie, and to sleep all bundled up in her fur coat.

The first few nights go badly. A distant, but still too loud, bell rings every fifteen minutes, and the roosters on a neighbouring farm crow their heads off at the crack of dawn. Weary and drawn, Daphne stares through the window. It is not yet daylight. She has a view over the white cottages of Fleury's winemakers and, beyond those, the roofs of a large manor house that is home to the Saint-Philippe orphanage. How is she going to adapt to this new life? The morning ablutions are unspeakably barbarous: cold water in a cracked basin, and each boarder must make her own bed! Never in all her life has Mlle du Maurier made her own bed. And she's not about to start now.

In the room next door are two younger girls, one of whom is a clumsy oaf named Henrietta, one of the few to have been impressed by the du Maurier name. In the blink of an eye, Daphne sweet-talks, charms, and enslaves her. From that point on, Henrietta will, very discreetly, make Daphne's bed for her every morning. As for the cold, Daphne complains about it so much to Muriel that her mother pays a supplementary fee to the school's management in order that Daphne and Doodie be allowed to light a fire in their room. Adrienne, the young maid, comes in to light it every morning.

Another downer is the formal prohibition on walking anywhere other than in the Camposenea park. An enthusiastic walker, used to invigorating hikes on the Heath, Daphne rails against this confinement. And her list of grievances grows longer: she doesn't like Mr. and Mrs. Sassisson's cooking and barely touches her meals. Is she being difficult in order to get attention? Maybe. She also complains about the timetable: the "inhuman" wake-up call at 7:15, prayers at 7:50, breakfast at 8:00, music at 9:45, classes from 10:15 until noon, the too-early lunch, and all those bells ringing at the most ungodly hours. An affectionate telegram sent by the actress and close family friend Gladys Cooper makes her smile: *Fondest love darling, thinking of you, Glads.*

But the worst thing is the humiliation Daphne suffers in her French course. There are four classes in Camposenea. In the First group are the "elite," the five or six most brilliant students, who speak perfect French. Next is the Second A class for those just below this level, then Second B for those with "passable" French, and Third for girls whose French is below average. After a test, which Daphne thinks she has aced, she finds herself in Second B. This is a blow to her pride. She, a du Maurier, with French blood flowing in her veins! It's unbelievable.

The only parts of this new existence that excite her are the weekly outings to Paris. The young boarders, accompanied by Mlle Yvon and Miss Engeler, take the train to Bellevue in a group and go to visit the Louvre, the Comédie-Française, the Opéra. Daphne, who is not especially musical, gets a shock when she hears Stravinsky's *The Rite of Spring,* conducted by the composer himself. That evening, in their room, while Doodie dances to a ragtime tune on the gramophone, Daphne writes in her journal, attempting to describe this strange, modern music that seemed to transport her to another world, then begins a letter to Tod. *Don't you love Paris? With its cobbled streets, shrieking taxis and wonderful lights and chic little women and dago*-like men with broad-rimmed trilby hats? I think that the Place de la Concorde, at night, after it's been raining, with all the lights, is too wonderful, it's all quite divine.*[2]

One evening in February 1925, on the train back to Versailles, Daphne sits opposite Mlle Yvon, the headmistress, a small, plump woman in her thirties with very dark hair and green, almond-shaped eyes. She speaks fluent English, with a strong French accent, and this only adds to her charm. A lively, sophisticated woman, she attracts a court of admirers from among the girls; in fact, Daphne realizes, the majority of the students seem spellbound by Mlle Yvon's ironic humour and sparkling smile. To begin with, after Daphne arrived at Camposenea, the headmistress's charm somehow passed her by, but now, here on the train, as Mlle Yvon's eyes rest on her—just for a few seconds—Daphne feels a strange pang, a sensation she had forgotten.

Mlle Yvon teaches only the Firsts, the elite students, an exclusive club over which she reigns supreme. The Firsts have the right to eat dinner at the same table as Mrs. Wicksteed, Miss Engeler, and Mlle Yvon, while all the other students must sit with one another. After the meal is over, Mlle Yvon and her favourites go to the "back room," a space reserved especially for them. The other students have to content themselves with dancing on the mezzanine or stifling their yawns as Mrs. Wicksteed reads to them out loud.

Above the sound of the music and Mrs. Wicksteed's quavering voice, Daphne pricks up her ears towards the "back room," listening out for every burst of laughter, every shout. Often one of the elite girls runs out in tears, face bright red, and another quickly follows to console her and bring her back. But what are they up to? Daphne wonders in a whisper directed at Doodie and her friend Sheila. It's the truth game, which they play with Mlle Yvon. Apparently, it's pretty strong stuff: you need nerves of steel.

Weeks pass, and Daphne quietly seethes. Why isn't she part of the group that goes to the "back room" after dinner? Why must she make do with these deadly dull evenings listening to Mrs. Wicksteed's readings? Because she's not in the group of Firsts? It's so unfair. Doodie is friends with two of the elite girls, but according to her it's impossible to even try to get into that closed group. Not that she minds: Doodie and Sheila seem perfectly happy with their dances on the mezzanine and their meaningless chatter with the Seconds and Thirds.

Daphne looks at herself in the mirror one morning, standing proudly at five feet three inches tall. She is a du Maurier, after all: her grandfather and her father would never have been afraid to enter that famous back room, to take part in their game, so what is she waiting for? Her father would have gone in nonchalantly, all charm. A boy's voice whispers in her ear. The voice of Eric Avon, ousted so long ago. Go on, Daph; you can do it. What do those girls have that you don't? You're the prettiest of all of them, and you've seen how Mlle Yvon looked at you, on the Versailles train. She's watching you with those cat eyes of hers; you know she is; you can see it; she's waiting for you to go and join them. Don't be frightened.

That evening, with a supreme insouciance that Gerald would have approved of, Daphne carefully chooses a book from the library—*Women in the 18th Century* by the Goncourt brothers—and makes a spectacular entrance into the "back room," walking in calmly, sitting on one of the chairs, and beginning to read. The conversation comes to a halt and the little group sitting in front of the fireplace stares at her. Their gazes are openly hostile. All of them wait for Mlle Yvon to ask this interloper to leave. But the headmistress's deep voice sounds welcoming, amused. *Come close to the fire, my child.*

It's a triumph.

Daphne is now part of the elite, and the other young girls must simply accept it, because Mlle Yvon seems to consider her the favourite of all her favourites. In Daphne's private journal, Mlle Yvon's first name appears very often. Fernande. Daphne's lessons, the outings to the Louvre and the Opéra . . . all these things are relegated to the background. The essential thing, from now on, is to be close to her, at meals, during visits to Paris, to be next to Fernande, at her right or her left, and what does it matter if the others notice this devotion and giggle about it? Half the girls in Camposenea have a crush on Mlle Yvon, after all. To comfort her, Doodie admits to having a weakness for Miss Vincent, the new red-haired teacher. Daphne questions herself, pouring her heart out in her journal. Crushes are the kind of thing her sister Angela has, rather ridiculously falling under the spell of almost everyone she meets, male or female.

Falling asleep in her sparsely furnished bedroom, hearing only the regular breathing of Doodie and that bell ringing every quarter of an hour, Daphne thinks about Fernande Yvon, about her theatricality, her sophistication. On waking in the morning, her first thought is for Mlle Yvon, asleep on the second floor, just above her, in the apartments reserved for the school's management. What is Mlle Yvon's life like? What secrets does she keep? Daphne wants to know everything about her. This desire consumes her, gnaws at her, and she knows that all of this is much, much more than a mere crush: it is fascination, it is adoration, it has turned into obsession.

One evening, Mlle Yvon accidentally drops her handkerchief on the mezzanine. Daphne discreetly picks it up. What a precious relic, this still-warm handkerchief, steeped in her scent. During an outing to Paris, Daphne buys a light, lemony eau de toilette, and pours a few drops onto the handkerchief. Later, in the back room, she hands the little cloth square back to the headmistress with a sort of courtly gallantry, like a gentleman spreading his cape over a muddy puddle so that his beloved may pass over it without dirtying herself.

Daphne's days revolve around Mlle Yvon's reactions. If Fernande pays her no attention, if she seems preoccupied, Daphne is dismayed; if she sends her a look of complicity, one of her devastating smiles, Daphne feels like singing and dancing on the lawn under the spring sun that shines down on Fleury.

Several times, she is bedridden by colds; hardly a surprise, as Daphne has always been fragile. She receives little gifts from her friends: books, chocolates. But what give her the most pleasure are the handwritten notes from Fernande Yvon, signed *F.Y.*, slipped beneath her door. One day, picking up one of these cards from the floor, she is the recipient of an unctuous smile from Marcel the groom, who is always lurking where you least expect him. He asks her if everything is all right. She glares at him disdainfully. What's it to him? In almost perfect French, she replies that everything is fine, thank you, and slams the door in his face, holding the precious card to her heart.

In April 1925, Daphne returns to Cannon Hall for the Easter holidays. Her parents are struck by how different she is: distant, mysterious, and thinner (and she had no need to lose weight). Her face is pale, her eyes dreamy. Her sisters are in on the secret: Daphne has told them about Mlle Yvon and what an important part of her life she has become. To her parents, she says nothing. She spends hours on end in her room, writing in her journal. She stands in the hall, waiting impatiently for the mailman every morning, and the only mail that matters to her are those letters from the other side of the Channel, the envelopes covered with French stamps and that instantly recognizable handwriting. She counts the days before her return to Camposenea. But didn't Daphne originally want to stay for just one more term? No, she wants to stay until the end of the year, to perfect her French, to master her grandfather's native language. Has she made new friends? Yes, lots of friends, she says nonchalantly. A secret smile. They know nothing. They must never know anything.

At Camposenea, spring has arrived, and Daphne finds Meudon and Fleury overflowing with greenery, flowers, scents. When she walks down Rue Banès to the train station, she always admires the houses that neighbour Camposenea: the villa La Source, with its lofty pediment and its orangeries, the Marbeau property and its chapel, the Villa Paumier and its immense gardens, its elm-lined paths.

On warm evenings, after dinner, Mlle Yvon takes her Firsts to the back of the villa, up the hill, close to the remains of Mrs. Panckoucke's Chinese pavilion. There, they can sit down and contemplate the view of Paris. The air is deliciously perfumed. Here, the truth game takes on another dimension: the questions are intimate, unnerving. If you were invisible, what is the first thing you would do? What is the most foolish thing you have ever done? If you were a meal, what would you be, and how should you be eaten? What is your most shameful dream? Have you ever swum naked? When was the last time you cried, and why? If you were a man, what is the first thing you would do? Who is your favourite person at Villa Camposenea?

Some girls turn white, or scarlet, and flee. Mlle Yvon snorts with laughter, her bright red fingernails covering her pretty mouth like a fan. My God, how timid these English girls are! All except for Miss du Maurier. That flint-sharp look in her blue eyes, that resolute chin, no, she is not afraid of anything, that one, and yet she still has all the charms of a girl of noble breeding, her finesse, her femininity. No question shocks or intimidates her; she gives as good as she gets with her replies, so assured and provocative, and then asks questions that disarm even the boldest of the other girls.

Tod is the only one who knows about the next stage of their relationship. Daphne is less open with her sisters, saving all her secrets for the letters she writes to her former governess, in which she admits her deep crush for Mlle Yvon. Could the headmistress be "Venetian"?* she wonders. It certainly seems that way! Mlle Yvon turns up in their bedroom most unexpectedly and is at her most alluring in the taxi on their way home from the opera. She even goes so far as to embrace the young girl in the backseat, something Daphne finds simultaneously sordid and thrilling. Oh yes, Daphne has been lured straight into the net, and she describes it all rapturously to Tod. Is it love? There is something secret, clandestine, compartmentalized about it: a whirlwind of intimate emotions, a powerful current that surges constantly, but of which she must not allow anything to show on the surface, about which she must say nothing, let nothing slip out; it is in the same disturbing, arousing vein as what she went through four years earlier with her cousin Geoffrey, an experience she has never forgotten. Some of the girls are jealous of her closeness with Mlle Yvon. Daphne has noticed those sideways looks, those whispers, that suspicion.

The finishing school will soon close its doors for the summer, and Daphne is filled with apprehension at the thought of this: How will she cope without the presence of the woman she now calls Ferdie? Daphne has seen her every day now for nearly six months, in classes, in the corridors, on outings, in the back room, at meals, and yet she is never alone with Mlle Yvon. Only in her journal does she dare to describe all her feelings, unburden herself freely of this passion. In her letters to Mlle Yvon she shyly attempts to reveal, without saying anything overtly, a hint of the fizzing effervescence she feels; she writes these letters in French, as best she can, taking care over her spelling, her grammar. Mlle Yvon responds to these letters with a simple look—a brief, discreet look, to which the others are oblivious—but in those green eyes is a promise that Daphne intercepts and treasures.

A wild hope is born in Daphne when Mlle Yvon suggests she come to spend a few weeks at the end of July in the Massif Central, where Ferdie is going for a treatment. Would Daphne care to go with her? Accompanying Ferdie to a spa resort in Auvergne? Is she dreaming? She immediately writes a letter to her parents, making clear the advantages of going on vacation with her headmistress. After all, what could be better for the progress of her French? To Gerald and Muriel's stupefaction, she happily gives up the prospect of a vacation in the sun of Capri and Naples in favour of studiously following Mlle Yvon to La Bourboule.

❧

Daphne still can't quite believe it. There she is, in the middle of summer, at an altitude of over twenty-five hundred feet, her lungs filled with pure air, looking down on the misty mountaintops of the Massif de Sancy, with Fernande Yvon by her side. Daphne's parents gave in so easily. In one of her most recent letters, her mother tells Daphne she thinks it an excellent idea, this studious vacation in La Bourboule; Mo has been told by her dear friends the P. family that it is a charming place and so fashionable: Sacha Guitry, Buster Keaton, all the top people go there. Daphne must write to tell her all about it! Daphne smiles as she replies to her mother's letter. The Italian mail is slow, and letters from her family arrive in Auvergne in dribs and drabs, while hers take a long time to reach her parents in Capri.

She is free. Never before has she felt like this, so independent. Every morning, Fernande goes off for her treatments at the Grands Thermes, a large grey building topped with surprising Oriental-style domes. What kind of treatment is Fernande having, exactly? Daphne doesn't know and Fernande has not told her. This adds to the mystery. While she waits for her friend's return, Daphne writes to her sisters, to Tod, and then fills pages and pages in her journal. Later, she goes for a walk in the town's peaceful, flower-lined streets, where she admires all the elegantly dressed people strolling around. She visits the neo-Romantic church built in white lava, the former casino with its pagoda-style roof that has been converted into the mayor's office. She crosses a bridge over the Vendeix, her fingers brushing the mosaics on its parapets. She sits on a bench and basks in the sunlight. She observes the tall sandstone façade of the Grand Hotel Metropole, with its black pointed rooftops, and spots her room, up there, on the fifth floor, with the wrought-iron balcony. She remembers the train journey that brought them here, her and Fernande. It was the first time Daphne had gone on such a long trip with someone who did not belong to her family. They'd had to catch a train at Austerlitz station and then, eight hours later, change at Clermont-Ferrand to take another, smaller one, which took them to the station here. Daphne watched the countryside move past, glorying in the wild, mountainous landscape. She had never seen the centre of France before, imagined that even her grandfather had never ventured as far as these green peaks.

They arrived at the hotel late and rather tired. She recalls her first dinner, alone with Fernande, far from Camposenea, far from everything. In the dining room, filled with the hubbub of conversations among the well-dressed guests, they ate a plate of Auvergne cheeses, a salad, and thin slices of local cured meat. Fernande, as talkative as ever, had made her laugh with her puns on the name Bourboule, inspired—according to their maître d'—by the Celtic name of the god of spring waters, a certain Borvo. They are in communicating rooms. Through the closed door, that first night, Daphne heard the quiet coughing of the headmistress, the sound of running water, then the squeak of bedsprings. It took her a long time to fall asleep.

At noon, Fernande returns from the spa, her skin pink and smooth. They eat lunch in the hotel, then take the cable car up to the plateau of Charlannes, which towers more than three thousand feet over La Bourboule. Daphne enjoys herself in the little oblong-shaped train that climbs up the mountainside like a caterpillar, digging a path through the huge pine trees. Up at the summit, the view is breathtaking. They sit at a shady terrace of the Hotel du Funiculaire, order tea, converse, and read. Since she has been here, Daphne has been reading, in French, the books of Anatole France, Paul Bourget, Jean Richepin, and, above all, de Maupassant. Reading occupies a large part of each day. She is pleased to be able to read in the language of her ancestors, and when she senses someone looking at her in the cable car, with *Une Vie* or *Bel-Ami* under her arm, she thinks that the person glancing at her must imagine her as French as Fernande.

They speak French together, always. From time to time, Fernande will correct Daphne's pronunciation of a word, a turn of phrase, but she is proud of her young student. It is generally Fernande who speaks and Daphne who listens, religiously. The headmistress is extremely chatty, and her young disciple never tires of hearing her deep voice, her throaty laughter. Fernande's sense of humour is irresistible, and Daphne is in thrall to her mischievous mind. They laugh loudly and heartily together. Between cups of tea, Fernande tells Daphne about her childhood in Avranches, in Normandy. Her father, a gardener named Ferdinand, was hoping for a boy, Fernand; oh well, she was called Fernande! Her mother, Maria, was originally from Aesch, in Switzerland; she is very close to her. As for Mlle Yvon's love life, it is like a novel. Daphne wonders if she is exaggerating a little bit. She had a fiancé, who died at the front; a cousin, who was madly in love with her but for whom she felt nothing; and then a dear friend, a young actor (quite well-known, according to Ferdie) who died in a car accident. And that's without even mentioning the fathers of some of her students, who have tried to seduce her behind their wives' backs, and that Parisian banker, so attentive, who was prepared to offer her financial advantages in return for . . . A shrug, a suggestive smile. Never has Daphne had such conversations with another woman. She is not shocked, simply dazzled. Why is Fernande, who will be thirty-two on her next birthday, still not married? She doesn't dare ask. Why this interminable list of admirers? Does she imagine she is going to impress her young student?

Daphne says nothing, listens closely. In spite of the attraction she feels for Fernande, she realizes she is capable of distancing herself, as if observing their table from afar, and later she will describe in her journal the precise content of these conversations, Fernande's expressions and mannerisms, but also the surrounding décor, the golden slowness of those afternoons in Charlannes, the play of shadows on the tea set, the persistent resinous smell of the pine trees, the laughter of the guests at nearby tables. She is learning how to narrate, recount, seize upon the tiniest detail, and transcribe it on paper, and even if no one else reads her journal, she takes a vital pleasure in this.

Fernande is affectionate, tactile. When they go out for walks, she holds Daphne's arm, leans against her; a passerby might see them as two old friends, happy to be together again. Sometimes, during meals, her fingers brush Daphne's. When Fernande tells a joke, when she bursts out laughing, she puts a hand casually on Daphne's shoulder. Does she have any idea of the excitement her touches provoke? Describing each scene in her journal, Daphne wonders: In a distant future, reading these impassioned pages devoted to Ferdie, will she feel embarrassed? But for now, she is only eighteen, and her whole life is before her.

At the day's end, the mail is distributed at the Hotel Metropole. Daphne is moved by a letter from Angela, in which she learns that Katherine Mansfield, her literary idol, who died two years ago, had once lived in Hampstead—in Portland Villas, very close to their own home. That window she saw, from her bedroom, lit all night, that window belonged to the novelist's house, a coincidence she finds magical. Fernande reads; frowning, she sighs, drums her fingernails on the table. Her mood is changeable, oscillating between giggles and preoccupied silence, and then mutating into irritated impatience. What is in those letters? Why doesn't she smile anymore? When Daphne asks her, Fernande replies that she is annoyed by *"un rien"*—a small thing, of no importance—and this response unsettles her young student. What is this "nothing"? Is it a word, a line, a disappointment, an unkept promise?

During dinner, while Fernande remains walled up in her discontent, Daphne again distances herself from the table, unknown to her companion, projecting herself outside the scene, as if photographing it with words. Nothing escapes her: the bitter creases around Fernande's mouth, the way she keeps shooting disillusioned glances towards the guests at the table facing them, the yawn she conceals with a weary hand, the forced smile that appears on her face when the mayor of La Bourboule, Mr. Gachon, who is dining at an emir's table, comes over to greet each guest. Then, as if by a miracle, without Daphne understanding why, Fernande's face relaxes: she gives her student a sly elbow when a woman wearing too much makeup walks past, takes another slice of tarte tatin. The pianist plays "Plaisir d'Amour," a tune Daphne loves. Her eyes meet Fernande's.

The vacation takes place under the August sun, punctuated by Fernande's treatment, outings to Charlannes, the reading of books. Each night, Daphne listens to the sounds coming from the room next to hers, her face turned towards the door that separates them. Soon, they will go back to Paris together, from where Daphne will return to Hampstead and Fernande to Normandy. After that, they won't meet again until classes start at Camposenea in early October. Two months without seeing each other, without speaking. Only letters. She stares at the door. Last night, Fernande half-opened it to say good night, dressed in a bathrobe, her long black hair flowing over her shoulders. Daphne was reading de Maupassant in bed and this sudden appearance startled her. She dropped her book. Then the door was closed again. She didn't get a wink of sleep.

Was it a message? An invitation? Daphne gets up, draws back the curtain, looks through the window. It is late, almost midnight. The square outside the hotel is deserted. She sees the bench where she sometimes sits during her walks, near the bridge. A pale moon shines in the night. Not a sound. She turns around, looks at the communicating door. A thread of light is visible underneath it. So Fernande is not sleeping either.

Suddenly Eric Avon's voice whispers into her ear, and it is his boy's heart that she feels beating, very strongly, inside her. Go on, Daph; open the door. What are you waiting for?

❧

It is their last day at La Bourboule. Tomorrow morning, they must wake early to catch the train. Their suitcases are almost packed. Daphne and Fernande have afternoon tea at Maison Rozier, the tearoom with the gold-and-blue mosaics in its storefront. They are sitting upstairs, overlooking the street and the passersby. Daphne is reading de Maupassant's *Le Horla*; Fernande is writing to her mother. From time to time, Daphne looks up from the page at the headmistress, observing her suntanned skin, her black, shining hair, her plump little hand, and she wonders, her mind buzzing, if it can be seen by other people, if the couple sitting opposite them have any idea, if it's written on their faces, hers and Fernande's, if their passion can be detected, their desire sensed. But no, nothing is visible, all they see is a woman in her thirties, concentrated on her letter, and another woman, younger, very studious, book in hand. The others see nothing, notice nothing; their secret is well guarded. As they leave the little town the next morning, Daphne knows she will not return to La Bourboule, but this is the place where she will have lived the most intense moments of her young life, instants that—even if they remain confined to the pages of her private journal—will have forged her.

On her return to Hampstead, Gerald and Muriel discover—to their intrigued amusement—a new Daphne, a real young woman, sure of herself, relaxed. She is cheerful, less timid, unhesitatingly accompanying her parents to cocktail parties, playing tennis at Cannon Hall with princes and viscounts, basking in a social whirl that, before, seemed not to interest her at all. But behind the sequined excitement of these soirées, Daphne still thinks about writing. Isn't it time she got down to it properly? These few weeks with Fernande have not solved anything. Good God, she'll never be a writer if she doesn't give herself the opportunity! She complains about this in her letters to Tod. *I try to write, but I find it boring . . .* [3] The ultimate irony is that her aunt Billy has lent her a typewriter and she hasn't even been able to change the ribbon.

September comes around, and she returns to Camposenea for her final term. To Camposenea, and to Fernande. Now Daphne is at last among the Firsts. This is a great satisfaction to her. The other young girls, envious, sense that something has happened between Mlle Yvon and Daphne during the summer vacation. Even Mrs. Wicksteed notices it; she doesn't say anything, but she becomes more vigilant.

On October 19, 1925—a cold, rainy day—Fernande Yvon celebrates her thirty-second birthday. Mr. Sassisson, the chef, makes her a cake. There is a party atmosphere at Camposenea. Daphne, sadly, has caught a cold and must stay in bed. From her room, she hears the sound of voices, laughter, the cheerful singing before the candles are blown out, and she seethes at being separated like this from the one person who means so much to her. After a bad night, Daphne wakes with a high fever. She shivers, coughs, complains of aches and nausea. She looks exhausted. One week later, she is no better. Mrs. Wicksteed begins to worry. The doctor is called. He diagnoses a bad case of flu and expresses concern about the state of the young student's lungs. Panic sets in. Gerald and Muriel demand her immediate return to Hampstead, but a Parisian specialist, after examining her, decides it is impossible for her to cross the Channel in her current state. She cannot stay at Camposenea either, as the temperature in the apartments is too low during this chilly November.

It is one of Muriel's close friends—Mrs. Miller, a rich American lady, married to an impresario—who offers to put up the young convalescent at her suite in the Hotel de Crillon in Paris. That way, Daphne can be looked after by her personal physician, a marvellous Swiss doctor. Everyone agrees with this idea, except Daphne. Leaving Camposenea means leaving Fernande. When Mrs. Miller's chauffeur arrives to pick Daphne up, she is struck down by sorrow, crying like a small child torn away from her mother. Bundled up in blankets, she sobs all the way from Fleury to the Place de la Concorde. In a vast, overheated room, pampered by luxury after the spartan conditions in the finishing school, she begs Fernande to come and visit her more often. Is Mlle Yvon being closely watched by Mrs. Wicksteed? Whatever the reason, Daphne doesn't see her as much as she wants, and that hurts. Daphne submits to the doctor's bizarre treatments: injections of volatile salt, electrified cushions placed on her abdomen, exposure to ultraviolet rays. The doctor's assistant claims that this procedure works miracles but does point out that the doctor's usual clientele consists of ladies of a certain age. After a few weeks of this, Daphne loses weight with frightening speed, falling below one hundred pounds. No one suspects that it is the absence of Fernande—whose every letter, every call, she awaits in a frenzy—that is making her waste away. After receiving yet another tearstained postcard from her daughter, bemoaning her fate at the Crillon, Lady Mo decides to leave right away for Paris, accompanied by Jeanne, who is now fourteen, to judge Daphne's state of health for herself.

It is early December 1925, and snow is falling over Paris. Jeanne catches a cold. Daphne is fraught with anxiety: tonight, Ferdie will come to have dinner at the Crillon; she will meet her mother for the first time. The doctor will be there, too, and Mrs. Miller. What might Lady Mo detect? Will she suspect something? During the meal, Daphne watches her mother on the sly as her mother observes Mlle Yvon. Fernande, dressed in a severe navy-blue suit, her black hair pulled back, is serious, attentive, professional; she acts like a headmistress with a student. Lady Mo is completely fooled. She finds Mlle Yvon remarkably efficient and energetic.

The doctor advises Lady du Maurier to send her daughter to Davos to continue her treatment. Daphne explodes. This is too much! She refuses to go to Switzerland; she will not leave Paris. After a few lively words with her daughter, alone in her room, Muriel finally yields. The doctor suggests Lady du Maurier bring her daughter back to Paris in early January to continue her treatment at a clinic in the 8th arrondissement for six weeks. Muriel asks Mlle Yvon if she could supervise Daphne's treatment in January, during the school holidays. She could stay in a little hotel near the clinic; Muriel would take care of all her costs. After that, when classes begin in Camposenea, Angela will arrive to watch over her sister in Paris, then accompany her to London in mid-February, at the end of the treatment. Mlle Yvon agrees: it is an honour for her to take care of Miss du Maurier's health. Daphne's face regains its radiance, and when the time comes for the headmistress to leave she says a polite, restrained goodbye to Mlle Yvon in front of her mother and her sister, knowing that Fernande will see the warmth and delight in her eyes, like a secret code.

The next day, Daphne, pale and very thin, accompanies her mother and sister to London. Daphne is happy to see her father and Angela again, but she is counting the days until her departure for Paris, when she will once again be with Fernande. As the Christmas festivities are in full swing, Daphne wonders what she is going to do with her life. What will happen to her? When she returns to London for good, next February, how will she settle down to her old routine, the walks on the Heath, the writing of poems and stories that she will never finish, the tall pile of novels that she will read, one after another?

In her journal, on New Year's Eve 1925, Daphne writes these words: *The finish of security. Doubt lies ahead. Adieu les jours heureux**.[4]

ىۋ

Every night, after the medical treatment at the clinic on Rue du Colisée is over, Daphne and Fernande have dinner together at Le Cheval Pie, a restaurant with a black-and-white, half-timbered façade on Avenue Victor Emmanuel, very close to the hotel where they are staying, on Rue de Ponthieu. A table is reserved for them, always the same one, near the chickens roasting on spits, the mouthwatering smell reviving Daphne's appetite. But what

---

* Farewell, happy days.

most entertains them is the little half-hidden step in the middle of the floor. A good number of customers regularly trip over it and fall flat on their faces right next to Daphne and Fernande's table. The two young women dissolve into infectious laughter and the waiters, accustomed to their bouts of hysterical giggling, wink at them while they help the customers to their feet.

Daphne comes back to life. Since her return, on January 4, 1926, since Fernande's beaming face appeared before hers on the platform of the Gare du Nord, she has felt happier than ever before. She suspects the doctor is a quack who is pocketing her parents' money with impunity for a harebrained treatment that is no longer needed because she is already cured, but she is in Paris, in this captivating city, Kicky's city, and she is with the person who matters more to her than anyone else in the world. She feels Parisian to the tips of her fingers, proud of her French blood, and Paris is opening itself up to her. She no longer has to visit it like a rushed tourist, with a herd of clumsy, badly dressed English classmates for company; she is free to stroll along its boulevards, to roam its avenues, its parks, the banks of the Seine.

The first thing she must do is follow in her grandfather's footsteps, walking or by tram, along the Right Bank. She stands dreamily outside 53 Rue Notre-Dame-des-Champs, imagining Kicky emerging from these huge double doors with his companions from the Gleyre studio; then she sips a lemonade at the Rotonde or Le Dôme Café, on Boulevard du Montparnasse. She takes notes in her journal, eating up every detail that the city offers her. Nothing escapes her: the smell of the air, so different from London; the passersby, more elegant and amusing than those in Piccadilly; the packed cafés, the noise, the traffic, the lit store windows, the exhilarating rhythm of life in this capital where Kicky's literary and emotional legacy leaves an indelible imprint on her.

Sometimes Fernande goes with her, but most of the time she is alone. She likes to walk up the Champs-Élysées, past number 80 where Kicky was born, to stroll down Avenue Kléber towards Passy and Rue de la Tour, to immerse herself once again in the atmosphere of her grandfather's first novel, going out as far as the Bois de Boulogne. The next day, indefatigable, she walks along the docks, beneath the rearing white walls of Notre-Dame; she leafs through the wares of the secondhand booksellers on the Seine. It is a personal version of Paris that she is forging, a Paris of the heart that she creates with her hiker's strides, her head filled with Kicky's nostalgic imagined world. Night falls quickly in January. Fernande is waiting for her at the Hotel du Rond-Point, and Daphne rushes back to see her. It is time to eat something after her exhausting explorations. Fernande has ordered brioches, eclairs, cups of hot chocolate.

Daphne's treatment is reaching its end. Fernande must return to Camposenea. When Angela arrives in Paris to take over from Fernande and accompany her sister back to London, she is shocked by the fragile, hypersensitive state of her younger sibling. Angela doesn't recognize this Daphne. Nothing seems to cheer her up or distract her. Leaving Paris is a tragedy for her: she feels like Kicky, torn from a city she loves so much, brutally uprooted. How can she bear this return to foggy London, so far from her darling Fernande, and submit to her parents' authority after escaping it completely for almost a year? She has never dreaded crossing the Channel as much as she does now. Her parents make an effort to be accommodating with her bad moods and lethargy. The only thing that soothes her at all is Muriel's suggestion that she learn to drive. Daphne throws herself into this, and after a few weeks of instruction from the chauffeur and her parents she is capable of driving her mother to the hairdresser, going shopping at Harrods. Another reason to smile: her own dog, which she names Jock, in memory of the Westie she had as a child on Cumberland Terrace. Jock and Daphne become inseparable: he sleeps in her room and sits by the window for her whenever she leaves Cannon Hall, eagerly awaiting her return. But beneath this apparent serenity, enough to reassure her parents, lurk the old ghosts of melancholy and boredom. In her journal, she gives free rein to her feelings of angst: *Everyone at dinner says how well I am looking. If only they knew what I felt like inside they'd talk differently. I guess I hide my feelings pretty well, if I want to. They don't know my mind is starving. Even if I read Claude Farrère, Zola and Maeterlinck. But it's when I get back into the house, and the same things happen every day, that I go into a silent frenzy, and a mist of hate comes over me for it all.*[5]

How can she motivate herself? She is not satisfied with the few short stories she's written, including "The Terror," which describes a child's nightmare, and "The Old Woman," which features a French peasant, nor with a long untitled poem that expresses her disenchantment. She loses heart.

She will never be able to write like Katherine Mansfield. As for being published one day . . . it's unthinkable. She dreams of leaving London, sleeps badly, loiters in the hallways of Cannon Hall. In March 1926, Jeanne suggests they get away for a few weeks, to Cumberland, that mountainous region in the northwest of England, famous for the beauty of its lakes, which inspired poets such as Wordsworth and Coleridge. Jeanne has friends who stayed at a farm near Derwentwater: Why not go there for a while? Muriel seizes this opportunity, certain that a change of air will do the taciturn Daphne good. And why not invite Mlle Yvon to join the girls when Muriel has to go back to London in order not to leave Gerald on his own for too long? Daphne is stunned by this suggestion of her mother's. Does she really not suspect anything? So this long-distance, secret passion of Daphne's doesn't show on the surface at all? She immediately writes to Ferdie. It will be like reliving La Bourboule: the walks, the pure air, the landscape. Ferdie agrees, to Daphne's joy.

In early April, Muriel, Daphne, and Jeanne leave for Cumberland by train. Muriel has rented rooms from Mrs. Clarke, the owner of the large farm. In her journal, Daphne describes the pleasure she feels at being surrounded by wild nature again, the hills, streams and rivers, the silver-shining lakes, the green smells of the trees and plants. She doesn't want to live in the city anymore, content with a walled garden. She enjoys the rhythms of days spent in nature, showing an interest in the farmers and their work, and even the charms of Parisian sidewalks seem to fade when faced with this need that grows inside her: to know the strength of the wind, the taste of the rain, the desire to touch the earth with her hands, to smell it, to feel it. Every morning, she leaves with her sister and her dog and goes off to climb peaks with magical names: Cat Bells, Causey Pike. With her mother, she visits Dove Cottage, the little white house that once belonged to William Wordsworth, left just as it was when he lived there; she walks through the rooms on tiptoes, thrilled by the sight of the desk where he wrote his most beautiful poems.

When Fernande Yvon arrives, ten days later, she brings the rain with her: huge thunderstorms and incessant downpour. This does not bother Daphne; in fact, she delights in the wildness of nature in the dark skies above, the heavy clouds, the wind that howls down the chimney. The bad weather is not to the taste of the sophisticated Frenchwoman, however: the dampness turns smooth hair curly, and, unlike the unperturbed du Maurier sisters, she is far from excited by the prospect of walking through a deluge. It rains every day. Fernande prefers to stay by the fire and chat to the farmers' daughter, with her muddy clogs. And one morning, Daphne hears her friend boasting about the renown of the du Maurier family to a dumbfounded Miss Clarke: Fernande describes Daphne's half-French grandfather, famous all over the world for his novels and drawings, and her father, who is undoubtedly the greatest living actor in England. Daphne can't believe it. Her Ferdie, lowering herself to such pretentious verbosity. This is a facet of the headmistress she has never discovered before. (Later, "doing a Miss Clarke"* will signify "overdoing it" for Daphne and Fernande.)

Back in London in late April, when she arrives at the small hotel in Russell Square where she is staying, Mlle Yvon finds a letter from Mrs. Wicksteed, the manager of Camposenea. Mlle Yvon has been fired. Her services are no longer required at Fleury. There is no explanation. Fernande is in shock, Daphne too. Why this sudden dismissal? Could Mrs. Wicksteed have suspected the true nature of their relationship? Daphne doesn't dare speak about this to Ferdie. And there is no way for her to verify the matter either way. All she can do is try to console Fernande and to encourage her in her idea of starting her own school in Paris. The next day, Daphne accompanies her to Victoria Station; she knows she won't see her again until the summer. Impossible to kiss her tenderly in public, except on both cheeks, Parisian-style. The train moves away, and Ferdie's gloved hand waves through an open window. Two months without seeing Ferdie. It is going to feel like a long time.

In early May 1926, while Daphne frets over the fate of her former headmistress, the country is paralyzed by a general strike that is carried out on an unprecedented scale and will last ten days. Workers protest against the lowering of wages and working conditions for miners. Gerald is panicked at the idea of having to cancel performances of his new play at Wyndham's Theatre, *The Ringer,* adapted from a book by his novelist friend Edgar Wallace. Despite London being blocked by striking workers, the premiere is a success and the play will have a good, long run. Daphne is interested in the prolific Edgar Wallace and his working methods. He has published dozens of books at an impressive rate; what is the secret of his writing? She asks him, as he often drops by Cannon Hall with his daughter Pat, who is the same age as Daphne. He admits that he is capable of "bashing out" a novel in a few days. Daphne stares, amazed, at this balding man with his affable smile, a cigarette holder always to hand. The only method that works, according to him, is discipline. An iron discipline. There is no other secret. No doubt he is right. She will have to force herself to write at least one page per day. Beyond her desire to be a writer, there is another desire, even more pressing: to be independent, to earn a living, no longer to rely, as her sisters do, on the pocket money given them by their parents.

At almost nineteen, Daphne already knows that she wants to live a long way from her family, a long way from Cannon Hall. She must provide herself with the means to do so. She shuts herself up in the little changing room above the tennis courts, with its musty smell of sweat, and sits there with a notebook and a pen. *I sit down all afternoon and do more writing. It comes very slowly, though. It's so much easier to think out vaguely in my head than to set it down in words. I wrote better at fifteen than now.*[6]

The coming summer is full of temptations for a pretty girl who loves to dance and laugh. The invitations pile up; Daphne is never short of devoted admirers eager to take her to a ball, or the theatre, or a garden party. Must writers hide away in a cave in order to write, she complains, when told that her car is waiting for her downstairs and she still hasn't found the earring she was looking for. Or maybe she must simply become less attractive, so no one notices her, so people don't whisper as she passes, That's the du Maurier girl, the prettiest of the three. She will write tomorrow.

~❦~

On the evening of July 15, 1926, Daphne arrives in Paris, at the Gare du Nord. Fernande has arranged to meet her at the café Le Dôme, at the Vavin crossroads. The next morning, early, they will catch a train from Montparnasse station to Lannion, in Brittany. Their ultimate destination is Trébeurden, the small fishing port on the Côte de Granit Rose. Her parents agreed without too much difficulty that she could accompany Mlle Yvon there. Paris is wilting under a heat wave. Sitting on the terrace of the Dôme, a place that always makes her think of Kicky, Daphne stays in the shade, her suitcase at her feet, and writes in her journal, discreetly observing the customers at the next table. To her amusement, they seem to be an illicit couple, the girl younger than the man, and their falsely casual attitude fails to conceal their nervousness. What point have they reached in their love affair? Where are they from? Daphne listens: they are British, which makes her smile. The man is cursing because he can't find a hotel room: there are no vacancies in the whole of Paris, it's outrageous. He pours wine clumsily, his face glowing and flushed; he's drunk already. The girl, who is not much older than Daphne, says nothing, biting her lips and looking lost, her face wan, dark rings under her eyes.

Daphne watches them, thoughtfully, and the story comes to her on its own: she sees its basic outline, knows how it will start, already knows the ending. She has no need to dig deeper or reflect. It's simply there. Leaning over her notebook, she doesn't notice that Fernande has slipped into the chair next to hers, so occupied is she with her writing; she no longer hears anything, she is caught up in her own momentum, whisked into a world that is not hers. When at last she glances up, Fernande is looking at her, warmly, tenderly. Daphne hugs her tightly—she is so happy to see her— then shows her the notebook with its pages full of words and whispers that she was inspired by the English couple next to them. She tells Fernande the story, and when her friend says, smiling, that it is a horrible story, Daphne bursts out laughing and nods, overexcitedly, yes, yes, it's a very dark tale, just awful.

Fernande has reserved a room in a hotel on one of the little streets off Boulevard du Montparnasse. She warns Daphne smilingly: It's not the Crillon, or even the Hotel du Rond Point, but everything else was full; she had no choice. On the doorstep, the manageress of the hotel looks them up and down with a contemptuous, mocking expression, as if she knew all about them, as if she didn't approve but had seen others just like them, and Daphne notes her white, puffed-up face, her dull red-dyed hair, just as she notes the shabby décor of the seedy hotel—a real *hôtel de passe*, she breathes to Fernande, who laughs loudly—and the murmurs behind the doors, the stained carpet on the stairs, the hideous wallpaper, the smell of something foul in the air, the chipped pitcher, the view over a dark court-yard with wet rags hanging from a clothes line. In the oppressive heat, undimmed by the fall of night, Daphne weaves her story, thinking about it constantly as she and Fernande have dinner in a brasserie on the boule-vard. She listens patiently as her friend complains about the heat wave, her exhaustion, the difficulties she is having setting up her school, and the story continues to construct itself inside Daphne's mind, until late at night, in the stifling humidity of the little room on the top floor.

The next day, on the train, while Fernande dozes, Daphne continues writing, rereading, scratching words out, correcting them. She gently wakes Fernande, hands her the notebook. Fernande deciphers the determined, resolute handwriting, taking a little longer because the story is in English, then, at the end, smiles, patting Daphne's wrist: but how on earth did she think of all this, what an amazing imagination she must have, and that end-ing . . . it's so dreadfully macabre! Daphne nods: she's not interested in romances or happy endings; she wants to grab her readers by the throat, never to leave them indifferent. That English couple, things were not look-ing good for them; you could see it on their faces, they were going to have a terrible night. Daphne takes back the notebook and, in a firm hand at the top of the page, writes a single word, the title of the short story.

"*Panic.*"

What a relief to leave the sweltering sauna of Paris for the coastal breezes of Trébeurden, to breathe its scents of seaweed and salt. The Hotel de la Plage is situated almost on the sand, next to the little port of Trozoul. Al-though "port" is something of an overstatement: there are only about thirty fisherman's dinghies here, and a few yachts. Daphne likes the sounds of the Breton names when she hears the locals pronounce them and repeats them herself, laughing as she rolls her r's: *Pleumeur-Bodou, Lan Kerellec, Goas-Treiz, Trémeur.* Fernande seems less preoccupied, more relaxed, happy to lie in the sun and smile. Daphne goes swimming every morning, discov-ering deserted coves where she can bathe nude, unobserved, in a turquoise sea. She likes to gaze at Le Castel, a rocky promontory that encroaches on the sea with a large rock that looks like a man's head in profile, and to admire the island of Milliau, which is sometimes accessible by foot at low tide. What a delight it is to walk on the still-wet sand, to discover, in the puddles that remain, what the sea has left behind it: the seaweed, the clams, the crabs that are a source of joy to fishermen.

In the afternoon, the two women go out near Perros-Guirec in a chara-banc and return tired but happy, their blood stirred by the sea air. While Fernande takes a nap during the hottest part of the day, Daphne roams in the hills of the little town, admiring the Gothic architecture of the Ker Nelly château, walking past an abandoned manor house and pausing there for a while, enchanted by the ruins of the high walls, the remains of the square tower, starting to daydream about what might have happened here, hundreds of years before. On Rue de Bonne-Nouvelle, the highest in the town, she notices the rectangular bell tower of an old granite chapel, by the side of the road. There aren't many people around as she slips inside, sits on a wooden bench, and admires the inner framework, in the form of an upturned ship's hull. Above the altar, she sees a retable representing the Virgin Mary in front of a maritime landscape, carved models of ships, inscriptions on the walls: *Pray for my son, out on the sea.* Suddenly every-thing snaps into place, just like it did on the terrace of Le Dôme Café. She leaves the chapel with the beginning of a story brewing in her head. She already has the first line: *It was hot and sultry, that oppressive kind of heat where there is no air, no life.* A sad tale about a naïve young woman, engaged to an unfaithful sailor, who comes to pray in this church.

Later, in the silence of the hotel room, while Fernande is still asleep, Daphne writes, sitting in front of the window, looking out to sea. From time to time, she turns to glance at Fernande, her black hair spread over the pil-low, one naked voluptuous shoulder revealed by the crumpled sheet. The title of Daphne's short story: "La Sainte-Vierge." During aperitifs on the ter-race (both of them drink Dubonnet Rouge), Daphne hands the notebook to Fernande, hoping for her approval, watching every expression on her face. Why are the young woman's writings so gloomy, so dark, when she herself is funny and cheerful? Better like that than the other way around, replies

Daphne, her nose turned up in a comical grimace that makes Fernande laugh. The summer days stretch out between sea, swimming, walking, and reading—de Maupassant, D'Annunzio, Voltaire. Every morning, from her window, Daphne contemplates the rolling hills of the little island of Molène, feeling an instinctive attraction for its wild, uninhabited appearance. One day, they rent a fisherman's boat to take a tour around it, admiring the fine sand that looks untouched, the white dunes. Daphne starts to daydream about living by the sea, as if Trébeurden's motto, "Ar Mor Eo Ma Plijadur" (the sea is my pleasure), had been written especially for her.

When she gets home in late August, Daphne's family is amazed by her radiance, her joie de vivre, even if none of them suspects how much she misses Fernande and France. In the dining room, after the evening meal one Sunday, Daphne asks her father to read the two stories and the handful of poems she wrote during her trip to Brittany. To her surprise, he seems proud of her, encourages her, is not put off by the darkness of the tales, even whispering to her tenderly that one day, he hopes, she will write novels even more famous than *Trilby*. *You remind me so much of Papa, always have done. Same forehead, same eyes. If only you had known him.*[7] Will she ever have the courage to work as tenaciously as Kicky, to embark upon a novel? Well, doesn't she already feel the same love her grandfather felt for Paris, the same curiosity towards the family's noble glassblowing forebears?

Every week, she waits for Fernande's letters. Her former headmistress has found a house in Boulogne-sur-Seine and already has two boarders with which to launch her finishing school. Daphne has only one desire: to go back to Paris, to see Fernande again.

Angela, in turn, reads her short stories and encourages her. Daphne decides to write in a more disciplined way in an unused room above the garage in Cannon Hall, but she lacks inspiration. One morning, at breakfast, as she is holding Ferdie's latest letter in her hand, her mother announces in a casual voice: *Your father and I have been thinking, that it would be a good idea if we could find somewhere, a house of our own, perhaps in Cornwall, where we could all go for holidays, instead of abroad. Edgar has been so generous over* The Ringer *that we could afford it. You'd like that, wouldn't you? Lots of swimming and walking.*[8] Daphne is mistrustful, detecting a parental plot hatched with the aim of dissuading her from returning to France and seeing Fernande. Her parents must by now have guessed at the intensity of the connection she shares with her former headmistress.

Grudgingly, with a shrug, Daphne agrees to accompany her mother and her sisters to Cornwall on September 13, 1926, to look at houses.

Though she cannot know it yet, this journey will turn her life upside down.

Part Three

Cornwall, 1926

Ferryside

Freedom to write, to walk, to wander, freedom to climb hills, to pull a boat, to be alone.

—Daphne du Maurier[1]

Fowey, Cornwall
November 2013

I t takes nearly four hours by train to get from London to the small town
of Fowey, in Cornwall, on the extreme southwest coast of England. This
is a maritime region, with a wild, craggy coastline studded with coves and
fishing ports. The wind blows hard; the sky is usually cloudy, the emerald
sea is controlled by the swell.

Walking through the narrow backstreets of the town, as steep as those
in Hampstead and Fleury, I understand why Daphne fell in love with this
place. Even in November, the light is glorious. Comparing the current reality with photographs of Fowey dating from 1926, I notice that there are
few modern constructions spoiling the beauty of the view. The façades of
the old houses are white, pink, yellow, or pale blue, those of stores and pubs
red or green. Here, the inhabitants smile, say hello, even to me, the stranger.

At sunset, I walk along the esplanade in the hills, towards St. Catherine's Point, where there are the ruins of a castle. I pass Whitehouse Beach
and the Fowey Hotel. I pass Readymoney Cove, an inlet amid this rocky
coastline with its pebble beach. I climb up to the ruins. The sea stretches
out into infinity.

I know that Daphne climbed up to this point, too, because she describes it in her memoirs. She stood where I stand now, she put her hands on this same balustrade, she looked out at the bay, where the River Fowey flows into the sea opposite the village of Polruan, which rises up on the hillside, its white and grey cottages standing out against the greenness. The sun disappears amid purple streaks, the seagulls screech above my head, and at the foot of the cliff, the backwash rumbles.

The next morning, under a clear sky, I go to the other side of town, out towards Bodinnick. Down by the estuary there is a white house, looking curiously like a Swiss chalet, with blue timbering. The figurehead of a woman is attached to the wall below the last window on the right, on the second floor. To cross the river, I have to take the little ferry that goes every fifteen minutes. As I approach the house, I make out the large white letters on the façade. *Ferryside.*

It was in this house that Daphne du Maurier wrote her first novel, at the age of twenty-two. Today, her son lives here.

⁓❧⁓

Since their train left Paddington Station this morning, Daphne has been staring out the window, bored stiff. She doesn't even feel like reading. Muriel, Angela, and Jeanne are excited by this trip and their mission: to find a house. But nothing seems to rouse Daphne from her torpor. She barely listens to her sisters or her mother, thinking, as always, about Fernande, about that magical summer that seems so far away at this moment, even though it is only two weeks since Daphne left Trébeurden. From time to time, she senses her mother's eyes on her, examining her, judging her, and she sighs: how tiring they are, her parents, and how little they understand her!

She dozes, barely touches her plate at lunch, refuses to join the others in swooning as the train crosses the impressive iron bridge of Saltash, built by the famous civil engineer Isambard Kingdom Brunel, which spans the River Tamar. They are in Cornwall now, her mother announces, and Daphne rolls her eyes, slumped in her seat. She could have stayed in peace at Cannon Hall, trying to write, tinkering with other short stories, other poems, instead of being dragged to the other end of the country against her will. Despite her bad mood, she cannot help noticing that the landscape has changed: luxuriant grass stretches out as far as she can see; the turquoise sea plays hide-and-seek with the train, the sky is streaked with beautiful shafts of light, as if the entire view had been painted with an infinite palette of greens, apart from the pink touches of spiked loosestrife, the scattered red of scarlet pimpernels.

The next morning, Muriel rents a car with a chauffeur to take them west towards St. Austell. The sun shines so warmly, it feels almost like summer. The car takes the seaside road and Daphne's pulse accelerates. She didn't sleep well, but she opens her eyes wide now, rendered speechless by the rocky coastline that spreads out to her left, and suddenly, at the top of the hill, as Fowey Bay opens up in all its splendour and she sees the immensity of the water, the jetties, the moored boats, the little houses clinging to the cliff side, her emotion grows so strong that she finds it hard to breathe. She feels as if she is coming home, to a land she loves, a place she belongs.

The car drops them at Bodinnick, at the bottom of the path, by the river. It is lunchtime; why not stop at the Ferry Inn, just next door? They could take the boat across the river after that. Daphne notices a large FOR SALE sign outside a house in poor condition, at the water's edge, next to the landing stage. They are told by a passerby that yes, it is for sale, its name is Swiss Cottage, it was previously used for boatbuilding, and only the upstairs floor is habitable.

During lunch on the terrace of the Ferry Inn, Daphne and her sisters cannot stop admiring the unusual Swiss Cottage below. It has something, this house, a charm, potential, they are all agreed. After coffee, the girls leave their mother to have a chat with the restaurant manager and go back down the path towards the river, entering the muddy land that surrounds the curious dwelling. There, they discover that the house is a troglodyte, built into the cliff itself, a detail that only serves to increase their love for it. The large, open space at the first floor of the house, through which a little stream flows, was used to build the hulls of boats, while on the second floor they made and stored sails.

Daphne stands by the water and sniffs the air, the odors of tar, rigging, rust, mingled with the saltiness of the tide. Suddenly she understands, shaking her head incredulously: Fowey is just like Trébeurden, that little piece of Brittany where she had felt so happy, so free, far from everything, far from London. Trébeurden and her secret love with Ferdie, writing, inspiration, and, beyond all of this, the incantation of the sea. Fowey and Trébeurden are twin mirrors facing each others in the two countries she loves, the country of her ancestors and the country of her birth, sister towns filled with the same colours, scents, and sounds.

Jeanne stands next to her and, noticing her agitation, slips an arm around her neck. Angela joins her sisters and together they look out at the uninterrupted flow of maritime traffic: fishermen's boats, sailboats, barges, large ships guided by tugs. The sailors notice the young women and blow their foghorn while waving to them. Later, they take the ferry with Muriel, walk through the streets of Fowey, then end up at the Fowey Hotel, where they stay for three nights, enough time to begin the process of buying the house, because yes, they have decided, all four of them equally enthusiastic, without even consulting Gerald, who gave them carte blanche, that Swiss Cottage will be theirs, that it will belong to the du Maurier family, no matter how much it costs, no matter how much work the place will need, no matter if it isn't ready before next summer. It will be their house, and they will name it Ferryside.

~*~

That autumn, the light of Fowey still glows in Daphne's eyes and in her heart, and she is uninspired by the dark room above the garage at Cannon Hall where she tries to work. Nevertheless, she sticks to her task and writes a few poems and short stories. The work on Ferryside has been started by the eager, indefatigable Lady Mo, who roams London in search of paintings, furniture, and chintz to her taste, while in Cornwall the roof is remade, staircases are built, ceilings lowered, bathrooms added, under the watchful eye of a contractor. Progress is rapid. Muriel and Gerald learn from J. M. Barrie that one of his dear friends, the novelist Sir Arthur Quiller-Couch, son of a Cornish doctor, lives in Fowey, in a large house that overlooks the bay, named The Haven. Barrie organizes a dinner in London so that they can all meet one another. Quiller-Couch and his wife are delighted to discover that the du Mauriers will soon be their neighbours. Their daughter, Foy, is a few years older than Daphne. In spite of this meeting with Arthur Quiller-Couch, nicknamed Q, a famous intellectual whose work she has admired since reading *On the Art of Writing*, the only thing that cheers Daphne up is a puppy, an adorable golden retriever that she takes for walks on the Heath every day, until she is out of breath. Gerald, as he was with Angela the year before, becomes possessive, watching over Daphne's walks, her nights out, wanting to know with whom she comes home, with whom she goes out. Daphne finds these interrogations unbearable, and they are even worse—frighteningly aggressive—when he has been drinking. Who does he think he is? Why doesn't her mother put an end to these accusations? Daphne is not doing anything wrong, just having a little fun. How does he have the nerve to preach to her when she knows he cheats on Muriel with the young actresses from his "stable"? Her vision of love, sex, and marriage grows even darker, and this shows in her writing—short, biting stories that feature manipulative and ridiculed women, spineless and ruthless men, guided by their sole desire.

She has to wait until November before she can see Fernande again. In the meantime, Mlle Yvon has opened her own school in Boulogne-sur-Seine, with two students, her new boarders. She has adopted a dog, a German shepherd named Schüller. Daphne feels at ease in the headmistress's modest house on Rue des Tilleuls, close to the woods. She would rather stay there than at a hotel, taking advantage of her status as Ferdie's favourite. Within a few days, she succeeds in winning over the fierce Schüller, and while Fernande gives lessons, Daphne goes out for walks. The two weeks pass quickly.

In Hampstead, faced with Gerald's interrogations and her mother's cool indifference, Daphne is relieved to be able to accept an invitation from the great family friend Edgar Wallace to spend the New Year holidays with his family in Caux, Switzerland, at the luxurious Palace Hotel. Angela goes with her. They have never tried winter sports before, and it is a revelation, especially for Daphne, who is naturally more athletic than Angela. Against a snowy fairy-tale backdrop, Daphne discovers the pleasures of skiing, sledding, and ice-skating. In the evenings, there are dances in the ballroom of the Palace Hotel, and the du Maurier sisters, free of the paternal yoke, prove immensely popular, Angela for her sense of humour and her contagious laugh, Daphne for her beauty and her talent as a dancer. They spend their nights at the bar, drinking, laughing, and dancing, along with all the other girls in their golden little world. The champagne flows, their heads spin, the boys flock to them, and kisses are distributed in a frenzy of casual flings. For the first time in her life, at nearly twenty years old, with admiring eyes watching her on the dance floor, Daphne feels beautiful, becomes aware of her seductive charms.

In March 1927, Daphne goes to Berlin with the actress Viola Tree, a close friend of her parents. Viola has professional engagements to attend during her stay: she has to meet a director, visit a few theatres. Though this is almost certainly a diversion deliberately created by her parents, Daphne submits without protest: Viola is a lovely woman, and the young writer is curious to discover Berlin. In her journal, she notes: *Complete efficiency.*

Quiet. Little traffic in the streets. Enormous amount of people everywhere. Complete luxury at the Hotel Adlon, where Viola, excited as a child, turned all the taps on in the bathroom full blast. We dine at a bourgeois café. How the Germans love their food![2] The next day, a walk in the Tiergarten pales beside Daphne's memories of the Bois de Boulogne: the passersby all look so dour and plain, and while the Kaiser's former palace in Potsdam is undeniably impressive, as is Frederick the Great's Sanssouci Palace, it still isn't Paris. No other city could ever take Paris's place in her heart. She goes back there in April, to stay with Ferdie for three weeks, and enjoys taking Schüller for walks in the woods, goes for solitary strolls along the Left Bank while Fernande gives classes, sits outside Le Dôme Café with the ghost of Kicky and drinks lemonade. Something has changed, though. Paris and Fernande both retain their appeal, but now Daphne is captivated by another place, a place she thinks about constantly. Fowey. The name of that town is on her lips all the time, Fernande complains, feeling abandoned. Daphne's mind is elsewhere: she dreams of returning to Fowey, of seeing Ferryside again after eight months of renovation work carried out energetically by her mother, and Ferdie, saddened, can sense it.

A few days before her twentieth birthday—May 9, 1927—Daphne takes a train to join up with Muriel and Angela, who have moved into Ferryside with the help of Viola and dear old Tod, who has gone to visit them. Daphne is stunned by the transformation in their new second home; her mother has performed miracles. On the first floor, Daphne discovers a vast, light-filled, comfortable living room where boats used to be made, and on the second floor, in place of the sail storeroom, she admires several pleasant bedrooms and a modern bathroom. On the top floor are her parents' bedroom, their bathroom, a large dining room, and a fully fitted kitchen.

The real miracle, though, is that Daphne has been given the green light by her parents to stay at Ferryside alone for a month, after the others leave on May 14. She still can't quite believe this. Did they give in to her pleas out of weakness? Have they simply accepted her obsession with Fowey? Whatever the reason, it is a demonstration of trust. A woman from the village will come and cook for her and clean the house, but apart from this nice, honest Mrs. Coombs and Biggins the gardener, Daphne will be alone for the first time in her life. The car leaves, with Muriel, Angela,

Tod, and Viola inside, and the heavy wooden door closes. Daphne jumps for joy, stroking the rough walls at the back of the living room, formed by the cliff face, caressing their cool crevices, singing at the top of her voice, and going outside through the room on the second floor, which has a door that opens on to the garden. She gambols in the grass, turning her face up to the May sun, and thinks how wonderful life is. She turned twenty yesterday and she is alone in her favourite place in the world. This is the best birthday present her parents could possibly have given her: this freedom, here and now.

Before she does anything else, she must master her new kingdom, get to know every nook and cranny of it. Daphne wakes early to the sound of seagulls and ship horns, eats a quick breakfast, puts on her sea boots and a pair of trousers (she can't stand skirts, which she considers impractical) and a blue-and-white-striped pullover, not forgetting the cap pulled down over her short hair. She looks like a sailor, and this pleases her. She walks, stick in hand, up the slope behind the house, turns right after the ruins of the St. John chapel, climbs the path towards Pont Pill, the peaceful estuary of the River Fowey that winds through the greenness of the ferns. A sign warns that the area is private, but she pays no heed and walks through the copses, intoxicated by the smell of damp earth, crossing through St. Wyllow and heading for Polruan. The sunlight filters through the dense foliage, a stream babbles close by, and behind a bush she discovers a shady, sparkling pond. She passes old quarries, disused lime kilns, barley silos, piles of coal. Down below, on the layers of mud that dry when the tide is low, she spots the framework of a schooner, with a figurehead still fastened to its hull. Fascinated, she rushes down the slope to take a closer look at the remains of this abandoned ship and reads the name still visible on its stern: *Jane Slade*. What was this ship's story? Where did it go? How dashing it must have been with this black-haired woman on its bow, her face lifted up in a smile, a bouquet of flowers held to her chest.

At the top of the steep path, in Lanteglos, on the road to Polruan, there is a little stone church that reminds Daphne of the simplicity of Notre-Dame-de-Kergonan, in Trébeurden. She likes to stop here and admire the old gravestones, the names of the dead overrun by a dogged orange lichen. One morning, she manages to decipher the name *Jane Slade 1812–*

1885 on one of the tombs. The same woman the shipwrecked boat was named after? Who was this famous Jane Slade? How could she find out? Daphne pushes the thick oak door, which opens with a creak, and enters the silence of a sacred space she respects, even if she is not a regular church-goer, feeling nourished by the sense of peace that emanates from these old yellow stone walls, these west-facing stained-glass windows that filter a hopeful light, these sculpted wooden benches worn away by the years. Here, as in Trébeurden, she can sense the fervour left behind by generations of sailing families who came to this church to pray.

When she goes back down to the village, the inhabitants she meets are all welcoming. They have come to recognize her slender, boyish figure, her long athletic stride, and they all wave to her, call her Miss Daphne. And she, in turn, is beginning to learn their names: the Bunnys, the Hunkins, Captain Bate, Miss Roberts . . . She goes by the dock, ob-serves the boats, noting their names, their shapes, imagining what they might be carrying, where they might be going, where they might stop over on the way. Everything about this maritime world interests her, and she gulps down the details. Sailors come to Fowey from all over the world to fetch cargos of clay and kaolin, down there, at Carne Point, at the modern, fully equipped landing stage. She goes there and watches the operations, becoming covered in white powder. This makes her laugh. She likes noth-ing more than listening to sailors, feeding on their stories of the sea, of storms, captivated by these men who spend more time on water than on terra firma.

There is one, in particular, whom she could listen to for hours: Harry Adams, a veteran of the Battle of Jutland, a big, strapping fellow, his fea-tures craggy with age, who is amused by this well-bred, angelic-looking young lady who dresses just like him. She wants to learn to sail? Perfect—he can teach her. He knows this estuary like the back of his hand. With his help, she learns in the space of a few weeks how to raise a sail, work out the strength and direction of the wind, steer, head out to sea. With him, she goes fishing, even in bad weather, and she doesn't flinch when she has to pull the hook from the mouth of a wriggling fish, she isn't afraid of the long eels they drag from the water near the jetties in the evening, after sunset. Sitting face-to-face in the fisherman's boat, they talk: he tells her about the history of Fowey, about his youth, his love of the sea. Does he, by any chance, know the story of the *Jane Slade*, the wreck of the schooner that lies at Pont Pill? Know it? Of course he does! He's married to a Slade, granddaughter of the famous Jane, and his brother-in-law, who runs a naval shipyard in Polruan, undoubtedly has some old letters lying around somewhere. Harry would be happy to find out, if she's interested.

In the euphoria of these first weeks, Daphne almost forgets what she has come to Ferryside to do: write. She gets down to work, writing a poem inspired by Jane Slade, then a short story, "And Now to God the Father," about a conceited London priest, every bit as dark and disturbing as her previous tales. In her journal, she writes: *I walk back by the loveliest lane imaginable, absolutely filled with peace and beauty. I could cry and laugh with happiness. I walk slowly, taking it in. Tired when I get back, and I read.*[3] She feels guilty, though: she is behind in her letter writing, she hasn't written to Fernande since she arrived here, nor to her parents, and the latest letter she receives from Aunt Billy only intensifies her guilt: *It's rather selfish of you, darling, not to write home and tell them what you are doing, when it's so kind of them to let you be down at Ferryside on your own.*[4]

Thankfully, Daddy isn't there—he is absorbed by his latest play—because Geoffrey, the dark handsome cousin she hasn't seen since that summer when she was fourteen, writes to her from Plymouth, where he is staying with his brother. Could he drop by and see her one day? She doesn't need to be asked twice. She picks him up at the train station, noting that he has aged—he is nearly forty-two now, after all—but the blue sparkle in his eyes is as flirtatious as ever. Immediately they strike up the same kind of naturally complicit relationship they enjoyed before, and which so worried Gerald: they laugh, joke, have fun together, going for a long, exhausting walk around Fowey and then having a drink outside the house as night falls. They don't touch each other, don't hold hands, but Daphne knows the old attraction is still there, even if the feeling between them has become more fraternal. Her cousin comes to spend the afternoon with her on several other occasions. When Gerald finds out about this, he phones his daughter, suspicious and inquisitive: What did they do? Where did they go? When is he coming back again? Later, she recounts this conversation to Geoffrey, who has a good laugh: Old Uncle Gerald, on the warpath again, they should make him believe the worst; that would be funny, wouldn't it? Daphne scolds him: he's crazy, irresponsible, her father would be furious. Suddenly Geoffrey grows serious: oh come on, she knows he's always been like that; it's in his nature, that irresponsibility, that lightheartedness, it's because of their cursed French blood, and that phrase makes his cousin smile, despite herself.

Her month of solitude comes to an end. In mid-June, Angela arrives from London with her Pekinese dog, Wendy, to take her sister back to Cannon Hall. Daphne is devastated at the idea of leaving Fowey. She must wait until the family vacation in July to sleep at Ferryside again, with her younger sister, Jeanne, when they go down to open the house up for the summer. There is an exciting surprise waiting for her: the gardener, Biggins, gives her a young dog—a cross between a spaniel and a sheepdog—named Bingo, who accompanies Daphne on her daily walks.

Gerald is going to visit Ferryside for the first time. The rest of the family worries about this. Will he love this house as much as his wife and daughters do? Won't he be bored, far from his club, his "stable," his theatre, his garden? In readiness for the summer, and to please Daphne, Gerald has bought a motorboat, the *Cora Ann*. While she waits for her father to arrive, Daphne learns to pilot the boat with her new friend, Harry Adams. She manages quite well, he tells her. In fact, his brother-in-law does have a packet of letters and other documents relating to Jane Slade, and he can show them to her if she's still interested: it all relates to the history of the Slade family and the construction of the ship. Daphne joyfully accepts, but she doesn't have time to read them because her parents arrive, along with their usual stacks of suitcases, their friend Viola, and their servants. The peacefulness of Ferryside is shattered.

The vacation begins in the worst possible way. It pours with rain. Muriel twists both her ankles and has to stay in bed. Viola slips on the docks outside the house, falling into the water and catching pneumonia. Gerald, who has never piloted a boat in his life, almost crashes the *Cora Ann* against the rocks. Daphne has the impression that her sanctuary has been invaded; she submits in silence to the permanent flow of elegant visitors who come and go all summer. Every morning, she escapes, going out to sea with Adams, sailing to Polperro with him, living the life of a sailor, in her trousers and jumper, her hair a mess, her face tanned, to the despair of her mother, who wishes she would wear dresses and keep her skin nice and pale.

In October, when the time comes to leave Ferryside, Daphne writes in her journal, sitting by the window of her second-floor bedroom: *I've just realized that I think of nothing nowadays but fishing, and ships, and the sea, and a sea-man's life. Adams and I go out and catch mackerel until after seven, and after dark we go up to the jetties and I catch a monster conger-eel, I'm sure it weighs about 30 lb. The river, the harbour, the sea. It's much more than love for a person. I don't know how I'm going to exist back in London. It's heart-breaking. To go away from this, the place that I love. I gaze for a long while at the sea. I tell the garden, the sea, that I shall be back soon. It all belongs to me now.*[5]

⚜

Twenty years old, and so impatient. She is dying of boredom in this damned city, London, when she could catch a train and escape to Fowey! How futile it all seems, accompanying her mother to Selfridges, carrying parcels, standing on a crowded Tube, rushing everywhere. Daphne daydreams that she is on the boat with Adams, feeling it sway on the rolling sea, hearing the shrill cry of the seagulls, breathing the salty odour of the breeze, imagining Bingo's joyous barking when she sets foot onshore again. There is only one way out: she must leave Cannon Hall. Winter arrives, with its grey skies. Ferryside is shut up. But there is still Paris. Yes, there will always be Paris. On an impulse, Daphne spends all her savings—more than thirty-five pounds—on a round-trip train ticket from Victoria to the Gare du Nord. She announces to her parents that she is going to France for a few weeks, and she says it so firmly, good lord, jutting out that bold chin of hers, that they don't dare say a word. She just packs her bags and goes. Rue des Tilleuls is waiting for her with open arms. How happy she is to see Fernande and Schüller again, and four new students. One unpleasant surprise is the presence of a certain Joan, an elegant, thin-faced brunette, American, a former boarder at Camposenea. Daphne remembers her, one of those snooty members of the "elite" who did not at all appreciate Daphne's entry into the back room. Now Joan is strutting around, leaving an affectionate hand on Ferdie's shoulder, whispering languorously into her ear. Daphne's enjoyment of this getaway is due less to Fernande than to the pleasure of re-discovering France. In her journal, Daphne writes in French, after a walk to Boulogne, on Rue des Menus, describing her freedom, strolling hatless along the streets of the Italian quarter.

The return to Hampstead in mid-December is, as always, painful. Her mother and her sisters have gone to Fowey to prepare Ferryside for the Christmas festivities. What has happened to her father? As soon as he gets up in the morning, his breath reeks of alcohol. He hangs around the house, whining self-pityingly. At a birthday dinner for Gladys Cooper, their actress friend, he gets drunk, and Daphne has to take him back in the car, alone, while he blubbers on her shoulder. She entrusts him to the servants, unable to bear his shamefaced expression when she leaves the room. Why has her mother burdened her with such a responsibility? It isn't up to her—his daughter—to look after him. Gerald is fifty-four, his hair is thinning, his long face is gaunt, the numberless cigarettes have wizened his skin, yellowed his teeth, and yet he still he thinks he's Peter Pan. He is a child. He is pitiful, even if the love she feels for him is unaltered. Her father, so vain, so self-centred, and at the same time so endearing and fragile. This complex personality simultaneously fascinates and repulses her.

Daphne takes the train with Gerald to Cornwall on December 21, 1927, to join the rest of the family. He is in a better state, but his blue eyes fill with tears as he watches the landscape speed past, his hands tremble, and he cries during lunch, though she has no idea why. She doesn't dare ask (does she really want to know the answer, after all?). Shouldn't he see a doctor? She doesn't know how to describe these recent days to her mother, how to put words to the crisis that her father is going through, how to disclose the drunken incident at Gladys's house. How can her mother bear such behaviour? What a farce marriage is! How do people manage to spend the rest of their lives together?

Daphne's anxieties fade in the face of the gaiety that reigns at Ferryside, the house decorated with holly and ivy, piles of presents, the Christmas dinner, all the festivities supplied by Muriel with her habitual expertise. This is the first Christmas at Ferryside, and it is a success. Geoffrey is there, without his wife, sick in hospital, and he seems to feel no remorse at all when he caresses Daphne's knees under the dining room table, under the very noses of her parents. But she no longer feels the arousal she felt six years before. The truth is that she pities Geoffrey, just as she does her father.

As the year ends, Fowey shivers under a fall of unexpected snow. 1928 begins with a series of domestic troubles: the boiler breaks down, and so does the oven. No more hot water, no more heating. Gerald complains, Muriel grows agitated, and everyone decides to head back to London. Everyone except Daphne. How can she make them understand—all these people who call her selfish—that she doesn't care about discomfort, that she finds it a thousand times more enticing to brave the cold of Ferryside than to be speared with boredom in Hampstead, that she wants to live without them, that she feels happy when she is alone? Is it really that complicated? Intense relief floods through her at the sight of them leaving on the ferry, headed for the train station. Quick, time for a walk with Bingo! She climbs the road up to Lanteglos, contemplates the silvery beauty of the bay, taking deep breaths, delighting in her solitude, finally at peace.

Back in the calm of the house, she gets down to work, wrapped up in a blanket, a hot water bottle on her knees. She sits facing the view she loves so much: the river, the passing boats, the ballet of seagulls. Here, in her room at Ferryside, the words come effortlessly; she doesn't have to wait for them as she does at Cannon Hall, in the room above the garage where nothing ever happened. Words fill the pages. Never before has she written with so much energy. Time passes, and she doesn't even realize. She is working on a new short story, so extreme in its darkness that she wonders if it's not a bit too much, perverted even, then decides not to worry about it. She keeps writing. Her heroine is a young girl who keeps a secret. She must find her a name, this beautiful brunette with her swan neck, her crazy eyes. A powerful, captivating name, the kind of name a man might scream or moan. She scrawls a few at the top of the blank page. *Jane*. No. *Olga*. Not that either. *Lola* . . . Perhaps. *May* . . . Suddenly her pen traces the letters of *Rebecca*. Yes, that's it: Rebecca! She will call her Rebecca. It sounds right, strong, the shivering *r*, the *b* forcing upper and lower lip together like a kiss, the two *c*'s stuck together, hard as a *k*. And that final *a*, a complaint, a groan. Rebecca lives in Bloomsbury, on the top floor of a tall building. What will we discover through our narrator, a young man dangerously attracted to her? What lurks behind the door of her attic apartment, in a round room, the walls covered in velvet, with thick curtains that muffle every sound? A disturbing truth. Rebecca prefers making love with a life-sized robot that she names Julio; this is her drug, her obsession, the only way she can feel pleasure. The title of her story? "The Doll." Daphne smiles as she imagines the look on her parents' faces. Maybe she shouldn't show this to her mother: What could she take from this cruel tale, after all, other than that men are just toys, replaceable at will?

The next day, Daphne is invited to tea by the Quiller-Couches, the friends of J. M. Barrie, in their house on the Esplanade. She wears a dress instead of her customary trousers, makes an effort with her hair. The atmosphere is cheerful and welcoming. Lady Quiller-Couch is charming, elegantly dressed in lilac satin. Daphne gets on wonderfully well with Foy, the writer's daughter. It is Foy who introduces her to Lady Clara Vyvyan, an eccentric author and indefatigable traveller who lives in the manor house of Trelowarren, near Helford. Foy and Daphne share the same passion for the sea and for boats. What's that, Daphne doesn't have a sailboat? But she absolutely must, now she lives in Fowey. This is now all Daphne can think about. The *Cora Ann* is a motorboat, fine for the river or for a calm sea, but really, there's no comparison. She talks about it with Adams and convinces her parents by showing so much enthusiasm that they can't help but be charmed. She has won: she will have her boat. But, in the meantime, she must return to London, to the damp February cold.

Daphne has polished up her dozen short stories and she is quite proud of them, despite the often sordid and chilling subjects, the texts marked by a cynical vision of sexuality that does not reflect her own life at all. In her stories, all is adultery, vanity, manipulation, madness. Her writing is biting, lively, incredibly caustic for someone so young. What do Gerald and Muriel think of it? Daphne couldn't care less. She wrote all the stories with passion, and that is what counts, not her parents' opinion. Her aunt Billy types them, then the stories are submitted to a literary agent, an acquaintance of Viola Tree, for an opinion.

The presence of Geoffrey, who has come to Cannon Hall to spend a few days before undertaking the long journey to Australia, lights up Daphne's winter. His wife is still convalescing in Brighton. Late at night, when everyone is asleep, Daphne meets her cousin in the living room, on the first floor, creeping downstairs on tiptoes. She is in pyjamas, and so is he, waiting for her in the dark. He draws her towards him and kisses her. A real kiss. Then another. A lover's kisses. Night after night, they meet in secret. She writes in her journal: *I suppose I oughtn't to let him, but it was nice and pleasant. I wish he could have been more light-hearted about it, though, and then I would have no compunction. But men are so odd. The strange thing is, it's so like kissing Daddy. Perhaps this family is the same as the Borgias! Daddy is Pope Alexander, Geoffrey is Cesare, and I am Lucretia. A sort of incest.*[6]

Despite the pleasantness of their kisses, Daphne warns her cousin in a long letter that he should pull himself together, stop lying—to his wife, to himself—and face facts. The day before his departure, Geoffrey thanks Daphne for her frankness; she is right, and he will conquer his own inconstancy, his weakness, but he has one last thing to tell her. Gerald came to speak to him last night, a scowl on his face, and asked him out of the blue, *Are you in love with Daph?* And Geoffrey replied, *I've been in love with her for seven years.* A bitter grin from Gerald: *Nothing can come of it, you realize that?* Geoffrey's reply: *I know, uncle, I know.*[7]

After saying goodbye to Geoffrey, Daphne stands by for a response from the literary agent regarding her short stories. The wait seems interminable. What if she went to see Fernande again? It is snowing when she boards the ship at Dover, but she doesn't care about the weather: Paris welcomes her, as always. In her journal, in French, she describes the smell of tobacco and beer that float by in the dusty streets, mingling with the odour of freshly baked bread. She longs to go back in time, to keep these moments forever. Sitting at Montparnasse café terraces in the early springtime, she amuses herself by detailing the faces of customers and passersby, reading Colette, Duhamel, D'Annunzio. One morning, Fernande hands Daphne an envelope with an English stamp, forwarded by Aunt Billy. The agent enjoyed her stories, he wants to see more; he is certain he will be able to find her a publisher.

✤

Daphne goes back to London for her parents' twenty-fifth wedding anniversary, celebrated in great pomp at the Savoy Hotel on April 11, 1928. She notices that her father does not like the portrait of Muriel his wife gives him—it's written all over his face—and when he tries to attach his gift for her, a bracelet, to her wrist, it turns out to be too small. *Oh dear, it was so pathetic,*[8] Daphne writes in her journal. Only her return to Fowey and the splendours of spring give her back her joie de vivre. She will be twenty-one soon, and a wonderful gift awaits her. Adams let it slip: his brother-in-law, Ernie Slade, who runs the shipyard at Polruan, is taking care of it in tandem with her parents: the du Mauriers will have a sailboat, but it will belong, above all, to Daphne. The most exciting thing is that she will be able to oversee the boat's manufacture from the beginning. She must start by choosing the wood that will form its keel. Daphne asks him if Ernie is from the same family as Jane Slade. The very same, laughs Adams, the same family who have been building ships in Polruan as long as anyone remembers. And what about that box full of letters? Isn't it time she took a look at that?

In the exhilaration of these moments, Daphne puts aside the stories she is supposed to write for the literary agent. The boat is the only thing on her mind, and she doesn't miss a single stage of its construction. She knows its dimensions already, meets with Adams every morning at the shipyard, watches the men as they saw, cut, sand the wood. Ernie Slade answers every question she poses, charmed by her fervour. Jane Slade was his grandmother, a hell of a woman; the ship was named in her honour. Would Miss Daphne like to keep the figurehead as a souvenir? Daphne obtains her parents' permission to have the wooden figure repainted and attached to the wall just below her bedroom window.

That same week, Adams knocks at the door of Ferryside while Daphne is drinking a cup of tea in the kitchen. He is holding a large box, which he hands to her with a smile: It's for you, Miss Daphne. The box is stuffed full of old papers—letters, documents, notes. All about Jane Slade. Alone, filled with wonder, she leans over these yellowed pages with their old-fashioned handwriting; her tea goes cold as she is transported to another age. She takes the box up to her bedroom, grabs a notebook, a pencil, and hastily draws a family tree for the Slades going back to the beginning of the nineteenth century. Chewing the end of her pencil, then her finger-nails, she dives back into her reading of the letters, only pausing to scrawl notes, and something begins to take shape. The colourful character of Jane Slade seems to dominate the entire family, leaving its imprint on her children, grandchildren, great-grandchildren, and the ship that bore her name continued to sail for a long time after her death.

Daphne gets to her feet and begins pacing her room. Isn't there enough material here for a novel? And it's all there, within easy reach. Of course, she'll have to work it, imagine the rest. Will she have enough energy to write a whole novel, she who hasn't even managed to complete any more short stories for the literary agent? As she sits down again and leafs through the letters, intoxicated by their dusty, damp smell, ideas come to her, effortlessly. She sees the path of the narrative open up before her. Jane Slade's son, the captain of the schooner, could also be a central character in the novel, connected to his mother by a timeless love.

The next morning, at the shipyard, Ernie Slade asks Daphne if she has thought about a name for the family boat. She talked about it on the phone with her father yesterday; he is as enthusiastic about it as his daughter, and they agreed that the boat should have a French name in honour of their French blood. Isn't that a good idea? It will be the *Marie-Louise*. The schooner will not be ready for weeks, though, as construction is behind schedule. Daphne is disappointed. As a birthday consolation, on May 13, 1928, her parents give her a flat-bottomed rowing boat, painted black, with a little red sail, just for her: the *Annabelle Lee*. This eases her irritability, and she celebrates her twenty-first birthday at sea with Adams, who admires the dexterity of her oarsmanship. Despite her fine bone structure, Miss Daphne rows like a real sailor. It seems strange to celebrate her birthday without her family, but she finds that she likes it. How many girls of her age would prefer to be out at sea rather than dancing in a bar? She opens a few presents: a pretty notebook from Viola, a red scarf sent by Fernande that matches the *Annabelle Lee*'s sails. And a card from Geoffrey, posted from Melbourne. Those Borgiaesque kisses in the darkness of Cannon Hall seem so distant now. In her journal, she writes, in French: *I no longer recognize my former actions.*

Summer comes to Fowey and with it the rest of the du Maurier family. There is a long parade of guests, and as the sun shines down, Gerald seems to reconcile himself to Fowey. On July 2, 1928, British women are given the right to vote, but this news has little impact on Daphne, who is growing impatient because the *Marie-Louise* still isn't ready. She wonders if Jane Slade suffered similar frustrations while waiting for her own ship to be built.

On September 13, the big day finally arrives. A bottle of champagne is ritually smashed against the bow of the *Marie-Louise* by Daphne. The sun shines and the east wind blows. Daphne's knees tremble: she has been anticipating this moment for months! The Slade family is there, and the du Mauriers too, all gathered on the pontoon in the Polruan shipyard. Everyone walks aboard: a solemn, precious moment. The schooner slowly leaves the port; then suddenly the wind fills the sail with a sound like a whip and Daphne's heart swells with joy. She takes the helm with a sure hand, feels the boat rear up, playing with the wind, and maintains her course under the watchful, protective eye of Adams. They leave the bay behind, and now they are out at sea, rushing over the waves, and she smiles, euphoric, the captain of the *Marie-Louise*.

A few weeks of sunlight and sailing, and then the autumn is here with its cold weather, and they must store the *Marie-Louise* in a depot in Polruan for the winter. They scrub its hull, clean out its interior, and cover it with a tarpaulin to keep out ice, salt, mould. Daphne oversees the operations for the first time, saddened at the idea of having to wait for spring before she can see her beloved boat again. Ferryside becomes calm again; only Angela, Daphne, and the dogs remain, and they must close the house up soon. Has she made any progress with her stories? She can't bear her parents asking her that question. Thankfully, they have left. No, she hasn't made any progress, and she feels guilty about it. Why has she grown so lazy? She dreams of independence, of being able to live at Ferryside without financial help, and she's not even capable of knuckling down to work. She has to get started again. Other girls of her age long to be married, to start a family. One day she might, too, perhaps, but for now writing is her priority: writing and earning a living from it, not having to depend on anyone else, whether it's a husband or her parents.

It is a pleasure to spend time with her older sister, an impulsive character, as dark as Daphne is blonde. Angela is always in a good mood, she laughs easily, never complains. But who is she really? Daphne wonders sometimes. Does it bother her to be the least pretty one, the sister no one notices? There is a lack of finesse to her features, she has a chubby face; her eyes are brown, not an intense blue like Daphne's. Angela's curves are no longer fashionable; in the 1920s, the style is for girls with slender, boyish figures. At twenty-four, she does not seem ready to find a husband any more than Daphne does, but in contrast to her sister, she enjoys going out, having fun. There is nothing timid about her; she is at ease in her parents' theatrical set, all those elegant, exuberant people who love to dance, smoke, drink, and laugh. The very people Daphne avoids. One evening, as they are walking along the Esplanade with their dogs, Angela admits that she too would like to write novels, like Kicky. This confession amuses her sister: Why not, after all? They have the same genes—Angela is a du Maurier, just like her, descended from the same artistic French lineage, and it is surely no coincidence that Jeanne paints and plays the piano.

One October night, while Angela is reading in her room, Daphne quietly leaves the house and crosses the river on the *Annabelle Lee*, her faithful dog Bingo by her side. She strolls through Fowey's silent streets towards St. Catherine's Point and climbs up to the ruins of the castle. The moon is shining on the black rocks, the dancing sea. Daphne can hear nothing but the lapping of the waves below. She thinks about the novel that is taking shape in her head, this book born of her passion for the sea and for Fowey. A shiver runs through her. Her novel will span four generations of a family, beginning with a powerful woman and her son, connected by a love that nothing can destroy. She can feel the book at her fingertips, but she must wait a while longer before she has the will and the perseverance necessary to write it. For the moment, it inhabits her. It is an imaginary land where she likes to wander, to lose herself, like Kicky's beloved "dreaming true" that provided so much inspiration for his own books.

Before going back to London at the end of the week, the du Maurier sisters have tea one last time with the Quiller-Couches. How lucky they are to live here all year round! Like Daphne, Angela has fallen in love with Fowey, and she tells her hosts, with her customary volubility, how much she finds pleasure in walking with her sister around town, especially up to Gribbin Head, above Sandy Cove, where the blue of the sea and the green of the countryside meet in perfect harmony. Daphne nods—a beautiful place, and as it happens she noticed, during one of their most recent walks, the grey roof of a distant house, just visible above the trees, inland. Lady Quiller-Couch pours her another cup of Darjeeling with a smile and says, Oh, that's Menabilly.

Daphne hears the name for the first time. She pronounces it herself, as a question. Arthur Quiller-Couch replies in his calm, deep voice that Menabilly belongs to an old Cornish family who have lived in Fowey since the eighteenth century. That manor house was built during the reign of the Virgin Queen; it's a very old house, its walls soaked with history. If those walls could speak . . . Daphne sits up suddenly in her chair, almost knocking over her cup of tea as her sister watches her, affectionate and amused. Couldn't they say a bit more? It sounds fascinating. What exactly happened at Menabilly? Q stands up and walks over to the large window, facing out to sea, takes a sip of his tea, and begins to tell the story. One has to go back, way back to the bloody Civil War between the Cavaliers and the Roundheads that raged from 1642 to 1645. Menabilly was sacked by the parliamentary soldiers; it was carnage. Daphne listens, spellbound. For a long time, it's been rumoured that Menabilly is haunted, Q goes on, because when a new wing was constructed in the last century the skeleton of a Cavalier was discovered in a secret walled-up room. Lady Quiller-Couch reminds her husband about the ghost of the lady in blue, who can be seen in the same window of one of the house's rooms. Daphne is restless with excitement: she wants to know who lives there now, how to reach the house. She is told that Dr. Rashleigh is the owner, but he doesn't go there anymore; he lives in Devonshire and has no descendants. He had a troubled childhood in Menabilly, his parents are dead, and the house hasn't been lived in for years. It must be in a terrible state by now. She wants to go there? It's a few miles from the bay, quite easy to find from the Four Turnings crossroads, but she has to cross through thick, overgrown woods, because nobody looks after the property.

Back at Ferryside, Daphne can still hear Q's voice resonating within her, explaining that, at its zenith, thirty years ago, Menabilly was a splendour— they used to go there for garden parties—but all that is over now; it's like the house in *Sleeping Beauty*. While Angela talks in the kitchen with Mrs. Coombs, who is making their dinner, Daphne examines a map of the surrounding area in a guidebook bought by Muriel. She locates the spot, marks it with an X, and triumphantly announces during the meal that, to-morrow, they will go to Menabilly, they will find the famous house. Angela strokes her cheek, teasing her: What is her obsession with Menabilly? Why is she so interested in it? Daphne, wolfing down her food, shrugs: she doesn't know how to explain it; all she knows is that she is attracted to the idea of this abandoned house. Later, when she goes to bed, her last thought is of that mysterious dwelling, buried deep in the woods.

The next day, in mid-afternoon, the sisters set out, with their dogs on leashes. It's a sunny day—no rain or wind—and Daphne admires the autumnal colours, the golden leaves, the still-blue hydrangeas. At the Four Turnings crossroads, they have to pass a lodge to open a huge rusted gate. They hesitate. What if the guard comes out and asks what they're doing? Daphne looks through the windows of the lodge. No one lives there anymore: the place is deserted. They are free to go on. Watched by the anxious Angela, Daphne manages to open the creaking gate. They enter a private driveway, pushing through thick undergrowth. As they advance, wide-eyed, the trees grow taller and the sky disappears behind their interlacing branches, like the vaulted ceiling of a cathedral. The sisters talk only in whispers now, even the dogs remain silent. The driveway meanders through deep greenery, and Daphne starts to daydream: she can almost hear the clatter of a horse's hooves, the squeaking wheels of a horse-drawn carriage, can imagine the costumes of another age: doublets, capes, three-cornered hats, and powdered wigs.

They walk for a long time—the dogs' tongues hang from their mouths; Angela's feet ache—but still no manor house. Have they become lost in this labyrinth of brambles? They feel as if they are going around in circles, tripping in the same potholes, struggling past the same claw-like branches. Angela hates this ghostly atmosphere; when darkness falls, she firmly declares that she's had enough, she wants to go back, she doesn't care about finding the house. The owls hoot, and other birds make frightening cries. A fox noses around somewhere close and the dogs growl. A clinging damp rises from the mossy ground. It's cold. Angela shivers. Finally, Daphne accepts defeat, for tonight. Reluctantly, she agrees to go home.

But how can they find their way back? A pale moon barely illuminates the shadowy path where evil-looking shapes seem to lurk, crouching in the blackness. Angela holds tight to her sister's hand, and it is the brave Eric Avon who, step by step, guides her towards the safety and warmth of home. The forest grows lighter at last, and they find themselves on a hill that slopes gently down towards the sea and a cove. No manor house any-where to be seen. They try to orientate themselves: they are in Pridmouth, at least two miles from home. How could they have walked so far? It's a long way to Bodinnick, and it's the middle of the night. When they finally arrive at Ferryside, they are worn-out and the dogs are panting with thirst. Mrs. Coombs says she was beginning to worry. But a fine meal is waiting for them. Angela asks her sister if she really wants to go back there; Daphne, eating her soup, answers with a frown: Of course, what does she think? They will leave nice and early tomorrow morning, without the dogs. She spotted a road on the map that does not go through the forest. Angela sighs, rubbing her aching feet and wondering what on earth has got-ten into her sister.

This time, they take Muriel's car, driving on another road that goes around the forest, towards Par, and park outside West Lodge and another gate, just as rusted as the one they saw the day before. Daphne pushes it open without difficulty. They walk through woods, anxious at the thought of meeting a guard or watchdogs, but they don't see a soul. Nor do they see a house. Have they gone the wrong way again? *Perhaps Menabilly has no wish to be disturbed, perhaps she wants to remain a house of secrets,*[9] Daphne whispers, and her sister points out to her that she is speaking about this house as if it were alive.

They come out on a wide lawn overgrown by weeds and bordered by trees, and Angela sees her sister's face light up. Who can she be looking at with such fervour, such love? Curious, Angela follows Daphne's gaze, and there is the manor house rising up in front of them: Menabilly, a large, two-story building, its shutters closed, its grey façade covered by thick ivy. They stand at a distance, listening out for any signs of life, but it is utterly silent, so they move towards it. One of the first-floor shutters is open, they notice. Through the dusty windows, they make out paintings on the walls, furniture covered with sheets, an old rocking horse with peeling paint. Angela finds the place gloomy, filled with sadness and solitude, but Daphne doesn't feel that way at all. That evening, she writes in her journal until late at night. *Menabilly has taken hold of me.*[10]

༖

Daphne's short stories have not found a publisher. She is bitterly disappointed. To console her, Aunt Billy gives them to her brother to read: Willie Beaumont is the editor of *The Bystander*, a popular magazine with a large readership. Uncle Willie is enchanted by "And Now to God the Father," a cruel tale featuring an odious parson, the Reverend James Hollaway, the heartthrob of London, but the story needs a little work, a prospect that does not enthuse Daphne. She prefers to leave for Caux in early 1929 with her friend Pat Wallace, Edgar's daughter. She wants snow, sunlight, pure air. To leave behind her parents and their social whirl. To leave behind her literary disappointments. Daphne is intoxicated by skiing and by the flings she enjoys in the evenings. In a letter to Ferdie, she confides: *I was kissed by two young men at the same time, and another man, married, kissed me outside in the snow.*[11] Dismayed, and certainly jealous, Fernande sends her in reply an angry, reproachful letter that makes her smile. Dear Fernande, so quick-tempered. But what Daphne doesn't know is that Fernande has warned Aunt Billy (whom she met in London, two years before) about her niece's "misconduct," and when Daphne returns to Cannon Hall a few weeks later, she is greeted by a stern-faced welcoming committee, including a father who is more suspicious than ever and a disapproving mother.

There is one pleasant surprise, however, amid this oppressive atmosphere: one of the young men she met in Caux (but not one of those she kissed) gets back in touch with her. His name is Carol Reed, he is Daphne's age, and she likes him. He is the illegitimate son of the actor Herbert Beerbohm Tree, the father of their friend Viola. Tall, dark, and slim, Carol is an actor and works at Edgar Wallace's film studio. With the cinema causing devastation to the popularity of the theatre, even the great Gerald du Maurier eventually finds himself obligated to move from the boards to the silver screen, a painful transition that is not particularly successful. Gerald is going through a rough time: his manager, Tom Vaughan, has just died, and the supervision of Wyndham's Theatre is complex, as is the thorny issue of income tax, which Gerald has never dealt with, leaving all the paperwork to Tom. Gerald's glory days are behind him, he has mountains of back tax to pay, no play to stage, fewer roles, and even the film industry is giving him the cold shoulder. And he's not getting any younger: what hurts most is seeing that face in the mirror each morning, bereft of its former charms. He becomes depressed, and that drives him to drink.

Two or three times a week, under Gerald's glowering eyes, Carol comes to Hampstead to pick Daphne up in his dilapidated Morris. They spend hours in cafés, smoking and talking. They go out to dinner, go to the cinema, then drive at top speed through London, kissing at every red light. They walk the streets, arms around each other's necks, and laugh as they climb scaffolding, enjoying the danger, then kiss again. When Carol takes her back, late, to Cannon Hall, Daphne looks up at the third floor, and behind the twitching curtain she perceives the severe face of her father, cigarette drooping from his lips as he watches them. As soon as she crosses the threshold, the rebukes begin. The pages of her journal are filled with her protests: *Honestly! They might have been born centuries ago. They treat me like a Victorian miss of 16, instead of being nearly 22.*[12] Angela agrees with her: you'd think their father wanted them to be nuns, locked up in a convent!

Gerald Borgia is back. The Sunday chats between father and daughter in the dining room are tense now. *Are you in love with Carol?* Daphne's reply: *He's a dear, I'm fond of him.* Gerald pours himself a glass. Bad idea. *Is he serious?* Daphne: *I don't know what you mean by "serious."* Gerald downs his glass in a single gulp, pours himself another. Daphne looks away. *Where do you go when the restaurants have closed?* She sighs. *We sort of drive around.*[13] How can she explain to him their walks by the Thames, all the way to Limehouse, the stories Carol tells, their complicity, their jokes, their kisses and caresses? Gerald wouldn't understand any of it. And the next morning at breakfast, it's Muriel's turn, her voice cold, her gaze contemptuous. *This coming home at one o'clock in the morning has got to stop. In future, you must be home by midnight. Really, it's the thin end of the wedge.*[14] Why such drama? They should be happy to know that a young man is in love with her, given their deep suspicion of her relationship with Mlle Yvon.

Will they never be content? Clearly, she can do nothing right in their eyes. How can she ever become a writer with parents like these on her back? It's hardly surprising, she thinks, sniggering to herself as she strides determinedly over the Heath, that there is something diabolic about her stories born in such an atmosphere, sordid, disturbing, so far from the image of the pampered heiress. And yet that is exactly how she looks, on the front page of her uncle's magazine, *The Bystander*, when it finally publishes "And Now to God the Father," slightly changed and shortened, in the spring of 1929. For this she receives a fee of ten pounds, a decent start. Uncle Willie insisted that she pose for the cover, and she played along: went to the hairdresser, wore an elegant beige trouser-suit, a gold necklace.

The magazine comes out while Daphne is alone in Fowey for a week. She makes a discreet visit to the local newsagent to buy a copy, somewhat embarrassed, her cap pulled down over her eyes, and can't get over the experience of seeing her words in print for the first time. She thinks about all the people who will read her story. Her first readers. The cover itself has little effect on her: that sophisticated image has nothing to do with her, with the real Daphne, dressed like a sailor, but she is aware that her name is a springboard, understands why her pedigree is mentioned, her illustrious grandfather, her famous father . . . to her, this seems normal, even if she must now make a name for herself.

That evening, Carol calls her from London: how proud he was to see his "darling Daph" on the cover of a magazine. He offers her his warmest congratulations. Daphne smiles: he's so sweet, this boy, she treasures their closeness, their giggling fits, the way they can tell each other everything or, equally, can stay silent but understand each other all the same. She adores his caresses, even if they do not possess the same forbidden passion as her secret affair with Ferdie. Carol's absence weighs on Daphne—she won't see him again for several weeks—but she has to face the truth: when she is here, she doesn't really miss anyone or anything. She is at peace with herself, in her domain.

One morning, Daphne gets up at five o'clock, crosses the river on her rowing boat, runs through the still-sleeping streets, and goes down to the beach at Pridmouth. The sun is rising; the sea is calm. The only other human being she sees is an old fisherman who waves to her from afar. The air is cool, coloured with a milky mist that slowly dissipates as she walks up the long road to the peak of the hill, to the house that awaits her. She finds herself on a grassy footpath, lined with wild hyacinths. At the top of the hill, she turns around, her face caressed by the breeze and the rays of the rising sun, and looks out over the bay spread out below her, the point of Gribbin Head straight ahead. She is welcomed now not by owls but by the songs of thrushes and robins. Daphne walks to the end of the lawn, and the house appears, mysterious, surrounded by giant rhododendrons: she has never seen them grow so huge, so red. Daphne turns to the house of secrets and stares at it like a lover. She sits in the dew-wet grass and keeps staring and staring, enthralled. How much time does she stay there? Finally she gets up, her legs numb, and approaches the house, flattening her hands against its grey wall, under the ivy near the front door. A shiver runs down her spine and she closes her eyes, abandoning herself to this dizziness, more powerful than love, stronger than anything.

❧

In late June 1929, as she prepares to spend the summer in Fowey, Daphne receives an unusual request from Rudolf Kommer, Viola Tree's impresario friend, whom Daphne met in Berlin two years earlier. He is contacting her on behalf of the famous American investment banker Otto Kahn, who wishes to invite a group of favoured people on a three-week cruise in the Norwegian fjords aboard his luxury steam yacht. The financier saw the cover of *The Bystander* and enjoyed reading Daphne's story, and he would like her to be part of the voyage. Daphne's first reaction is to refuse: she doesn't know anyone on the ship apart from Kommer, she would undoubtedly be the youngest person on board and would probably be bored stiff, and besides, what about her clothes? She has no outfits chic enough for this kind of occasion. Her family is amazed: How can she turn down such an opportunity, she who adores the sea, ships, travel? And surely this trip would prove a great source of inspiration: it might make a novel one day. As for her wardrobe, all it would take is a few trips with Angela to Lillywhites in Piccadilly, and Muriel's dressmaker could quickly make her several evening dresses. Daphne is not convinced.

She meets Carol that evening at the Café Anglais in Leicester Square. She tells him she has no desire at all to bow and scrape to a bunch of toothless old farts, stuck on a boat. Carol listens, laughing: she's so funny, his "Daph," when she imitates other people, sarcastic and scathing, more than slightly provocative. Well, then, she should stay, he says, kissing the back of her hand, her palm. She should spend the summer with him in London and leave the old farts to their cruise. On the red backseat in the Café Anglais, while the band plays "You Were Meant for Me"—their favourite song— Daphne kisses her lover and doesn't notice the time passing . . . My God, it's one in the morning, what a nightmare; her parents must be waiting for her now, wild with rage, on the doorstep. She can already see Gerald's "Borgia" face. They must go now, drive at full throttle to Hampstead, prepare for the worst. Strangely, not a single light shines at Cannon Hall. All is silence. Daphne stealthily emerges from the Morris, blows a few kisses to Carol, slips inside the house, and rushes up to her bedroom, relieved.

The next morning, war is declared in the du Maurier family. Muriel's face is cold as stone. As she wrote to Carol this morning, this is the last warning she will give them: if the rules are not respected, if Daphne is not back before midnight, they will not be allowed to see each other again. Daphne is speechless. The crisis is unexpectedly diverted by poor Angela, who is suffering from acute appendicitis. Carol scrawls a letter of apology to Sir Gerald and Lady du Maurier. But the harm is done, on both sides. There is no way Daphne can endure the coming weeks in the company of her parents. So, what if she decided to accept Otto Kahn's invitation?

On the platform at Victoria Station, in early July, Daphne gets to know her travel companions, not such old farts after all, even if she is the youngest person in the group. There's Lieutenant Colonel George, with his pretty wife. Two married ladies, without their husbands. A big, strapping, funny man and a tall, shy, bearded man, both single. Their host, Otto Kahn, is waiting for them in Hamburg with his friend Rudolf Kommer to set sail on the *Albion*. They are accompanied by a ravishing blonde, Irene. But which one is her lover, Daphne wonders mischievously, Otto or Rudolf? Or maybe both? The steam yacht is incredibly luxurious: each cabin has its own bathroom, the living room and dining room are decorated with great pomp, and all the meals are prepared by a chef.

Destination Copenhagen, Stockholm, and Oslo. The further north the yacht moves, the longer the opaline sun stays in the sky: here, in high summer, the sun never sets. During meals on board the ship, Daphne gets to know Otto Kahn better. He is an affable and distinguished man, in his sixties, with silver hair and moustache. She is flattered that this rich, world-famous financier, a great art collector and patron, is so interested in her and seems to enjoy their philosophical discussions. She, in turn, asks him about the construction of the immense Oheka Castle, his property on Long Island. He eagerly describes the building, which is every bit as grand as any French château, with more than a hundred bedrooms, its name a contraction of his own (Otto Hermann Kahn). He is the richest person she has ever met. His wealth does not impress her all that much, but her natural curiosity gets the better of her: she wants to know more about the spectacular rise of this Jewish millionaire, born in Germany.

The cruise continues and during the white nights on the bridge, as the guests sip champagne, Kahn seems to neglect Irene, the pretty blonde, and show more interest in Daphne. He is old enough to be her grandfather; she is not amused. How to discourage the gallant Mr. Kahn? She coaxes the shy, bearded man from his shell, and he in turn is besotted. Even the lieutenant colonel knocks on her door while his wife is napping to "have a chat"; Daphne gently sends him packing. The only one not to fall under her spell is Ralph, the big, burly man, whose nose is buried in a book with the surprising title *The Sexual Life of Savages*. In her journal, she describes the stopovers: *Oslo made no great impression on me. The fjords were another matter. This beauty is too much. It's defeating, utterly bewildering. Beauty most exquisite. Blue and ice-white, mountains high and aloof with green, thick trees, yet utterly desolate, no humanity. Somehow, profoundly unhappy. I thought of the boy who would run away to sea in the white twilight in the book I must write one day, but he wouldn't be in a steam-yacht, he'd be sailing before the mast.*[15] Though she relates her onboard conquests in great detail in the journal, she takes care not to mention them in letters to her family, or to Carol.

One sunny morning, Daphne is sitting on the edge of a fjord with Otto Kahn. The others have stayed on the yacht. A worrying situation. Facing the magnificent view, he tries to kiss her, once, twice. How can she reject him firmly, but with grace? There is no question of letting him get what he wants. She stands up suddenly, removes her dress and her underwear, watched by her stupefied host, and dives naked into the cool waters of the fjord. A risky manoeuvre, but it works. Kahn does not move, watching her swim with a bitter little smile on his face, then hands her the towel when she comes out, shivering. That is as far as he will go. The forty years' difference between them put an end to his hopes of any funny business. During a later stopover, he offers to buy her a mink coat. She declines, replying impishly that fur is for old women, then points towards a silver dagger: That is the kind of thing she would like more if he insists on buying her a gift, and who knows, maybe it would come in useful one day?

The yacht is now heading south. The weather is changeable, the sea less calm, the ambience on board no longer quite so pleasant. Rudolf is sulking, and so are the two ladies; the lieutenant colonel's wife avoids Daphne's eyes. Irene drinks too much at lunch and has to be escorted, reeling, to her cabin. When she returns from the cruise, Daphne does not tell anyone much about what happened, but the whole story is recorded in the pages of her journal. From time to time, she looks at the dagger given to her by Otto Kahn, dreamily caresses its handle, and smiles.

London, in the heat of late July, and Daphne has an important meeting (thanks to Uncle Willie) with Michael Joseph of the prestigious literary agency Curtis Brown. Their offices are on Henrietta Street, in Covent Garden. He has read all her short stories and enjoyed them, but he feels certain that she is ready to write a novel. Doesn't she already have an idea for a novel in mind? Daphne admits she does, an idea that has been brewing inside her for the past year. So what is she waiting for? Hesitation. Then she decides to trust this man, even though she doesn't know him at all, and to explain, blushing darkly, that what is preventing her from writing is her family and that the only solution would be to shut herself up in the house in Cornwall after summer so she can work in peace. To her surprise, Michael Joseph takes her seriously. He suggests she continue to write short stories if she wishes and then they will see.

Ever keen to distance herself from Cannon Hall, Daphne spends a few weeks in Boulogne with Fernande. Her finishing school has grown in size and will move in time for the new academic year to a building in Neuilly-sur-Seine. Laid low by a cold caught at the end of the Scandinavian cruise (about which she will reveal no details to the oversensitive Ferdie), Daphne evades her questions. So, when is she going to write this novel of hers? She is just like her cousin Geoffrey, soft and weak! Despite the quinine that deadens her mind, Daphne defends herself spiritedly: She is nothing like him: how dare Ferdie compare her to him? She's not just some piece of driftwood, at the mercy of the current. She will write her novel, very soon, and one day Ferdie will be proud of her—she'll see!

To console Daphne and to calm her down, her friend promises to take her to Fontainebleau, to see Katherine Mansfield's grave. As soon as she is over her cold, the two women set out. In the verdant little cemetery in Avon, Daphne and Fernande find the tomb, covered by a simple white slab marked with the dates *1888–1923*. The caretaker tells them that the famous novelist, who died of tuberculosis at the age of thirty-four, was originally buried in a mass grave due to the family's financial problems but was transferred here later after the intervention of her brother-in-law. Touched, Daphne leaves a bouquet of roses, squeezes Fernande's arm, and whispers that she wishes Katherine Mansfield could know how much she owes her, how much she is inspired by her work. To write as well as her: Is that even possible? Fernande tenderly pats Daphne's cheek: perhaps Katherine Mansfield is looking down on her, encouraging her from above, who knows? . . .

The pilgrimage to the author's graveside stimulates Daphne's imagination. Armed with a new fountain pen, she starts writing in Fernande's living room in Boulogne, and suddenly the words come easily; she is able to slip inside her characters' minds; an entire story is told in a single sentence. *The themes are a bit depressing,* she writes in her journal, *but I just can't get rid of that. Ideas for stories crowd thick and fast, like people waiting for a train.*[16]

Daphne arrives in Fowey at the end of summer, 1929, with her parents, her sisters, and various guests. What a joy it is to be back in her boat, on the sea, with her fishermen friends. And back near Menabilly, which still captivates her. She wants to show the secret house to Jeanne and one of her friends, Elaine, as well as their cousin Ursula, Uncle Willie's daughter.

The four young women take the forest path from Four Turnings: the very track where Angela and Daphne got lost. They walk for hours through the dense undergrowth, almost give up, then finally manage to locate the house and reach it from behind, coming first to the most recently built wing. They notice a half-open skylight; what if they tried to get inside? Daphne cannot resist the idea of seeing the house's interior, and she is the one who leads the way, goes in first. The four girls advance amid sepulchral silence, finding walls covered with spiders' webs, patches of brownish fungus in every corner, dusty floors littered with debris, and endless dark corridors. They eventually reach the oldest, noblest part of the house, and Daphne recognizes the large living room she had seen through the window with Angela.

She is finally here, in this long room decorated with family portraits, with furniture protected by dustcovers, with the old rocking horse that has not moved in years. Next to this room is a large dining room, and beyond that a library containing hundreds of books. What happened between these walls? What secrets is Menabilly hiding? Why does all this stir her feelings so? The other young ladies do not like the feeling of abandonment, the silence, the shadows, whereas Daphne wishes she could stay here longer, climb the grand wooden staircase, touch the remains of the peeling scarlet wallpaper that reminds her of the rhododendrons. They leave through the little window, which Daphne carefully closes behind her. While she catches up with the others, a huge white owl flies out of an upstairs window, startling her.

All evening, Daphne cannot rid her mind of images of the house. Why is she so possessed by a past that is not even hers, haunted by the memories of an abandoned manor house?

~※~

October 3, 1929: a cool, grey day. Daphne unlocks the door of Ferryside, with Bingo at her heels. The house smells stale and damp. She goes straight up to her bedroom and looks out of the window, at the estuary and the sea, as she does every time she arrives here. The day has come. It will be today, she knows it; she has waited so long for this moment. Today, she is going to begin her novel. Nothing else matters. She is leaving behind her father's growing financial worries, which have forced him to sell their famous surname to a brand of cigarettes. The transition from theatre to film seems as painful as ever, especially as he has to wake at dawn to be ready for the start of each day's filming. Gerald would rather play his old roles onstage—*Dear Brutus, Peter Pan*—but the audience demand is no longer there. And Carol, who wants to marry her: he's a sweet boy, but really, what an idea! How would she be able to write if she became his wife? He understands: he is kind, patient; she's right, he'll wait, she must go to Fowey to work, alone, he knows how much she needs that. Mo and Gerald agreed that she could go to Cornwall for two and a half months on condition that she stayed with Bingo at Miss Roberts's house, across the road, so that the old lady can take care of her meals and keep the house clean. She will be able to write only in her bedroom at Ferryside; the rest of the house will remain shut up. Daphne accepts this deal without objection, even though Miss Roberts's little house has no bathroom and only an outside toilet. At least Daphne knows that the housekeeper will never cast a contemptuous look at her muddy boots or her perpetual pair of trousers.

The rain starts to pour down; the wind picks up; the sky grows dark. Daphne sits at her desk, wraps a wool blanket around her thighs, fills her pen with ink. On a blank page, she writes the date, and the title of the novel, which came to her just like that—*The Loving Spirit*—then a few lines from a poem by Emily Brontë:

Alas, the countless links are strong,
That bind us to our clay,
The loving spirit lingers long,
And would not pass away.

She begins. Jane Slade becomes Janet Coombe. Fowey is renamed Plyn. While the storm howls outside, Daphne writes in a rush, unhesitatingly. Janet is a tall, stocky brunette with powerful hands and a moody, melancholic nature, in love with the sea; she dreams of escape, freedom, wishes she had been a man. She is engaged to Thomas, her cousin, and even though she does genuinely love him, even though she is happy to start a family with him, she cannot help imagining another life as a sailor, without attachments, aboard a ship sailing around the world. When night falls, Daphne puts down her pen, wraps herself up in her oilskin, locks the house, and walks back to Miss Roberts's house. The next day, she is back again. A ritual begins. After lunch, made by her landlady, she goes for a walk with Bingo before returning to her desk.

She is possessed by her novel; it is all she sees. She smiles tenderly as she reads through Carol's letters, then forgets them completely. She has eyes only for Janet and her nocturnal walks in the hills of Plyn; she lives only for her freedom-starved heroine, with whom she secretly identifies; she follows her up to where the wind whips her long black hair, where Janet has a vision that turns her life upside down, the vision of a man who looks just like her: he has her eyes, her hair, and one night he comes to talk to her at the cliff's edge.

Lost in her book, Daphne is unaware when the world of finance collapses on October 24, 1929, in Wall Street. She has no idea that her devoted admirer Otto Kahn and other stock-market big hitters are suffering a black week that will mark their lives forever. She writes in a frenzy, six or seven hours per day, holding her pen so tightly that a callus forms on her middle finger. After the birth of her second son, Janet realizes that little Joseph is the incarnation of the vision she had on the cliff, that he represents that loving spirit, the son who is almost a bodily part of herself, her double. Daphne has no doubt that the connection she is describing between mother and son is excessively close, almost incestuous, but she accepts this. Within a month, she has finished the first two parts, which tell Janet's story, then Joseph's, and the construction of the ship that bears her heroine's name. Without pausing to rest, she throws herself into the next part, about Christopher, the grandson, third generation of the Coombe family. He does not get along with his father, Joseph, does not share his passion for the sea. There are conflicts, and Daphne writes even more passionately, inhabited by her characters. Her only form of recreation is the weekly Sunday dinner at the Quiller-Couches' house, with Lady Vyvyan, as lively as ever. On November 17, she finishes her third chapter. In a few days, she must return to London, as agreed with her parents, and she will not come back to Fowey until the New Year. Her novel must wait. Her only source of happiness is seeing Carol again. During the Christmas holidays, she thinks constantly about the unfinished manuscript that waits for her at Ferryside. She is racked by doubts: Isn't it too long, too boring? Has she worked at it enough? Will the book find a publisher? Will she find readers?

Daphne returns to Cornwall in early January 1930 and is reunited with her dog (who stayed with the gardener while she was gone), Miss Roberts, and her book. It is impossible to write in Ferryside now, because of the cold and the snowstorms, so she works in her landlady's cramped living room. The final part of her text causes her a few difficulties. The fourth generation of the Coombe family is symbolized by Jennifer—the daughter of Christopher and great-granddaughter of Janet—who is only six when her father dies at sea. Daphne is not entirely convinced by this character. How can she make her more captivating? What if she has lost the plot of her story? While the snowflakes cover the roof of the little house, Daphne day-dreams, pen in hand. Miss Roberts is humming in the kitchen, presumably unaware that she is preventing her lodger from concentrating. What would Katherine Mansfield do in her place? On January 16, during another storm, Miss Roberts and Daphne are startled by the explosion of a distress flare. The woman next door announces excitedly that a ship has crashed into Cannis Rock, not far from Menabilly, the house Daphne loves so much. The next day, Daphne goes to the cliff top in Pridmouth and looks down at the three-mast ship, a hundred feet long, its iron hull damaged, run aground on the rocks at the mercy of the waves. Its name: the *Romanie*. She knows she will never forget this vision of a shipwreck.

She finishes the novel in late February. Ten weeks of work: Daphne is drained, exhausted. Doubts prey on her, as always. She has to admit that the final chapter was longer and harder to write than the previous three. Jennifer is not her favourite character; she feels closer to the wildly roman-tic figures of Janet and Joseph. The sea is less present in the final chapter, the ship too, and she was not as inspired by describing London in 1880. She fears her readers will sense all this. To celebrate the completion of her book, Daphne walks up to the little church in Lanteglos and prays in silence by Jane Slade's grave. The Quiller-Couches know a secretary who can type up the manuscript, and Daphne hands over her precious pages to this Mrs. Smith. Two weeks later, Mrs. Smith brings her the first two parts. The sweet, rotund lady is her first reader. What will she think of it? On the doorstep, Mrs. Smith smiles. She tells Daphne she found the book fascinating and can hardly wait to type up the rest! Hope is reborn. When Mrs. Smith has finished, she mails the typescript to Hampstead, where Daphne is once again staying. The packet is enormous—my God, did she really write all that? Her family is proud. Angela manages a slightly forced smile, admitting that she too is trying to write a novel, but it is nothing like Daphne's.

Now she must drop off the heavy parcel with Michael Joseph, on Henrietta Street. But there is no way she's going to pace the floors of Cannon Hall, waiting for her agent's response. Daphne takes refuge with Fernande. Her former headmistress is now in Neuilly-sur-Seine, at 44 Rue de Chézy, a much bigger house (named Les Chimères) than the last one, with a large garden, a tennis court, and a dozen boarders from various parts of the world—England, America, Norway, South Africa—plus a team of teachers. Fernande works constantly, giving classes, recruiting students; she seems happy but tired. Their relationship has changed, the passion and affection giving way to a serene, deep friendship.

A postcard from Michael Joseph is awaiting Daphne when she returns from her Parisian outing. He very much liked *The Loving Spirit* and is submitting it immediately to a few publishers. He will keep her informed as and when he hears anything. Daphne becomes ever more anxious. She seems to see every fault in the book in unforgiving close-up, its longueurs, its weaknesses. She goes back to Montparnasse and spends her afternoons reading at Le Dôme Café. The wait feels endless. Daphne conceals her impatience by walking along Avenue de Neuilly and visiting the market, breathing in the powerful smells of cheese, buying a still-warm baguette and nibbling it as she crosses the Seine towards Puteaux.

At breakfast on March 30, 1930, Fernande hands out the mail to her boarders, as she does every morning. Daphne receives a letter with the logo of the Curtis Brown Agency on the back. She opens it feverishly and reads it, hand on mouth. Fernande, impatient, asks her what's going on. Daphne shrieks, jumps to her feet, almost knocking over the coffeemaker and spilling it on the two South African sisters, Dagmar and Lucila. Fernande asks her again, and Daphne hops around the dining room table, shouting with joy and making Schüller bark. Janet, Kitty, Iris, Honoria, Millie, and Mary all sit in silence, taken aback, and the other professors stare wide-eyed; then Daphne pirouettes towards Fernande, brandishing the letter: Can she believe it? Her novel is going to be published by Heinemann, first in England, and then with Doubleday in the United States! Isn't that extraordinary?

༄

No more procrastination. Those days of no one taking her seriously . . . they're over. On May 13, 1930, Daphne turns twenty-three. She no longer thinks of herself as a dilettante; she is a writer on the verge of being published. She begins revising her novel, under the shrewd supervision of Michael Joseph. The publisher, Heinemann, thinks it too long. Daphne learns to cut her own words efficiently, unsentimentally, resigned to the loss of whole passages that she had so enjoyed writing. Infuriatingly, the book will not be published until the following year. The world of publishing is full of delays of which, for the moment, she has no comprehension; she knows nothing about how books are manufactured, marketed, distributed to bookstores, launched, and publicized. All of this she will learn soon.

The machine has been set in motion. Nothing now can prevent Daphne from writing. Nothing and no one. Certainly not her parents. Are they proud of her? Probably. Do they realize the scale of her ambitions? Possibly not. Ideas are forming in her head, like blossoms on tree branches in springtime. While she waits for the still far-off appearance of *The Loving Spirit* Daphne throws herself into a new novel. What, already? her family exclaim. She smiles, a little mockingly: Yes, already, that's what her life is now, she's a writer, she writes, haven't they understood yet? This time, there is no need to isolate herself in Fowey. Aunt Billy lends her a secretary's office on Orange Street. Each morning, early, before her parents or sisters are awake, she goes there, and works all day, stopping only for a brief lunch with Carol.

She is not talking to anyone about this book, not yet. She is letting it come out of her, giving it free rein. It has a different voice from the last one, a man's voice, and it's written in the first person. The narrator is Richard, twenty-three years old. Is it strange, identifying with a male hero? Not really. She is guided by Eric Avon, as she has been ever since she was ten. She has absolute trust in this secret boy who lives inside her, unknown to everyone else. Dick—as Richard is generally known—is a young man of good family who is disowned by his father, a famous writer, apalled by his son's pornographic poems. Dick attempts suicide in the opening pages and is saved at the last moment by an older man, Jake, a strange fellow with a shady past, who takes him on board the *Romanie,* a merchant ship headed north.

In the dusty office on Orange Street, while spring is blossoming in London, Daphne meticulously re-creates the blue-and-green landscapes of her cruise with Otto Kahn, describing those Nordic cities bathed in white light. And, to her great pleasure, she becomes what she has always dreamed of being: a boy. It is the first time she has written as "I." She realizes that this book—modern, impertinent, audacious—risks shocking people. Oh well. She would rather have an impact than leave readers indifferent. One of the book's central themes is love: not love with a capital *L,* but the sex, disgust, and doubts it arouses. In Montparnasse, Dick meets Hesta, a young music student, of American origin. How Daphne enjoys describing Paris, which she considers hers; it is the French part of her that narrates Dick's wanderings through those places she knows so well, the bars, the restaurants, where she has so often sat to observe passersby. Despite his money worries, Dick leads an idle life, postponing the idea of marriage and finding a small apartment on Boulevard Raspail where he spends his days in bed with Hesta, feeling sure that he will become a famous writer, and becoming mired in his own laziness. He cannot escape his need for paternal approval, and his manuscript is rejected by a publisher: a crushing moment. Having left Hesta and regained a little common sense, Dick will become a boring office employee, his turbulent youth now consigned to the past.

Daphne hides skilfully behind Dick—her screen, her protection—and who can doubt, reading this book, that the young female author knows all about the mechanics of carnal love, that she has tasted pleasure in the arms of an experienced older woman, then with an enamoured young man, that she now understands the full powers of the secret and the forbidden? Only her sisters know almost everything about her clandestine life, and when she speaks to them about it, it is always under the cover of the code they have developed together: "wax,"* "spinning,"* "Cairo."*

In two months, the novel is completed. On July 18, 1930, Daphne scrawls *The End* and takes the Tube home. She doesn't feel like talking, shuts herself up in her room, seeking rest. In silence, lying on her back, she smokes a cigarette and stares at the ceiling. She likes this solitude, this exhaustion, that no one else could ever understand.

In late July, Daphne sends the novel to her agent, along with a short note. The book is titled *I'll Never Be Young Again*. She grows nervous. How can she prepare herself for another person's reactions? No member of her family has yet read the first book; they are patiently waiting for its publication, set for February 1931. And here she is, already having "bashed out" another one, radically different. As has become her custom, Daphne leaves Hampstead and goes to meet Fernande for a few weeks in Brittany—in the town of Quimper—taking with her a photograph of herself taken by Cecil Beaton, the famous photographer and a family friend. At the bottom of the glazed paper, on the right, she has written the words: *For Fernande, August 1930*. It is not until later, in Fowey, that she will receive the phone call she has been expecting from her agent. He likes this new book, very surprising, it won't be so easy to promote, because the main character is so lacking in charisma, it's hard to identify with him, he's a selfish and sometimes vain young man, and the book's themes are resolutely modern, which might trouble certain readers. Listening, Daphne grimaces, imagining Q's face when he reads the book; she already feels sure he won't like it. Anyway, better not to think about that for the moment, particularly as the book won't be published until 1932. What did her agent like best? The descriptions of Scandinavia and of Paris. The latter were especially masterful. He understands that she can change style, genre, that she is not the type of writer who will always remain faithful to one subject. He is astonished by her eclecticism, at only twenty-three years old, and wonders what on earth she might come up with next. Swept away by Michael Joseph's enthusiasm, Daphne feels liberated, euphoric. But she will have to learn to dismiss other people's views and judgements. As she heads out with Bingo towards Readymoney Cove, it strikes her that writers should never be afraid of anyone, or anything, except the fear they may no longer be able to write.

While she waits for the publication of *The Loving Spirit,* Daphne spends several months in Fowey, becoming closer to Foy Quiller-Couch, a treasured friend, and to Clara Vyvyan, despite the latter being twenty-five years older than her. Carol has gone to the United States to shoot a film. She doesn't miss him. Or not much, anyway. He is slowly fading from her life. Q suggested to Daphne that she write to Dr. Rashleigh to ask his permission to roam around the grounds of Menabilly. To her surprise, he agrees, and she goes there regularly, still stirred by the same passion for the large, empty house.

One day in November 1930, Foy and Daphne go for a horse ride on the rocky, deserted moors of Bodmin, located to the north, near Launceston. They stop at a granite hostelry with the exotic name of Jamaica Inn, which makes Daphne laugh. The wild moors around Bodmin take root in her fertile imagination. There are no trees or grass for miles around, no roads or villages, no signs of life at all. The two young women get lost, wandering across an endless arid landscape, the wind buffeting them, overlooked by huge blocks of craggy rocks. There is no way of finding their path again, and when a storm suddenly breaks above them, the rain pouring torrentially down on them, they panic. Numb with cold and soaked to the bones, they try to take shelter in the ruins of an abandoned farm. Time passes. Night falls. They are alone in this vast, lunar, inhospitable space. Exhausted, Foy suggests letting the horses guide them by instinct. In the small hours of the night, when they are starving and on their last legs, no longer believing they will find their way, the tall chimneys of Jamaica Inn rear up before them, illuminated by flashlights. The hostelry's managers had begun to worry and had sent out men to search for them on the moors. They are welcomed with a hearty supper of eggs and bacon. While they warm up by the peat fire, Foy elbows her friend in the ribs: And what if Daphne wrote a novel about their disastrous outing?

༄‿༄

One December morning in Fowey, Daphne receives a check from her publisher for *The Loving Spirit:* sixty-seven pounds sterling. It's not a huge sum, but it is money she has earned herself, alone, with her pen. She also receives her author copies of the book and is surprised by the emotion she feels at holding her first published novel in her hands. Daphne signs one for her father and mails it to Hampstead, still under the spell of this unexpected emotion. A few days later, Gerald calls to tell her how much he liked it. This is a relief. The other members of her family—Aunt Billy, Uncle Willie—plus Tod and Q, write her complimentary letters about the novel. Will the critics be this favourable, too? Daphne doubts it. But she doesn't let these negative thoughts affect her. She looks ahead: she still has such a long way to go, so many stories to imagine. *The Loving Spirit,* even if Daphne is not ashamed of it, already seems part of the distant past, written at a different point in her life.

She uses her first earnings to return to France in the New Year, to stay with Fernande on Rue de Chézy, in Neuilly. In early January 1931, a third novel demands forcefully to be written. This is not the story of her misadventures on the moors with Foy—she puts that aside for later. This is a new direction, far from the romantic melodrama of *The Loving Spirit* and further still from the narcissism of young Dick, lost in his frantic pursuit of pleasure. The hero forming in her mind is named Julius Lévy, born in Puteaux, France, in 1860, the son of a Jewish Algerian immigrant and a Christian peasant girl.

On the first floor of the house on Rue de Chézy, Daphne sits down at Fernande's desk, in the living room with a window overlooking the garden. In this large room filled with books and flowers, she is able to write undisturbed, barely even hearing the classes being taught in the adjoining rooms, the whispers, the footsteps of the students on the stairs. Sometimes, Fernande pokes her head through the door, impressed by her young friend's concentration. Daphne raises her eyebrows mischievously: and to think that not so long ago, Ferdie was comparing her to her poor, sluggish cousin Geoffrey, accusing her of lacking energy and motivation! How times have changed. Her first novel will come out in a month, the second the following year, and here she is already at work on the third, which will see the light of day in 1933. Fernande smiles and tenderly strokes the pale forehead leaning over the pile of pages: she never doubted it; she always knew that Daphne would be a great novelist.

The book that is taking shape is volcanic, brutal, disturbing. There is nothing sympathetic about Julius Lévy. Even as a child, he is capable of throwing his kitten into the Seine, of coldly watching as his father murders his adulterous mother. Where does he come from, this cruel being, consumed with ambition, cunning and fearsome? He has none of the golden sophistication of Otto Kahn, who made such an impression on Daphne. In her journal, the young woman writes: *No ships, no wrecks, no boys running away to sea. Julius, I see him as child, an old man. I must follow him throughout his life, from the 1870 war between France and Prussia. I must look up all the history of the siege of Paris. I must work like a fury.*[17] But it is rather the book itself that is a fury, overflowing with shocking, macabre images, like young Julius's liaison with a twelve-year-old prostitute, like the apocalyptic childbirth suffered by Rachel, Julius's wife, a rich heiress who will give him a child.

Daphne puts the vile and fascinating Julius aside and goes back to London to celebrate the publication of her first novel, on February 23, 1931. Armed with the famous du Maurier name, her publisher has arranged a few advertisements and articles to support the book's release. In the excitement of these weeks, Daphne does not know that Angela too has written a book, *A Little Less*, a love story between two women, which she has not shown to her family and for which she has attempted to find a publisher, secretly and without success. Angela flits from party to party, hiding her sadness and disappointment behind her evening dresses, and warmly congratulates her younger sister on the publication of *The Loving Spirit*. The critics are generally positive towards this family saga, influenced by the Brontë sisters. The *Times* of March 10, 1931, hopes that Miss du Maurier will, with time and experience, be able to follow in the footsteps of her illustrious grandfather. The *Spectator* encourages her to distance herself from her artistic emotions. The *Observer* and the *Times Literary Supplement* are emphatically enthusiastic. The *Saturday Review* is less so, complaining of an overabundance of pathos and an incomprehensible dialect, while nonetheless saluting the young novelist's promise. The *New York Herald Tribune* is warmly encouraging. When her publisher tells her that they are ordering a second print run of the book, Daphne is delighted, but she keeps her feet on the ground. She is thinking about the next one and has only one desire: to get back to the ruthless Julius and his meteoric rise. She accepts an invitation to the American embassy from her New York editor, the famous Nelson Doubleday, but feels out of place; she is by far the youngest person there. Even so, she is enchanted by the friendly, welcoming Doubleday, with his kind smile and his impressive moustache.

Back in Fowey, Daphne breathes easier, as always, dividing her time between walks, outings on the *Marie-Louise*, a weekly dinner with the Quiller-Couches, and the writing of her book. She has no wish to return to London. Her days and nights are haunted by Julius Lévy, with his sharp eyes, his appetites, his dizzying ascent. He moves to London and becomes a powerful, feared, respected businessman. Nothing can stop him. He only loves one person other than himself: his daughter, Gabriel, a slender girl with blonde hair and blue eyes. She is his obsession, his adoration. A hint of incest. Daphne worries that she is overdoing this aspect of the story. Will Gerald recognize himself in this image of the monstrously jealous father who cannot bear his daughter going out at night, who cannot accept the idea that she might have lovers, who waits at the top of the stairs to reprimand her? How will he react? Ultimately, though, that doesn't really matter to Daphne. The essential thing is that she has freed herself from her father's influence by fictionalizing him in these (admittedly shocking) pages. She is not afraid anymore. There is a tangible distance between them. She knows now that, in order to write, she must not fear anything at all. Otherwise, there is no point in writing.

One day in mid-July 1931, Daphne is woken at dawn by the telephone. Her parents are sleeping upstairs in Ferryside. She rushes to answer it. The call is from a nurse in the hospital in Ripon, a small town in Yorkshire. Angela has had a car accident, but everything's fine; she is not seriously injured. She will need about a week of treatment there before rejoining her family. Angela arrives seven days later, her face covered in bruises and her neck bandaged. When their parents return to London in mid-August, the sisters remain in Fowey, one to write and the other to rest.

In September, Daphne is in her room, pen in hand, still lost in the world of Julius, when her sister calls her, sounding agitated. *There's a most attractive man going up and down the harbour in a white motor-boat* [sic]. *Do come and look.*[18] Intrigued, Daphne goes upstairs to join her sister, who is standing by the window. Angela hands her Gerald's binoculars, the ones he uses to watch birds. The man in question is just her type: tall, dark, handsome, muscular, and elegantly dressed. The next day, this magnificent man in his thirties is back again, this time accompanied by a friend (less attractive, as Angela notes) and they begin speeding back and forth past the house in the white motorboat with the curious name of *Ygdrasil*. So who is this handsome helmsman? They find out the answer from their neighbours: He is Major Browning, a young soldier with a brilliant career, educated at Eton and Sandhurst, recipient of the Distinguished Service Order and the French War Cross, obtained in 1917, when he was only nineteen years old. He is currently attached to the 2nd Battalion of the Grenadier Guards in Pirbright.

Daphne forgets him quite quickly: she is close to finishing her novel and does not allow herself any distractions. In November 1931, *The Progress of Julius* is completed, and in January 1932 she sends it to Michael Joseph, who does not seem overly perturbed by its darkness or its terrifying end. Daphne says the unsayable, daring to describe the vile act Julius performs on his daughter, and if the reader is left stunned, that is precisely what the author wants. The book will be published in the spring of 1933. *I'll Never Be Young Again* is set for May 1932, and preparations are under way for its publication. She already has to pose for a few photographs, something Daphne endures rather than enjoys. Her agent sends a well-known photographer, Miss Compton Collier, who specializes in taking portraits of famous people, to capture a series of pictures. Daphne warns her agent: she is not going to change, she will wear her usual jumper and trousers. Her only compromise is to put on bit of lipstick. Miss Collier accepts these demands without complaint, and Daphne poses in the living room at Ferryside, looking a little rebellious with her raised chin, her defiant gaze, hands wrapped round her knees, a cigarette drooping from her red lips. A curious portrait, both masculine and feminine, and one that amuses Daphne, who feels as if Eric Avon is making an unexpected first public appearance.

⁂

In April 1932, while she is convalescing at Fowey after an appendectomy, Daphne is told by the managers of the Ferry Inn that handsome Major

Browning is back in town again. He arrived on the *Ygdrasil* and has admitted to George Hunkin, a friend who works at the shipyard in Bodinnick, that he would very much like to meet Miss du Maurier. Daphne is secretly flattered. The next day, she receives a short note at Ferryside.

> *Dear Miss du Maurier, I believe my late father, Freddie Browning, used to know yours, as fellow members of the Garrick Club. The Hunkins tell me you have had your appendix out and can't do much rowing yet, so I wondered if you would care to come out in my boat? How about tomorrow afternoon?*
>
> *Boy Browning*[19]

Daphne replies by return of post that she would be delighted.

April 8, 1932: a sunny day in Fowey, with a cool breeze, the perfect combination as far as Daphne is concerned. Major Browning comes to fetch her outside Ferryside, hatless and magnificent. He holds out his hand to help her aboard the *Ygdrasil*. She suspects Jeanne is spying on her from the window above. She and the major have to sit very close to hear each other over the roar of the wind. He explains that his first name is Frederick, but that everyone calls him Tommy and he would be happy if Daphne would do the same. Daphne already knows his nickname—Boy—because she read it in the papers. She knows he earned it by being awarded the prestigious War Cross when still very young. "Boy," that word so idolized by Daphne, by Barrie, by the whole du Maurier clan. She asks him what *"Ygdrasil"* means and Tommy's response is that the name comes from ancient Nordic mythology and means "the tree of destiny." But the boat too has a nickname, *Yggy*. She watches Tommy's hands on the helm, manly hands, supple and tanned. Up close, she notices that his eyes are green, his smile radiant. Tommy: she used that name in her childhood story *The Searchers*. Never in her life has Daphne felt so attracted to a man. Carol pales in comparison: a charming fellow, of course, but one for whom she feels a sort of brotherly affection. Boy Browning is not afraid of the gusting wind, nor the waves, and he steers his boat with strength and skill. Daphne laughs with him as the two of them are soon soaked by the spray. She can hardly believe how easily they get along, the pure happiness she feels in his company, as if they have known each other for years. After their outing, she shows him the *Marie-Louise*. He loves boats as much as she does, loves the sea, salt, wind, just like her.

In Ferryside, Tommy and Daphne sit in front of the fireplace and talk about everything, while Jeanne discreetly remains upstairs. Conversation is effortless and pleasurable. He has something he must confess to her. The reason he came to Fowey for his leave was because he wanted to meet her. She is amazed. He goes on, telling her how much he enjoyed *The Loving Spirit*, with its evocation of the sea and sailing, his two passions, then he came across a magazine article about Miss du Maurier in Fowey, at Ferryside, and there was a photograph of her . . . He doesn't say any more, just smiles. On the doorstep, he asks her if she is free tomorrow. He has another two days in Fowey before he must return to his unit. She nods, waves goodbye, watches him ride away on the water, then closes the door with a sigh of ecstasy. Jeanne comes hurtling downstairs and the two of them stand by the window to watch the handsome major at the helm of his boat. Jeanne pinches her cheek, teases her, what a lovely "menace"*! And Daphne replies that she has never felt so "menaced" in all her life!

Two days together, sailing, walking in the hills of Fowey, sitting by the fire and talking. They discuss the book that brought them together, the books yet to be published, which might surprise him. They talk about their families: Tommy about his mother and his sister, Daphne about her whole clan. When he has to go, Tommy kisses her for the first time, and she shivers at this masculine contact. One week later, he turns up early in the morning while she is sawing firewood in the garden; he drove all night to be with her. With a teasing smile, Daphne remarks that the army seems to be very generous with its leave at the moment. He shrugs, equally mischievous: not much is going on at the moment, and an officer friend of his agreed to do his job for him, so—if she'll put down that saw—the *Yggy* is ready to go! Daphne looks forward excitedly to each of the major's visits. He is there for her birthday and meets Mo and Gerald, who end up inviting him to dinner. He makes a good impression on them. How could he do otherwise?

Amid this whirlwind of romance that fills her mind, Daphne is confronted with a less pleasant aspect of life as a writer: the first mixed reviews, bad reviews, or simply the absence of any review at all, with merely a brief résumé of the book's plot. *I'll Never Be Young Again* has just been published, and it perplexes journalists and readers alike, surprised by the absence of the romance they found in her first novel, disturbed by the crudeness of Dick's adventures. But her agent reassures her that the novel is selling well despite all this and she will soon be receiving checks for much bigger sums. Daphne realizes that she will be able to plan on a future of financial independence. However, she must face up to the unfavourable opinions of people she respects, such as Tod or Q, who is severe in his criticisms of the book, denouncing its vulgarity and its cynicism. Aunt Billy echoes these sentiments. The members of the Garrick Club in London are outraged: How can a young lady of their rank permit herself to be so knowledgeable and brutally honest about sexuality? Only Gerald and Angela offer her any succour, her father whispering a few well-chosen words of encouragement and her sister genuinely adoring the book and comparing it to Hemingway. Daphne does not let the negativity grind her down; she believes a novelist must be free, must not write for other people, and must learn not to fear their reactions. In truth, what most interests her in this early summer of 1932 is Major Browning, who makes regular trips to see her.

During an outing on the *Yggy* on June 29, Daphne lets Tommy know just how attracted she is to him; she is the one who makes the move—there is nothing shy about her—but Tommy has his principles. This will not be some casual fling, like the one between Dick and Hesta in her second novel. They are serious, and now they talk about marriage for the first time. Daphne is simultaneously thrilled and panic-stricken. Marriage? It's so quick, a little crazy, but at the same time she likes that, the speed, the craziness. She is in love with this man, who attracts her as no man ever has before. The feelings she has for him are much more powerful than any she had for Geoffrey or Carol, and they have so much in common. Yes, she wants to become this man's wife, in spite of her desire for independence, of her secret former passion for Fernande, of everything she has ever said about marriage in the past. She draws a line under what she has experienced with Ferdie: that's in the past, it's behind her, and she has never considered herself one of those women with "Venetian"* tendencies.

In fact, she shares her father's oft-expressed repugnance for homosexuals. The boy in her accepts defeat; she begins to leave him behind, and Eric Avon curls up in his box somewhere deep inside her, nestled in the shadows.

Will Tommy give her the freedom to write? Does he expect a devoted, attentive officer's wife? Daphne can hardly boil an egg, never mind make a bed. But who cares! She sweeps away her doubts and succumbs to the joy of being loved by this brilliant, funny, charming man who is madly in love with her. And by becoming Mrs. Browning she will free herself forever from her father's grip. The first thing to do is write to her mother, to Carol, and to Fernande and tell them everything. How will they take the news? No time to think about that: she writes the three letters in a rush and mails them straightaway. Next, she heads for Pirbright, in Surrey. At Tommy's army camp, she is shocked and proud to see him in his uniform. Then she travels to Rousham, Oxfordshire, to meet his mother, Nancy, and his sister, Grace. *Sweet and kind*, she notes in her journal. *It's all like a dream, and sometimes I feel I am a ghost, with a path laid out before me, and a picture of every moment.*[20]

When Muriel reads Daphne's letter out loud at Cannon Hall, Gerald breaks down in sobs. According to Mo, he cried out, *It isn't fair!*[21] But he changed his mind, she tells her daughter, because his dear brother Guy was a soldier and would have approved of this nephew with all his medals. Gerald and Mo are expecting a London wedding at the Guards Chapel, an expensive white dress, flowers, a sumptuous garden party. Daphne cuts them short. *Oh, no, nothing big*, she writes to them. *Just yourselves, as Angela and Jeanne are away. Down at Fowey, at Lanteglos church, where Jane Slade was buried. Early in the morning, July 19th, and the Hunkins as witnesses.*[22]

Muriel is disappointed—she would have so liked to mark the occasion properly for this first of her daughters' weddings—but Daphne has made her decision: it will be quick and without any "fuss." She is twenty-five, after all; she's not a child anymore! The press, of course, takes note of this union between the young novelist with the famous name and a distinguished major ten years her senior. On July 8, 1932, an article in the *Daily Telegraph* gushes: "Miss du Maurier, who is slim, with curly fair hair and bright blue eyes, was the unconscious starter of the 'hatless movement' which the younger set have taken up so enthusiastically. She speaks French without an accent and spends two months of the year in Paris. Major Browning is one of the youngest majors in the British army and an all-round athlete."

The evening before the ceremony, Muriel irons the blue cotton twill outfit that her daughter will wear; Daphne didn't want to get married in white either, nor to have a sophisticated hairdo. Gerald complains about a wedding at eight o'clock in the morning, he has always hated getting up early. Daphne's cousin Geoffrey gatecrashes the wedding, and no one dares ask him to go. Daphne, Gerald, Muriel, and Geoffrey leave Ferryside on the *Cora Anne,* heading towards Pont Bridge in the golden silence of early morning, followed by Tommy and the Hunkins on the *Ygdrasil.*

Daphne, nervous, does not utter another word, climbing the steep path up to the church with her long, determined stride, face serious, watched closely by her parents. She admires the beauty of the surroundings, the little church isolated amid the splendours of nature, its sculpted wooden benches. She wanted a quick ceremony, a simple registry wedding, but when Tommy whispers his consent in a shaky voice, staring straight into her eyes, in this stunningly romantic setting, she feels herself submerged by a wave of emotion. Later, after a brief breakfast at Ferryside—no speeches, no flowers, no celebrations—the newlyweds put on their favourite sailing outfits and, aboard the *Ygdrasil,* leave with the tide, towards the bay. It is Daphne who has chosen the site for their honeymoon: Frenchman's Creek, near the Helford River, a calm, secret place, where the boat berths amid scented greenery, sheltered from any prying eyes. *We couldn't have chosen anything more beautiful,*[23] she writes in her journal.

These are the last lines that Daphne writes in those pages. Her journal, which she has kept scrupulously since the age of twelve, stops dead.

❧

Becoming Mrs. Browning is not an easy task, despite the love she feels for her husband. Marriage deals a blow to her precious freedom. How will she manage to write? The newlyweds move into a cottage at the back of the garden in Cannon Hall, on Well Road. One night, Tommy wakes up screaming, soaked with sweat and terrified. Daphne tries to comfort him and succeeds in calming him down, but the nightmare recurs the next night and then again the following week. She doesn't dare ask him about it, imagining that it is connected to the horrors of war, experienced fifteen years earlier. Tommy has still not spoken to her about the Battle of Cambrai in November 1917, in Gauche Wood, where he fought for several days in woodlands strewn with eviscerated corpses.

Watching him leave for the army base every morning, handsome and proud in his medal-covered uniform, she is the only one who knows that her husband, the leader of a hundred men, sobs in the middle of the night like a little boy. And then there are those stomach aches that have plagued him since childhood and that mystify the doctors. There is a fragility to Tommy that she never suspected, and that makes a big impression on her. Even his collection of teddy bears, his "Boys," which he takes everywhere with him, and which amused Daphne at first, now seem to betray a secret weakness.

For the first time, Daphne confides in her mother. When Tommy leaves, she walks over to Cannon Hall, sits with Muriel in her boudoir, shares her morning tea, and asks her advice about domestic, feminine matters. Mo is only too happy to respond, delighted by this new closeness with her daughter. What Daphne fears most, her mother quickly realizes, is the role of military spouse that she must now adopt. How boring it all is, having to greet all those women, share those tiresome dinners, those insipid conversations, uphold her position.

At Christmas, Daphne discovers she is pregnant and joyfully announces the fact to her husband, her parents, her sisters. It will be a boy, she feels sure. No one dares to contradict her. In anticipation of the birth—due for July 1933—a nanny named Margaret is hired. The nanny is shown the nursery, already painted blue, and shyly points out to Mrs. Browning that the child might turn out to be a girl. Frowning, Daphne replies firmly that it will be a boy.

The Progress of Julius is published in May 1933, when Daphne is seven months pregnant. Fully occupied by her impending motherhood, she only distantly follows the appearance of reviews. The ones in the *Times* and the *Observer* are quite positive, those in *Punch* and the *Saturday Review* more mixed, the former criticizing her novel for "materialism at its ugliest." Graham Greene judges her prose to be "bookish," but for him the novel is "saved by its energy" and "admirable vigor." One of Daphne's friends and neighbours, the novelist and biologist Leo Walmsley, is horrified by the book and admits it. Unperturbed, Daphne writes to him on May 26, 1933: *Yes, of course it's overwritten, but then in a sense it was deliberately done. I wanted to ooze blood and diarrhoea all over it. Yes, I suppose romantic stuff is happier to write and to read, but perhaps it's the old French blood that make me want to dig under the surface to find the creepy, crawly slugs, and cut out the sentiment!*[24]

Her family is not especially thrilled either, and they tell her so, very honestly. Only her father keeps his thoughts to himself. What does he really think of this harsh, sordid novel and the pitiless light it shines on father–daughter relationships, largely inspired by his own Borgiaesque excesses? He prefers not to say. He is not feeling well anyway and has to take things easily. From the garden, where she reads a book, Daphne sees him smoking a cigarette at his second-floor bedroom window, staring out at the view of his beloved London. What is he thinking about? His lost youth? His waning career? His financial worries? Is he proud of her? Probably, because she is still aware of the fervour and power of his love for her. But for now, he is still the most famous member of their family. Daphne has not overshadowed him; her three novels have not made a huge impact, they are nowhere near the bestseller lists. Is it possible that his own fame will one day be eclipsed by his daughter's?

For Daphne, this book is better than her first, and in spite of some less than favourable reactions (Q, for example, has banned the novel from his library), she is unfazed. Michael Joseph confirms to her that the book is selling just as well as the previous two, despite the paucity of good reviews, and that he is confident that she has a great future. Daphne listens to him, saying nothing, but is impatient for the moment when people will no longer cite her name alongside references to her father and grandfather.

At home, on July 15, 1933, Daphne gives birth to a baby girl. When the child's sex is announced to her, she instantly feels disappointed, barely even glancing at the sweet infant who is handed to her. She was so sure she would have a son. Later, she writes to Tod, giving her details of the agony of childbirth: *Of all the hellish performances, so beastly degrading, too, lying on a bed with legs spread-eagled and feeling exactly as though one's entire inside plus intestines and bowels are being torn from one! Pheugh! The child is flourishing. Exactly like Tommy, but fair hair and blue eyes. Nice skin, never red or pasty. Name of Tessa.*[25] Little by little, Daphne grows closer to her baby, even if Margaret does most of the hard work, spending the whole of each day with Tessa. Will she be able to find time to write? It's possible, but it isn't easy, getting used to this new life. The Brownings leave their cottage on Well Road and move to Surrey. Tommy has just been named second in command of the 2nd Battalion Grenadier Guards. Daphne organized the move, without enthusiasm. For two years, their address will be the Old Rectory, on Portsmouth Road. Will she finally be able to write now, in this pleasant redbrick house, surrounded by grounds? No, because Gerald has health problems. Already, at Christmas, he seemed uncomfortable and complained of pains. Growing thin and shrivelled, he looks older than his sixty-one years. In late March 1934, the doctor diagnoses cancer of the colon and informs him that an operation is unavoidable. Gerald must be hospitalized, a prospect that throws him into a panic; he can't bear hospitals. The operation goes well and the tumour is removed, but Gerald is very weak when he returns to Cannon Hall.

Ten days later, when Daphne comes back from a walk with little Tessa, Margaret is waiting for her on the doorstep of the Old Rectory, looking tense and pale. Daphne understands immediately, not even listening to the nanny's few stammered words. When she reaches Hampstead, Daphne knows that she will remember this day—April 11, 1934—for the rest of her life. It is, ironically, her parents' wedding anniversary—their thirty-first. Her mother, so elegant, so perfect in all circumstances, is a broken woman, her face disfigured by tears. Daphne holds her tight, comforting her as if she were the mother and Muriel her daughter, surprised, in spite of herself, by this strange moment, because the two of them have never been physically close. Muriel pronounces a few words in a broken voice. Gerald loved Daphne so much. Daphne knows. She was her Peter Pan of a father's favourite, loved with an intensity so powerful it felt suffocating at times, all-consuming. Jeanne and Angela, both devastated, join the grieving huddle.

Gerald's death is front-page news. The articles about him all sing his praises, acclaiming his career, emphasizing his unique charm. Even George V sends a letter of condolence to Lady du Maurier. Muriel wants a private ceremony, for family only, and she has to fight to keep the press and curious onlookers at a distance. The day of his funeral, Daphne does not go to the little church in Hampstead with her mother and her sisters. She walks over the Heath, alone, with two pigeons in a cage, to the place where their father took them when they were little girls, when he told them about his walks with Kicky, and she frees the birds. Watching them fly away, high into the springtime sky, she thinks of her father.

She knows, now, that her next book will not be a novel. It will be the first biography of Sir Gerald du Maurier, written by the one person who knew him best in the whole world—his daughter.

᪣

When her agent, Michael Joseph, reads the opening pages of Daphne's biography of her father, he discovers an astonishingly frank portrait, devoid of all deference. In the hope of advancing Daphne's career, he suggests she sign a contract with a new editor, a certain Victor Gollancz, a dynamic, ambitious man who successfully launched his own publishing firm, Victor Gollancz Ltd, in 1927. Gollancz's author list includes the likes of Isadora Duncan, Ford Madox Ford, and George Orwell, and he is renowned for his eagerness in using advertising to sell books, capable of buying a whole page of a daily newspaper to announce his latest publication. His black logo (the bold letters **VG**) and the bright yellow and magenta colour scheme of his covers are instantly recognizable.

When she meets him for the first time in his office on Henrietta Street, a stone's throw from the offices of Curtis Brown, Daphne is captivated by this sparkling man, who seems so thrilled to be publishing her and who speaks about her biography with great passion. Suddenly, rather hastily, she forgets all about Heinemann and everything they have done for her and her first three novels. She likes Gollancz's fervent enthusiasm and believes that if she is ever going to be successful, it will probably be due to a man like him. She doesn't care if some people find his use of hype somewhat vulgar.

Victor Gollancz takes Daphne and her agent out for a drink at Claridge's to celebrate the contract they sign in May 1934. This is the first time Daphne has spent time in the presence of a publisher, apart from her brief meeting with her American editor, Nelson Doubleday. She knows that it is not out of vanity or a lust for fame that she wants her books on the best-seller lists, but purely to preserve her independence, so she can live by her pen. Victor rubs his hands, certain that he has found his flagship author: she has everything she needs to appeal to a wide readership, her name, her beauty, her youth, those first three novels, the latter two with their whiff of sulphur, and of course the highly promising biography on the life of her celebrated father. In the hushed surroundings of Claridge's, while they toast their agreement, Daphne wonders if this portly editor, with his little glasses and his shaven head, who looks at her both greedily and respectfully, will be the architect of her first major success. She wants to trust him. After all, isn't Victor a charmed name, the herald of future greatness?

Daphne writes this book in four months, at home in the Old Rectory, while Margaret looks after Tessa and Tommy devotes himself to his battalion. It is not a classic biography, with dates and a chronology of events and a catalogue of places. In her words, Gerald comes back to life, along with his unique sense of humour, his prowess as an actor, his imitations, and his sometimes infantile jokes. It is all described clear-sightedly: his pampered childhood, his first loves, his meeting with Muriel Beaumont, his famous "stable" of actress-fillies, his peculiar relationships with his daughters, his unhappiness when they turned from children to women. With great empathy, Daphne exposes her father's faults and contradictions, his selfishness, his most intimate doubts, his fear of germs, even a simple cold.

Gerald: A Portrait is published in October 1934 by Victor Gollancz. Gerald's actor friends and members of the Garrick Club are, once again, shocked by Daphne's frankness. How can a girl depict her own father with such realism? Daphne's friends and family fully approve the book, however, and congratulate her. The *Morning Post* expresses a few reservations but praises the young writer's "staggeringly candid" approach, while the *Times* salutes this "portrait seeing deeply into his nature, written without a trace of malice." The book sells well as soon as it comes out, and the royalty cheques start to mount up. Daphne received an advance of a thousand pounds and will receive 20 per cent on the first ten thousand copies sold. But the absence of Gerald, and the first Christmas without him, diminish her feelings of happiness. Cannon Hall has been put up for sale, and her mother and sisters have moved into the cottage on Well Road where she lived until Tessa's birth.

It is painful, bidding farewell to this childhood home. She remembers hurtling down the stairs with Jeanne, recalls the games of cricket with Gerald on the lawn. She even finds herself missing his "Borgia" face. Her youth is fading. She is the wife of a highly respected soldier, mother of a little girl who will soon be two years old. Sadness overwhelms her. It is the end of an era, a new path in her life, which she embarks upon with a feeling of bitterness.

She must start writing again. What else can she do? In the summer of 1935, the tireless Victor encourages her, asking her to think about a novel; she should strike while the iron is hot from the success of her biography. Daphne divides her time between Surrey and Fowey, escaping the tedious small talk of army life whenever she can, to her husband's displeasure. Her mother needs her, too, because she is suffering without Gerald. How can Daphne make them all understand, without hurting them, without creating conflict, that her priority is not her child or her marriage or her mother or her sisters, but her writing?

↝❧↜

Gone is the time when Daphne could just dash off to France and spend a week with Ferdie in Paris or shut herself away in Ferryside. She no longer has any freedom in her daily life, but she preserves it in her head. Victor is curious to learn more about her new novel: Couldn't she tell him a little more? Daphne reveals that her heroine is Mary Yellan, twenty-three years old, and that the story takes place at the beginning of the nineteenth century, in Cornwall, on Bodmin Moor. Daphne is inspired to write this book by memories of her childhood reading, the fantastic atmosphere of novels that held her spellbound such as *Treasure Island,* but also by that disastrous outing with Foy Quiller-Couch, five years earlier, when the two of them got lost on the moors. Victor asks excitedly what the title is. Daphne's reply: *Jamaica Inn*. That is all she will tell her editor.

Daphne writes on a typewriter, an Oliver No. 11 that she learns to use two-fingered. The household becomes accustomed to the clattering noise that goes on for several hours a day. Tessa soon understands that her mother must not be disturbed when she can hear this noise. The first draft is completed within a few months, and Victor is the first to read it. From the opening pages, read in his office on Henrietta Street, he knows he has a hit on his hands. There is a captivating dramatic tension to the story, and a cast of characters some of whom are appealing, like Mary and her poor aunt Patience, and others terrifying, such as Joss Merlyn, Mary's brutal, drunken uncle, and the disturbing vicar Davey, with his ivory mane and his white irises. Victor knows that readers will be fascinated by the poignant story of a young woman whose mother has just died, and who goes to live with her uncle and aunt, owners of an inn located on windswept marshland. From the moment she arrives at this sinister tavern, the young girl suspects the worst: that her relatives are involved with pirates, that ships are being deliberately wrecked in order to pillage their cargoes, and that her aunt and uncle are part of a shady trafficking operation to dispose of these stolen goods. Victor is aware that it's not a light, simple novel: some scenes are difficult. Reading it again, however, he realizes that Daphne has forced herself not to sugarcoat the story. He congratulates his new author on her wild, fertile imagination. And to think she is only twenty-nine! He is convinced that filmmakers will show a keen interest in the rights and organizes an impressive publicity campaign.

The novel is published in January 1936, and Daphne receives the same advance and the same royalty percentage as for the biography of her father. The book is an instant hit, even before the first reviews appear, and within a few months *Jamaica Inn* has already sold more copies than Daphne's first three novels put together. Despite the death of George V on January 20, 1936, which dominates the news agenda, the reviews salute the power of the young author's prose and the descriptions of Cornwall. And yet—and this bothers her—almost all of them emphasize the debt she owes to the Brontë sisters: a house filled with mystery and dread, a Gothic atmosphere, heroes inspired by Heathcliff or Rochester. As if she hadn't created anything new at all! Thankfully, the reviewer for the *Spectator* of January 24, 1936, writes: "I do not believe R.L. Stevenson would have been ashamed to have written *Jamaica Inn,*" praise that delights Daphne. It is her first bestseller, but despite her excitement, she senses that she can do even better, and Victor encourages her in this belief, persuaded as he is that the rise of Daphne du Maurier has only just begun. For the moment, she protects herself, refusing all interviews, all events where she might have to meet her readers. But the fan letters soon pile up, forwarded by her publishers, and she is astonished by these letters sent from all over the country—and then from the United States, too, when Doubleday publishes the novel. She replies conscientiously to all of them, using her typewriter.

Victor was right: a film production company wishes to buy the screen rights for the novel. The company in question is Mayflower Pictures, run by Erich Pommer, a German producer who has worked with Marlene Dietrich, and the British actor Charles Laughton. The director they have in mind is Alfred Hitchcock, who knew Gerald du Maurier well, having produced the 1930 film *Lord Camber's Ladies,* directed by Ben Levy and starring the beautiful Gertrude Lawrence opposite Daphne's father.

Rather than enjoying her newfound fame, Daphne concentrates on the next book; she explains to Victor that she does not yet have an idea for a new novel, but she would like to write a history of the du Maurier family, going back to her great-grandfather's time and ending with the births of Kicky's five children. Her editor would have preferred another juicy novel in the same vein as *Jamaica Inn,* but he has no desire to clash with his young protégée.

While Daphne begins the book, using her father's family archives, which Mo has kept, and researching birth and marriage certificates, she receives the news she has been dreading. One evening in March 1936, Tommy enters the Old Rectory with a strange expression on his face, and she guesses what he is about to tell her. For three years now, she has been able to merely play at being an army wife without really investing herself in the role. But now Tommy's regiment has been sent to Egypt for an indefinite period, and he has been put in command. Daphne's duty is to follow her husband.

How will she be able to survive in this dusty, despised city of Alexandria, in this appalling heat, with these deadly dull people, these interminable expat dinners where the other guests look her up and down like some curious beast, where she can read on their lips: Mrs. Browning, that's the writer Daphne du Maurier, didn't you know? They must think her very shy, because she always keeps her distance. The house is pleasant, though: located at 13 Rue Jessop, it overlooks the beach at Ramleh, where Tessa and Margaret frolick. Tommy is gone all day with his troops in the desert. Daphne tries to make progress on her family biography but is bereft of energy and inspiration. Why did she ever start this book? She should have waited for an idea for a novel to come to her. From her window, she looks out at the smooth sea and feels sorry for herself. Her only pleasure is swimming. It had been easy to write the biography of her father, because she was simply remembering a man she had known closely all her life; she knew how to shine a light on his virtues, his faults, his obsessions. Her task on this new book is much harder, because she knows nothing about her ancestors, apart from what can be gleaned from their letters. She has to breathe life into them, add flesh and blood to the dates and places, treat them like characters from one of her novels. But this is not a novel, she reminds herself, as she sweats inside a sticky bedroom, behind closed shutters, in the slow, hot afternoon hours. She begins her account in 1810, in London, with little Ellen, who will later marry Louis-Mathurin Busson du Maurier, the son of emigrants from Angers, Kicky's father. In September 1936, Daphne finally manages to finish the book, but she is not proud of it: *Done about 100000 words,* she writes to her editor, sending him the typescript via friends who are returning to London (lucky so-and-sos!). *I feel it is something of a tour de force to have written it in an Egyptian summer.*[26] She suspects that her dialogue is contrived, artificial, that her characters seem lifeless and unsympathetic. How she missed the freedom allowed by a novel as she wrote these pages.

Margaret, the nanny, is worried by Mrs. Browning's paleness and weight loss, which she finds alarming. She remarks that her employer is eating less and less, that she spends her days locked up in her room, lying on her bed with a cool, damp cloth on her forehead. Even her deadpan sense of humour seems to have been dented. Tessa, who is nearly three, is growing ever livelier, despite the oppressive heat. She is an amusing, outgoing little girl, but her energy exhausts her mother. One morning, Margaret is so concerned by Mrs. Browning's state of health that she calls the doctor.

She is expecting a child. Upon hearing these words, Daphne, overwhelmed, bursts into tears. But after the initial shock, she feels hopeful again, because she knows that she will finally be able to return to England, even if only for the birth of the child, due in the spring of 1937. She misses her homeland, her mother and sisters, and her faithful Tod, too, whom she has never lost touch with since 1922, and Foy Quiller-Couch. Nearly a year without all those people: it's a long time. On December 11, 1936, Daphne listens attentively to the abdication speech of Edward VIII, who announces from Windsor Castle that he is giving up the crown to marry the woman he loves, the divorcée Wallis Simpson. How Daphne would have liked to listen to this speech in the company of Mo, Angela, and Jeanne, to share this historic moment with them. In the meantime, she finally receives a letter from her editor. Victor's verdict is positive; he finds *The Du Mauriers* extremely well written and interesting, he believes in it. Daphne is reassured but already feels quite distant from the book. Alfred Hitchcock, meanwhile, has bought the film rights to *Jamaica Inn,* and a screenplay is being written. She wonders if the film will be true to her book, if her characters will appear on-screen the way she imagined them.

Daphne leaves for England, at last, on January 16, 1937, aboard the *Otranto,* with her daughter and Margaret. As soon as she breathes the sea air of "her" Cornwall, she feels alive again. Her mother and her sisters now live in Ferryside, and she is overjoyed to see them again. She has to return to Alexandria after she gives birth, however; she cannot abandon Tommy, who will be there for a long time yet. But for now, she can look forward to a few months in England, and she is determined to enjoy them. She spends several weeks in Fowey, following the publication of *The Du Mauriers* from afar. The reviews are generally favourable—the *Observer* talks of the book's "sheer entertainment value"—but sales are sluggish. Daphne was expecting this and is unfazed by this half failure. Q is highly appreciative of the book, as are Tod and Ferdie, and their compliments are significant to Daphne. So, what about a new novel? Yes, she has a vague idea in mind, something quite dark, macabre, but it's too early to talk about it.

As her pregnancy nears its end, she resigns herself to having a second daughter, and her instinct is proved right this time: on April 2, 1937, a baby girl is born in the apartment of Queen Anne's Mansions that the Brownings have rented in Westminster, not far from St. James's Park. That very morning, Angela had taken her younger sister out for a ride in her new car, a Morris Eight, with minimal suspension. This must have had an effect on Daphne, because the baby was born two weeks early. *The child literally whizzed out!* she writes to Tod. And Aunt Angela says that the baby resembles *a little red radish.*[27] Daphne so wanted a son, but she consoles herself with the thought of "third time lucky." Tommy is back in England for a three-month leave, and it is he who chooses the name of their second daughter, Flavia.

The new king, George VI, the brother of Edward VIII, is crowned on May 12, 1937. The country is in a state of jubilation, and the next day Daphne's thirtieth birthday is celebrated by her family. The young mother smiles, laughs, opens her presents, eats her cake, but secretly she is thinking about the novel that awaits her. She daydreams about it constantly. The ideas come together, slowly but surely. The crucial thing is finding the time to write. Not easy, with a husband and two children, even if she does have permanent help. How can she rediscover the solitude she so badly needs? Angela says she has made progress on her own novel, but clearly she does not need the same kind of isolation that Daphne does. Angela is thirty-three, still plump, still unmarried, but she doesn't care; her joviality is infectious, and she clearly prefers the company of women, making endless trips all over Europe with her lady friends. Her greatest pleasure is a long train journey. She has the same love of extravagance as her father, always travelling first class, always staying in the most luxurious hotels, to Daphne's amusement. Angela's novel is centred on Verona, the disgraced heroine, who makes the wrong choice and pays the consequences. Daphne listens, nodding. She is not worried by having a novelist for a sister, she is proud of her, just as she is proud of Jeanne, who wants to go to art school and to make her living as a painter. Even though Daphne is married and has children, the bonds between her and her sisters are as strong as ever.

Little Flavia seems more fragile than her sibling, so Daphne decides to leave the two children under the supervision of their grandmothers—Nancy Browning and Muriel du Maurier—as well as their nanny, Margaret. Daphne has no intention of taking a newborn and a three-year-old to the furnace of Alexandria, where Tommy must return from July to mid-December 1937.

Five months to get through. Resigned, Daphne follows her husband. But on the ship that takes them back to Egypt, while she stares out through the porthole at the sea, she is not thinking of the two children she has left behind, nor of her mother or sisters, and she forgets everything that surrounds her on board: her husband, the other passengers, their conversations. She goes to her cabin to retrieve her notebook and begins taking notes. Later, in the stifling humidity of her room on Rue Jessop, Daphne paces the floor and bites her fingernails as she did when she was young. There are ripped-up pages strewn over the floor. She has thrown away a whole first draft because she wasn't satisfied; she is going to start again at the beginning. Over and over, she sits down, opens her notebook, rereads her words, stands up again. There is, ironically, a shrub named the daphne that flowers all year round and needs a little sunlight but must, above all, have its roots well planted in damp, fertile soil. Is it the heat that is making it so difficult for her to write? She has been here for more than a month now, and she is not getting anywhere. Daphne has the impression that her brain is turning soft. When she tries to type, her fingertips stick to the keys. She has been sleeping badly ever since Flavia's birth and swallows a sleeping pill each night. Consequently, her slumber seems heavy and she is drained when she wakes up. She is still as uninterested as ever by the army-wife parties she is obligated to attend. Why does she feel so ill at ease in society, so desperate to escape other people's eyes, just like she was as a child at Cannon Hall, hiding behind the flower beds during those hated Sunday lunches?

How she would love to be elsewhere, anywhere but here, close to the desert, how she would love to be under the rain; how divine it would be to stand in the light, scented drizzle in Fowey, now, to be cold, to shiver, to snuggle inside a thick coat, to walk in the wet, green grass, to breathe the pure air, to stroke the rough bark of a tree, the velvety, dew-speckled petals, to stare out to sea as the waves crash against the cliffs. To walk in the grounds of Menabilly, to put her hands on its grey walls, to feel again that shiver of intense pleasure.

She picks up her notebook. *A beautiful home . . . A first wife . . . A wreck, perhaps at sea . . . A terrible secret . . . Jealousy . . .* [28]

Daphne concentrates, closes her eyes, forgets Egypt, projects herself into the misty coolness of Fowey, and she thinks of Milton, the immense house that had so enchanted her as a child, with its impressive balcony, the servants lined up in front of the majestic staircase, the housekeeper, Mrs. Parker. She should use that tall, black silhouette. She should use the shipwreck she saw, and which left such an impression on her, in Pridmouth, in January 1930, that smashed ship, the *Romanie*, at the mercy of the waves. She sees herself again, rummaging through the drawers in the Old Rectory, finding those love letters that Tommy had received from his previous fiancée, Jeannette Ricardo, whom he was supposed to marry on March 25, 1929. The engagement had been broken off. Why? Daphne didn't know. The feminine handwriting, sloping and determined, traced in black ink, haunts her still. Why did Tommy keep those letters? Perhaps he had never been able to forget the woman who signed those letters *Jan*, with an outsized capital *J* that eclipsed all the other letters. Daphne had found a few photographs of the young woman, a sophisticated beauty with black hair, looking sublime in her sheath dress. She must have been a perfect hostess, one of those women who know how to receive guests, arrange flowers, make conversation with anyone, be elegant and composed in all circumstances. Daphne had tidied away those letters and photographs, with jealousy pinching her heart. She should use that jealousy, now, excavate it, fictionalize it, exploit it. Find a name for this sumptuous mansion . . . *M* like "Milton," *M* like "Menabilly" . . . Manderley, the name comes to her, Manderley, an immense old building, its noble splendour slightly worn away by the years, the twin of Milton Hall, with clock towers and parapets, like the Villa Camposenea.

In the silence of her stuffy room, Daphne repeats the name out loud— *Manderley, Manderley*—and a sentence fills her mind with a sort of sober grace, the feeling, or rather the instinct, that she is not mistaken, that she has found, unhesitatingly, the right words, like a bolt of cloth that falls perfectly. *Last night I dreamt I went to Manderley again.* The novel's title, she already knows, will be *Rebecca.* The same name she used for her evil heroine in the strange short story "The Doll," written ten years earlier and never published. Rebecca, the first wife . . . Dark haired, stunningly beautiful, talented. A perfect creature with a boyish figure, capable of taming a stallion and raising a sail in a raging storm, who writes in an elegant, sloping hand and signs her name with a huge capital *R.* Dead in tragic circumstances, at sea. That same roaring sea that can be heard from the large house hidden behind trees, up on a hill, sheltered from prying eyes. The high gates, the long, winding driveway, the rhododendrons, the azaleas, the hyacinths, the little granite cottage on the beach at Pridmouth, all the magic, all the mystery, of Menabilly . . . Daphne sucks it all up greedily and breathes it out onto her imaginary Manderley.

She abandons her typewriter for the moment, writing directly into the black notebook. Chapter after chapter, she builds the novel. It will begin with an epilogue, something new for her, a way of accentuating the tension: the suspense that already existed in *Jamaica Inn,* and which she wants to emphasize even more here, so that the reader is compelled to continue reading, unable to put the book down. Rebecca's husband, a widower, is Henry de Winter. Daphne is not sure that Henry is the right name for him, it's a little dull for her tastes, but she keeps it for the moment. He's in his fifties, an attractive but gloomy-looking man, very reserved. It is de Winter whom the female narrator meets in Monte Carlo, when she is merely a travelling companion to the vile, rich American lady Mrs. Van Hopper. The narrator has no name: Daphne can't think of one for her and decides she doesn't need one, because she likes the idea of this very young woman—a shy orphan, badly dressed, with her bitten-down nails, lank hair, and flat feet—remaining in the shadows. And yet she becomes the second Mrs. de Winter, to the stupefaction of Mrs. Van Hopper, who makes it clear to her, with a loathsome laugh, that she will never be able to replace Rebecca, that she will never be the true mistress of Manderley. As soon as she arrives in this vast house, described by Daphne as a character in its own right, the young Mrs. de Winter realizes, with a sinking heart, that the old American lady was right. At the foot of the great staircase, the servants stand motionless, awaiting the new wife of Henry de Winter. A tall, black figure stands out, with a horrifyingly white face, unsmiling, unwelcoming. This is Mrs. Danvers, the housekeeper, with her ever-clinking bunch of keys. She it is who looks after Manderley. She it was who looked after the first Mrs. de Winter. She has never gotten over the death of Rebecca. *Rebecca.* The novel resonates with those three ghostly syllables, signifier of the first Mrs. de Winter, who died a year ago and has left behind a vertiginous void filled with secrets, doubts, dread, and nightmares.

When Daphne leaves Alexandria in mid-December 1937, she has already written a third of the book. The family reunion worries her, in spite of her joy at seeing her daughters again. She fears that little Tessa will demand her presence, as will the eight-month-old baby. When Daphne informs her mother that she plans to meet her in Cornwall, so she can write, leaving her daughters for a few weeks longer with their nanny at her mother-in-law's house, Mo is shocked and does not flinch from telling Daphne so. How can she make her mother, and all the others, understand that the book is more important than anything, that she lives only for Manderley, that place in her psyche that haunts her night and day? Like Peter Pan, she has created her own Neverland, and no one else can enter it. It upsets her, that her mother can think her cruel, so she attempts, rather clumsily, to explain herself and her feelings in a letter. *I should get no work done. What a strain.*[29] Muriel gives in, and Daphne leaves for Ferryside, to work relentlessly on her novel.

At the beginning of 1938, the Brownings move again: Tommy is transferred to Hampshire, near Fleet. Daphne thinks herself lucky: She attaches so much importance to houses, and she takes an instant liking to the one they are to inhabit, Greyfriars, with its gabled roof and its large garden bordered with a forest. It is there, in the green-walled living room (because her bedroom is too small), that she makes progress on the book, sitting in front of the window with her typewriter, and whenever she looks up she can see the trees and little Tessa playing on the lawn, wrapped up against the cold. Never has she invested so much of herself in a novel; never has the writing of a book taken such possession of her. Her previous characters— Janet Coombe, Dick, Julius Lévy, Mary Yellan—were never given this psychological depth, this sensitivity to even the faintest emotion. Through the evocation of the innermost thoughts of her heroine, and a narrative that fluctuates between daydreams, past and present, Daphne knows just how much she owes to her grandfather Kicky and his "dreaming true." The magnetic darkness of Svengali leaves its imprint on the pale features of Mrs. Danvers, who nurtured "Venetian"* feelings towards Rebecca. As for Manderley, the luxurious manor house could no longer be visited again, except in dreams.

Three months later, Daphne types the final full stop of the story. Now she must reread it, armed with the blue pencil she uses to remove long-winded sentences, repetitions. Her spelling is not the best—a childhood weakness that she never grew out of—but she knows that the text will be corrected before its publication by Norman Collins, one of the young editors at Victor Gollancz Ltd. She sits on the sofa with her pen and reads every word of the thick manuscript out loud. This takes her several days. Henry de Winter . . . no, that name doesn't suit him at all. This central character, so enigmatic and attractive and yet so cold, needs another first name. George? Paul? Maxim . . . Yes, that's it, Maximilian de Winter. Elegant, cosmopolitan. His friends call him Maxim. There was only one person who called him Max, and that was Rebecca.

Before sending the corrected manuscript to Victor, Daphne hesitates. She dreads those uncomfortable moments, when the book no longer exists, lost in a no-man's-land of waiting for her editor's opinion, between the final corrections and publication. The ending is left ambiguous: What will her readers think? Is there a risk they will feel lost? And that dull, nameless heroine, who exists in Rebecca's shadow: Isn't she just a bit too clumsy, too self-effacing? What will Daphne do if Victor thinks the book too sinister and macabre, or simply overdone, sliding into melodrama? In April 1938, Daphne finally writes to her editor: *Here is the book. I've tried to get an atmosphere of suspense. It's a bit on the gloomy side. The ending is a bit brief and a bit grim.*[30]

Norman Collins is the first to read it, and he devours it in two days, then bursts ecstatically into Victor's office. Victor reads it next, and when he calls Daphne his voice is excited, jubilant; she can hear it right away. At Victor Gollancz Ltd, they rush to prepare the ground for the novel's publication in the first week of August. Victor has set an initial print run of twenty thousand copies, but he has a feeling he will need to reprint it very soon, certain that the book will double its sales within a month. He also feels sure that he will be able to sell foreign translation rights; up to now, Daphne has not been published in any other language. As for the cinema, he has no doubts: the film rights will be snapped up in no time. Hitchcock has had a few problems with the shooting of *Jamaica Inn,* which is due for release the following year, 1939. Michael Joseph has already informed Daphne that her story has been radically transformed, and not in a good way. She expects the worst. But, for now, her mind is fully occupied by *Rebecca.*

While she waits, Daphne spends several summer weeks in Hampshire, touched by the enthusiastic responses of booksellers who have read advance copies of the book. Sunbathing in a deck chair, she encourages Flavia, who is taking her first steps on the lawn while Tessa plays with her father. The sweetness of light-filled afternoons, evenings enjoyed as a family. From time to time, Daphne gets up to put a new record on the gramophone. The rousing voice of Charles Trenet, a young French singer she adores, rings out in the garden: *Y a d'la joie!** She sings along with him, in her almost perfect French accent:

> *C'est l'amour qui vient avec je ne sais quoi*
> *C'est l'amour bonjour bonjour les demoiselles*[†]

Daphne closes her eyes, sips a vodka gimlet, sings some more, thinks about Paris, about Fernande, about Kicky, about Montparnasse, about that French blood she's so proud of. She has the strange feeling that this is the calm before the storm. Could this novel change her life?

～※～

It is a hurricane. Hurricane *Rebecca,* sweeping everything before it. In a single month, the book sells forty thousand copies. The publishers order a reprint. And that is only the start. Daphne du Maurier is the name on every-

---

* "There is joy!"
† "It's love, coming with I don't know what / It's love, hello hello ladies"

one's lips. Who *is* this woman, only thirty-one years old? For the first time, Victor pressures Daphne: she must agree to do interviews, events; she must speak on the radio. She is fiercely opposed to the idea, but Victor insists. Reluctantly, she gives in. Her first interview takes place in her own home, at Greyfriars, with the journalist Tom Driberg, an effeminate man in his thirties with slicked-back hair, a rising star at the *Daily Express*. With typical humour, she admits to him that she hates London, loves gardening, is uninterested in cooking, drinks very little, is utterly indifferent to fashion, adores her quiet life in the countryside, and loathes public speaking. What does she read? Nothing very contemporary: the Brontë sisters, Anthony Trollope, and the poems of William Somerville. Her working day? From 10:00 am to 1:00 pm, then from 3:00 pm to 5:00 pm, every day except Sunday. The journalist asks Colonel Browning, who is present during the interview, if he ever knew a "Rebecca." The colonel's reply is succinct. *No.* When the article is published, Daphne is described as "a successful novelist, wife of a colonel and daughter of an actor." Further on, Driberg makes a misogynistic barb: "In her conventionally comfortable drawing room, Daphne du Maurier looks more like a subaltern's pretty little wife than a colonel's wife."

In late August 1938, the important bookstore Foyles, on Charing Cross Road in London, invites Daphne to a prestigious literary lunch organized by Christina Foyles. Two other, less famous novelists will be present. Daphne is dragged there by her editor. She warned Victor beforehand: she will not speak; she has nothing to say. All those eyes on her, all those people wanting to ask her questions, shake her hand, get their books signed . . . it's torture. Later, she writes angrily to Foy: *Writers should be read, but neither seen nor heard.*[31] Daphne has no desire to be part of any literary circle, to meet other authors. All this to sell more books? It's a waste of time. Victor takes all this on the chin. But the growing and spectacular success of *Rebecca* is more than enough consolation. It has sold one hundred thousand copies in Britain before the American edition, published by Doubleday, appears in late September 1938, with every sign that the book will replicate its UK success. The offers pour in for translation rights. The French rights are bought by the publishing house Albin Michel.

The British public falls for Daphne's harmonious face, her intensely blue eyes, her elegance. She goes on the radio, for the BBC, and her voice seems made for the airwaves, soft but powerful, feminine. The spotlight is hers, just as Victor predicted. And the more she refuses interviews and media appearances, the more eager the press and public are to find out more about this young novelist. The more she hides, the harder they seek.

By the year's end, Victor has been proved right. The American edition has sold two hundred thousand copies. Nelson Doubleday is exultant. These figures make Daphne's head spin—she finds them hard to believe—but the royalty checks that start flooding in make her proud. This is the independence she always dreamed of, as a teenager. The other side of the coin is the press reaction, which is often pitiless. The *Times* scornfully declares: "There is nothing in this book beyond the novelette." The *Christian Science Monitor* judges the book "morbid" and predicts its author will be "here today, gone tomorrow." The *Canadian Forum* deplores the novel's "mediocrity" and labels its heroine "impossibly inept."

It is painful to read these articles, like being stabbed in the chest. Daphne learns to put on her armour, to protect herself; she thinks of Kicky, who in difficult moments would repeat softly to his children, *A quoi bon?** She takes great pleasure in the good reviews, though, and thankfully there is no shortage of them. The *New York Times Book Review* writes: "Daphne du Maurier's gift is telling a story studded with shimmering truth." The *New York Herald Tribune* is eulogistic: "Intense, dazzling . . . a credible and endearing heroine." The *Saturday Review* salutes "a touching and moving story." And the book continues to sell. And to sell.

During the 1938 family Christmas in Fowey, Daphne sees her old friend Arthur Quiller-Couch. He congratulates her on her success and seems sincere. But he utters a little phrase that will haunt her for a long time afterwards: *The critics will never forgive you for writing* Rebecca.[32] In early 1939, Daphne begins to sense that Q is right. Even while the sales figures mount, she feels her book is being misunderstood. No, it is not a Gothic romance; no, it is not a corny little love story; it is the tale of an all-consuming jealousy and its murderous consequences. Is it her publisher's fault? Victor has hyped the novel up as something very romantic and commercial.

---

* "What's the point?"

Behind the story of a house, a man, and two women lurks a much darker and more disturbing truth, that of a psychological war disguised by muted violence and suppressed sexuality. The critics did not think it necessary to explore Maxim de Winter either: a complex personality, gnawed at from within, at once reserved and irascible, full of words left unsaid, whose very surname suggests cold, sterility, a burial under snow that has stunted the growth of everything. Why is *Rebecca* so quickly categorized as "mass-market fiction" intended for starry-eyed girls and romance-starved women? Why is the legacy of the Brontë sisters always raised, to the detriment of Daphne's work, considered inferior and popular? Victor deplores this reaction but manages to console his author with the phenomenal sales that show no signs of abating, even amid the growing political tensions rocking Europe. Tommy warns his wife and their friends: war will be declared in a matter of months. It's inevitable.

Despite these gloomy predictions, Angela's first novel, *The Perplexed Heart,* is published in February 1939 by agent and editor Michael Joseph, and the du Mauriers toast the event together. For press and public, the novel may as well not exist, swallowed up in the path of Hurricane *Rebecca*. The few reviews it receives are negative, repeatedly comparing Angela to her sister. With guts and humour, Angela insists she will not change her name: she is proud of being a du Maurier, and she has just as much right to the moniker as her famous sister. And she continues to write. As does Daphne. Not a novel this time—she still doesn't have an idea in mind—but she would like to bask a little longer in the ambience of Manderley, so she thinks about the possibility of adapting *Rebecca* for the stage. The idea excites her. After all, she is the daughter of actors; she has grown up in a theatrical atmosphere. Daphne sets to work with a pleasure she has never known before. How strange and enchanting it is to return to the imaginary world she created, one year later. First, she must construct a single setting: Manderley's immense entrance hall, with a view over the magnificent garden. No descriptions here, of the kind that usually enliven her novels; she must limit herself to dialogues, give life to her characters purely through their voices, their mannerisms. Although Margaret, the nanny, is absent with a migraine, Daphne somehow manages to finish her adaptation while at the same time taking care of Tessa (six) and Flavia (nearly two), an achievement that leaves her exhausted. *I must say,* she admits wearily to Tod in a letter, *I'm not one of those mothers who live for having their brats with them all the time.*[33] The play does not end in the same way as the novel; it is much more positive, a real happy ending. The curtain falls as Mr. and Mrs. de Winter embrace, at peace and in love. The ghost of Rebecca has been exorcised. Manderley is transformed from a temple of death into a bastion of love. Why? Because war is approaching, because Daphne has suffered so many reproaches for the ending of her novel, because she has the power to make that change, because writers can do whatever they like, because she is free.

The Brownings leave their pretty Greyfriars home in the summer of 1939 and move to Hythe, in Kent, so that Tommy can be closer to headquarters. The house is less charming, the garden not so pleasant. Fernande comes to visit the family for a week. This is the first time she has seen Daphne's children. Although still plump and nearly forty-six, Fernande is as lively and vivacious as ever. Tommy does not find her interesting, this Mlle Yvon; in truth, he seems increasingly preoccupied as he rises through the ranks of the army. Consequently, Daphne must put up with a constant parade of colonels and generals in her new house.

Hitchcock's film adaptation of *Jamaica Inn* is a disappointment. The screenplay bears almost no resemblance to the novel at all, with the darkness of the original abandoned in favour of an unsubtle comedy. Her fears are realized: she recognizes neither her own characters nor her own plot. *Don't go and see it, it is a wretched affair,*[34] she writes to Victor. The reviews are merciless. When the famous producer David Selznick, flush with the success of *Gone with the Wind,* adapted from Margaret Mitchell's novel, decides to buy the film rights to *Rebecca* for ten thousand pounds and assigns Alfred Hitchcock to direct it, Daphne is distraught. What will he do to her *Rebecca,* that bald, thick-lipped, and frankly unfriendly little man, with whom she feels no connection at all? He has already made a travesty of Mary Yellan and Joss Merlyn. How can she trust him after that? She writes to David Selznick, begging him not to resurrect the first Mrs. de Winter on the screen: Rebecca must remain draped in mystery. Selznick reassures her: he is keeping a close eye on Hitchcock, making sure the screenplay is reworked until it respects the arc and ambience of the book.

uriel du Maurier and her three
ughters, Angela, Jeanne and, to
e right, Daphne. 1912, London.

rryside, the house Gerald
Maurier bought in Fowey,
ornwall in 1926. Today Daphne's
, Christian Browning, lives
ere with his family.

Daphne and her dog, Bingo,
at Fowey in 1930.

n 1940 Alfred Hitchcock adapted *Rebecca* for the screen, starring Laurence Olivier
nd Joan Fontaine. Judith Anderson (on the right) played Mrs Danvers. The film, like
he book, was a worldwide success.

Daphne and her three children, Tessa, Flavia and Kits, in front of Menabilly in 1945.

Daphne and her husband,
Sir Frederick Browning, at
Menabilly in 1944.

aphne on the beach at Pridmouth in front of the wreck of the *Romanie*, 1944.

Daphne poses on the grand staircase at Menabilly, beneath the portrait of her father, Gerald. Late 1940s.

Daphne at Menabilly with Kits, Flavia and Tessa.

...cnic on the beach at Pridmouth
...ith Kits and Flavia, 1944.

...aphne photographed outside the
...ederal Court Building in New
...ork City, 1947, during the *Rebecca*
...lagiarism case.

Daphne at 70, in 1977.

Irritated, Hitchcock uses a secret pseudonym in his screenplay for the second Mrs. de Winter—Daphne de Winter, a nickname that causes much amusement in the Hollywood studios. Daphne is apprehensive; she fears that her work is slipping away from her. Laurence Olivier, the biggest English film star of the moment—who played the dark, tormented Heathcliff in the adaptation of Emily Brontë's classic, *Wuthering Heights*—is cast as Maxim de Winter. Daphne is thrilled by this. But he would like his wife, Vivien Leigh—Scarlett O'Hara in *Gone with the Wind*—to be the second Mrs. de Winter. With her green eyes and ebony hair, Vivien is far too beautiful to be Maxim's shy second wife, Daphne protests; she looks more like the bewitching Rebecca! Thankfully, it is the more prosaic-looking Joan Fontaine, sister of Olivia de Havilland, who is finally chosen.

In early September, Hitchcock begins shooting in California. At the same time, Germany invades Poland, and a few days later, on September 3, 1939, the United Kingdom and France declare war on Germany. Daphne is aware that her little world is crumbling. She writes to Angela: *We are still here (Hythe) hanging on, and I rush to the lav whenever the post arrives in case there is a letter from the War Office ordering Tommy off. I can't bear to think of it.*[35] She tries to make her sister laugh by describing the exercises organized by first-aid centres to combat gas attacks: *Last week, a maniac came to lecture us, and with a face devoid of any humour, went into fearful details of gas possibilities. She then whipped out lots of little phials from her attaché case all filled with gas and rammed them under our noses, muttering savagely with a wild gleam in her eye.* At the end of the same letter, Daphne adds soberly: *How is the "Muse"? I don't feel like "musing" myself. I don't think I could lose myself in a fictitious story whilst living in such uncertainty.*[36]

Here it is again, that short, hard word that she hated so much as a little girl: "war." It is everywhere. But now she is a mother, she is the one who must protect her daughters, her mother, her sisters. In January 1940, Tommy is appointed commander of the 128th Infantry Brigade—aka the Hampshire Brigade—and goes off to Hertfordshire with his men, while Daphne and the children take refuge in Fowey, with Muriel, Angela, and Jeanne. Even Fowey, her sanctuary, is transformed by the war. There are soldiers on every street corner, and the feeling of peacefulness is gone. In the mornings, they read the newspapers, with their announcements of the first bombardments, the first deaths. And yet she can still be overjoyed by the good reception accorded to the play version of *Rebecca,* which is performed for the first time in London, at the Queen's Theatre in March 1940.

But even this is nothing compared to the huge success of Hitchcock's film, which reaches cinemas in the spring of 1940, while the war rages in Europe. The Olivier-Fontaine double act causes a sensation. Mrs. Danvers is masterfully interpreted by Judith Anderson. Daphne adores the film, a genuine success, with its sombre black-and-white images perfectly reflecting the atmosphere of her fictional world. And the copies of her novel are flying off the shelves once again, while translators all over the world rework her words in other languages. In April 1940, Daphne receives a letter from her French editor Robert Esménard, from the publishers Albin Michel. *As you know, after publishing your admirable* Rebecca *in France, I have now acquired the French language rights for* Jamaica Inn, *as I am extremely eager to ensure that I have exclusive rights over all your works in France.*[37]

Unperturbed by the deadly Luftwaffe raids, the ominous advances of the Nazi army in Scandinavia and Holland, Hurricane *Rebecca* continues to blow mightily. Muriel, Angela, and Jeanne have to get used to it. This proves all the harder for Angela, who has just published her second novel, *Weep No More,* dismissed as "ridiculous" by *Kirkus Reviews*. No one talks to them about Gerald anymore. No one talks to them about anyone except her, the world-famous Daphne du Maurier.

❧

Her greatest joy is the knowledge that she is pregnant again. Even if, as Daphne feels sure, it will be *another lumping daughter,*[38] as she writes with weary irony to Tod, she is wildly happy to be carrying new life inside her during these troubled times, while the country fears invasion. In July 1940, Tommy is posted to Hertfordshire. As it is impossible to find a house in the current climate, the Brownings move in with a distinguished couple of the same age: Christopher Puxley, a gentleman farmer, and his wife, Paddy, are childless, and they welcome paying guests to Langley End, their taste-fully decorated Lutyens-style house. Daphne writes to Angela, who has gone to Scotland for nine months: *We are still most happy and comfortable with the P's, who are heavenly. I'm rather worried about Mummy and the children in Fowey. On Tessa's birthday, bombs dropped in the garden beyond ours, and in the harbour. I do feel we should all be together. I'm quite prepared to see us all interned because of our name! Specially if the Pétain government turn nasty and madly ally with Germany!*[39]

She misses writing. To fill this gap in her life, Daphne agrees to write a short book of patriotic fables on the suggestion of a friend, the tennis player Bunny Austin, who is involved in the organization Moral Re-Armament, in order to give courage to the British people. She entrusts publication of the book to her former publisher, Heinemann, as she doesn't think Victor Gollancz will be interested. It is not easy, writing optimistic short stories, for someone who has always preferred to explore darker ideas. Not without difficulty, Daphne produces ten short stories. Royalties will go to military charities and families in need. To her surprise, *Come Wind, Come Weather*, which she expected to quietly sink into obscurity, quickly sells 250,000 copies. The *Rebecca* effect, undoubtedly, because the quality of the writing, Daphne is well aware, leaves something to be desired. Mo and Tommy like these simple stories, which feature ordinary people confronted with the very real fears of the war. The only person who is less than delighted by the book is Victor. No matter how much Daphne protests that she didn't think he would be interested in such *propaganda*, he makes clear his displeasure and warns her that she must never publish anything with any-one else again. Message received, loud and clear.

Even in the midst of war and pregnancy, Daphne does not lose her char-acteristic deadpan sense of humour. In this peaceful corner of Hertford-shire, north of London, she and her daughters feel safe. To Angela, she writes: *I'm feeling pretty fat, with two months still to go, but thank heaven am not fat all over, or square, and don't lurch.* More seriously, she admits that sirens and air-raid warnings are not part of their daily life. *All goes well here and no alarms of great magnitude. We seem to be getting off pretty lightly. Think this bit of Herts must be in a quiet pocket. Actually, about twenty Nazi* planes flew over us on their way to Luton, eight miles away, the other after-noon. It really was rather an exquisite sight, so remote and unreal, those sil-very creatures like birds humming above us.[40]

Not long before the birth of the baby, in October 1940, the Brownings move to a neighbouring house, Cloud's Hill, for a few months, so they can await the new arrival in more serene surroundings, despite the worries caused by the war. Tessa (seven) and Flavia (three) are finally reunited with their parents. Daphne is haunted by a single fear: that her husband will be sent to France. In Fowey, Muriel and Jeanne have had to leave Ferryside, which has been requisitioned by the navy. They are staying on the Espla-nade, in town, while Angela prolongs her stay in Scotland. Jeanne puts aside music and painting to enroll in the Women's Land Army, a paramilitary agricultural organization, dating from the First World War, that sends women to the fields to take over the roles of men sent to the front, with its members devoting themselves to farming activities to produce and sell veg-etables at the local markets. The work is arduous, but Jeanne performs it very willingly.

Daphne gives birth to a boy on November 3, 1940. At last, her dream comes true. Tongue-in-cheek, she describes the agonies of childbirth to An-gela: *Suddenly those violent pains started, and luckily Sister had everything ready. She shoved a gas and oxygen contraption into my hands, which needless to say was useless, and the doctor was sent for and barely approached the bedside before I felt the most violent explosion and the baby shot out of me like someone taking a header, and yelling as it did so! And then I heard Sister say "Oh, good, won't they be thrilled" and I realised it was a boy. "One's son" at last! Christian Frederick du Maurier Browning.*[41] She is deliriously happy. Tommy gets to hold the newborn in his arms during a quick visit between two secret missions on the south coast. Tessa and Flavia realize, to their amazement, that their mother is no longer the same person since the birth of little "Kits." She is the one who bathes him, not Nanny. She kisses and cuddles him for hours, rocking him in her arms and staring rapturously into his eyes. The little girls walk around on tiptoes, feeling unwanted. Never have they received such affection, such love, from their mother.

In early 1941, the Brownings move back in with the Puxleys. The girls like sweet Paddy and the white living room where "Uncle" Christopher plays the piano, melancholy airs that echo through the large house. The war seems far off, hardly real, yet the truth is that the conflict is now in its third year and Germany's thirst for conquest shows no signs of diminishing as its army invades Bulgaria, then Yugoslavia, then Greece.

❧

Daphne has not written a novel in three years. Her time has been taken up entirely by Mrs. de Winter, Kits, and the war. For the new book that Victor is demanding, she does not want to do something in the same vein as *Rebecca:* she would prefer to create a plot that will soothe and console her readers. The world is at war, after all, and she senses that her writing has been changed by this fact: it is less dark, less macabre. Witness the change she made to the ending of *Rebecca* when she adapted it for the stage; witness, too, the optimistic stories of *Come Wind, Come Weather.* She feels like writing a story set in the past, a tale of the sea and adventure along the same lines as *Jamaica Inn,* but without its horrors. She feels like writing about love, passion, sensuality. A handsome, grey-walled house like Menabilly, a secret cove like the one she and Tommy went to for their honeymoon, on the River Helford. A heroine in her thirties, beautiful and rebellious, who is wilting in London with her dreary husband. Brown, curly hair . . . white skin . . . A French pirate, from Brittany . . . who might bear some slight resemblance to Christopher Puxley, with his calm movements, his slow smile.

Daphne has to face up to the aggravations of life as a mother. The nanny falls seriously ill; Tessa catches measles, and then so does Flavia. The baby is exhausted by his first bad cold. Dona St. Columb, her heroine, who wishes she had been born a boy so she could live freely, and Jean-Benoit Aubéry, the Breton pirate, must wait. Flavia (four) is the most affected by her illness. Daphne anxiously watches over her, day and night. It is the first time she has felt this close to her second daughter, and throughout her long convalescence, Daphne sits on the edge of Flavia's bed with the typewriter on her knees. From time to time, the little girl opens an eye, surprised and happy to have her mother all to herself. She is not in the least disturbed by the clatter of the typewriter keys.

In the spring of 1941, it is Daphne's turn to be sick, as she comes down with pneumonia. The doctor orders complete rest. She sleeps, and she reads. Angela publishes a third novel, *A Little Less,* with Michael Joseph: this is the infamous "Venetian"* novel that she wrote in secret twelve years before and was roundly rejected. The book's publication gives rise to much gossip in London society, but the reviews are both rare and severe: "cheap . . . lush mush . . . a literary failure," proclaims the *Saturday Review of Books.* From her bed, Daphne writes encouragingly to her sister, congratulating her for her boldness and suggesting that she try writing comic short stories rather than novels. It is not easy to be Daphne du Maurier's elder sister and to want to be a novelist, but Angela refuses to give up. She already has the idea for her next novel in mind; it will take place in Cornwall. For now, she joins her mother and sister in Fowey, in the little house on the Esplanade. And, following Jeanne's example, she enrolls in the Women's Land Army.

When Daphne is finally able to get out of bed again, her family realizes how thin she has gotten, how pale and weak she appears. She cannot go up or down stairs. Christopher Puxley has to carry her. A delightful man, the very opposite of Tommy, who comes back home during every leave with the weight of the war on his shoulders, his face ravaged by anxiety, stomach twisted by some unexplained pain. Christopher smokes his pipe in the evenings and says barely a word, contemplating her with a gentle smile. Daphne likes to lounge on the sofa and listen to him play, admire his beautiful hands. Her favourite tune is Debussy's "Clair de Lune," which Christopher plays with such sensitivity. Little by little, she regains her strength and starts writing again, imagining herself back in the seventeenth century and the ambience of Navron Hall, the St. Columbs' seaside home, an old house, long uninhabited, where Dona flees one night on an impulse, with children and nanny in tow, infuriated by the superficiality of society life in London. The bold, mischievous Dona is capable of dressing up as a highwayman with her accomplices and robbing terrified old aristocrats. *A romance with a big R,*[42] Daphne tells Victor in a letter, knowing full well that the critics will, once again, ridicule her for choosing to exploit a popular genre. But what does it matter? People are being killed by bombs and the newspapers are full of the horrors of war; in this climate, she does not have the heart to write something sad. She takes the subversive attraction between a Breton pirate and an English lady and throws herself yearningly into her tale, describing the slow and delicious temptation, the looks, the silences, just like those between her and Christopher Puxley, the voiceless connection that must not be mentioned, that must never be confessed, but which unlocks the secret door of her writing.

The French pirate is tall, dark, and silent, with passionate eyes and the pleasant fragrance of pipe tobacco floating around him. His hands are long and beautifully shaped, and she imagines them playing a piano or caressing a woman; yet these are hands capable of taming a sea storm, of pillaging a ship, of cutting a man's throat. His ship, like Rebecca's *Je Reviens*,* like Daphne's own boat, has a French name: *La Mouette*.† The liaison between the pirate and the lady remains as secret as the silent creek hidden at the end of the large garden. Each evening, as darkness falls, the lady disguises herself as a cabin boy and goes sailing with the captain of *La Mouette*. But her husband, Lord St. Columb, begins to question his wife's long absence. He arrives at Navron without warning, along with greedy Lord Rockingham, a former suitor of Dona's. The secret of the creek is revealed. The life of the charming pirate is in danger. . . .

The novel *Frenchman's Creek* is published in September 1941, and, as Daphne expected, the reviews are not kind. The *Times Literary Supplement* even compares the book to "dope," labelling it facile. Not that Victor cares: the readers vote with their hard-earned pounds, and the book is another bestseller. As for *Rebecca*'s sales figures, they are now approaching a million copies. Paramount Pictures snaps up the film rights to *Frenchman's Creek*; the film will be directed by Mitchell Leisen, and already there are rumours that Joan Fontaine, fresh from her success in *Rebecca*, will play the willful Lady Dona.

Tommy is promoted to Major General in November 1941 and is given the onerous task of shaping thousands of men into an airborne fighting unit, in collaboration with the Royal Air Force. Daphne's husband is now an authority in the army. Have they really been married for ten years? Daphne

---

* "I return."
† "The seagull."

can hardly believe it. It seems to her only yesterday that they first went out together on the *Yggy*. Ten years of marriage, and a husband who is now never there, sucked into the eye of the storm. And yet she is in danger. Not the same kind of danger as her husband. Here she is, in a beautiful house, safe from enemy bombardments. In a sweet bubble of peacefulness, with an attractive host. Too attractive, probably. And who is himself some-what dazzled by this witty, pretty, world-famous novelist. How could he not succumb to the charms of Daphne du Maurier? Particularly when he sees her every day for two years, her slender figure, her grace, the de-lightful sound of her laughter. The servants whisper, troubled. Aren't Mrs. Browning and Mr. Puxley spending too much time together? And poor Mrs. Puxley, who seems blind to it all . . . Daphne tries to reason with herself. This is not love; it is just a fling, a crush, that's all, a few embraces, a few caresses, a close friendship, not an all-consuming pas-sion, nothing too serious. But the danger is there, all the same. It lurks, it prowls, as it does around *La Mouette,* which waits for Dona every night at the foot of Navron's garden, as it does in the sensual smile of the French pirate, in the jealousy of Lord Rockingham. The danger of the forbidden, always so captivating.

One morning, Paddy Puxley looks at her with eyes that are no longer warm or welcoming, and Daphne finally understands, with pain and shame, that the time has come, in the spring of 1942, to leave Langley End.

There is only one place she can possibly go.

Fowey.

❧

Readymoney Cove, that little creek she has always loved. Facing out to sea, a white, square cottage with a grey roof, and a garden filled with yellow roses, opening directly on to the beach. Daphne takes care of renting it and settles the children and the nanny there. The rooms seem cramped and dark after Langley End, and the kitchen is tiny. Daphne arranges her office in a long, almost corridor-like room. The girls protest that their new bedroom is regularly invaded by black beetles; apparently, it's because the house used to be a stable.

Daphne adopts her usual defence to life's vicissitudes: she writes, submerges herself in a new novel. No time for anything else; Daphne is like a workhorse wearing blinkers. Tessa, now almost nine, goes to school on the Esplanade, close to the house where Mo, Jeanne, and Angela are staying. That makes only two children in the house during the day, but it feels like more because of Kits's fiery temperament. At eighteen months old, her son is an irresistibly impish little blond boy, idolized by his mother, and every bit as spoiled by her as Gerald was by Big Granny, which makes Muriel smile. It is Kits who, day after day, is covered with kisses, endlessly hugged, in a way that Daphne's daughters never were. In her novels, the heroines love only their sons, passionately. Real life is no different.

The novel she is writing now is a family saga, *Hungry Hill*, a sprawling historical novel in the same vein as *The Loving Spirit*, which tells the story of five generations of an Irish family, the Brodricks. Enough of romance, of ladies and pirates, Daphne is moving up a gear; she wants to be taken seriously, wants the literary critics to finally show an interest in her. She delegates all domestic tasks to Margaret and the cook, Mrs. Hancock. She remains deaf to Kits's screaming and does not leave her office before lunch. At teatime, the children are allowed to enter her lair and she reads to them the adventures of King Arthur and the Knights of the Round Table. Even Kits falls silent then, bewitched by the melodious voice of his mother and the voyages of those men in armour.

Daphne discovers that one of her childhood friends, Mary Fox, their former neighbour in Hampstead, has just moved to a house nearby, providing her with the ideal companion for her daily walks. During the autumn and winter of 1942, Daphne works hard. She will not admit to anyone that the idea for this novel was inspired by Christopher Puxley: he often talked to her about his Irish ancestors, even showed her a few letters, enough to embellish the narrative structure and preserve a secret link with him. There is the distinct impression, during this time, that Daphne is rushing headlong to escape her everyday life, losing herself in the meanders of a dense story in order not to have to think about the sad letters her husband sends, weighed down with his military responsibilities, a man approaching his fifties who feels too old for this war and misses his family. She fears for Tommy's life, now he is the Major General of the Airborne

Forces Division and has been sent to North Africa for several weeks to help out with preparations for the Desert War.

With Ferryside having been vacated by the navy, Muriel, Jeanne, and Angela do all they can to organize a festive Christmas in spite of the wartime restrictions. They toast the publication of Angela's fourth novel, *Treveryan*, "dedicated with much love to my sister Daphne," the dark tale of siblings under a family curse, set in an elegant manor house by the sea. *Kirkus Reviews* judges the book better than its predecessors, even if the author "tends to overwrite her dialogue and overplay her hand." Sales remain modest, but this does not worry Angela, who has already found the inspiration for her next novel.

Daphne's morale is at its lowest point. Outside, it rains constantly. The final corrections of *Hungry Hill* seem to drag on forever. In February 1943, she is woken by the arrival of a telegram. Tommy, not long back from North Africa, has had a glider accident. In a panic, she rushes to his bedside at the air force base in Netheravon, Wiltshire, 125 miles from Fowey. Her husband's shoulder and knee injuries are sufficiently serious that he is sent to Readymoney Cove for two weeks to recuperate.

The children had almost forgotten that their father smelled like a combination of lavender water and Woodbines, his favourite brand of cigarettes. When their mother brings him home, he is grouchy, agreeing only grudgingly to stay in his bed with his leg bandaged. When he is finally able to walk again, with the aid of a stick, Daphne and the children accompany him along the Esplanade and Tommy insists on saluting every G.I. who emerges from the huge American army base recently set up in the wooded hills behind Readymoney. The little port of Fowey is invaded by the American fleet, and civilians are no longer allowed to sail there. Tommy tells the children that, when the war ends, he will build a new boat and take the whole family out to sea. Listening to him, observing his gaunt face, Daphne realizes what a terrible mark the war has left on their lives: things will never be the same again. Even if Daphne's life does not appear so very different from the way it used to be—visits with the children to see her mother at Ferryside, lunches with the Quiller-Couches, high teas with Clara Vyvyan in Trelowarren, walks with Mary Fox, writing, and proofreading—she has a husband who chose armed conflict as a career.

Fearfully, she watches him leave again, stiff-backed in his uniform, his shoulders already burdened by the weight of the battles to come.

Hungry Hill is published on May 5, 1943. Daphne is annoyed by the book's appearance: the paper is of poor quality, thin and transparent, like the pages of a telephone directory, and the letters are tiny. But Victor had no choice: the printers, too, are suffering from wartime restrictions. She waits eagerly for the reviews, allowing herself to hope that she will finally be accorded the eulogistic articles she so desperately yearns for, that she will be congratulated on the seriousness of her work, that she will at last read that Miss du Maurier does not write mere mass-market mush for lovesick girls. But not one journalist champions the book. Its structure is judged to be clumsy, unsubtle, its prose stiff and convoluted, the characters unappealing and lifeless. The *Observer* wonders a little maliciously if Miss du Maurier had intended to write her story directly as a screenplay, without any attempt to make it literary or novel-like. Even though the film rights are bought by a production company, Daphne is cruelly disappointed. She remembers Q's little warning: *The critics will never forgive you for writing* Rebecca. Her disenchantment is intensified by the dangerous nature of the missions Tommy is given in North Africa, by this war that seems never-ending. When Tessa and Flavia's school is requisitioned by the American army, Daphne transforms her office into a classroom to educate her daughters. Helping Tessa (nearly ten) with her multiplication tables and Flavia (six) with her alphabet seems to her the best way of diminishing her own anxiety and disillusionment. The girls are thrilled by these unexpected lessons given by their mother, who goes from talking about the death of Joan of Arc (her favourite tomboy) to the devastation of the plague. She encourages them to turn some of Chaucer's tales into theatrical productions. They are fascinated by her geography classes, which she embellishes with bizarre drawings on cards, and beg her for more.

One day in the spring of 1943, Daphne takes Tessa and Flavia for a walk with their aunt Angela and whispers to them that she is going to show them her house of secrets, her favourite place in the whole world, the mansion that inspired Manderley, in *Rebecca*. She leads them patiently along an endless, overgrown driveway and, just when the girls can't bear it anymore, when they are hungry and thirsty, she finally points out the large grey house emerging from a red cloud of rhododendrons. The place is silent. The grass is waist-high. Confused, they watch their mother walk up to the house, her eyes shining, and caress the ivy-clad walls, touching her lips and her cheeks to the stone façade as if she were kissing it. This house is called Menabilly, she tells them, and no one has lived here for twenty years. It is the first time her daughters have heard this name. Their mother pronounces it with the reverence of one in love, her voice soft and dreamy. For a long time, she sits in front of Menabilly, her face transformed by happiness. Tessa gets bored—she's not interested in this house, she wants to go home—but Flavia watches her mother speaking in a low voice to Angela. Daphne seems filled with an intense joy.

Finally, it is time to leave. Daphne takes her daughters by the hand, turns around one last time, and offers a secretive smile to that abandoned house enveloped in silence. As they walk away through the undergrowth, escorted by the singing of doves, she is still smiling, because she knows, now, who the new mistress of Menabilly is going to be.

PART FOUR

CORNWALL, 1943

MENABILLY

❦

It makes me a little ashamed to admit it,
but I do believe I love Mena more than people.
—DAPHNE DU MAURIER[1]

Fowey, Cornwall
November 2013

Y ou want to go to Menabilly? *Impossible.* Visit it? *You must be joking.* See
it? *No one sees Menabilly.* Menabilly is inaccessible. The Rashleigh
family, who have owned the mansion since the sixteenth century, wish it
to remain that way. I observe the property on Google Maps: the house appears, seen from above, a pale square surrounded by greenery, then the sea,
very close, an emerald ribbon touching a rocky coastline. But this is not
enough. I want to see it with my own eyes.

It is surprisingly bright, this late in the year, and the cool air smells of salt,
grass, damp earth. Holding my map, I leave the Menabilly Barton farm and
turn right towards the little beach at Pridmouth. The quiet footpath descends towards the sea, and I hear its murmur grow louder as I approach.
The beach is scattered with large grey rocks covered with lichen, the same
grey as the granite cottage that sits almost at the edge of the sand. The same
cottage that inspired the one in *Rebecca,* a place of mystery and tragedy. Apparently, you can rent it by the week. It sleeps eight and is almost always
booked up. To the right, a wooden footbridge climbs up towards a large red-
and-white beacon that stands on the hill at Gribbin Head. To the left, an
uneven road and a rusted winch. Daphne used to come here every day,

with her children or alone, accompanied by her dogs, even in bad weather. In the summer, she liked to swim and sunbathe here. Going back up the path, I am aware of walking in her footsteps and I try to walk like her, quickly, with long strides.

Menabilly is only a few minutes' walk from where I stand now, but as I have been warned, there are signs with STRICTLY PRIVATE in large letters on all of the high gates. I could, at my own risk, approach the house by that secret path that goes under the trees; I could ring the bell at the lodge, which is no longer abandoned as it was when Daphne first visited, and ask the guard if I could meet the owners. The Rashleigh family decided long ago not to give any interviews or information about their famous tenant, who spent nearly twenty-five years in the mansion. Since the publication of *Rebecca* in 1938, Menabilly has exerted a magnetic attraction over readers from all over the world, who continue to travel all the way to Fowey in the hope of being able to explore the property that was such an inspiration to the author. Like me, they find the way barred. So I must use cunning, if I want to get any closer to the house. There is, I have been told, only one path that allows the mansion to be seen from a distance. You must climb above the farm, walk along the coast, go past fields enclosed by wooden fences, climb farther up to Polkerris, and, at the junction, take a right, towards Tregaminion Chapel. The bright green pastureland that overlooks the sea is usually deserted, but when I pass a woman there, she greets me with a polite smile, which I return.

While I continue along my path, I think about the moment when I discovered *Rebecca* in English, at eleven. I read it several times. Then, at sixteen, I read the French edition, a gift from a friend. *Translation by Denise Van Moppès, 1940.* I immediately noticed that there had been cuts made in the French version; they were too significant not to be noticeable, particularly if you knew the original text as well as I did. Altogether, about forty pages had been removed.

From a distance, I see the clock tower of the little church. I am almost there. I can't stop thinking about that translation. Daphne had a perfect understanding of French. Did she compare that edition with the original version? Did she realize just how many of her descriptions had been shortened? I discovered that the translator had, here and there, performed a disappearing act on the heroine's reminiscences, her obsession with Rebecca, and her thoughts spreading into daydreams, all of Kicky's influence. The rhythm of the book had been altered, losing much of the atmosphere that Daphne had so meticulously created. But what most upset me was the fatal diminution of two essential scenes, the first with Mrs. Danvers in the large bedroom in the west wing, stripped of its dramatic tension, and the second with Maxim, the climax of the book, that moment when the truth is revealed—what happened in the cottage on the beach where Rebecca used to go with her lover—of which an entire page of dialogue is missing. I have not been able to find any trace of a correspondence between Daphne and her French publishers, Albin Michel, concerning the translation of *Rebecca*.

I reach the chapel and look south, over the fence and the sheep grazing in front of it. There is no one else here. A golden light pierces the low-hanging clouds. In the distance, the roof of Menabilly's north wing is just visible through the trees. I feel the same emotion I felt outside Cannon Hall. A little patch of roof is all I will ever see of the house that Daphne du Maurier loved so passionately.

❦

Summer 1943. Daphne is thirty-six years old. Her royalty payments are pouring in, making her a wealthy woman, so much so that she starts to complain about the high rate of income tax she must now pay. She has no desire to buy dresses, cars, works of art. There is only one thing she wants to spend her money on, but it is not for sale. How unbearable, that vision of Menabilly, neglected, left to rot year after year. One morning, she has an idea: call her lawyer in Fowey, Walter Graham, to ask him to contact Dr. Rashleigh and find out whether it would be possible to perhaps rent Menabilly. It's a long shot, obviously, and she doesn't mention the idea to anyone else. She braces herself for a refusal. But, one week later, her lawyer gives her an unexpected reply: the Rashleighs agree. Mrs. Browning can live in Menabilly in exchange for a rental payment to be determined and subject to a contract that they will draw up. Jubilation and incredulity. The lawyer warns her that the house is in a deplorable state: the roof might collapse at any moment, damp has infiltrated the walls, but Daphne interrupts him: she is so moved, so happy, she has not felt anything like this since Kits was born three years ago. Her mother and her sisters attempt to dissuade her. She must be crazy: there's no running water, no electricity, no heating; it's impossible! While Tommy fights the war on the front, Daphne fights for Menabilly. Walter Graham enters into lengthy, ill-tempered negotiations with Dr. Rashleigh. After a great deal of hairsplitting, an agreement is reached. Daphne will rent the house for twenty years, and she will pay for all work carried out on it. Does this give her cold feet? Not at all. She manages to obtain some government aid for the renovation but finances most of it herself.

For the moment, she does not tell her children anything about this. They see her leave every morning with Margaret, armed with brooms, mops, and cloths. A stranger in a suit, carrying a large box filled with mysterious maps, spends several evenings at Readymoney Cove, shut up in the office with their mother. One day, pressured by their constant questioning, she finally admits that she is preparing a surprise for them and that they must wait patiently for it to be ready.

Dressed in her trousers, jumper, and boots, Daphne spends her days at Menabilly with her team: lawyer, bricklayer, roofer, plumber, electrician.

Whenever she is told that something is not possible, Mrs. Browning becomes offended, then begs them, asks them, to see what they can do. The renovation takes six months, and Daphne is inordinately happy as she directs the building work. Electricity, water, and heating are installed, doors and windows are changed, the roof is entirely replaced, dust and saltpetre removed, the walls repainted. And all this in wartime. It's a miracle.

Menabilly comes back to life. The ivy is trimmed, and sunlight again enters the house. The long rooms regain their old nobility. Daphne feels overwhelmed by love. Is it wrong to love stone as if it were a person? A house that isn't even hers, that she will never own. Does it matter? She lives here now, and she will for the next twenty years—a long time. She will be fifty-six then, she will be old; she will have time to get used to the situation. She has moved in her own furniture, recuperated from storage, and has bought new furniture, too, and in December 1943, the three dumbstruck children discover their new abode. On the doorstep, their mother announces with a dazzling smile: *Welcome to Mena!*[2]

"Mena" bears no resemblance to the abandoned mansion of the previous summer. The wooden floors shine once again, a fire blazes in the large living room hearth, the flowered wallpaper matches the fabric on the chairs and sofas. The old rocking horse waits for them in front of the sparkling stained-glass windows. Stunned, the children walk through to the book-lined library where a baby grand piano stands on a white carpet and the wood-panelled walls are decorated with engravings of hunting scenes. They find their grandfather Gerald's bronze bust and walking sticks, the caricatures drawn by their great-grandfather Kicky. They run up the grand wooden staircase, admire the portrait by Whiting of their mother and their aunts when they were children, with the little dog Brutus in Jeanne's arms. On the second floor, they find long red-carpeted corridors, their parents' bedrooms, and other bedrooms, most of which look out over the garden, and then their own room, a beautiful space, painted green, with images of Peter Pan pinned to the walls, and with three beds—a sight that makes Tessa cry, because she refuses to sleep with her younger siblings. Margaret firmly but gently puts an end to her tantrum.

Daphne has planned everything for Tommy's return during the New Year holidays, down to the smallest Christmas decorations. Her mother and sisters are openmouthed with admiration. How did she do it? Daphne wonders, seeing her family united in front of the Christmas tree, in this house she loves so much. She believed in it, she wanted it, she got it. But she must admit that she's exhausted now. She will need twice as many servants to look after the children, the housekeeping, the cooking, the garden. There is always a fire to be lit, a child to be watched over, an object to be repaired, wood to be chopped. Daphne manages to find a retired schoolteacher from Tywardreath, who comes by taxi three times a week to give Tessa and Flavia lessons. Will she soon be able to think about a new book? She will have to get back in the saddle after the half failure of *Hungry Hill,* which did not sell as well as Victor had hoped. She feels like writing a few short stories, perhaps a play, while she waits for the idea of a novel to start "brewing."*

Daphne orders new stationery for her correspondence with a simple letterhead that makes her swell with pride: MENABILLY, in red letters, and to the left a winged crown, the Browning family coat of arms. From January 1944, in her new house, Daphne remains faithful to her "routes."* The maid, Violet, wakes her at nine o'clock with the breakfast tray: coffee, and toast with honey. The children come in to give her a kiss and a hug, and at ten she starts work, sitting behind the desk in her bedroom with its faded wallpaper decorated with white roses. She uses a new typewriter, a portable Underwood Standard. Kits (four) is the only one allowed to stay with her while she writes. This is unfair to Tessa and Flavia, but that's just how it is. He plays with his collection of lead Indians until Margaret comes to fetch him without disturbing Mrs. Browning. Daphne does not stop writing until one o'clock, when she always eats lunch alone. At two comes the children's favourite moment, when the four of them go for a walk. In good weather, they head down to the sea at Pridmouth and play games around the wreck of the *Romanie*, the remains of which are still there. If it rains, they explore the mysteries of the forest. Carrying a long stick, wearing her jacket, trousers, and boots, Daphne guides them, tirelessly energetic. She always pauses to chat with Mr. Burt, the handyman and part-time gardener, who works hard, armed with a scythe, accompanied by his dog, Yankie. A quick stop to let Kits play on the swing, and then it's time for tea.

Daphne sips her China tea alone in the library, then goes back to her room to work, until it is bathtime, when she sometimes takes over from

Margaret. The children's bathtub is high and deep, with ball and claw feet. The water used for washing comes from pumping a distant pond, located near the gates that lead to the house. It is supposedly filtered, but it always looks greenish and leaves marks on the enamel, as well as in the children's blond hair, which amuses them no end. After their supper, Tessa, Flavia, and Kits come in to kiss their mother, in the library where she reads the newspapers near the fire, with the old gramophone playing a Rachmaninoff tune. She changes her clothes for her solitary meal, wearing a long embroidered jacket with velvet trousers and a silk blouse.

The children's bedtime takes a while; Kits does not like the dark—they have to light a little night-light—and the girls are scared, because Mr. Burt told them about a ghost, a lady in blue who roams the empty bedroom next to their father's walk-in wardrobe. And then there are the rats, which have never left the attic and which, all night long, make noises in the ceiling above their heads. And that's without even mentioning all the bats that fly around outside the window at sunset. When the children complain to their mother about this, she invents such funny stories about bats and rats that they end up laughing with her and making the best of the situation. Their mother's new nickname is Bing, inspired by her beloved dog, Bingo, her faithful companion at Ferryside.

Besotted with Menabilly, Daphne is able to bear the coldness of the house in that first winter, unlike the children and Margaret. With its high ceilings, the house is almost impossible to heat, and the corridors are always freezing. The children get ear infections and chest infections, but Daphne's morale never wavers, especially with spring just around the corner. She looks happier than she has ever been. Her dream has come true: she is the mistress of Menabilly. Does she suffer from Tommy's absence? Of course, but she has built herself an enchanting and exclusive refuge, sheltered from everything, and that is enough. Spurning the dark heart of the war, Daphne locks herself away in her imaginary world, where she reigns like an empress over her characters. Nothing else matters.

American soldiers regularly discover the path to Menabilly and ring at the door of the mansion, a copy of *Rebecca* in hand. Is this where the great novelist lives? Daphne forgets how famous she is. She is intimidated by the prospect of meeting her readers, and prefers to hide on the parapet that surrounds the roof, leaving ten-year-old Tessa to answer the door to unexpected visitors. A tried-and-trusted speech: _Daphne du Maurier is out, and she won't be back until evening._ Undaunted, the G.I.s come back the next day, with their books to sign, and sometimes Daphne yields, smiling at them and tracing her name on the flyleaf of their books.

While Daphne retreats into her bubble at Menabilly, Tommy becomes a lieutenant general at forty-seven years old, the commander of the 1st Airborne Division. In the spring of 1944, vast preparations are secretly in progress for D-day. Husband and wife see each other briefly in May. Every morning, Daphne writes to him, and the mailman brings her several letters each week in return from Tommy. The envelopes are stamped with the Browning seal and the missives invariably begin with _My own beloved Mumpty._ The words are scribbled in haste and signed _Your devoted Tib, with all the love a man's heart can hold,_[3] with Xs for kisses, sent by the eight favourite teddy bears that the lieutenant general still takes everywhere with him.

The entire coastline, from Exmouth to Falmouth, is tense with excitement and nerves on the eve of the Normandy landings, of which Daphne and her family know nothing, but which they all hope for. She imagines how hard her husband must be working during these crucial hours. The authorities ask Mrs. Browning to organize a top-secret lunch at Menabilly for about sixty American war correspondents who are in the region incognito. Under a shroud of secrecy, Muriel, Jeanne, and Angela help her to host the lunch. Her own cook, the nanny, and the maids have been sent out on a picnic for the day, so they do not suspect anything. Menabilly is invaded by an efficient American team led by a chef who prepares a festive meal in a battery of saucepans and platters bearing the insignia of the U.S. Navy. It is a great success, which must never be spoken of.

On June 6, 1944, Angela and Jeanne call their sister, feverishly excited: while they were taking care of their tomatoes for the Women's Land Army, they noticed that, by evening, there was not a single American ship in the bay. Daphne spends her days listening to the radio, on the alert for anything concerning the airborne divisions, the ones that are supervising Tommy's men in Normandy. She knows how furiously her husband is working to fight the Nazis and their allies, and even if the first reports of the landings are positive, he is not out of danger yet.

In September 1944, Daphne's anxiety is at its height. Tommy is a key element in the preparation of the biggest airborne operation of the war, code-named Market Garden. Conceived by General Bernard Montgomery, its objective is to parachute Allied divisions behind German lines in order to capture strategically important bridges that will enable the ground troops to enter Germany. The most remote target is the city of Arnhem, Holland, situated on the Rhine. Not everyone is convinced of the soundness of the idea behind this massive operation. Tommy publicly expresses his doubts to General Montgomery: *We might be going a bridge too far, sir.*[4] The battle rages for nine days, the Germans resist, and strategic mistakes put the operation in peril. On the bridge in Arnhem, the order is given for the Allies to withdraw. Seventeen thousand soldiers are killed. When he returns for a leave, in October 1944, Tommy is exhausted. A luxurious weekend with his wife at Claridge's in London is not enough to soothe him, and Daphne realizes just how psychologically scarred her husband is by that defeat. What kind of a man will he be by the end of this war, when he used to have nightmares, as a young man, because of what he experienced in Gauche Wood? Will he ever be able to vanquish the demons of Arnhem?

In November, a gala evening is organized at the Troy Cinema in Fowey in honour of the film adapted from *Frenchman's Creek*, directed by Mitchell Leisen. Daphne, looking glamorous in a long dress, attends with her mother and her sisters. She dislikes the Californian Technicolor sunsets, so far removed from the Fowey estuary, and suppresses a shudder of disgust at Joan Fontaine's red wig. But, despite the extravagance of the costumes, which she disapproves of, the film is quite well done, and she is happy to learn that the book is selling again as a consequence. Victor knows that Daphne is finishing a play; he would have preferred a novel, and she promises him one for next year. The play, *The Years Between*, tells the poignant story of a colonel who disappears at sea and whose widow, Diana, overcoming the ordeal, manages to forge a new life, falling in love with another man. Then it is that her husband, whom everyone thought dead, returns. Daphne tried to give a glimpse of her happy isolation at Menabilly, that selfish well-being she feels, far from her husband, that no one would ever be able to understand or accept. In December, the play is staged at Wyndham's, her father's old theatre, and it proves a success.

One December morning, Daphne receives a letter from her French editor, Robert Esménard. *Dear Madame, Delighted as I am that the mail is now being delivered once again between our two countries, I hasten to enter back into correspondence with you in order to keep you up to date on the distribution of your works in France. Our publishing house did everything it could to ensure the successful publication of* Rebecca. *As you surely know, the representative of Curtis Brown in France has given me a general option on all your productions. I would like to express here, once again, the esteem I feel for your wonderful talent.*[5] More good news accompanied this letter: the release of French royalty payments, which had been frozen during the war. Since its first appearance in France, in 1940, *Rebecca* has sold five hundred thousand copies, and it is still selling.

At the end of 1944, an even greater distance is put between the Brownings: Tommy is appointed Lord Mountbatten's chief of staff in Ceylon, in southern Asia. Daphne is saddened by his departure, but her next novel is "brewing"* nicely; this will be the first book she has written in Menabilly, and she is eager to get started.

❧

She will write the history of the mansion, using what happened within these walls during the English Civil War, between 1642 and 1649, a series of conflicts that led to the fall and then the execution of Charles I and the establishment of a new regime, the Commonwealth. Daphne will return to that tormented period in Menabilly's past and excavate the legend of the mysterious walled-up room and the skeleton of the Cavalier dressed in a royalist uniform. Full of hope, she sends a letter to William Rashleigh, the family heir, who lives near Plymouth. Could she have access to documents, private letters? He refuses, but Daphne is undeterred and tries his daughter, who is better disposed. Miss Rashleigh gives the author the family tree and files relating to the years that interest Daphne, a mine of information that delights her. The Cornish historian Alfred Leslie Rowse, a friend of the Quiller-Couches, also provides some primary source material. For several weeks, Daphne immerses herself in history books, pores over letters, examines maps, sketches out the novel's structure. Victor is relieved to learn that she is writing again; Daphne is his flagship author, his biggest earner, with advances of three thousand pounds per book and royalties of 25 per cent. She promises him she will finish it by July 1945.

On a night with a full moon, just after Daphne has begun writing the novel, she stands close to her bedroom window and thinks she hears the muffled thunder of hundreds of galloping horses; she makes out the clinking of harnesses and the animals' panting breath, as if a whole army were encircling Menabilly. She opens the window and leans out to observe the silent garden. Nobody there. The next morning, she tells her children about this strange sensation and they listen, wide-eyed.

Her new heroine is Honor Harris, a young royalist who truly existed, and the story begins in 1620 when she is only ten years old. Even at that age, she is already a compelling character with a bold, insolent temperament that stimulates Daphne's imagination, a tomboy in the same swaggering, fearless vein as Janet Coombe, Mary Yellan, Rebecca de Winter, and Dona St. Columb. Her older brother Christopher has just married the fiery Gartred Grenvile. The Grenviles are one of the most powerful families in Cornwall. Ten years later, Honor's destiny is dramatically altered, and it is Gartred's younger brother—the irresistible, impetuous Richard Grenvile—who is the cause.

Locked away in her room, Daphne leaves the care of the children and the house to migraine-stricken, overworked Margaret. What a bore, all these material necessities, when the only thing that counts is Honor Harris. Things get done without Mrs. Browning—shopping, cleaning, cooking—so why should she take care of all that, when there are others who can do it? She no longer drives, has not been behind the wheel of a car since her wedding day, and she doesn't miss it. No one disturbs her. No one dares. From time to time, she gets up from her desk (who could imagine that just writing for hours on end would cause such pain to one's entire body?), stretches her numb legs, massages her stiffened fingers. Standing up, leaning against the window, she smokes a cigarette and looks out towards the slim blue line of the sea, lost in her thoughts. She does not see the children playing at the edge of the woods, nor Mr. Burt, the gardener, hard at work; she is in the seventeenth century, amid the murderous violence of the revolution, she hears the crowd shouting, the cannons booming, the crossfire of muskets; she sees the sack of Menabilly, bastion of royalists, the furniture on fire, the torn clothes, the smashed mirrors. She sees the secret room, impossible to locate, buried somewhere in the mansion that she has searched so many times in vain. She will recount, once again, her love of Cornwall, the sea, the violence of storms, the scented rain, the wind that sweeps everything before it, and her passion for this house, stronger than anything she feels for man, woman, or child. She will describe the war, how it changes the course of a life, describe the agony of waiting suffered by women who are not at the front but who feel it in their flesh just as men do, who hide fugitives, surrender to invaders, protect children and houses, heal wounds, but who, like Honor, hold their heads high, with faith in the future. Daphne mixes the insurrections of 1648 with what she understands of the current global conflict and the complexity of military strategies, she who has a husband fighting in the thick of the action. The book is dedicated to him, in fact, and its title is *The King's General.*

On May 8, 1945, the day after Germany's unconditional surrender, Daphne, her mother, and her sisters listen to the radio as the Allied governments announce the official end of the war in Europe. This does not mean that Tommy will be coming home, however; he is still kept abroad by his military career. When Daphne thinks about his return, she is torn between joy and fear: How will they pick up the threads of this marriage weakened by his long absence? How will she explain to him that she has become attached to her solitude, that she now likes nothing more than writing, alone, in Menabilly, following her "routes,"* surrounding herself with silence? Daphne unearths an old military redingote that used to belong to Tommy and puts it on for her lone dinner in the library. With her blonde hair now showing hints of silver, Daphne looks feminine, beautiful, but suddenly formidable, as if that purple and gold jacket accentuated a previously concealed power. Sometimes, late, as night is falling, Flavia and Kits stealthily descend the stairs to spy on her while she dreamily plays a few chords on the piano. To them, Daphne seems dazzling and unreachable. In the end, they go back upstairs in silence and slip into their beds without waking Tessa.

Daphne finishes the book in July 1945 and sends it to Victor, highly satisfied, who plans to publish it in a blaze of publicity (the war is finally over!) with a print run of seventy-five thousand copies in 1946. Despite the tiredness she always feels after completing a novel, Daphne must manage her household. Flavia has broken her arm, falling off Mr. Burt's pony, and Margaret is again tormented by migraines. Poor Mrs. Hancock, who does all the cooking for the family, cannot do everything on her own. For a while now, Daphne has had an idea in mind, and she can't stop thinking about it. Why not try it? It would, after all, be the perfect solution. Yes, she will ask Tod, dear Tod, her favourite governess, to come and work at Menabilly. Daphne and Tod have remained close over the past twenty years, writing to each other on a regular basis. Tod has already met Daphne's husband and their three children. She must break the news gently to Margaret, who has been in the Brownings' service since Tessa's birth, explaining to her that Tod will not be replacing anyone but will take care of the children's education. Tod is not certain that she can start work for Daphne straight away, however, as she is under contract with her current employers, an aged couple in Yorkshire.

One night in September 1945, while they are in bed, the children learn from the beaming Margaret that the war is officially over, and they rush downstairs to the library and noisily announce the good news to their mother. She looks up at them, puts down her newspaper, and responds with unexpected severity: *Yes I know it is, go back to bed this instant.*[6] Crestfallen, they troop back upstairs, baffled by their mother's strange attitude. They are waiting for just one thing now, the return of their father, but that is not going to happen immediately: Tommy must first go to Singapore, where he will oversee the demobilization of hundreds of thousands of men.

Miss Maud Waddell, alias Tod, arrives at Menabilly in October 1945, preceded by her numerous suitcases and her watercolour painting materials. A small, renovated apartment awaits her in the oldest part of Menabilly, the west wing. She moves in, organizes her lessons with Tessa and Flavia every morning, and in no time at all she manages to smooth over the frequent misunderstandings between the two sisters, while making herself liked by Margaret. Daphne is so happy to see this familiar face again, to hear the rich, deep voice that resounded through her childhood, her sentences that invariably begin with *My dear*. Daphne had been a similar age to her daughters when Tod arrived in Cannon Hall in 1918. How distant that period seems! Listening to Tod make her daughters recite their multiplication tables, Daphne sees herself with Angela and Jeanne, sees her father again in the garden at Hampstead, lighting a cigarette, always ready to clown around, and she is seized by a nostalgia for her childhood days. Daphne is one of those writers who prefer looking back to looking forward, who is capable of filling entire pages with what was, a place, a trace, putting words to the fleeting moment, the fragile memory that must be bottled like a perfume. Tod has known her for almost thirty years; she has seen her become a novelist, watched as the talent of that determined, solitary, book-hungry girl blossomed into fame, and now she is here to help her in her role as a mother and wife. Tod's searching eyes do not miss a beat. Acute and understanding, never judgemental, she sees Daphne's all-consuming preference for little Kits, to the detriment of his sisters; she sees the magic spell that "Mena" has cast over Daphne when it is, in reality, just a big, cold house lost in the forest, infested by rats and bats. Like Fernande, she is the sentinel of Daphne's past, the privileged witness to her youth, one of the few to understand her complex nature. It is out of the question that Tod should join Daphne for a drink in the evening, or eat with her when she sits alone in the library, dressed in the crimson redingote, nibbling her light meal. Tod knows better than anyone how much Daphne likes her solitude. What will she do when her husband returns?

New residents arrive at "Mena" at almost the same time as Tod: two young goats given to Tessa by her godfather. They are both females, but the children insist on calling one of them Freddie, after their father, whose real name is Frederick. The other is named Doris. With their gentle eyes and adorable bleating, they bring joy to everyone . . . until the morning when Daphne finds them happily settled on her bed, having already eaten her nightgown and made a good start on her silk robe.

Soon after the goats' arrival, Victor warns Daphne that she will have to submit to another photo session to help publicize the book—and this time it will be a family portrait. The photographer will be Miss Compton Collier, the same lady who immortalized Daphne at Ferryside thirteen years before, in 1932. She has lost none of her theatricality, turning up at Menabilly in her tweed suit, followed by an assistant, soaked with sweat and buckling under the weight of the cameras, tripods, and bags he must carry. Flavia and Tessa have a fit of the giggles, which they overcome only with difficulty. While Miss Compton Collier sets up her equipment, she suggests to Mrs. Browning that she change her clothes. Daphne firmly declines this offer, believing that her outfit is perfect: beige linen trousers, a white shirt, and a cardigan. The look on the photographer's face sends the girls into hysterics again, and this time their mother joins in.

The session is not off to a good start. Mrs. Browning and her children cannot keep a straight face. Miss Compton Collier finds this regrettable and becomes angry. She suggests bringing in the goats, which she has spotted grazing in the distance, to create a diversion. While Tessa and Flavia fetch them over, and the photographer is hidden behind the camera beneath a vast black cape that blocks out the light, Doris and Freddie, panic-stricken by the sight of this ominous shape, rush at it, heads down and horns out. Helpless with laughter, Daphne and her children hurry to the aid of Miss Compton Collier. The goats are banished, the tweed suit readjusted. Thankfully, the photographer possesses a sense of humour, and she too is able to joke about the misadventure. The photo shoot is a success.

∾❧৩

In early 1946, Daphne becomes Lady Browning, after the knighthood given to Tommy, who is now Sir Frederick Browning. She is pleased by this distinction. Tommy is still not back from Asia—*I honestly don't think that there is going to be much chance of a man getting back soon,*[7] he tells his wife in one of his letters—and he is counting the days until he can be reunited once again with his family. This return weighs on Daphne's mind. How will they be able to reforge their old complicity, now that she is in the grip of Menabilly? This house, her very own Manderley, grown from the same magical soil as Uncle Jim's Neverland, this place where she always enters alone, to which no one else possesses the key.

While she waits for Tommy's return and the publication of her novel, Daphne enjoys her tranquility in Fowey. In November 1945, she signs a contract with her French publisher Albin Michel via the intermediary of her agents Curtis Brown and Michel Hoffman for the publication of three of her books: *Gerald: A Portrait*, *The Du Mauriers*, and *I'll Never Be Young*

Again, her second novel. Her sister Jeanne, after spending the last few years working in the fields for the Women's Land Army, has been able to return to her canvases. Her pictures are delicate, luminous interiors and still lifes. Her works are exhibited in St. Ives, about thirty-five miles from Fowey, where a community of artists has been established. For Muriel and Angela, who are more interested in Jeanne's work than Daphne is, Bird has inherited her grandfather's artistic talent (she is already using Kicky's old easel), and they feel certain she is set for a great career as a painter. Jeanne, their mother's favourite, is a pretty thirty-five-year-old with blonde, curly hair, but she does not have the same striking beauty as Daphne; her features are less harmonious, her personality more reserved, sometimes even a little cantankerous. Flavia and Tessa prefer the company of their comical aunt Piffy, always good for a laugh. Angela is relieved that her work in the fields, which she hated, is over and that she can now start going to the theatre again, travelling, can re-establish her friendships with actresses, aristocrats, women of the world, friendships and loves that she mentions only to her sisters. She is horrified by the Dantesque vision of London, devastated by the Blitz, and irritated by all those people who no longer dress up to go to the opera. Her fifth novel is published in the spring of 1946 by her cousin Peter Llewelyn Davies, who has founded his own publishing house. Michael Joseph has retired, and the young man who replaced him rejected Angela's book. *Lawrence Vane* does not arouse any interest in the press, despite its bold subject matter: it is the story of a young concert musician who goes blind at the zenith of her fame and marries her pen pal, Paul, a possessive man who has never revealed to her that he is mixed-race, with an Indian mother. One acerbic review in *Kirkus Reviews* goes as far as advising people not to borrow the book from a library. The *New York Times Book Review* criticizes the book, "told with flat British restraint that doesn't whip up ardent sympathy for the lovers." Angela, used to such reviews by now, keeps smiling. During a vacation in Italy, at a fashionable hotel—the Bella Riva, on Lake Garda—she is signing her name in the register when an affable customer walks up and thanks her for her help with her nephew. Angela raises her eyebrows, and the woman goes on: *You and your husband were so kind to him . . .* Angela interrupts her with a smile: *I expect you think I am my sister, Daphne Browning?*

I am Angela du Maurier.[8] The woman recoils, looking angry, and tells her husband, *It's only the sister!* She turns on her heel and leaves Angela gaping. How many times has Angela heard that phrase? *It's only the sister.* She should write a book about it, one day. Her memoirs. Why not? In the meantime, she is planning to write a collection of short stories.

A young editor at Gollancz, Sheila Hodges, works with Daphne on the proofs of *The King's General,* her eighth novel. Aware that her grammar and spelling are far from perfect, Daphne recognizes the importance of this correction work, is happy to accept the editor's suggestions, and does not become offended when her mistakes are pointed out to her. She has great hopes for this novel's publication, after the mediocre reviews and disappointing sales of the last one. But the newspapers' coverage irritates her more than anything. Reviewers appreciate the powerful love story between Honor Harris and Richard Grenvile, but condescendingly emphasize it to the detriment of the rest of the novel, reducing the book to the status of a simple romance. Her in-depth research is not even mentioned, nor is her skill in mixing fact with fiction. Though she is indignant about this, Daphne's good humour is restored when Victor tells her about the excellent sales figures and about the juicy offer for film rights of sixty-five thousand pounds.

But, in truth, it is not the literary world that occupies Daphne's mind in the summer of 1946. Tommy has just been appointed Military Secretary of the War Office in London.

He will soon be back, after six years of absence.

❧

The woman in the mirror confirms what she sees: Daphne is beautiful, her skin tanned, her eyes shining, her ash-blonde hair set in attractive waves at a recent visit to the hairdresser, her slender figure accentuated by a chic suit. No one would guess she was thirty-nine. Tommy returns on the day of their wedding anniversary, July 19, surely a good omen for their reunion. His latest letters have been full of life, love, joy at the prospect of seeing her again, and fear that she will be disappointed, that she will find him changed, no longer the same man. She waits for him on the runway of the RAF airport in Northolt, near London. Tommy's airplane finally arrives, and her stomach is in knots. The doors open noisily, his tall figure appears, walks quickly down the steps, and she starts to rush towards him, then holds back, and it looks as if he is holding back, too: he doesn't hug her, just pecks her on the cheek. Perhaps this is because of the presence of his team, because they are not alone? But Daphne is also left wondering about that beautiful brunette in her early twenties: her name is Maureen, apparently, and she is Tommy's assistant.

This is all it takes for Daphne to feel invisible: the lack of warmth in Tommy's clumsy embrace, and the presence of the disturbingly pretty Maureen. They spend their first night together in the small, gloomy apartment on the sixth floor of Whitelands House, on the King's Road in Chelsea, near Sloane Square, that Tommy has rented for his new job. The rooms are narrow, the floorboards creak, and the air smells faintly of gas. The Brownings spend a night together without tenderness, without love. But Tommy is probably tired, exhausted in fact, and things will be better at Menabilly, where he is going for a six-week vacation before taking up his new office in London. After that, he will take the train to Cornwall every weekend to see his family. Daphne had made her feelings clear: there was no question of her leaving Menabilly to move in with him in the capital. Was she too intransigent? Too attached to her independence?

Tommy falls asleep, and Daphne's thoughts race. When was the last time they "waxed"*? It seems an eternity ago. It's been a long time since they've done any "spinning"* or had "Cairo,"* but of course there was the war, the war that drained all desire, the war and its attendant woes that had such an effect on her Boy. Her handsome, green-eyed Boy is nearly fifty now, and looks it. She watches him sleep and wonders what happened to the magnificent young man on his white boat. And what about her? Since she last saw him, Lady Browning has fallen madly in love with a house. How can she explain that to her husband? It's not the kind of thing that can be explained, only observed.

At Menabilly, Tommy is shocked by how much his children have grown. Tessa (thirteen) is a willowy adolescent with blue-grey eyes, Flavia (nine) is a gap-toothed, short-haired tomboy, and Kits (five) is the apple of his mother's eye. That summer, Margaret leaves the family's service. The children are saddened to see her go, but happy to have their father again.

How he has changed! His wrinkled forehead gives him a permanent worried look. And whereas their mother almost never gets annoyed with them
or raises her voice, whereas she is so smiling and patient and funny, their
father flies into a rage over nothing, seems unable to relax. Sometimes he
is in such a foul mood that the only thing they can do is keep out of his
way. Quite often, Tommy refuses to have anything to do with the two main
obsessions in Daphne's life: "Mena" and Kits. Is this a manifestation of his
jealousy, a desire for revenge?

Occasionally, Tommy forgets his wretchedness for long enough to have
fun with Kits and Flavia at bathtime. In the still-greenish water, he organizes merciless naval battles with a large sponge and a fleet of wooden
boats. Later, in the living room, if his good mood lasts, there will be a cata-
clysmic cushion fight, then he will pursue the children through the long
corridors, buzzing like a bee, deaf to their pleas. When Tommy smiles like
that, it is like the sun emerging from behind the clouds.

Their favourite activity? The mini-Olympics organized in the living
room on the orange carpet, with four disciplines determined by their
father: boxing matches, hurdles races, long jumps, and horse races. The
spectators are Daphne, Tod, Tessa, and the eight "Boys," Tommy's teddy
bears, who have been through two wars with him. The victor is presented
with a silver cup that Tommy won back in his Eton days, and two shillings.
Sometimes, Tommy can be cuddly; he likes to hold Flavia's hand, sitting
peacefully on the sofa, while listening to *Swan Lake*.

The three children are now old enough to eat their evening meals in the
dining room with their parents and Tod. Tommy monopolizes the conversation: politics, local events, the boat he wants to have built. Tod is the only
one who responds to him, because Daphne picks at her food, her eyes distant.
Well, what do you think, Duck? (This is Tommy's nickname for her, and she
calls him the same thing in return.) Daphne comes back to the present,
looks at her family, and smiles. *Well, I can hardly say, Duck,* she replies vaguely.
Tommy gives her a gently scornful look and sighs: *Woman, you live in a dream!*
He has frequent arguments with Tod and the atmosphere deteriorates. He
and Tod do not get along. One night, at the table, the governess complains
about a persistent throat infection. Eyes sparkling with sarcasm, Tommy hands
her a carving knife: *My dear Tod, why don't you cut it?*[9] Tod is not amused.

She leaves the table, and sulks for a week, until Tommy, at the urging of his wife, is forced to apologize, somewhat ungraciously.

Most often, to get away from Menabilly, Tommy spends his time on the water, as if he wanted to catch up on all those years lost to the war. These are the only moments of sweetness with Daphne. His new boat, the *Fanny Rosa*—named after the heroine of *Hungry Hill*—is a robust fishing boat with a blue-green hull and rust-coloured sails. It sleeps six. But its great disadvantage is that it tends to pitch rather violently. Kits and Flavia are the ones most affected by seasickness, drawing the contempt of their father and their older sister, an experienced skipper. Tommy's assistant, the pretty brunette Maureen, comes to stay for a few weeks. The whole family falls for her kindness, her sweet smile, and Daphne forgets her brief spurt of jealousy. Muriel and Angela visit Menabilly once a week, arriving in the large Hillman, which Mo drives as if she has never learned how to get out of first gear. Muriel does not like walking and insists on driving the car down to the beach, jolting along the uneven path. *God help you all,* Tommy mutters mockingly as he watches them leave. Kits and Flavia open the gate; Daphne accompanies her mother in the car, holding a picnic basket, while Tod takes her painting supplies; Angela and Tessa come last, dawdling as they chat. The picnic consists of egg and tomato sandwiches, which are delicious, except for one time when Tod sat on them, reducing their meal to a squished mess. The family passes hours on end splashing around in the natural pools formed by rocks or swimming in the sea, while Tod sits in the shade and paints. At the end of the day, Muriel spends half an hour reversing the car up to "Mena." The Hillman's engine whines painfully, attracting the notice of other bathers and walkers, who laugh at the spectacle of the elegant old lady grappling with her motorcar amid the stench of burning rubber.

One day, the children, playing in the garden, hear a loud explosion and a group of men arrive from the beach with a wounded man on a stretcher, his leg half torn off. The war may be over, but its memory is never far away: the land mines on the beaches must be defused, all along the coastline. In a grove nearby, a cow had been blown up into a tree, and hung there, dead. This does not prevent the children having fun in the forest, left to their own devices. With some neighbour youngsters, they build tree houses and make camp in the bushes, then come home late at night, disheveled and starving.

Deep in the forest, two ladies live in a cottage named Southcott: Miss Wilcox and Miss Phillips, vaguely mysterious creatures—witches, according to Daphne—and the children suspect that those ageless ladies, one of whom has strange opaque, thoughtful eyes, will one day end up in a book.

The only person Daphne dares confide in about the slow wreckage of her marriage is her faithful Fernande, in a few disillusioned letters. She describes to her the summer of 1946 as it comes to its end and Tommy prepares to return to London for his job. From now on, she explains to Ferdie, their relationship is entirely platonic: they go sailing together, watch the birds, walk around Fowey like good friends, like a brother and sister. Tommy seems rested, tanned, more peaceful, but this summer break has not brought them any closer. Daphne had insisted on having her own bedroom, partly out of selfishness, partly out of apprehension. Was she wrong to do so? That ham-fisted manoeuvre seems to have sounded the death knell to their physical intimacy. So many times in the night, she confesses to Fernande, she would get up, gently open the door, and see that Tommy wasn't sleeping either, that there was a shaft of light beneath his bedroom door. She tells Fernande about her uncertainty: Should she go to see him, take him in her arms, kiss him? But she remained motionless in the doorway, sad, troubled, and then wearily went to her bathroom to swallow sleeping pills, cursing herself when she woke in a fog the next morning. Daphne spent the whole summer watching out for a signal that never came. But what if her husband was doing the same? Maybe he too would stare hopefully at her door? Maybe he didn't dare knock on it either? They spent the summer missing each other, she complains in the letters to her confidante.

As autumn draws near, Daphne decides to act. No more hesitation, she wants to give herself a chance to strengthen their marriage. Despite her dislike of London, she goes there once a month on the train, dressed in her city clothes—suit, high heels, coat—to see Tommy. But only more disillusionment awaits her: her husband's time is monopolized by his new job. Every time she visits him, she feels sidelined, unimportant, even if he does tell her in detail about his recent trip to bombed-out Berlin. All his conversations revolve around the devastation wreaked by the war. In the face of this relentless pessimism, Daphne feels powerless. What can she do in London? Visit Christopher Puxley? This makes her feel better, even if it's not a very good idea. She also sees Carol Reed again: not only has he married since she last saw him, but he is now in the middle of a divorce. She bumps into her old friend Pat, Edgar Wallace's daughter. Her past is all around her, bringing with it feelings of nostalgia, and she surprises herself with the bitter observation that she is coming to resemble her father who, as he grew older, always looked backwards, not forwards. Her youth has slipped between her fingers. In the mirror is a woman with greying hair, whose assertive chin gives her an almost severe look. Daphne does not like what she sees.

There is always writing, but for the moment nothing comes; nothing is "brewing."* No novel in sight. No short stories or plays either. The winter of 1946–47 that descends on Fowey is worthy of Siberia. At "Mena," the water freezes in the pipes; the power goes out. The children have to sleep in their clothes and coats, under piles of blankets. Snow piles up in the garden and the forest, and the house is cut off from the rest of the world for a whole week. The children build enormous snowmen and sled down hills on metal trays. It is so cold that Tessa keeps the goats, Doris and Freddie, in her bedroom. This is a disaster, as they get into Tommy's closet and eat his favourite coat, an heirloom from his father. When he sees what they have done, Tommy yells with rage and hunts the terrified goats through the house with his bow and arrow. His curses make the servants blush.

The cold spell lasts all winter, the temperature finally rising with the arrival of spring. But Daphne and Tommy's marriage just seems to grow ever colder. Not that this is visible from the outside. For their children, their friends, and even Maureen—Tommy's assistant, who is becoming increasingly close to the Brownings—they still appear the perfect couple: handsome, athletic, funny, complicit. No one suspects the invisible barrier that is rising between them. And still Daphne doesn't write: the clatter of the Underwood has been silenced.

During the first sunny days of 1947, Daphne suggests to her husband that they go on vacation, to a neutral country unaffected by the ravages of war. She hasn't been abroad for nearly ten years. She believes that this trip will provide them with the stimulation they need and convinces Tommy. They head for Switzerland, with its lakes, its pure air, its peaceful countryside. Two weeks of walking, resting, reading . . . and yet there is still no intimacy between them, physical or emotional. Saddened, Daphne does not talk about it. She suffers in silence, concealing her feelings from everyone. Her pain is doubled by her inability to write. No love, and no book. She misses writing as much as she misses those sensual moments with her husband. She has been seized by a sort of intellectual barrenness, making it impossible for her usually fertile imagination to rain down ideas. And this is compounded by the sensual aridity affecting her most intimate desires. Unlike many authors, Daphne has never lived in fear of writer's block. She has never lacked inspiration before. All that remains to her now is the pleasure of living in Menabilly, with the coming summer, in the company of her friends, Maureen, Foy Quiller-Couch, Clara Vyvyan, Carol Reed, Mary Fox, her mother and her sisters, and her children: Tessa, gracious and perspicacious; Flavia, shy and dreamy; and Kits, the centre of her universe, in all his perfection.

Daphne is forty years old, the age that her father so dreaded, but in the summer of 1947, playing and sunbathing on the beach at Pridmouth with her children, never writing a word, she is still as beautiful as ever. Her books continue to sell, all over the world, and in France, *I'll Never Be Young Again* is being translated for Albin Michel. Michel Hoffman, her French agent, informs her that the novel will be translated by Mlle Van Moppès (who recently married and became Mme Butler), the same woman who translated *Rebecca* and *Jamaica Inn*. Daphne does not know this Mme Butler, but she places her trust in her. She is unaware that her translator is also a novelist, that her first novel, *Dormeuse,* was published by Grasset in 1932, when she was twenty-five. Daphne has been told by Michel Hoffman that Mme Butler was authorized to "modify" the text in order to adapt it for French readers. Daphne decides to trust her on this matter, too, and in September 1947 Mme Butler thanks her for her confidence in a letter.

To coincide with the release of the film version of her novel *Hungry Hill*—directed by Brian Desmond Hurst and starring Margaret Lockwood and Denis Price—a team of journalists arrives at Menabilly to record an interview with Daphne. She cowrote the screenplay for the film with Terence Young. The reviews are bad, especially the one in the *New Yorker*: "The interminable British saga of several generations, which could only interest those mentioned in their will." Daphne is disappointed, having enjoyed this first collaboration with Terence.

In the black-and-white images of the TV interview, the author emerges from the impressive manor house, followed by Kits and Flavia. Daphne wears a trouser-suit, à la Marlene Dietrich, her hair flowing over her shoulders, and her stride is long and elastic, like an overgrown adolescent. She walks around, hands in pockets, the mistress of her kingdom, then—after pushing Kits on the swing—she sits nonchalantly on a stone bench, in a boyish pose, with one foot lifted up on the seat. Daphne looks radiant, at the zenith of her life and career, but what no one sees is the crisis that rages inside her. Menabilly remains her fortress, the guardian of all her secrets.

A telephone call fills her with dread, one evening in September 1947. She must go to New York. Her American editor, Nelson Doubleday himself, is the one who asks her. Daphne hangs up, feeling nervous and worried: another accusation of plagiarism against *Rebecca!* Six years earlier, the *New York Times* ran an unsettling article citing the numerous similarities between *Rebecca* and a novel published in 1934 that Daphne had never read—*La Successora* by Carolina Nabuco, a famous Brazilian novelist—which had a comparable narrative structure, a second wife, a large mansion. Daphne's editor had vigorously defended her, rejecting all suggestions of plagiarism, and thankfully no one had followed the story up. Then another complaint hit Nelson Doubleday's desk, almost at the same time, lodged by an unknown author, Edwina MacDonald, who was convinced that Daphne du Maurier had drawn inspiration from her earlier novel, *Blind Windows,* another story of remarriage that Daphne had never read. In 1942, Daphne published a cutting letter in the *New York Times*, in which she sarcastically asked Miss Nabuco and Mrs. MacDonald if they could work out which one of them had written her book. The case dragged on, before Doubleday's legal team once again managed to quash it without any intervention from Daphne. And yet it was still not finished. With Mrs. MacDonald now dead and the war over, her son decided to take the matter to court. This time, Daphne has to appear in person, in New York, to explain to the judge how and why she wrote *Rebecca* in 1938. The thought terrifies her. Of course she did not plagiarize anyone—there is not the slightest doubt about that—but the idea of publicly describing the mechanics of writing, that very intimate, very particular process, makes her fearful, as does the prospect of facing the crowds, the press, the photographers, of answering indiscreet questions that expose the darkest secrets of her soul, as a writer and as a woman. Yes, she must go there; she must even stay a few weeks, possibly even a month, because such trials can be protracted. Resigned to this fate, she reserves two cabins on the *Queen Mary*: one for Kits and herself, the other for Flavia and Tod. Tessa will not come, as she is about to start boarding at her new school, St. Mary, in Oxfordshire, a prospect that excites her: she is eager to make new friends and to get away from "Mena." She is the only one of the three children not to like the old house's peculiar atmosphere. As for Tommy, he will remain in London to work, and Maureen will look after him. Daphne and her family will stay with Nelson Doubleday and his wife, Ellen, in their house on Long Island.

The first thing she must attend to is her wardrobe. For more than a decade now, Daphne has been living in trousers and sailor jumpers, her children wearing the same old rags. In the United States, she knows, she is a star author, and there is simply no way she can attend the trial dressed in her casual Menabilly clothes. She also suspects that Barberrys, the Doubledays' luxurious Long Island home, is a society magnet, which only serves to increase her anxiety. She does not know Ellen Doubleday, but she has heard about her elegance, and imagines she must look like those bejeweled, emaciated American ladies she dislikes so much, such as Wallis Simpson. Miss Tryel, the local seamstress, works like a slave to produce clothing worthy of the occasion in time for the family's departure: matching outfits in navy blue and red for Kits and Flavia, suits and evening dresses for Daphne. The next priority is a family visit to the hairdresser. A cut and a perm for Daphne—the cut a little too short, the curls a little too tight, perhaps, she thinks regretfully—but she refuses to dye her few grey strands. Tessa gives up her long braids, Flavia is given a new hairstyle with a fringe, which suits her, and Kits is proud of his boy's haircut.

Daphne travels to America for the first time in her life. Tommy and his assistant, Maureen, come to bid them goodbye, on this cold November day. The *Queen Mary* awaits them in Southampton. The children are so excited: never in their lives have they seen such a huge ship, over a thousand feet long and capable of carrying more than two thousand people. Their comfortable cabins are filled with flowers, and Flavia is thrilled by the small, mahogany-panelled bathrooms. The first night goes well: the sea is calm, no one gets seasick.

The next morning, while Daphne is with Tod and the children in her stateroom, there is a knock at the door. A slender, dark-haired lady in her early fifties stands there, holding a bouquet of white roses. Behind her is a steward carrying a basket full of gifts. The woman smiles and introduces herself: Ellen Doubleday. She has come in person to welcome the famous novelist published by her husband, to make sure she arrives safe and sound. The children and Tod are charmed by their new companion. But for Daphne, the feeling is more intense than that. She cannot take her eyes from this gorgeous vision; she is bewitched by the elegance of her publisher's wife, her graceful movements, her hazel eyes, her velvet voice, her refinement, her distinction.

While she listens to Ellen Doubleday, while she accepts the roses, the gifts, her heart is pounding, and it is a boy's voice that whispers in her ear—the voice of Eric Avon, whom she locked away in his box, so long ago, back when she first met Tommy. Eric Avon comes back to life, sparkling and resplendent, hammering with both fists against the lid of his box, shouting out that he is alive, he is here, real, now, just as he was at Camposenea, when he became intoxicated by the scent of Fernande Yvon's handkerchief, and the feeling is so powerful, so feverish, that Daphne cannot speak; she can only observe Ellen Doubleday in silence, transfixed, her hands writhing, her breathing fast.

All the way through the crossing, Daphne remains dazzled by Ellen, admiring her clothes, soothed by her soft voice. There are rumours that Greta Garbo is on board the *Queen Mary*, but Daphne couldn't care less: all she sees is Ellen, as if this woman's presence has woken her from a hundred-year sleep. When they arrive in New York, there are a Buick and a Cadillac waiting to take them to Oyster Bay. Barberrys is only thirty years old, but looks more ancient, a lovely house with pale walls overlooking a yacht-speckled bay, with terraces and beautiful gardens. There are nineteen bedrooms, each one decorated with tasteful luxury; a swimming pool, tennis courts. After Menabilly, with its cold drafts and its rats and its green water, the Doubledays' heated house is a wonder. The Brownings are welcomed as if they were part of the family. Ellen rules over her home and her servants like Rebecca de Winter, no detail escapes her. Nelson, tall, stout, and greying, is just as friendly as Daphne remembers him from their meeting in London in 1931, the one and only time she had seen him before. But beneath the veneer of perfection, Daphne detects a discreet tension between the Doubledays, she notices Nelson's mood swings, his fragile health, his tendency to drink one glass too many, his wife's worried looks.

The trial begins, and it truly is a trial for Daphne. The prosecution lists forty-six parallels between *Blind Windows* and *Rebecca*. They seem determined to make Daphne confess, in spite of everything, that she read Mrs. MacDonald's story before writing *Rebecca* and was inspired by it. They question her relentlessly. As she stands in the witness box, it requires a concerted effort from Daphne not to dissolve into panic. Miss du Maurier reads the *Times Literary Supplement*, does she not? So Miss du Maurier must have seen a review of Mrs. MacDonald's story published on May 20, 1928? Daphne replies as calmly as possible, but her heart is pounding beneath her new suit. She feels intimidated by all the eyes in the courtroom trained on her. She was only twenty-one in 1928, she says; she was writing short stories, one of which was published in the *Bystander* magazine, but she had not begun a novel, and no, she never read that review in the *TLS*.

The prosecutor Charles S. Rosenschein is remorseless, and so is his colleague Arthur L. Ross. They take it in turns to grill the author with a barrage of questions. Miss du Maurier knew the author Edgar Wallace, did she not? Yes, Daphne replies, she was friends with his daughter Pat in the twenties and thirties. Smiling triumphantly, Ross holds up one of Edgar Wallace's books, published by John Long Ltd. He opens the book and shows the court an advertisement for other novels published by John Long Ltd, one of them, *Blind Windows* by Edwina MacDonald. Miss du Maurier must certainly have seen this ad, he insists; she can't possibly have missed it. The defence lawyers object and, when it is Daphne's turn to speak again, she manages to say, in a phlegmatic voice that conceals her inner torment, that she never saw those advertisements.

Every afternoon, Daphne emerges from the courtroom drained of all energy. The trial seems interminable—there is no way it will be over in a few weeks—and she is already exhausted by it. At Barberrys, Ellen awaits her return and pampers her, making her Earl Grey tea, cinnamon toast, sitting next to her on the sofa in the magnificent living room with its view over the bay. *Not a word, Daphne dear, until you have something warm inside you, no sir.*[10] She often ends her sentences with this peremptory *no sir,* which makes the children laugh. Later, the two women will share a light meal in Daphne's room, because she feels too tired to dine with the others downstairs.

On the weekends, as Daphne feared, the Doubledays have guests over. But Ellen is so warmly welcoming and enthusiastic that Daphne ends up having fun at these spectacular parties. The mistress of the house insists on taking her shopping at Saks Fifth Avenue, so that her husband's star author can shine during these dinners in her honour. Daphne does not object; how could she say no to Ellen? Mrs. Doubleday's maid had thought that one of Lady Browning's evening dresses, made by Miss Tryel, was a nightgown, a misunderstanding that sent Daphne and her children into hysterics. When Daphne descends the wide staircase to meet the guests, dressed in a new outfit, a gift from Ellen, her children admire her, dazzled by the transformation in their mother. All eyes on her, Daphne du Maurier shines.

As the end of the trial nears, in mid-December 1947, Daphne prepares like a boxer about to enter the ring for one last fight. She knows she must do everything she can to convince the judge she did not plagiarize anything. Her lawyers reassure her, but Daphne cannot help feeling afraid: if she loses this case, it will cost her a great deal of money and, even worse, be a blow to her reputation.

Daphne enters the witness box, hands trembling and mouth dry. But her voice is clear, assertive, melodious. Her voice is a powerful weapon. She explains that she began writing *Rebecca* in 1937, when she was in Alexandria with her husband. She describes the unbearable heat, her desire to go home to Cornwall, and in one hand she holds up her little black notebook, the one in which she wrote her first notes for the novel. She speaks for a long time, not rushing; she is the daughter of actors, capable of remaining on the stage for hours. Those anonymous faces, those eyes staring at her, all those people who have never written a novel in their lives . . . what can they understand of the writing process? What do they know of the doubts that assail novelists? Do they believe, these strangers listening to her now in the silence of this austere Federal Court in Foley Square, that a book is written just like that, built on a single idea? That all the author has to do is follow that idea, placidly, sheeplike? They could never imagine how nebulous and complex a novelist's thoughts are, how filled with contradictions and subconscious impulses, nor how degrading it feels to stand there, facing them, to have to coolly analyze her inspiration as if it were merely a recipe for a meal, to have to expose the intricate mechanisms behind this intimate alchemy, the labyrinthine workings of her brain.

Why should writers be obligated to explain themselves, to reveal the secrets of their art? What would they make—all these lawyers and journalists, these ladies and gentlemen of the jury—of her secret jealousy towards beautiful, dark-haired Jan Ricardo, Tommy's first fiancée, this woman who (as she read, perplexed, in the newspaper) had thrown herself under a train in August 1944, when she was married to Mr. Constable-Maxwell, when she was mother to a two-year-old girl? Must she confess that she searched through her husband's desk drawer, that she read love letters to him sent by another woman? What would they make of Eric Avon, who has urged her to explore her masculine side since she was ten years old and who is now banging on the inside of his box as if he sensed the importance that Ellen Doubleday would have in Daphne's life, a sudden, dizzying thunderbolt of love capable of ridding her of her writer's block?

Not for anything in the world would Daphne admit to them the true genesis of her novels; not for anything in the world would she reveal that a book came from a visceral feeling, that her characters are sorts of "pegs,"* a code word of her own invention, hooks on which she hangs a personal blend of fantasy and truth. The prosecutors, Rosenschein and Ross, are right: yes, writers are liars, con artists, constantly reinventing other people's lives, using smoke and mirrors to mislead their readers, concealing themselves under a smooth, kind, generous façade in order to facilitate their lying. They are supreme falsifiers, because their world, like the world of actors, is created from mystification, illusion, appearance; in this way, and only in this way, are novels born. But Daphne says nothing of all this. She follows through with her plan, choosing her words prudently, calmly, not raising her voice, not flinching as she explains how she imagined Manderley as a cross between Milton Hall and Menabilly, the first house captivating her as a child and the second exercising an enchantment over her life that still holds her spellbound today.

When she leaves the witness box, she is pale, but her head is held high, and it seems to her that Kicky and Gerald are applauding from somewhere up above. Arriving at Barberrys, she collapses. Ellen sits at her bedside for hours on end, and in spite of her exhaustion, Daphne savours this delightful closeness. How happy she feels, in this cozy bed, in this enveloping comfort, and, above all, in the glow of that velvet hazel gaze, with the touch of that soft little hand which she holds tightly. The judge will deliver his verdict in January 1948, but Doubleday's lawyers have no doubt: Daphne has nothing to worry about: she won hands down. Why not spend Christmas here? Ellen suggests. Daphne could continue her recuperation at Barberrys. Daphne is tempted, but Tommy and Tessa are waiting for them, and everyone is ready to spend Christmas together at "Mena" after their long absence. The tickets are booked on the *Queen Mary,* and the time has come to say goodbye to the Doubledays. Once again, their cabins are filled with gifts and flowers; Ellen has even given each child one present to open for each day of the crossing. The return trip is spoiled by the terrible weather, however, the *Queen Mary* enduring one of the most horrific journeys in its history. There is nothing to do but lie in their beds as the ship violently rolls and pitches all the way to their arrival in the Channel. When Daphne finally reaches Whitelands House, in London, she is so worn-out, so thin, so pale, that Tommy calls the doctor. His verdict: Lady Browning is exhausted and is in need of complete rest. Her despondency resembles the hollowness she felt during her separation from Fernande, in November 1925. Who could imagine, twenty-five years on, that the person she is missing so desperately is none other than Mrs. Nelson Doubleday, her publisher's wife?

⁓✻⁓

Daphne returns to "Mena" for Christmas 1947. Tommy has been named Comptroller and Treasurer to the young Princess Elizabeth and her new husband, Prince Philip, the Duke of Edinburgh, at Clarence House, a prestigious position he is proud to accept, and which means he will spend the majority of his time in London, assisted by the faithful Maureen. But for the still-weak Daphne, Ellen is the only person who matters; she sends her letter after letter, confessing her feelings, trying to describe this *coup de foudre,* this thunderbolt of love. From her bedroom, she writes: *Go right back into the past and see D. du M as a little girl like Flave, very shy, always biting her nails. But never being a little girl. Always being a little boy. And growing up with a boy's mind and a boy's heart.* Writing to Ellen, she at last admits what she thinks she is: a strange hybrid, a woman with the soul of a boy, an oddity she has never confessed to anyone before, keeping the secret for so many years. To Ellen, she can—she must—tell everything about the being that lives deep inside her: Eric Avon. *A boy with nervous hands and a beating heart, incurably romantic, and wanting to throw a cloak before his lady's feet. At eighteen, this half-breed fell in love, as a boy would, with someone quite twelve years older than himself who was French and had all the understanding in the world, and he loved her in every conceivable way.*[11] However, there is no question of her wanting to confess any "Venetian"* tendencies to Ellen. *By God and by Christ, if anyone should call that sort of love by that unattractive word that begins with "L," I'd tear their guts out,* she makes vehemently clear.

While preparing "Mena" for the New Year festivities, Daphne continues her interminable correspondence with Ellen, watching out for the mailman's red van with the same impatience she used to wait for letters from her darling Ferdie. Walking through the forest to gather mistletoe and holly branches so she can decorate the house, she is already thinking of the next letter she will write to her: *And then the boy realized he had to grow up, and not be a boy any longer, so he turned into a girl, and not an unattractive one at that, and the boy was locked into a box forever. D. du M. wrote her books, and had young men, and later a husband, and children, and a lover, and life was sometimes lovely and sometimes rather sad, but when she found Menabilly and lived in it alone, she opened up the box sometimes, and let the phantom, who was neither girl nor boy but disembodied spirit, dance in the evening when there was no one to see.*[12]

Christmas, this year, is spent with Muriel, Angela, Jeanne, and Aunt Billy, Mo's sister, plus another Angela, a good friend of Piffy's, whom everyone calls Shaw, accompanied by their turbulent Pekinese. The Browning children have never believed in Father Christmas; Daphne has always told them the truth, disapproving of those fables children are encouraged to believe, and they recognize the presents under the tree wrapped by their mother, the ones in crumpled paper with lopsided ribbons. During the Christmas dinner, as the guests laugh loudly and Tommy carves the turkey, kicking the dogs out of the room, Daphne thinks about Ellen, who must be celebrating at Barberrys with her husband and children, Madeleine, Pucky, Nelson Junior, and Neltje, and the smile fades on her lips. Is Ellen wearing that black-and-red dress that suits her so well? At the end of the day, when the guests have left, Daphne goes to her bedroom, closes the door, and begins a new letter, looking up continually at the photograph of Ellen that now stands atop her chest of drawers. *I pushed the boy back into his box again and avoided you on the boat like the plague. Watching you at Barberrys was very hard to bear. You looked lovelier every day. It just defeated me. I wanted to ride out and fight dragons for you, and bring back the Holy Grail.*[13] What if, one day, someone were to read these letters, these private missives in which she pours out her heart, strips herself bare? Her husband, or Ellen's husband? She doesn't think about it; these pages are a sort of liberation for her, and the more she confides, the lighter she feels, as if the act of telling Ellen everything is a balm for her soul. Daphne lies down, exhausted, and as she dozes, Kits silently joins her in bed and falls asleep beside her. Downstairs, in the empty living room, Tommy looks for another bottle of champagne, but it's all gone, so he pours himself another gin and tonic, smoking cigarette after cigarette. His bad mood gets the better of him and he starts kicking his presents. Tod and the girls leave him to his rage.

Ellen's replies arrive in dribs and drabs and reflect their author: gentle, comforting, levelheaded. For six letters sent from Menabilly, only two come from the United States. Ellen explains to Daphne, with infinite tact, that she feels a deep friendship for her, but that this affection could never be transformed into anything else. Daphne is not downcast by Ellen's gentle rejection because she refuses to recognize it for what it is. Thanks to Ellen, her new "peg,"* she is inspired once more and she begins "to brew" a new novel; she feels herself come alive again, grow stronger, regain her sense of humour, and laugh with her loved ones, especially seven-year-old Kits, who seems to have inherited his grandfather Gerald's talents for mimicry and mockery. The code words she used with her sisters when she was young are now part of the daily vocabulary of the Browning children, remaining a mystery for guests, who are never able to guess their meanings. And in truth, it is not easy to imagine what is meant by "crumb,"* "royal,"* "waine,"* "honky,"* and "Nanny."* The children also know the meaning of "Robert,"* because Daphne, traumatized by her own mother's silence concerning menstruation, explained it all to them, even Kits.

On January 14, 1948, the verdict of Judge Bright and the jury members on the *Rebecca* affair is finally delivered: Miss du Maurier did not plagiarize Edwina MacDonald's *Blind Windows*. Relief all around, but Daphne has already moved on to something else. In the silence of her room, she writes—for Ellen, and about Ellen. No one will know, though: it will be their secret. Daphne feels as if she is breathing in Ellen's perfume, *L'Aimant* from Coty, with its scents of peach, jasmine, rose, and vanilla, a fragrance that suits her perfectly. By February 1948, Daphne has already finished it: a play, *September Tide*, written in barely two weeks, the story of a widow who falls in love with her daughter's husband, a young painter. An impossible love. How good it feels to hide herself behind this young man, to adopt Eric Avon's voice, to reveal in this way her attraction to the dazzling fifty-something woman, the mother of his new wife. Could anyone read between the lines, detect the feelings she has for Ellen-Stella? No, Daphne has covered her tracks too well. The one recognizable element, a source of amusement to her friends and family, is the décor of the living room at Ferryside, faithfully reproduced down to the sounds of foghorns and the backwash and the cries of seagulls. It feels good to write so quickly, with so much pleasure, to embellish a fantasy that will soon be played out onstage, made public, but the true meaning of which will be understood only by Ellen and herself. It is dangerous to be loved and desired by a writer; she went through this with Christopher Puxley, the "peg"* for her French pirate. That story left a bitter aftertaste, not to mention the Puxleys' torpedoed marriage. Despite the danger of this new "Ellen peg," she cannot resist the voracity of the desire to write that grips her once again, to the point that the rest of her life seems colourless and bland, and she emerges each evening from her room staggering like a junkie.

On the other side of the Atlantic, Ellen is shocked by the advance of her husband's cancer; the doctors give him only one year to live. He is recovering from a last-chance operation, and Daphne's letters to her friend are full of tenderness. At Fowey, spring finally arrives, with the hyacinths and rhododendrons in bloom. Angela has a short story collection, *Birkinshaw*, published by Peter Llewellyn Davies, which vanishes unnoticed; this time, however, she is stung by its lack of success. The only way to battle her disappointment is to start on a new novel, and between two vacations this is what she does. As for Jeanne, she has moved to St. Ives to pursue her artistic career more seriously; she meets the painter Dod Procter there, with whom she embarks on a series of journeys to Africa.

❧

At Menabilly, next to Gribbin Head, is the hut where Captain Vandeleur lives—a name that might easily have come from one of Daphne's novels. Flavia claims he looks like a large, cap-wearing toad with bulging eyes. Captain Vandeleur is employed by the Rashleigh family to maintain and watch over the vast domain of Menabilly. He lives alone with his dogs and spends his days wandering the woods, paths, and fields of the farm. His garden includes a beautiful bed of camellias, Daphne's favourite flower. There are twenty-eight vases to be filled with flowers at Menabilly, one of the few domestic tasks carried out by Lady Browning, and unfortunately there are very few camellias in her part of the property. It is tempting to pilfer a few from Captain Vandeleur, but this involves quite an operation. Kits and Flavia cycle along the path that leads to his hut, to check whether his car is in the garage. If the way is clear, Daphne quickly walks over there, secateurs in her pocket, while the children stand guard. She hastily cuts a few, here and there, from the profusion of white, pink, and red flowers, then hurries back home, followed by her escort. One day, Captain Vandeleur catches her red-handed. While she attempts to conceal the flowers behind her back, embarrassed, he tells her, with gentle irony, *Good evening, Lady Browning, how nice to see you. Do please let me know if you would ever like some camellias, as I should be most happy to give you a flower or two.*[14]

Only once did Captain Vandeleur blow his top. Carol Reed came to spend a few days at "Mena." He was a film director now. After dinner, Carol made Daphne laugh by announcing, like some juvenile prankster,

Let's have a huge bonfire! That rhododendron bush by your writing hut, you said yourself its height spoils the view of the sea.[15] In a rush of enthusiasm, he went off to find paper, kerosene, and matches, followed by the children. After a few minutes, it was all ready, and the bush caught fire in a very cinematic way, a huge orange burst lighting up the night, accompanied by a loud crackling noise. The flames rose up in the dark sky and the nearest neighbours arrived, looking amazed. *We thought t'was the blinking house on fire, like in the film* Rebecca,[16] joked one observer. While everyone was admiring the fire, Captain Vandeleur appeared, followed by his dogs. Upon discovering that the fire had been started by one of Lady Browning's guests, he seemed wild with rage. *You will be hearing from the estate, Lady Browning, and no doubt Dr. Rashleigh,*[17] he said, furious, as he was leaving. Thankfully for Daphne, she never received any complaints from her landlord regarding Carol's bonfire. But Captain Vandeleur sulked about it for quite a while.

He is not the only man in a bad mood: there is also Tommy, who takes his work at Clarence House very seriously and finds it exhausting. No one in his office suspects how tired he is, except Maureen, his devoted assistant. Boy Browning, complain? Never! He goes back to his small apartment at Whitelands House every night, alone and depressed, succumbing to one glass of gin, and then another. Little by little, alcohol becomes a pernicious influence in his life, along with cigarettes. Daphne knows this, guesses it; she thinks of her father, who had gone down the same road, and feels powerless. On Friday evenings, Tommy arrives late at Menabilly, having taken the last train from Paddington; he smiles at the idea of returning to the *Fanny Rosa* and his family, but his joy is short-lived. By Sunday morning, knowing that he must leave again that evening, his face darkens, his stomachache returns, and he locks himself away in his melancholy. The hardest moment, for him, is when he has to pack his suitcase, with his teddy bears that still go everywhere with him. Kits, unwittingly, finds a new nickname for his father. Daphne asks one morning where Tommy is, and Kits replies, *In his room, moping.*[18] Moper. A soubriquet that will stick to him and that he will never be rid of. And yet he and Daphne enjoy some pleasant moments on the *Fanny Rosa* in that summer of 1948, sailing to Falmouth with Daphne at the helm, and for a few days she has the illusion that they have rediscovered their old closeness. It is a fleeting impression.

The challenge, in the autumn of 1948, is to decide who will play Stella Martyn. Every famous actress over forty is in contention: Diana Wynyard, Carol Reed's delightful ex-wife; Gertrude Lawrence, a close friend of the playwright Noël Coward, fresh from her success in *Pygmalion:* and the great Shakespearian actresses Fay Compton and Peggy Ashcroft. Daphne is invited to London to meet the casting directors, and Tommy takes advantage of this trip to introduce her to Princess Elizabeth and her husband, moments that she narrates in detail to Ellen in a letter. The princess is *sweet, but sort of shy,* and the prince *a "menace,"** except too fair and pale.*[19]

Fifty-year-old Gertrude Lawrence finally obtains the role. Daphne is not thrilled by this; she thinks her too old, dislikes her dyed hair, her artifice, and, above all, the fact that she is one of those actresses who once belonged to her father's "stable," with Daphne in no doubt as to the nature of their relations at the time. Gerald and Gertrude met in 1930, on the set of *Lord Camber's Ladies,* produced by Hitchcock, and they played opposite each other in a play by John Van Druten, in London, in 1932. "Gertie," with her cheeky wit, her fleshy lips, her piercing voice, her Cockney accent, her swearwords, her booming laughter, her dancelike gestures . . . no, none of this is right for Stella-Ellen, the epitome of class and distinction. However it isn't Daphne who has the last word, but Irene Hentschel, the play's director. Daphne attends the first rehearsals, but she is infuriated, ill at ease; she feels as if she is witnessing a travesty of her work. No, that's not right: Stella would not stand like that; she wouldn't kiss Evan in that way. Daphne keeps quiet, bites her nails. She is so annoyed that she has to swallow two pills to go to sleep every night.

Breathing in the atmosphere of the theatre, however, Daphne realizes that she is in the grip of an unexpected pleasure: reliving the ambience of her childhood, as if she might find her father again amid these dusty, familiar smells of dressing rooms and scenery, while enjoying the company of stage managers and actors, a unique and special world that she has missed. She thinks about Gerald as she watches her characters evolve on the stage, as if he were standing next to her in the wings, observing and joking.

Gertie, a will-o'-the-wisp, has a *je ne sais quoi* reminiscent of Gerald in the way she clowns around, the way she is always the centre of attention, the way she absolutely has to win over everyone she meets, instantly. Gertie is capable of losing her temper over a trifle, flying into a rage, and unleashing a volley of insults, an exhausting and fascinating creature. Daphne knows exactly what makes her tick, because her father was the same—except that he would never have used a swearword. The most unexpected thing is the way Gertie inhabits the character of Stella, takes possession of it, adding her own personal touch, her emotions, and Daphne realizes, to her growing confusion, that Gertie is instinctively appropriating what Daphne tried to capture of Ellen, as if Gertie, on the stage, is channelling Ellen's personality. How is that possible? The magic of the theatre? The talent of the actress? Daphne opens up about it in her letters to Ellen, describing how Gertie, quite unconsciously, puts on an American accent, which makes Daphne miss Ellen even more. Once, she says, it was too much to bear, and Daphne had to leave the theatre.

The first night is set for the end of November 1948 at the New Theatre in Oxford. After that, the play will be performed at the Aldwych Theatre in London, from December 15, with Michael Gough as Evan and Anne Leon in the role of Cherry. Gertie's American husband, Richard Aldridge, comes from New York for the occasion. All of London rushes to see the play performed at the Aldwych. Queen Mary, Princess Elizabeth, and Princess Margaret go, too, accompanied by Tommy. It is a success, Gertrude Lawrence's comeback, a triumph. *September Tide* will be performed for months and will mark the birth of a deep friendship between Gertie and Daphne. Daphne calls her Cinders, after Cinderella, while Gertie calls her Dum, for her initials. During the dinner to celebrate the first night, Michael Gough, the handsome young actor who is playing the part of Stella's son-in-law—visibly charmed by Lady Browning, as so many people are—asks Daphne how she invents her characters. She replies, with a mischievous smile, *Most of my characters are based on real people, only sometimes are they invented out of thin air.*[20]

Thanks to Gertie, Daphne's desire to go out is rekindled; once again, she enjoys making herself beautiful, having lunch at the Savoy, at the best table, where Gertie flirts outrageously and hilariously with the waiter. Daphne wears a new perfume created by Germaine Cellier, *Vent Vert* from Balmain, leaving an audacious, green scent in her wake—an avant-garde fragrance described in the press by Colette as having *the bittersweet tang of crushed plants. The kind of thing that will please those she-devils of today.* Daphne likes to go to Dover for the day with Gertie, to visit Noël Coward, who wrote the hugely famous play *Private Lives* just for Gertrude, his childhood friend. At White Cliffs, Noël's spectacular white villa, built into the cliff, Daphne rejoices in the company of actors such as Katharine Hepburn and Spencer Tracy, enjoying the sometimes scabrous, mordant, droll conversations. She succumbs to the champagne that flows like water, the wreaths of cigarette smoke, the open-throated laughter, to that sparkling atmosphere that her father was so good at distilling when they lived at Cannon Hall. Swept along on this wave of sociability, she accompanies Tommy to a ball at Buckingham Palace, in a shoulderless lilac dress lent to her by Molyneux, on the astute recommendation of Gertie. Later, in a letter to Ellen, she describes the outfits and fineries glimpsed at the palace.

Daphne's newfound joy is tempered by the death of Nelson Doubleday, at fifty-nine, on January 11, 1949. It is time now for her to console and comfort her friend, to be present, even if she is distant in a physical sense. Her passion for Ellen is undimmed and as secret as ever; no one knows to what extent Ellen haunts her days and nights. In February 1949, the idea of a novel germinates, and she is able at last to get back to work. First piece of business: leaving her bedroom, which is too noisy, too close to the sounds of slamming doors and footsteps. She moves a table, chair, and typewriter into a rudimentary little cabin at the bottom of the lawn, heated by an oil stove, where she is tranquil. She calls it her hut.

Her novel is personal, inspired by the world of the theatre, rediscovered with such glee, and her own family. The title? *The Parasites*. The family's name is Delaney: a clan of wealthy, bohemian artists, whose father, Pappy, is a famous opera singer and mother, Mama, a famous dancer. The beautiful Maria (the heir to Gertie's extravagance), the illegitimate daughter of Pappy and an Austrian actress who died in childbirth, is now a spoiled and idolized actress, married to a rich, kind man. Niall, a composer, is the son of Mama, his father unknown. Celia is the Delaneys' only legitimate child, and since the death of her mother she has spent most of her time looking after her sick father. Daphne enjoys exploring a new, satirical side to her imagination, and the book's tone is at once maliciously amusing and languid, slightly weary. Her caustic gaze oversees a series of journeys, hotel rooms, previews, dazzling parties, featuring her egocentric, arrogant characters, but the heart of the book is the emotionally incestuous relationship between Maria and Niall, a theme she already touched on in *The Loving Spirit* and *The Progress of Julius*, and which obscures the light of happiness. It is Charles, Maria's miserable husband, who proffers the truth (a truth that would certainly make Jeanne and Angela du Maurier smile): *A parasite. And that's what you are, the three of you. You always have been and you always will be. Nothing can change you. You are doubly, triply parasitic; first, because you've traded ever since childhood on that seed of talent you had the luck to inherit from your fantastic forebears; secondly, because you've none of you done a stroke of ordinary honest work in your lives, but batten upon us, the fool public who allow you to exist; and thirdly, because you prey upon each other, the three of you, living in a world of fantasy which you have created for yourselves and which bears no relation to anything in heaven or on earth.*

Finishing the novel several months later, Daphne suspects that it will disconcert readers, who risk being unsettled by that new tone, half-cruel, half-disillusioned, never mind the three main characters, wallowing in a selfishness that, although comic, is utterly reprehensible—and very difficult to identify with. Another pitfall is the book's structure, which is ambitious to the point of being confusing, with the narration moving between "I" and "we," as if Niall, Celia, and Maria were speaking together, and it is sometimes hard for the reader to work out who is narrating. Angela is enthusiastic, convinced that Gerald would have loved it, while Gertie already sees herself playing the role of Maria, and Victor seems thrilled. He is banking on a first print run of one hundred thousand copies.

When *The Parasites* is published, in the autumn of 1949, Daphne discovers she was right to beware the book's critical reception—*dingy*, according to her. In the *Daily Herald*, the famous poet and literary columnist John Betjeman shoots down the novel almost angrily, reproaching Daphne for her "heavy, dull and obvious sentences," written only "to titillate the public and secure sales." Victor sends him a stinging letter in defence of the novel and its author, the first time he has done such a thing in twenty-seven years as a publisher. There is one pleasant surprise, however: Ivor Brown, another eminent journalist, writes in the *New York Times Book Review* that the book is "magnetic" and wonders why so many of his fellow critics persist in scorning Daphne du Maurier's work for being "so wickedly readable."

Daphne has developed thick skin, and she no longer lets the book's reception affect her, accepting that it will not be a great success and instead concentrating on an event that overwhelms her as a mother: the departure of eight-and-a-half-year-old Kits for his first boarding school, West Downs, in Hampshire. No matter how she tries to reason with herself, to get a grip on her emotions, she remains inconsolable after her beloved son has gone. Her reddened eyes draw the sarcasm of Angela, there to eat lunch. *Pull yourself together for a start, Bing!*[21] she tells her sister, in an irritated tone.

Flavia, age twelve, finds herself alone at Menabilly. Tod gives her lessons every morning, and in the afternoons she goes walking with her mother for a few hours. What a privilege, having her mummy all to herself! They are accompanied by Mouse, Daphne's new Westie, and even when it rains they walk along the beach to the Gribbin, dressed in rubber boots, jumpers, and oilskins. Daphne grows closer to her daughters, whose very different personalities she enjoys. In the letters she sends each week from her boarding school, and which begin with *My darling Bing,* Tessa writes openly and humorously to her mother, signing off *With all my love, from your little pup.*[22]

Soon after Kits's departure, Daphne joins Ellen in Paris, in September 1949, for a long-planned trip to Italy, just the two of them. Ellen had postponed this journey on numerous occasions, as if she doubted her friend's motivations. The week proves hurtful and sad for Daphne, with Ellen calmly but firmly putting things straight on the very first night: no, there is no possible "Venice"* between herself and Daphne. At last Daphne admits, to her pain, that the fervour she feels for Ellen—a mix of hope, delusion, and idolatry—will never be reciprocated. Prey to a bitter melancholy, Daphne watches Mrs. Doubleday walk so elegantly through the Tuscan light, and the idea of a novel comes surreptitiously to her mind. The story of a beautiful and irreproachable widow around whom floats an obscure aura, a barely visible cloud beneath the veneer of perfection. Angel or demon? Manipulator? Victim? Executioner? Daphne scrawls a few lines in Kicky's favourite notebook, which she takes everywhere with her. It is hard for her to distance herself from this romantic disappointment. Writing will help. When she returns to Menabilly, she is cheered by

Gertie's joyful, almost childish postcards from Florida, begging her to come and visit. Not that this prevents her sending a few vicious, resentful letters to Ellen, which she will later describe, when apologizing to her friend, as her *gin & brandy* letters. Thankfully, Ellen retains her sangfroid and is not angry with Daphne for very long.

It is once again Ellen, unattainable, inaccessible, who provides the driving force for her new novel, though still no one suspects a thing. The whole complex range of her feelings for Ellen is at work here: her gratitude, her passion, but also her bitterness; everything she has experienced since that day of enchantment on the *Queen Mary* in November 1947, three years ago already, and also the bereavement she is attempting to go through for this impossible love. By writing about the "Ellen peg"* perhaps she will be able at last to get it out of her system, to drain it, to vanquish it forever?

So, that trip to the United States . . . Why not? To feel the sun on her face again, and the warm welcome of husband-less Gertie, who is waiting for her there. Tommy is busy with his duties in London, Tessa and Kits are at boarding school, and Flavia is being chaperoned at "Mena" by Tod. The way is clear. Struggling against her fear of flying, Daphne takes the airplane during this cool early spring of 1950, landing in the tropical mildness of Florida. She discovers, to her amazement, the white beaches of Naples, the fine sand, the long pier stretching out into the blue-green water, so warm compared to the English Channel. Gertie is as puckish and bewitching as ever. Impossible to resist her pranks, her humour; being with "Cinders" is like rediscovering her youth, sharing the same teasing camaraderie she once shared with Carol, the jokes, the complicity, the giggles that Daphne so desperately needs. Gertie, fifty-two? Impossible. She is youth personified, and her irreverence, her wit, her charm remind Daphne so much of Gerald. As for Daphne, she no longer feels forty-three; she is Eric Avon once again, the perpetual adolescent who runs along the beach, hair blowing in the wind. Eric Avon admires Gertie's sinuous figure, finds her beautiful, takes her hand. He could never take Ellen's hand; she always pushed him away, gently but firmly. At sunset, Eric Avon savours a Sea Breeze on the terrace. His pale thigh rubs against Gertie's tanned thigh. He laughs at her jokes, succumbs to her generous warmth, to her ocean-salty kisses. Life is offering him a brief interlude of happiness, pleasure, and sensuality, so why not take it? In this sunny refuge, there is no one to judge Eric Avon, no one to reprimand him, to order him back to his box, to lock him in and throw away the key.

∼✻∽

At "Mena," during her daily walks in the woods with Flavia and Mouse, Daphne makes a discovery: an old granite monument, engraved with the Rashleigh family's coat of arms, hidden behind thick vegetation. Daphne crouches down and, with her daughter's help, pulls the leaves from the crumbling stone. It will be perfect for Daphne's new hero, Philip; here, he will sit down and daydream, alone beneath the trees, with only birdsong for company. Once again, Menabilly is the setting of a novel. Though never named, it is the manor that belongs to Ambroise Ashley, whose surname recalls that of the Rashleighs. For this tenth novel, Eric Avon writes in the first person, as with *I'll Never Be Young Again*, this time in the person of Philip Ashley, the narrator, a twenty-three-year-old orphan, Ambroise's nephew.

Each morning, Daphne goes to her hut, emerging three hours later, when Tod rings the bell, to eat a quick lunch, then working again until 7:00 pm. An oil lamp illuminates her desk, and to keep warm she wraps a blanket around her knees, as she used to do at Ferryside when she was writing *The Loving Spirit*. On her desk is a dictionary (rarely consulted, as it annoys her to have to break the flow of words so she can open it), a Thermos of coffee, and some Fox's Glacier Mints, her favourite sweet. Sometimes her fingers freeze on the Underwood and she stares vacantly through the little window. She recalls her Floridian escapade, feels the sun on her skin again, tastes Gertie's secret kisses. Then she thinks about the ascendancy Ellen has over her, against which she must fight. Her only weapons are words on paper, her only strategy to construct a novel around Ellen's influence in order to destroy it.

As with *Rebecca*, the story that is taking shape explores jealousy and obsession, but considered from a man's point of view. Daphne describes this new book in a letter to Fernande as *rather sinister and a bit creepy, and you will never really know whether the woman is an angel or a devil.*[23] The woman in question is Rachel, a petite brunette in her forties, with large hazel eyes, a distant cousin of both Ambroise and Philip Ashley, and the widow of a

Florentine count. In a notebook, Daphne makes a detailed plan, and then the opening pages come to her suddenly. What she wants is a disturbing atmosphere similar to those of *Jamaica Inn* and *Rebecca*, an atmosphere lacking in her most recent novels. A return to the nineteenth century, to horse-drawn carriages, crinolines, and redingotes. Rachel has none of Rebecca de Winter's fatal, flamboyant beauty. She is gentle, reserved, covered by a mantle of class and distinction, a woman who never raises her voice and is, at first sight, unremarkable. But beware. Rachel is the kind of woman for whom a man might do anything. A woman to make you lose your head.

Another Philip disturbs Daphne's concentration in April 1950: the Duke of Edinburgh, Princess Elizabeth's husband, invited to Menabilly by Tommy. Prince Philip will only spend one night there, but the family is thrown into a panic by this princely visit and the house is cleaned from top to bottom for the man Daphne nicknames P.P. The blue room, "Blue Lady," the best in the house, is reserved for the prince (despite it being haunted, though no one has ever seen the ghost), and his valet will sleep in Tommy's walk-in closet, close by. The bodyguard won't be far away either, in the bedroom known as "Little Arthur," also haunted, according to Flavia, by the noisy ghost of a little Rashleigh, who died at the age of seven within those walls. Daphne asks her young housekeeper to make sure that everything is impeccable in the prince's room. The housekeeper replies with a smile that she doesn't see why Lady Browning is making such a fuss: the prince is a human being, like any other. Infected by the general fluster, and mocked for it by Tod, Tommy starts polishing everything he sees. He decants port left, right, and centre, while Daphne laments that there are only four presentable knives and the candelabra must be repaired. At the last minute, new wineglasses are bought and the children ordered to tidy their rooms, while Daphne agonizes over what to wear: *Oh, Duck, do you think I have to put a skirt on?*[24] She feels like Maxim de Winter's second wife, gauche, timid, and incapable, and makes her children laugh by telling them that she is bound to trip over while shaking the prince's hand or spill her cup of tea.

When it comes to setting the table for their very important guest, Tommy is unable to remember in which order the little and large forks should be put and he loses patience. Everything was going so well, with new place mats and candlesticks, and the salt and pepper cellars polished to such a sheen that you can admire your reflection in them, but this thing with the forks makes him click his tongue (bad sign), gnash his teeth, then go red: *Christ, why haven't we got a butler? Why is everyone so bloody hopeless in this house? You two get the hell out of here!*[25] This last remark is addressed to Flavia and Kits, back at "Mena" for their school holidays. Tod makes a comment on how tables are set in France, which only serves to stir up Tommy's wrath. *What the bloody hell have the bloody French got to do with it? Silly arse!*[26] With this, Tod, incensed, goes up to her rooms. Daphne, as usual, does not deign to get involved with household preparations. Ignoring the conflicts around her, she concentrates only on arranging flowers in the house's twenty-eight vases. P.P. is due to arrive around 4:00 pm, and after a moment of hesitation—should they stand in front of the gates in order to salute the royal Daimler as soon as it comes into sight?—the family ends up waiting outside the front door. Daphne and Flavia curtsey, while numerous suitcases are taken from the trunk of the car. P.P. is thirty years old, very tall and cheerful. The valet seems taken aback that there are no servants to carry the luggage, so the bodyguard takes care of this. Later, the prince greedily eats the dinner prepared by Mrs. Burt, the gardener's wife. Daphne has finally swapped her usual pair of trousers for a very elegant dress that used to be Ellen's. The next morning, Tommy gets up at the crack of dawn to set the breakfast table himself. When the prince leaves that morning, the children accompany the Daimler to the gates on their bicycles and P.P. gives them a big smile and a wave of farewell.

With Prince Philip finally gone, Daphne is able to get back to her own Philip, a tall, lanky, charismatic, dark-haired man, behind whom she is delighted to hide, taking more pleasure in the writing than she did when incarnating the immature and egocentric Dick. It is impossible not to become attached to Philip, not to be moved by his urges, his stubbornness, his loyalty, not to feel as outraged as he does when he learns one morning that his dear uncle Ambroise, the man who has looked after him since the death of his parents, is, at over fifty years old, going to marry a distant cousin encountered during a trip to Florence. Ambroise, an inveterate bachelor, marrying a perfect stranger? Incredible! And yet this is, horribly, the truth. But what most disturbs Philip are the vague, muddled letters Ambroise writes to him from Tuscany, letters that portend the worst.

When Ambroise dies suddenly and inexplicably in Italy, Philip ponders the matter fearfully. Who really is this cousin Rachel? There is only one way to find out. He must confront his uncle's widow. He must go to Florence right away.

Sitting in her hut, impervious to the rest of the world, Daphne writes in a fever, devoting herself to perfecting the character of Rachel, the enigmatic heroine with the name that is at once soft and harsh, a woman as charming as she is disturbing, the twin sister of Ellen Doubleday down to her composed voice, her dancer's gait, and her velvet-brown eyes . . . this Ellen-Rachel is the most complex, most inspired, most personal "peg"* of Daphne's career, her greatest secret. Not forgetting Florence and the golden light of that disastrous trip with Ellen. This is how novels are nourished—on their authors' passions and obsessions, all those things that cannot be exposed overtly to the outside world for fear of appearing insane, all those things that idiot judges and lawyers have never even imagined or anticipated, all that is woven in a writer's soul: fragments of truth and fantasy, a personal clay moulded and fired at will in the twisting curves of a labyrinth of intimacy forbidden to visitors and onlookers.

Philip is bewitched by Rachel, as Daphne was by Ellen: possessed, hypnotized, to the point of losing sleep, to the point of banging his head against walls, swept away by a hurricane of emotions that rages within him. The way her story slowly tightens its grip, each sentence polished to a shine, gives Daphne an intense pleasure that she hasn't felt since *Rebecca*. The fate she reserves for Rachel is chilling. This novel will, she knows, satisfy her publisher and her readers, stamped as it is with the peculiar brand of subtle psychological horror that has contributed to her fame.

Meanwhile, in France, it is once again Mme Butler, alias Denise Van Moppès, who translates *The Parasites*—a little too hastily, apparently, as in April 1950, Albin Michel ask her to *review her translation very seriously*. While her younger sister is busy writing, Angela publishes her sixth novel with Peter Llewellyn Davies, *Reveille*, a family saga with political overtones. There is not a single review in the press upon publication. At forty-six, Angela feels the time has come to write her memoirs, and it is at Menabilly, in the living room, while her sister is finishing her novel fifty yards away at the end of the garden, that Angela embarks upon the story of her life. As for Jeanne, while she is travelling with Dod Procter, a renowned artist belonging to the St. Ives movement, she meets Noël Welch, a petite, intense-looking, thirty-year-old brunette who writes poetry. There is electricity between them, instantly. Jeanne is distancing herself from Fowey, from her sisters and mother. She is the most reserved of the three, Muriel's favourite, the baby of the family who now wants to break free, leaving her older sisters to look after their ageing mother at Ferryside.

Tessa, sixteen, is interested in France and her ancestors, and her command of French, taught to her by Tod, is good. Relations between Tessa and Daphne have grown close; in her letters, Tessa confides in her mother, telling her about the spark she feels for Ken Spence, Tommy's godson. *My darling Bing, I was so menaced* by him I didn't know what to do! My God, it's so wonderful to be able to tell all this to one's mother, I must be the only person in the world to do so! But don't tell anyone!*[27] Daphne tears herself away from her novel, deciding to take her eldest daughter to discover Paris in June 1950. She has arranged things with Fernande; after a few days in the capital, they will go to her house in the Yvelines, about twenty miles from Paris, where Tessa will spend the summer, under Ferdie's care. Tessa has never taken a plane before, and she is perturbed at seeing her mother look so tense during the short flight, eyes closed, as if this were her final journey. Daphne and Tessa are welcomed to Paris by a charismatic young American man, Frank Price, who runs the Doubleday office in Paris and is thrilled to be able to show Tessa the City of Light. Frank lives in a large apartment on Rue de la Faisanderie, in the 16th arrondissement. He offers to put up Lady Browning and her daughter there—why go to a hotel when they can stay with him? They accept. Tessa suspects her mother is rather "menaced"* by the charming Frank. He is funny and clever and looks a little like the young actor Danny Kaye. Frank takes them out to dinner at the Eiffel Tower, where Tessa tastes *côte de boeuf* in Béarnaise sauce for the first time. After that, they go to the bar at the Ritz and then a nightclub in Montmartre. Frank tells the teenage girl, moving rather stiffly on the dance floor, to relax. In Paris, Daphne seems to come back to life: she is laughing, rejuvenated, and easily mistaken for her daughter's elder sister. The apartment on Rue de la Faisanderie, a short walk from the Bois de Boulogne, is magnificent, with its high ceilings, its crystal chandeliers, and a succession of rooms with communicating doors. A few days later, they go to see Fernande, who lives in Mesnil-Saint-Denis with her mother, an old lady who does not speak a word of English and whom Daphne calls Maman. When Tessa returns at the end of August, in time for Fowey Regatta, which she refuses to miss, her French is as good as Daphne's. She is delighted by her first taste of France and talks about it constantly. Fernande and she went to see *Manon Lescaut* at the Opéra, and there is nothing more beautiful than Paris at night. Daphne smiles at the thought that Paris has cast a spell over Tessa, too; Kicky would be proud of his great-granddaughter's accent.

❧

My Cousin Rachel is published in July 1951, with a first print run of 125,000 copies. To Daphne and Victor's joy, it is as resoundingly successful as *Rebecca*. The critics are unanimous: Daphne du Maurier, at forty-four, is at the zenith of her literary powers. "Spectacular, surprising, masterful," announces the magazine *The Queen*. The review in the *Guardian* is even better—"It is in the same category as *Rebecca*, but is an even more consummate piece of storytelling"—while the critic from *Kirkus Reviews* raves: "A gifted craftsman, and spinner of yarns, Daphne du Maurier excels herself." The ambiguous ending, a method already used in *Frenchman's Creek* and *Rebecca*, and which can leave some readers frustrated, does not seem to disconcert anyone this time. Whether Rachel is a poisoner or not, readers still love her story. The film rights are sold for fifty thousand pounds sterling in the same month the book first appears, and Richard Burton, a rising young star, is cast to play Philip Ashley, with the beautiful Olivia de Havilland, Joan Fontaine's sister, in the role of Rachel, directed by Henry Koster. An article in the *News Chronicle* names Daphne as the best-paid novelist in the country. As her royalties increase, however, so does Daphne's generosity: she is never hesitant to help her friends and family financially. Even Margaret, her former nanny, benefits from Lady Browning's munificence to open a little shop.

Still basking in the glory of *Rachel*, Daphne goes to London in September 1951 to attend a literary cocktail party given by Ellen at the Ritz.

Although she rings the bell for Mrs. Doubleday's suite, no one answers. A young woman in her twenties is also waiting on the doorstep. Tall, dark-haired, dark-eyed, she introduces herself as Oriel Malet, a writer published by Doubleday. In contrast to her womanly curves, she has a voice like a little girl's. As the two of them wait in the luxurious corridor, Daphne makes the young brunette laugh with her ironic remarks. They discuss literature and Paris, because Oriel is a Francophile and her godmother is the French actress Yvonne Arnaud. Oriel did not recognize the famous Daphne du Maurier, but she is already under the spell of this distinguished forty-something with her pretty, suntanned face and her scathing wit.

When Ellen arrives, late, with a cohort of guests, followed by waiters bringing *petit fours*, flowers, and champagne, Oriel at last realizes—to her stupefaction—who this mysterious, acerbic blonde woman actually is. The author of *Rebecca* and *My Cousin Rachel*! The guests chat, glasses in hand. There are other writers here, plus journalists, and that tease Frank Price. In a few recent letters to Fernande and Ellen, Daphne admitted "spinning"* with Frank, whom she saw again in Paris and London in the spring of 1951. Nothing too serious, just a few kisses, one of them in the restaurant La Tour d'Argent, in front of a magnificent view of Paris, but also in front of all the other customers. Was she testing out her seductive abilities? Either way, she behaved like a teenager and is faintly ashamed of her behavior now.

After a glass of champagne, Daphne sneaks out and finds herself face-to-face with the intimidated Oriel Malet in the lift. She is interested in this young woman with intelligent eyes and invites her to get something to eat at her apartment in Whitelands House before she catches her train back to Cornwall. While Daphne packs her suitcase, Oriel admires the photographs of dogs, boats, and children, particularly one of a mischievous-looking blond boy: *One's son, it's my French blood, I expect!*[28] She thanks Oriel for coming to keep her company that night, as Kits went back to boarding school that very afternoon and she had been dreading the empty apartment. After a quick supper, Daphne and Oriel say goodbye. This is the beginning of a long friendship and a rich epistolary correspondence. But on board the night train that takes her back to Fowey, Daphne does not think about that meeting, even less about her *son*, alone in his dorm, nor of Ellen or Gertie, her usual obsessions. Something dark and sinister is hatching inside her: a collection of short stories that she already knows will shock her family and friends, her readers, the press.

She has to get this darkness off her chest, no matter what. She mustn't be afraid to explore the extreme, to offend people, to shock them. It's like those grey hairs she's getting—why dye them? Why pretend? It is time to put blondeness, softness, behind her. What emerges on paper is morbid, disturbing. Sometimes, Daphne stops herself when she is in full flow and smiles pensively as she looks at the photos that Gertie mailed her, snapped during another trip Daphne took to Florida: two figures in bathing suits on the beach, laughing, entwined, brazenly beautiful. On the backs of the pictures, Gertie scrawled a few libertine phrases that Tommy unfortunately saw one morning, Daphne having stupidly left the photos on the desk in the library. Cup of coffee in hand, cigarette dangling from his lips, he had put the photographs back without a word. After that, Daphne hid them away in her hut, to have them close to hand, so she can admire the blue sky and Gertie's impertinent smile and dive once again into the torments of her poor, mistreated characters.

Oriel Malet, recovering from a motorcycle accident, comes to spend a few days at Menabilly in October 1951, on Daphne's invitation. One morning, they are crossing a straw field with Mouse, near the farm in Menabilly Barton, and they see dozens of birds circling in the sky. Daphne tells her friend she has always loved birds, just as her father did. Gerald used to watch them with binoculars, for hours: *I've often thought how "nanny"** it would be if all the birds in the world were to gang up together and attack us.*[29] Oriel feels sure her friend, whom she now calls Bing, has found a subject for one of her short stories. Daphne imagines incomprehensible attacks by sparrows, robins, quails, thrushes, larks, metamorphosed into killers of human beings. Storks, partridges, and seagulls join this murderous flock, descending on houses, smashing shutters and windows with their beaks, swooping down chimneys to peck out the inhabitants' eyes. Is climate change to blame for these violent attacks? No one knows. The authorities are powerless, and it's every man for himself. One brave farmer, Nat, barricades himself in his house with his family while around them, chaos reigns. The story ends in a crepuscular atmosphere, with no hope for the future. Oriel thinks it brilliant, and terrifying. She will not be the only one.

Even though Daphne's stories are set in peaceful locations—the Côte d'Azur, Hampstead, Cornwall, the Alps—the ambience is instantly suffocating. In "The Apple Tree," a widower is obsessed by a small tree that reminds him of his dead spouse, whom he never loved. Nature will avenge itself pitilessly on him. In "Monte Verità," Daphne chooses, somewhat perversely, the name of her editor, Victor, for the narrator of a symbolic story that touches on sects, sexuality and moonbeams. *My next story—I hope to get on with it when the dreary cold goes—is one you will hate,* Daphne writes to Oriel about "The Little Photographer." *About a sensual, rather foolish woman, who through idleness, lets a honky* man from a shop make love to her, and then when he begins to get serious, she gets frightened, she only meant it as a pastime, but I shan't tell you how it ends.*[30] The sordid one-night stand between the rich Marquise and the young disabled man is horribly cruel, but Oriel doesn't hate it at all; on the contrary, she loves it and asks for more. "Kiss Me Again, Stranger" narrates a macabre fling in a cemetery between a bloodthirsty cinema usherette and a naïve mechanic, and "The Old Man" reveals a family secret, its final sentence leaving the reader stunned.

While Daphne mercilessly plumbs these murky depths, Angela publishes her memoirs, still through their cousin Peter Llewellyn Davies. The title is ironic: *It's Only the Sister.* The book retraces her childhood, her career, her beginnings in the theatre, her love of the opera, her travels, her books. Her prose reflects her personality: chatty, sparkling, full of humour. There are generous extracts from letters written by Daphne, an unexpected gift for her younger sister's innumerable admirers. Family photographs complete the package. For once, this publication is greeted with a warm welcome, and Angela's spontaneity and wit are certainly a big part of that. But it does now seem impossible for Angela, nearly fifty, to ever escape her sister's shadow. The same is true for Jeanne, despite a few prestigious exhibitions.

It is early 1952 and *My Cousin Rachel* is about to be released in the United States, when Ellen Doubleday suggests that Daphne come to New York to promote the book. Why not ask Oriel Malet, who is also bringing a book out, to accompany her? The two novelists take a night flight in first class, their tickets paid for by their publishers. Oriel, who has never visited America, is very excited. As for Daphne, despite her fear of flying, she is secretly thrilled at the prospect of seeing, in that same country, that same city, the two women who are more important to her than any others. It is simultaneously an ordeal and an exultation to find herself with Ellen again, as serene and distinguished as ever. Daphne's passion has dimmed now, even if her feelings for Mrs. Doubleday retain traces of their former wild intensity. Daphne's suffering is less, though, as if the fact of having bumped off Rachel Ashley on paper had, thanks to the "Ellen peg,"* been enough to dull her ardour. What remains, after that, is a solid friendship. It is also a joy to see her beloved Gertie again, filling Broadway theatres for the past nine months alongside the Russian-born actor Yul Brynner in the musical comedy *The King and I*.

One evening, Daphne and Oriel go to the St. James Theatre on 44th Street to watch Gertie in the role of Anna, the English governess hired by the King of Siam. It is a breathtaking performance. Gertie twirls through sumptuous sets in ball gowns designed by the ultra-fashionable Irène Sharaff, and the duo she forms with the charming Brynner, who has shaved his head to play the Eastern sovereign, is a delight. At the show's best moment, the famous song "Shall We Dance?," Anna, dressed in a voluminous pink satin crinoline, teaches the king how to dance the polka, and the couple pirouette at vertiginous speed like spinning tops. Daphne is frightened, gripping tightly to her armrests. As the curtain falls and applause rings out, her Cinders looks suddenly exhausted, withered: Is she overdoing it? The play lasts three hours, and she sings and dances throughout—and she's been doing it eight times per week since March 1951. Not only that, but the famous prink crinoline weighs more than seventy pounds, Gertie later admits a little boastfully.

When they are alone in the apartment belonging to Gertie and her husband, Daphne notices how unwell her friend looks; she hadn't detected it under the thick stage makeup. Numbed by a torpor that is alien to her, Gertie admits to Dum that she has had a few medical exams, but that the doctor hasn't found anything. Curled up in front of the TV set watching bad soap operas, Gertie seems lonely and fragile, and Daphne, unsettled, feels an urge to protect her. Sometimes, the old Gertie bursts back into life, to Dum's joy, as one evening when their limousine, stuck in a traffic jam, is passed by some lout, and Gertie lowers the window to yell, *Fuck you, we're in a hit!*[31]

During their stay in New York, and when Daphne's busy schedule allows it, she and Oriel visit the Frick Collection and the Cloisters museum and go for brisk walks around Central Park. *My Cousin Rachel* is acclaimed upon its American release, and the book sells just as well as it had in Great Britain. Here too, Daphne du Maurier tastes triumph, thirteen years after *Rebecca*. Now it is time to return to Europe, to Menabilly, where Daphne must finish the short story collection, which Victor plans to publish in the spring. On the return flight, she thinks about Gertie, incandescent in her pink dress. Gertie, her ray of sunshine, to whom, as she was leaving, she gave a heart-shaped brooch. They will see each other again soon, very soon. So why, then, does she feel this pang of anxiety? When she gets back to Menabilly, Gertie still haunts her thoughts.

꧁꧂

As Daphne no longer drives, it is Angela who takes her to London, one cold February day, to meet up with Tessa. Arriving in the capital, Daphne notices that all the flags are at half-mast. Intrigued, she asks a sad-looking shopkeeper for an explanation. The king has died in his sleep. The highly sensitive Angela begins to weep, while Daphne is rendered speechless. George VI was only fifty-six, one year older than Tommy. Daphne thinks about her husband, who has been in Africa for the past few days with Princess Elizabeth and her husband. Tommy will have to escort the new Queen of England, twenty-five years old, back home, on this day of bereavement: February 6, 1952. Does the Princess at least have something dark to wear in her suitcase for the airplane's arrival? The whole city, the whole country, is in mourning. Black is everywhere: in windows, on doors, on clothes, in people's hearts. On the square outside Buckingham Palace, despite the icy rain, a crowd gathers until late at night in tribute to the late king. At Sandringham, where his body rests, people mass outside the castle gates. When the funeral train rolls towards London with the royal coffin aboard, people rush to the railway tracks to bid farewell to George VI, who is buried on February 14, 1952. The Brownings attend the funeral service at St. George's Chapel in Windsor. Daphne feels sure that her husband's career will evolve as a result of this royal death. And she is right: his new position will be Treasurer to Prince Philip, at Buckingham Palace, still assisted by Maureen. Lady Browning will have to take part in the commemorations, festivities, and galas for Elizabeth II, sumptuously crowned the following year, in June 1953, although the solitary mistress of Menabilly finds such social duties tedious.

In the spring of 1952, most of the reviews of Daphne's short story collection are virulent. Victor had predicted it; many people consider Daphne du Maurier a "romantic" author and are horrified by the violence and the sordid nature of her stories, particularly the journalist Nancy Spain, of the *Daily Express,* who claims that these nauseating tales draw their inspiration from "malformation, hatred, blackmail, cruelty and murder." She expresses her repugnance with such bile that Victor picks up his pen for the second time to defend Daphne. These unfavourable reactions have no effect on the novelist, who long ago became immune to them. Her readers devour the collection, and Hitchcock, once again, buys the film rights, to "The Birds." Her family and friends are also disconcerted by the book's tone. Daphne finds herself in the same state of mind as when *The Progress of Julius* caused so much offence, twenty years before. No, she certainly isn't a romantic author—what claptrap! Good God, don't these journalists understand how important it is for a writer to experiment, to explore dark avenues in order to reinvent herself? Daphne has just turned forty-five, she's not a kid anymore; her hair is grey, her childlike face is lined . . . it's time they gave her a break from that image of a writer of old-fashioned melodramas! While Daphne is being critically damned and commercially successful, Angela publishes her seventh novel, *Shallow Waters*. Again, there is not a single newspaper review of her book, an ode to her youth and the world of the theatre, the story of an actress who will abandon all artistic leanings in order to concentrate on being a mother. Angela consoles herself by remembering the warm welcome that greeted her autobiography the year before.

In Paris, it is Albin Michel's turn to publish these dark short stories. Daphne's translator, the all-powerful Mme Butler, has her say once again, making clear her reservations about "The Old Man" and "Monte Verità," which she finds "not very credible" and "boring." [32] In her opinion, it would not be "very desirable" that these stories should form part of the collection. So Daphne must accept that they won't be published in France! Michel Hoffman, her agent, suggests replacing them with two other stories, "No Motive" and "Split Second."

In another reverse for Daphne, Henry Koster's film version of *My Cousin Rachel* has just been released and it is a disappointment, even though she enjoys the acting work of young Richard Burton, playing the impetuous Philip Ashley to a T, and is very glad that some of the scenes were shot in Cornwall rather than Hollywood. The unctuous, irritating Olivia de Havilland bears no relation to her conception of the enigmatic Rachel. With her convoluted bun and her middle parting, she looks like the Duchess of Windsor. When Flavia enthusiastically declares that the actress reminds her of Ellen Doubleday, however, Daphne falls silent, momentarily troubled.

Tommy is busy building a new boat; he has to replace old *Yggy*, which has come to the end of its seaworthy life and now rests in the garden at Menabilly. The *Ygdrasil II* is also a motorboat, but bigger and faster than its predecessor. It is only out on the water that Daphne and Tommy rekindle their old closeness. Tommy now sets to work on his latest project—designing a sailboat, to be named the *Jeanne d'Arc*. It will be pricey, but Daphne doesn't have the heart to refuse him.

With the return of the good weather, Daphne accepts an invitation from her great friend Clara Vyvyan to go hiking with her, first in Switzerland and then the Rhône Valley. A robust walker in spite of her sixty-two years, Clara fascinates Daphne with her Gypsy-like appearance, her dry, copper-hued skin, her sparkling eyes, and her endless memories. Lady Vyvyan has been around the world, alone with her backpack, from Greece to Alaska, from Montenegro to Canada. Daphne has read and enjoyed her travel books, published by Peter Owen Publishers.

During the summer of 1952, Daphne's letters to Oriel retain their mischievous spirit, recounting her excursion with Clara, who does not share Daphne's ideas of comfort: Lady Vyvyan is capable of sleeping in a haystack, while Daphne needs her *awful ritual of creaming my face, and my hair in pins, and breakfast in bed!* Another panic arrives when she gets her period while climbing in Switzerland. *Lady Vyvyan will despise me if I don't walk up a mountain because of Robert.* What shall I do with the Robert* things? I see myself furtively changing behind a glacier.*[33] The house has not emptied after the summer. Tod is recovering from an operation on her varicose veins and Maureen from the removal of her tonsils. Tommy is out on the boat from dawn till dusk. Fowey Regatta, which takes place every year at the end of August, has been a great success, and the famous dancer Margot Fonteyn, a friend of Tommy's, comes to spend the weekend at "Mena." *Tommy is rather menaced* by her, awfully nice and easy, and reminded me of a Red Indian,*[34] she tells her young friend. The weather has been glorious; Daphne goes swimming every day and has never been more tanned. Tessa, nineteen and gorgeous, has invited a young man home. *Tommy and I went for a short cruise in the boat to the Helford River, I did this on purpose so as not to be there to make conversation!*[35] The only sad lines in this summer correspondence concern Gertie. Daphne confesses to Oriel that the lawyer Fanny Holzman, a close friend of Gertie's, wrote to warn her: Gertie is seriously ill. She fainted onstage and had to be replaced at the last second by her understudy, Constance Carpenter, and it may take her a long time to recover.

Three days later, when Daphne gets back from a walk along the shore, she is handed a telegram. Her heart contracts as she opens the little envelope, and she has to concentrate to decipher the few words it contains. Gertrude Lawrence died of cancer on September 6, 1952, in New York. Daphne stands in the entrance hall, suddenly numb. She can't hear anything—not Tommy, asking her if she's all right, because she looks so pale, nor the voices of her children as they play outside on the lawn, nor the barking of Mouse, her Westie. Maureen gently takes her by the arm and offers her a cup of tea. Tod leads her towards the sofa. Still Daphne says nothing. Her face is white and the telegram a crumpled ball in her hand. The telephone starts to ring: it's Oriel Malet for Lady Browning. Daphne struggles to her feet and puts the receiver to her ear. Oriel was shelling peas in her kitchen when she heard the news on the radio; she immediately thought of Bing. Daphne nods, stammers something about being shattered, thanks Oriel, and hangs up.

Daphne won't say much for several days. Her family and friends watch in astonishment as she withdraws into a catatonic sadness. So Cinders was really that important to Daphne? And yet they had only been friends for a few years. The truth is that no one guesses at the depth of Daphne's feelings for Gertie; no one knows about their closeness, their secrets, their frolics. From her bedroom, Daphne follows reports of the funeral, learning that her Cinders was buried in her pink crinoline and that the lights on Broadway were dimmed for three minutes in tribute to the actress with the Cockney accent. How can she explain to her loved ones that she feels as if she has lost Gerald again, eighteen years after his death? Daphne recalls her grief on the Heath, watching the two pigeons she'd released from their cage fly away, on the day of her father's funeral. Gertie and Gerald, fanciful and capricious, impish and beguiling, are gone forever.

⁓⁂⁓

The only way to survive this bereavement is to write. But try as she might to find inspiration—shutting herself away in her hut, going for walks with her dog on the Gribbin—nothing "brews."* The coming winter horrifies her. Flavia has just gone away to boarding school and, for the first time, "Mena" seems too empty to her. She misses Kits, of course, but also her daughters—and that is new. She is united by a deep tenderness to Tessa and Flavia, even if her son remains her favourite. Daphne takes an interest in Tessa's love life and likes her first boyfriend, Ken, but there is another "menacing"* young man in the picture. She enjoys her long philosophical discussions with Flavia, in whom she recognizes her own sensitivity and inclination towards daydreaming. Now there is only Tod and herself in the house, and her old governess often gets on her nerves.

In desperation, Daphne suggests to Victor that she write a nonfiction book about Mary Anne Clarke, her ancestor, Kicky's maternal grandmother, in the style of her biography on the du Mauriers. She had wanted, a while back, to write a play based on the life of her famous eighteenth-century forebear, convinced that Gertie would be ideal in the role of such a dazzling character. Then Gertie passed away. So why not return to this germ of an idea by writing a novel dedicated to Cinders? But first of all, Daphne must do some research, because she doesn't know very much about the tumultuous life of her great-great-great-grandmother, the bawdy effigies of whom, inherited from Gerald, show a buxom lady in low-cut dresses pursued by vicars and kings. There is no question now of going to London to visit the British Library; she is too fond of her reclusive life at "Mena." She could ask Oriel Malet, who lives in the capital, to help her, and she could call on the services of young Derek Whiteley, an assistant at her publishers.

Her heart isn't in it. Writing becomes a chore. In spite of the ample documentation gleaned by Oriel and Derek in libraries, Daphne's progress is laborious. She admits to Victor and Sheila, her editors, that this is a novel *written with the head, not the heart.*[36] And yet the life of Mary Anne Clarke, who quickly climbs the ladder of high society despite her humble origins, is not lacking in spice. Like Daphne, she laments being born a girl. Clever, ambitious, and attractive, Mary Anne is not content to be the submissive wife of a lazy, drunken husband or to raise his four children in the slums of London. A feisty heroine in the style of Dona St. Columb or Honor Harris, Mary Anne decides to exploit the most advantageous part of her resources: herself. Becoming the Duke of York's mistress, she makes use of information gleaned between the sheets, indiscreet pillow talk.

Daphne is bedridden by a bad case of flu for several weeks in March 1953, and when she starts work again, in April, her prose seems to her watered down, insipid, bereft of its usual vigour. What is happening to her? She doesn't recognize her own sentences. Will this book be as much of a struggle to read as it has been to write? Won't her readers be bored to death? And then an even darker apprehension grips her: Once she is finished with this novel, what will she do with her time? She is capable of spending hours in the sun whenever it appears, sitting on the lawn, with her back to the hut. She writes to Oriel: *I wish I knew what it meant to love the sun so much.*[37] She also tells her young friend about what she is reading and how she is finding a certain comfort in the works of Carl G. Jung, whom she finds "nicer" than Freud or Adler: *He does say that the ordinary life of an artist or writer can never be satisfactory, because of this awful creating thing that goes on inside them all the time, making them Gondal.*[38]* "Gondal," a new code word between Daphne and Oriel, borrowed from the Brontë sisters, means "the world of the imaginary."

In the autumn, thirteen-year-old Kits goes off to Eton, where his father went before him. It is Tommy who goes with him for his first day. Daphne feels enormously proud, watching him leave, so handsome in his black morning coat.

September 1953 brings a new obligation: a stay at Balmoral Castle in Scotland, the royal family's summer residence. There is no way to get out of it: Tommy has already postponed the trip once before, the previous year, when he was slightly injured in a boating accident. The young queen has just been crowned, and the Brownings' presence is fully expected. As always, Daphne is thrown into a panic by the need to pack suitcases, wear long dresses and jewellery, inhabit the role of Lady Browning, and forget the writer. Even the place's beauty has no effect on her, so ill at ease does she feel. She is plunged back into the crippling shyness that used to overcome her on Sundays at Cannon Hall; she does her best to smile, to keep up with the conversations, but she is counting the days until she can go home again. The constant curtseying and the formal clothing leave her exhausted. The only moment of joy is when the Queen Mother, a great lover of her books, asks her about the novel she is working on now. Daphne tells her about the life of her amoral ancestor and explains that she has not yet decided what she should censor, or not, for the book. The Queen Mother responds enthusiastically by begging her to not leave anything out.

Upon their return to Menabilly, a sizable surprise awaits the Brownings. Tessa announces to them that she wishes to become engaged to the young man she has been dating for a while now, a soldier named Peter de Zulueta. She is only twenty! Daphne likes the young man in question—good family, elegant—but she is not completely convinced. Tommy feels the same reservations. But their daughter is so fervent that they end up agreeing. The wedding will take place the next year, in March. For now, Daphne concentrates on the final pages of *Mary Anne,* which she finishes, with difficulty, in the autumn of 1953. She sends it to her publishers with a note addressed to Victor: *You'll have to be ruthless, don't pass what is doubtful.*[39] And, in fact, the book will require considerable rewriting, carried out by Sheila. This does not bother Daphne, who feels no real attachment to the novel. She finds it dull and thinks it reads like journalism. Her only consolation is that it does not contain even a hint of romance. *I'm done with romance forever,*[40] she writes ironically to Sheila.

❧

The big event in March 1954 is the wedding of Tessa Browning to Captain Peter de Zulueta of the Welsh Guards. It is the kind of wedding that Muriel would have loved Daphne to have, a church ceremony at St. James, in London, followed by a party for several hundred people at the Savoy, as Tommy has recently joined the hotel's management committee. Tessa's robe is silk brocade, and her veil has a train several yards long. Her chief bridesmaid, seventeen-year-old Flavia, wears gold satin. The young couple emerges from the church under a guard of honour formed by the raised swords of the groom's officer friends. The newlyweds will honeymoon in Switzerland.

Her daughter, married! Carrying the young bride's lily, Daphne feels her heart melt as she looks at her, so pretty, so fresh-faced. At her age, all Daphne's dreams were of independence. She observes her husband, who has traded his Moper melancholy for a more affable expression. He looks very elegant in his impeccably tailored morning coat and an immaculate silk shirt, a white carnation in his buttonhole. Everyone seems to know him, greeting him as "Boy," and Daphne notices the admiring glances he receives from other women, their gazes lingering on his tall frame, his distinguished face. Even now, at fifty-eight, Boy Browning still has the same effect on women. Is she completely crazy, leaving this man alone all week in London, insisting on having separate rooms in Menabilly for the last eight years? They talk on the phone every morning, but is that enough to keep a marriage alive? Tommy has made new friends, has become passionate about the ballet, which leaves Daphne cold. He has become a committee member of the Royal Academy of Dancing and in his spare time is writing the script of a ballet, based on Tchaikovsky's opera *The Maid of Orleans*. In London, Tommy goes out, accepts invitations, never misses a musical comedy or a show, and when he arrives at "Mena" on Friday evenings, he tends to sink into a torpid apathy, a glass of gin always at hand. Has Daphne pushed herself too hard, locking herself away for selfish reasons, in the name of writing and creativity? And in the end, what has it gotten her, all that ambition—a novel that will come out in a few months' time, for which she feels nothing but shame? During the reception, Daphne listens to these alarm bells going off inside her, but she quickly silences them. She will think about this tomorrow.

Her first priority is to get away: to take a trip with her beloved Clara, this time in Greece, a country she has never been to before. Under a burning sun, the two women visit the islands in boats, on buses, and on donkeys, climbing hills and sleeping under the stars. Daphne gets her fill of savage nature, flowers, little hillside churches, Greek blue skies, accumulating as much energy and vitality as she can in order to deal with her return to England and the much-dreaded publication of *Mary Anne* in June 1954. Victor has ordered a print run of 125,000: Too optimistic? The *Daily Herald* goes first, with this ambiguous line: "A book which will bring delight to the hearts of circulating libraries and acute nausea to critics." The *West Morning News* warns its readers that the novel is "a disappointment." One of the book's few champions, the *New York Herald Book Review,* finds Mary Anne "a lively lady." *Catholic World* does not hold back, calling it "a slipshod and thoroughly unpleasant book" with a "nasty and immoral" heroine. *Kirkus Reviews* is a little more positive: "not top drawer du Maurier, but a sure best-seller." Her friend the historian Alfred Leslie Rowse, though not generally fond of historical novels, at least appreciates the acuity of her research, which is some comfort to her.

Victor takes her out to lunch at the Criterion in Piccadilly to celebrate the book's publication, but Daphne is filled with ennui. What happened to the pleasure of writing? At twenty years old, she used to line books up one after another, insatiable for more. Is the death of Gertie responsible for this scarcity of inspiration? Or is it the inexorable approach of that dreaded passage in a woman's life? Daphne will be fifty in three years' time, after all. Next year, she will certainly be a grandmother. She has no right to complain, she reminds herself, sipping her champagne: she has a husband, three children, a magnificent house, and her books are bestsellers. So where, she wonders, looking at the neo-Byzantine décor of the restaurant as Victor orders dessert, does this feeling of emptiness come from? It is as if a long black ribbon were slipping between her fingers: her father held it, Kicky too . . . perhaps the du Mauriers have this sadness in their blood, and Daphne has handed this ribbon on to dreamy, sensitive Flavia. Angela, though unsuccessful as a novelist, seems untouched by this hereditary gloominess; she continues to flirt with women, to travel, and has never married. Does her solitude pain her? No, she loves her Pekinese dogs as if they were her children. In the drawer of her bedside table, Angela keeps the timetable for the Orient Express, and just looking at it is enough to inspire her. As for Jeanne, the youngest, the artist, she perhaps held this black ribbon in her hands for a while, but she has met her soul mate in the person of the young poet Noël Welch. Jeanne and Noël have chosen to live in the heart of Dartmoor, north of Plymouth, in a setting of hills, streams, and waterfalls. Daphne envies them their cottage, with its novelistic name Half Moon, where Jeanne paints, far from her sisters and her mother and Fowey. Over coffee, while Victor lights his cigar, Daphne thinks bitterly that her two sisters enjoy a freedom that she does not possess. She is no longer free because she has run out of ideas.

When a publisher asks Daphne to write the preface to the new edition of *Wuthering Heights*, she seizes the opportunity. In October 1954, she suggests to Flavia and Oriel, who are fourteen years apart in age, that they go with her to visit the Presbyterian "Parsonage" in Haworth, Yorkshire, where the Brontë children grew up. It is a pleasant, studious vacation, in spite of the cold that leaves circles of frost on their windowpanes each morning. Watching her mother take so much pleasure in following the footsteps of her favourite novelists, Flavia suspects that she will one day write a book related to the Brontës. The new preface is written quickly, and Daphne leaves Yorkshire with a feeling of work well done and future inspiration. The Brontë she is most interested in, she admits to the two girls on the train home, is Branwell, the unsung, unfortunate brother, who was nevertheless just as talented as his sisters.

Soon after this literary getaway, Daphne receives a letter from her publishers, Doubleday. The lease on the large apartment on Rue de la Faisanderie will not be renewed after Frank Price's departure, and it will remain vacant for six months before the next tenant moves in. How would Daphne like to take advantage of this fact, given her love of Paris and France? To move back to the city she so adores, to write in a room overlooking chestnut trees, to go for strolls in the nearby Jardins de Bagatelle . . . it's a tempting prospect. But she cannot leave "Mena," nor Tommy, who comes to see her every weekend. If she lived in Paris until next spring, it would put further strain on their marriage. She has a different idea: Flavia and Oriel could occupy the apartment, one to learn French, the other to write, and that way, Daphne could go to visit them occasionally. Both girls are game: How could anyone turn down an offer like that? They arrive at the Gare du Nord in freezing rain, but even that does not dampen their enthusiasm. The winter of 1954 is one of the harshest since the end of the war, and the girls shiver in the vast apartment, even more so when the building's boiler breaks down. Flavia enrolls in art courses in Kicky's former studio on Rue Notre-Dame-des-Champs, while Oriel starts writing a novel. But after a week, they are so fascinated by Paris that writing and painting are neglected. Daphne goes to visit them several times, and each time she feels her love for France surge up again. When she goes to Rue de la Tour in an attempt to resuscitate Kicky's old Passy in a now-modern Paris, Daphne feels a frisson of excitement that she has not felt for a long time. Why not explore, once and for all, those famous French roots of hers? Go in search of the Bussons du Maurier, in Sarthe? That's it, the subject of her next novel: finding the traces of those aristocratic glassblowers from whom she is descended, seeing their châteaux, their houses, visiting their graves. Kicky and Gerald would be so proud. The time has come to lay claim to her French blood.

While she is organizing this trip, Daphne almost chokes as she is leafing through the French translation of *Mary Anne,* published by Albin Michel in late 1954, a few copies of which she has just received from her agents. The cause is her translator, Denise Van Moppès, alias Mme Butler. Lady Browning writes a long, angry letter to Michel Hoffman in Paris, who in turn hastens to contact her French publishers. *I must make you aware of a very serious mistake committed by Mme Butler in her translation of* Mary Anne. *On the last page of the novel, there is the word "starling," which of course means "étourneau" or "sansonnet," and which Mme Butler unfortunately decided to translate as "un million de petites étoiles" ["a million little stars"], presumably confused by the similarity between the words "star" and "starling." I do wonder how a translator of Mme Butler's professional reputa-*

tion could have allowed such a gross error, particularly as the scene in question takes place in broad daylight. As the author wrote to me, her readers must wonder what stars are doing in the sky over London on the morning of the Duke of York's funeral![41] Daphne was able to spot this error because she speaks fluent French. Now that her novels are published in over thirty languages, however, Daphne knows that she must trust her translators, as she isn't able to read all those other languages to search for any inaccuracies. She learns through her agent that Mme Butler has translated Hemingway, Thomas Mann, Koestler, and Henry James, that she is highly respected in the profession and also publishes her own novels under her maiden name. Albin Michel hastens to correct Mme Butler's mistake, but the translator herself does not write an apology to the author.

❧

Daphne gives advice to Flavia and Oriel, who have become thoroughly Parisian. Dress warmly, even to go to the Louvre. Don't wear stiletto heels, because they slip on the frozen sidewalks. Don't walk alone in the Bois de Boulogne (when Daphne did it, twenty-five years ago, she had the terrifying Schüller, Ferdie's German shepherd, on a leash, to discourage any aggressors). Learn to use the Metro, not easy to begin with. Get in touch with Doodie (Daphne's childhood friend, an amusing and welcoming woman, now the highly chic Comtesse de Beauregard, who lives on Rue Barbet-de-Jouy).

Daphne is now a grandmother, at the age of forty-eight. Tessa gives birth to little Marie-Thérèse on February 15, 1955. Watching her daughter breastfeed, Daphne cannot help feeling moved. She remembers Tessa's birth, twenty-one years before, recalling her disappointment because the baby was a girl. Tessa does not seem at all disappointed by the sex of her child, however; on the contrary, she radiates pride. Kits catches measles in April, and Daphne is at his bedside in "Mena" when she learns by telegram that Fernande has been hospitalized in Rambouillet. Poor Ferdie: she demanded that Lady Browning should be personally informed. Daphne can't do much, from where she is, and her son is her priority. In a letter to Oriel, Daphne gives her the phone number for the house in Mesnil-Saint-Denis and asks her to call to find out more. Yes, this is cowardly. Ferdie will always remain in her heart, but for a while now Daphne has been irritated by her friend's detailed accounts of the difficulties and rivalries she is facing in the mayor's office at Mesnil. Flavia and Oriel obediently visit Mlle Yvon during her convalescence in her house in Yvelines, bringing her avocados, which she adores. Ferdie, in her sixties now, weakened and bedridden, would have so loved to see her Daphne again. Thirty years earlier, Daphne would have been at her side, holding her hand. Will she see her again one day soon? In May, Daphne celebrates her forty-ninth birthday quietly at home with her family, and remarks that her daughter Tessa is a wonderful mother to her baby, completely unlike Daphne at that age. Summer passes peacefully. Tommy's assistant, Maureen, marries a very nice fellow, Baker-Munton, nicknamed Bim, who becomes another close friend of the Brownings. In a letter to Victor, who is impatient to know when her next novel will arrive, Daphne replies frankly: *Everything I write comes from some sort of emotional inner life and the ordinary emotions are absolutely stagnant in me these days, so the unconscious has just got to work on its own, I can't do anything about that.*[42]

Not until September 1955 is Daphne able to start planning her journey. Because she doesn't drive, the trip is complicated to organize. In the end, it is her sister Jeanne and Jeanne's partner, Noël, both experienced drivers, who accompany her to France. Daphne possesses a few documents—letters, birth and death certificates—that she used when writing her biography of the du Mauriers in 1936, as well as the famous engraved crystal tumbler, passed on to her by Gerald. Her first task is to find the Angevin forebears of Louis-Mathurin Busson du Maurier, Kicky's father, born in London in 1797. His father was French, a master glassblower, originally from Sarthe.

Daphne has marked on a map some former glass factories: Coudrecieux and Chérigny, in Sarthe, and Le Plessis-Dorin, in Loir-et-Cher. In the Forest of Vibraye, she finds a place where the soil consists of a very fine powder of ground glass, which she touches with her bare hands. Afire with excitement, on her hands and knees, she calls out to Jeanne and Noël: her ancestors' former glassworks must have been here! A police van passes by chance in this remote area and stops. Two suspicious gendarmes ask the ladies what they are doing there. Daphne's perfect French allows them to avoid an unpleasant situation. For a week, they stroll through villages full of stone houses in Sarthe, in search of the ruins of glass factories. In the grounds of the Château de Chérigny, in Chenu, nothing remains of the factory. Intrigued by Daphne and Jeanne's surname, the owner of the château points out a small farm nearby called Le Maurier—perhaps that is a clue? Not to mention the Château du Maurier, in La Fontaine-Saint-Martin, a few hours by road from there. Following his advice, the three women go to the farm, then to the château. Daphne is puzzled: in *Peter Ibbetson*, Kicky always talked about a château, but according to his granddaughter's research, none of their ancestors were born in the Château du Maurier. Later, Daphne makes a major discovery while ferreting through the local registers. A certain Robert-Mathurin Busson du Maurier, master glassblower, was born in September 1749 on the humble farm of Chenu, at the place known as "Le Maurier." Her great-great-grandfather!

At the Auberge du Bon Laboureur, in Chenonceaux, where they spend a few nights, Daphne announces to Jeanne and Noël that, despite this fascinating news about the forebear born on a farm, rather than in a château (how Kicky would gasp, if he knew!), she does not have the strength, or the desire, to dive into the paperwork, the work she did on *Mary Anne* being too fresh in her memory. She will have to hire several assistants to do more in-depth research. There is so much still to find out: dates, places, clarifications. It is no longer a question of inspiration, but of documentation, which she finds discouraging. Noël and Jeanne, the poet and the painter, just as dependent as Daphne is on inspiration and their own whims, fully understand and support her.

The beauty of the Angevin landscapes, the autumnal colours, the châteaux and manors, the scenes of daily life in these villages will seep into the pages of a future novel. This arrives sooner than expected. Towards the end of their stay, in an animated market square near Le Mans, Jeanne and Noël notice that Daphne has stopped in her tracks; she seems magnetized by a stranger who is getting out of a car. Jeanne elbows her: Why is she staring at that man like that? Who is he? Daphne comes out of her trance: she was convinced, for a few moments, that it was a man she knew, a friend of Tommy's. She would have staked her life on it. During dinner, Daphne is strangely silent, with a dreamy look on her face. Jeanne watches her mischievously, and asks if Bing isn't seriously "brewing"* since seeing that man. Daphne laughs: she hasn't stopped thinking about it, she has an idea, a starting point, and it feels so good to be inspired at last, to think of nothing but that. Jeanne and Noël press her: What exactly does she have in mind? Daphne looks out of the window, towards the old town of Le Mans, the lights on behind curtains, the darkening sky, the footsteps echoing through medieval alleys. She sips a mouthful of wine and tells them that it will be the story of a man who, one day, by pure chance during a trip, meets his double, a man who looks exactly like him. No one can tell them apart.

At last! Surrendering to the enchantment of a novel that takes over her life, thinking about it day and night, taking notes at any moment, in her bath, with wet fingers, on soaked paper, never mind, a few words scrawled urgently, important, essential, because, as in "Hansel and Gretel," these scraps of words form a secret path that will lead her to the book she wants to write. And that's it: she locks herself away in her hut, concentrates on her story, and everything else, as usual, fades away. She imagines an ordinary Englishman, tired of his daily grind, who during a trip to Le Mans meets his doppelganger in a bar: an Angevin count, Jean de Gué. Manipulated by his false twin, who slips a sleeping pill into his glass, John wakes up the next morning in an unknown hotel, dressed in the count's clothes, with the Frenchman having vanished into thin air. A chauffeur is waiting downstairs to take him to the château that belongs to the de Gué family. John discovers that he is the head of a vast domain and a glassworks on the verge of bankruptcy due to spiraling debts and mismanagement. His personal life is even more complex: an old mother addicted to morphine, a pregnant, sickly wife, a precocious daughter, and two mistresses, his calculating sister-in-law and a highly perceptive beauty who lives in the village below the château. No matter how much John explains the truth of what has happened, no one believes him. And so he is obligated to live the life of Jean de Gué, a cunning, deceitful, and selfish man, with a shady past as a collaborator. When he realizes that he is trapped in the skin of such a reprehensible character, John does his best to improve the man's image and rescue the family business. But nothing turns out the way he hopes it will.

Daphne is proud of this book, *The Scapegoat*, finished in June 1956, written in six months with such intensity that she is driven to bouts of fever. In

March, she asked Oriel to send her a missal. *Someone has to die soon in my book, and I feel I must have a French missal before she does so I can feel myself at her funeral. Don't go to any expense, any shabby little book will do, actually the shabbier the more I shall like it!*[43] Publication is not set until March 1957, but Daphne already feels the need to write to Victor, ordering him not to make his usual boasts about Daphne du Maurier's phenomenal sales figures, because she believes this makes the literary critics hostile or indifferent towards her. In a letter to Oriel, Daphne makes fun of her editor: *I'm sure if he said "This book has sold no copies and nobody who has looked at it can understand a word," the critics would be nice, for once!*[44] Victor Gollancz's commercial methods, though responsible for helping build her fame, now annoy her. Daphne would prefer a quieter, subtler approach and plans to send her book to writers she admires. Why not André Maurois, for example (whose *Olympio: The Turbulent Life of Victor Hugo* she has just read in French), given that the story takes place in France? She senses that, after twenty years as a published author, she needs other ideas to support her novels; she can no longer depend exclusively on the bedrock of her faithful readership.

John, the central character, expresses himself in Eric Avon's voice to produce a dense, dark, tense, and ultimately pitiless novel written in sober, simple prose. It is a tale about duality, a theme that has fascinated Daphne since her childhood, since she realized her father was capable of playing evil Captain Hook and kind Mr. Darling in the same play. She already touched upon the theme with Maxim's two wives: the diabolical Rebecca and the angelic second Mrs. de Winter, and in *My Cousin Rachel,* whose heroine is either a saint or a poisoner. But this time, Daphne adds what she has drawn from her journey across the Channel, a French touch of which she is very proud. She hopes that the complexity of the narrative structure will finally procure her the respect and recognition of those critics who have, up to now, pigeonholed her simply as a popular novelist devoid of literary calibre.

When the book is published in the spring of 1957, Daphne's hopes are fulfilled. For *Kirkus Reviews,* it is "faultless." Nancy Spain, the *Daily Express* journalist who was so scathing in her review of Daphne's short story collection five years before, is full of praise, as are the *Spectator,* the *New*

York Times Book Review, and the *Daily Telegraph,* who even compare her to Henry James. In France, Albin Michel has the book translated by the inevitable Mme Butler, tasked in writing to *review a number of suggestions, as the literal translation of the English title will not work.* A letter from Michel Hoffman, Daphne's agent in Paris, describes Lady Browning's anger at the French title suggested by Mme Butler. *Lady Browning asks me to tell M. Esménard that she is extremely disappointed by his choice, and that she finds* John et Jean *weak and puerile. It is a title, she says, for a children's book. Furthermore, Mme Daphne du Maurier believes that, for France, the title is even more important than it is for England.*[45] Robert Esménard does not wish to risk upsetting the most famous English novelist on his roster, so he chooses the literal translation of *The Scapegoat: Le Bouc Emissaire.* Daphne is relieved. Another source of happiness: Alec Guinness, one of her favourite actors, has been approached for the role of the Comte du Gué, and the screenwriter Gore Vidal is already at work on the screenplay. The icing on the cake is a letter from André Maurois complimenting her on the novel.

Amid such joy, who could guess that 1957, the year Daphne du Maurier turns fifty, would turn out to be one of the darkest of her life?

∼❧∽

She didn't see it coming. Not at all. Except perhaps in those recurring dreams of a sea at high tide, those terrible anxiety dreams where she swims vainly against the water as it floods back and submerges her. In the private clinic of Lord Evans, the queen's personal doctor, Daphne waits, biting her nails as she did when she was a little girl, her stomach full of butterflies.

Monday, July 1, 1957. Another date engraved in her memory. The telephone had rung late at night. It was Maureen, Tommy's assistant: Daphne must leave Menabilly, come as quickly as possible to London, Sir Frederick was sick, very sick. In the train, Daphne watched the landscape move too slowly past the window. She had not told anyone: not her children, nor her sisters, nor her ageing mother. She is waiting to get a grasp on the nature of the problem. What had Maureen said, exactly? That Daphne's husband was suffering from nervous exhaustion, that he'd been hospitalized in a clinic near Harley Street.

Only in the waiting room does Daphne remember the tiny warning signs, picked up three years ago during Tessa's wedding, during the party at the Savoy. She had not wanted to see them. She had taken refuge in her books, her glorified "Mena." And yet there had been happy moments for Tommy and her, like the birth of Paul, Tessa's son, in April 1956, and Flavia's wedding, two months later, at the tender age of nineteen, with a captain in the Coldstream Guards, Alastair Tower: a church ceremony at St. Peter's, near Eaton Square, Flavia looking divine in white tulle, wearing Daphne's pearl tiara. And not forgetting her fiftieth birthday, celebrated last May. And that trip with Tessa, also in May, to Saint-Paul-de-Vence, in France, just the two of them, Tessa driving the car they had rented at the airport in Nice, and that charming hotel, La Résidence, in the hills, and that man who had called out to them while they were walking, they are such pretty young ladies— can he accompany them?

Daphne gets to her feet, looks through the window towards Weymouth Street. Big Ben tolls three o'clock. Why did she insist on her desire to be alone? Isn't it her selfishness that is to blame for scuttling their marriage? Now she must face up to the truth, accept her share of the responsibility. She remembers the recent, irrepressible desire to paint that she hid from those around her, those garish, clumsy canvases that she produced, unbeknown to everyone, in her hut. She had felt obligated to surrender to her urge, buying materials in secret so she could reproduce in paint what she saw in her mind, most often vast expanses of reddish earth.

At last a nurse comes to fetch her. Daphne follows her through a warren of white corridors. Her husband is lying in bed, his face emaciated and exhausted, his body all skin and bone, looking suddenly ten years older. Tommy starts to sob. Daphne is dismayed: Boy Browning doesn't cry. At a loss, she sits beside him, holds his hand, tries to comfort him. She questions him gently, but he doesn't reply. He looks like a broken man. All Daphne can do is console him by repeating that she is there, he can count on her, she is his wife, she will look after him. He has, undoubtedly, worked too hard, driven himself to exhaustion. He must rest now and he will be fine, she is sure of that. In the meantime, they'll have to see if they should cancel the party for their twenty-fifth wedding anniversary, planned for July 19 at "Mena," for close friends and family only. Tommy has not spoken a single word. His gaunt cheeks are streaked with tears. Before she leaves, Daphne talks with the doctor in his office. It is a nervous breakdown, aggravated by Sir Frederick's alcoholism and the poor state of his liver. Tommy will have to spend several weeks at the clinic and follow a treatment. Lady Browning can come back the next morning. Until then, no visits.

Stunned, Daphne heads for Whitelands House. It is hot and humid, this July day. She opens the windows wide to air the apartment. Why this sudden collapse? She knows how fragile her husband is, has not forgotten those nightmares he's had since the beginning of their marriage, nor his psychological state after the loss of so many of his men during the disastrous Operation Market Garden, in 1944. But why now? What happened in the last few days? No matter how hard she searches, she can find no answer. Was he more "mopey" than usual? She didn't notice, if so.

The sound of the telephone startles her from this reverie. A strange woman on the other end of the line. She doesn't introduce herself and speaks in a jumbled rush, never taking a breath: she has been Sir Frederick's mistress for more than a year, she loves him; she is worried about him; he collapsed because he could no longer bear living a double life and succumbed to the temptations of alcohol. All of this is Lady Browning's fault.

Devastated, Daphne hangs up. She wants to throw up, and her legs give way beneath her. She collapses in a chair, her head in her hands. Tommy, unfaithful. Her Boy, in another woman's arms. She looks at the unmade bed and disgust overwhelms her again. How many times has that woman come to this apartment? How many times has "Cairo"* taken place in this bed? Tears well in her eyes, and she lets them fall. Who is she, this mysterious woman? What is she like? Brunette, blonde, younger than her? Pretty, sensual, funny? Probably some toady whom he met in his amateur ballet circles, those shows she wouldn't go to with him, out of boredom, indifference. Never has Daphne felt so humiliated, so hurt. What a fool she was, what an idiot, not to have suspected that this might happen, not to have understood that Tommy felt abandoned during those long weeks here, alone in this gloomy apartment that she hates even more now. And the separate rooms that she insisted on for the last ten years. What an imbecile! Racked with pain, she imagines her husband's hands on the strange woman's body; she sees them kiss, caress, flesh bared. Unbearable visions.

Daphne is trembling less, but the nausea and the dizziness still trouble her. And what about her? She too cheated on her spouse. She was not a faithful wife. Did he suspect? Did he suffer because of it? She thinks again about the day Tommy read those words that Gertie had scrawled on the backs of the photographs taken in Florida. Guilt overwhelms her. It must have hurt Tommy so much. Daphne cries again, submerged in sorrow and shame. How can she speak to him about all this? What can she say? She paces the little apartment, her nerves raw.

There is only one thing to do. Write to him. That is all that is left to her now, her pen. Words on paper. Tell him everything, the truth, and don't wait another second. Daphne sits at Tommy's desk and, for a laborious moment, nothing comes. Then she forces it, and it's as if a dam bursts under the pressure of her writing: everything surges out, everything she has to reveal. It is all her fault, the sadness that he has endured for years. She cheated on him with Christopher Puxley and she hates herself for it, as she does for her obsessive passion towards Ellen and then Gertie, both linked to writing. It is a very long letter, stained with her tears, which she concludes, despite herself, on a determined tone: they must overcome this crisis; they must get through this ordeal, they will do it, they love each other, don't they? In spite of taking a double dose of sleeping pills, she spends a restless, infernal night.

The next morning, looking tired, Daphne takes a taxi to the clinic. Tommy is in the same state as yesterday, his green eyes filled with tears as soon as he sees her. He remains silent. Daphne cries with him, squeezing his hand as tightly as she can. She looks at his withered, handsome face, caresses his large, noble forehead, whispers to him that she loves him, that she will always love him. She forgives him, he must forgive her, too; they will find a solution, they have to. She slips her letter into his hand and, after one last kiss, leaves the room, leaves the clinic, as fast as she can, phones her friends and family, returns to "Mena" to gather her strength.

In the train that takes her to Cornwall, Daphne realizes how hard she is going to have to fight—not for herself, but for a loved one. For the first time in her life.

❧

Taking refuge in the calm of her hut, on July 4, 1957, Daphne writes a long letter to Maureen Baker-Munton, Tommy's assistant, one of the few in the inner circle to be aware of the real reasons behind Tommy's moral and physical collapse. To the others, Daphne has given the "official" version: Sir Frederick is overworked and needs rest. To Ellen, her great epistolary confidante, she does not say very much, failing to mention her husband's infidelity. The wedding anniversary party is cancelled. Daphne confesses to Maureen that the only things keeping her going are swimming and spending time with her increasingly fragile mother. *It was like being faced with a great jigsaw puzzle, or a pack of cards, and trying to fit the right bits into the right squares, and get the suits of cards right.* Each of her books reflects part of her, she admits, and *The Scapegoat* is the story of her and her husband. *We are both doubles. So is everyone. Every one* [sic] *of us has his, or her, dark side. Which is to overcome the other? Can Moper, and can I, learn from this? I think we can.*[46]

Covent Garden is the code name Daphne gives to her husband's London-based mistress, a woman who mingles with ballet circles, Boy's passion. But what should she think about that young woman who works in a shop in Fowey and whom Tommy has regularly taken with him on boat trips since last summer? At the time, Daphne paid no attention, mocking the shopgirl's infatuation with her husband and cruelly baptizing her Sixpence as if to emphasize her humble origins. Daphne suspects her husband must have had an affair with her, too, and her paranoia goes up a notch. Even her heroine Rebecca returns to haunt her: Tommy could go mad with jealousy like Maxim de Winter, lose his mind, and shoot Daphne because she made the mistake of prioritizing her writing over her marriage. *The evil in us comes to the surface,* she writes to Maureen. *Unless we recognize it in time, accept it, understand it, we are all destroyed, just as the people in* The Birds *are destroyed.*[47]

After three weeks in the Weymouth Street clinic, where he is given electric shock therapy and massive doses of antidepressants, Tommy is taken by car to Menabilly in late July by Daphne's cousin Peter Llewelyn Davies, whom she trusts. The doctors consider Tommy to be sufficiently recovered to start work again after a month's vacation. Sir Frederick will need the permanent support of his wife, and he must not touch a drop of alcohol. Daphne waits for them, apprehensive. When Tommy emerges from Peter's car, he looks stooped and dreadfully pale. He is also markedly silent. Is he really cured?

It is a stormy, rain-lashed summer. Tessa arrives with husband and children in tow, followed by Flavia and her new spouse, then the beaming Kits, the only one who can give their mother her smile back. At nearly seventeen, he is a handsome, mischievous prankster, the spitting image— according to Daphne—of Gerald, the grandfather he never knew. It is a blessing to have the house filled with the sound of children's laughter, in spite of the bad weather. Daphne devotes herself to the little ones, showing herself to be a patient, attentive grandmother, reading them stories, taking them to the beach. The children call her Track or Tray, after the funny nicknames given her by Kits, when he was small. Their grandfather is Grampy.

Tommy continues to be a serious concern. He has never stopped secretly drinking and spends a lot of his time in front of the television, which Daphne bought in 1956. She describes him to Oriel in a letter as being like Kay, hero of the story that frightened her so much when she was a child, *The Snow Queen*. Moper is like the little boy with the sliver of glass in his eye, seeing reality through a distorted lens. But for Daphne, too, this is a turbulent period. She frightens Oriel with a few incoherent phone calls, whispering to her that a major attack is brewing in London, that unknown people want to harm the royal family, that she must avoid public places, no longer take the Tube. Oriel does not know how to react to these unexplained anxieties. It is Kits, with his clownish personality, who ends up poking fun of his mother and making her aware of her ramblings. She should just write a novel, instead of bothering them with her nonsense!

At the end of summer, Daphne agrees to spend more time in London to be close to her husband when he returns to Buckingham Palace. The doctors have made her understand that he is no longer in a fit state to be left alone. It is a painful choice, as she hates the capital and that apartment, which she nicknames the Rat-Trap. *Moper seems better and more cheerful,* she writes to Oriel. *But he's still what I call very "quiet", and one doesn't know if he's just plain tired or has things on his mind. I know I am doing the right thing.*[48] It isn't easy to give up Menabilly. It also means giving up writing, solitude, and freedom. Daphne also suffers from having to dress like a city dweller, in suits and high heels. One day, unable to bear the hat she is wearing anymore after returning from a cocktail party, she throws it in the Thames, watched by dumbstruck passersby.

Daphne has not written anything since the publication of *The Scapegoat*. In a letter to Oriel, she confesses: *No, I have no writing plans at the moment,-can't, but there is always Bramwell waiting, and after what has happened lately, I should say material for a dozen 'tec or crook novels!* I told old Victor work was on the way, but I could do nothing at the moment, because my family life was a bit disorganized with being backwards and forwards to London. I didn't go into details, and did not say Moper had not been well.*[49]

Since July and the crisis she is going through with Tommy, Daphne has not felt at ease, as if a dark cloud were hovering just above her head. She still dreams of the high tide swallowing her and wakes up each morning with her stomach in knots. And then, at the end of November 1957, the news comes that her mother has passed away. After lying in a coma for several weeks, Muriel finally dies at Fowey, nearly eighty years old, after seven years of illness. Already afflicted by what she is suffering with her husband, Daphne is deeply upset by the death of her mother, to whom she had grown closer in recent years. Muriel had mellowed with age, finding a way to show her tenderness towards the daughter who was always Gerald's favourite. After a private funeral in Cornwall, Daphne and Angela take her urn to Hampstead, to the little cemetery where the du Mauriers lie. Though upset, Daphne manages to say her farewell to Lady Mo, whose *Narcisse Noir* perfume still lingers in the air at Ferryside.

The traumatic events of the last six months have exhausted Daphne. *I don't know who I am,* she writes to Oriel at the year's end. *I can cope when I am here, but once home, it's such torture to come back to the Rat-Trap. I always seem to be in a train. Moper's physical self is better, but I don't think his mind is all right. I dread him getting into the hands of the psycho boys*

---

* detective novels.

again.[50] For Daphne, Tommy-Kay still has the fragment of glass in his eye, and that scares her. He is not as he was before. In London, he spends hours sitting at his desk, methodically filing his papers, and when he finds himself at "Mena" he seems at a loose end, silent and preoccupied. Daphne wonders how she will hold up if things stay as they are. She is overwhelmed by melancholy. Perhaps she should have chosen to live with Tommy in London after the war ended? If she'd done that, might she have avoided this situation? Would she have been able to write *The Parasites, My Cousin Rachel, Mary Anne, The Scapegoat*, her short stories and plays, away from "Mena"? She feels incapable of working in the Rat-Trap. Her artistic output here consists solely of strange paintings, always produced in secret, when Tommy is at the palace. *My only pleasure is to paint the horrible view from my bedroom at the flat, all strident and screaming, because of my hate, with glaring chimneypots and those awful Power Station Battersea things, belching evil smoke. Bing's paintings are very out of proportion, like paintings done by madmen. (Perhaps I am!)*[51]

Since her mother's death, she has had no more "Robert."* A strange, hesitant sensation, like being in limbo, a feeling she detests. Her life seems less intense, more nebulous, without the lure of a new "peg"* to excite her. Is this what it is to be in one's fifties? A dreary, arid plain devoid of fermentation, and the prospect of living with a husband in decline, soon to be retired, driven to drink, not forgetting the depressing spectacle of those once-radiant Llewelyn Davies cousins transformed into potbellied, grey-haired whiners? And she herself must now note the spread of wrinkles in the mirror, must sigh over her white hair. How distant it seems, her ebullient youth! What does she have left? Her sense of humour, thank goodness, most often resurrected by Kits, the only person capable of making her laugh hysterically. Bitterly, Daphne understands the melancholy her father felt as he aged; she sees him again in Cannon Hall moping around in front of his bedroom window, looking out at the view of London he loved so much.

The short stories hatched from this discontent, published in 1959, are as disturbing and troubling as those that appeared in 1952; this time, they do not explore the characters' relationship with death, but the meanderings of madness and the unconscious mind. Daphne abandons herself to them, convinced that if she does not get them down on paper she will lose

her mind. Writing becomes her life jacket, her way of fighting against paranoia and the anguish that has invaded her life. In fluid, often chilling prose,
wavering between dreamlike fancy and pitiless introspection, each text highlights a breaking point, and that is what Daphne titles the collection: *The
Breaking Point*. Daphne writes the stories in London, at the Rat-Trap, and at
"Mena," taking refuge in her hut. "The Blue Lenses" describes the terrible
side effects suffered by a patient who is given temporary lenses after an eye
operation. When she wakes up, the vision she has of other people is terrifying. "The Chamois" explores the intimacy of a marriage in crisis during a
hunt in Greece, so subtly disguised that even Victor doesn't guess it is about
the Brownings. An amateur painter tips over into murderous insanity; an old
man falls for a young waiter on vacation in Venice, leading to disaster; a girl
becomes a woman one stormy night and loses the key to her childhood.
Even if some of the themes are familiar—psychological duality, the blurred
border between reality and imagination, rich animal symbolism—Daphne
opens the door for the first time on the unknown by using mystical and
supernatural elements. She boldly explores this new vulnerability, like a sub-
marine plumbing the dark depths of the ocean, as if these stories were
shields to keep madness at a distance, confining them to the safety of pages
in a book. Writing as the ultimate protection, a guardrail.

❦

Is it a good idea, this trip? One year after the crisis of July 1957, Daphne
and Tommy go on vacation together in France, to witness the filming of
The Scapegoat in Sarthe, near La Ferté-Bernard. The director is Robert
Hamer, an Englishman who already worked on *Jamaica Inn*. The casting
is impressive: Alec Guinness, Nicole Maurey, and Bette Davis, in the role
of the elderly mother. It is the first time Daphne has visited a film set, and
she is awed by the sight of all these actors, set managers, technicians, all
here because she wrote a novel. But her enthusiasm does not last long,
because she realizes how far the screenplay has strayed from the book. The
atmosphere between Bette Davis, acting like a diva, and the rest of the cast
is turbulent. Annoyed and disappointed, Daphne writes to Ken Spence,
Tommy's godson and Tessa's ex-boyfriend, who has become a close friend:

Not one word of mine in the screenplay, and the whole story changed. I think it will be a flop.[52] Their vacation is a flop, too, with Tommy lost in sadness and silence. Is this how the rest of their life together will be: dark, morose, apathetic? What happened to Boy and Bing, hair blowing in the wind as they sailed on their boat, magnetized by their love of the sea? This melancholy, sixty-something man is her husband, the man she will have to learn to live with again, because the plan is for Tommy to leave Buckingham Palace and retire to Menabilly. The prospect fills Daphne with dread.

And yet there are happy moments, as when Kits, eighteen years old and just out of Eton, decides, with the support of his parents, to attempt a career in the cinema, beginning with an internship on the shoot of the new Carol Reed film, *Our Man in Havana*. After that, young Kits will move into the London apartment with Tod, who will look after him. To celebrate this new departure, Daphne gives her son a camera, which he uses to shoot a short film at "Mena." Tommy plays the bad guy and particularly enjoys murdering Tod. Another moment of happiness: the news of Flavia's first child, due in August 1959. The new housekeeper at Menabilly is Esther Rowe, a twenty-eight-year-old brunette, lively and cheerful, always smiling, with a strong Cornish accent. She it is who takes breakfast in bed to Tommy and Daphne, who prepares their lunch, keeps the house clean. Mother to a little boy, she lives with her husband, Henry, in a cottage on the Menabilly estate. She is the house's ray of sunshine. When, one day, Tommy finds her energetically scouring the kitchen stairs, he tells her off, remarking that slavery was abolished long ago!

Daphne agrees to take part in a long interview for a French magazine, *Marie-France*, due to be published in late June 1959. The article is set to be at least eight pages long. The journalist, Françoise Perret, is given permission to meet Daphne at Menabilly, along with her photographer. This is a rare privilege, as Daphne generally does not give interviews, hates telling journalists about her life. She has a reputation as a recluse, which she quite likes. But this proposal wins her over because the magazine is synonymous with France and the prospect of speaking French with Mme Perret seems a pleasant diversion in a trying time.

The interview lasts an entire afternoon. In front of the lens, Daphne relaxes, bursts out laughing, cigarette in hand, dressed in faded jeans, a white shirt, and a coral-pink cardigan. The photographer immortalizes her in the living room, on the main staircase beneath the portrait of Gerald that Daphne loves so much, and then, as it is a sunny day, outside in the garden, near her hut, where the relic of the hull of Tommy's first boat, the *Yggy*, lies. The novelist admits with a laugh that she doesn't know why her heroes are so tortured, because she herself is very optimistic. Maybe she is too happy? Has life been too generous to her? She talks about her childhood, about her adored father and his death in 1934, still the most terrible ordeal of her life. She mentions the positive influence of Tod, who is there for the interview, and divulges her love of Cornwall and Menabilly, which she must leave one day, because the lease comes to an end in three years' time, in 1962—a *tragedy* for Daphne, who would love to be able to die within these walls. She won't know how to live, she insists, away from Menabilly. She remembers her romantic first meeting with Tommy in Fowey, just after the publication of her first novel, *The Loving Spirit*, their private wedding ceremony, the simple blue suit she wore that day. All the things she has never told to any journalists she reveals now: her writing process, the long daily walks that allow her to think, the six hours a day she spends writing in her little wooden hut, her need for solitude, the fictional characters who come to meet her. She takes five days to write a short story, one year for a novel. As soon as a book is finished, she forgets about it, she explains, detaching herself from it and never reading it again.

Unabashedly, Daphne talks about her age—fifty-two on May 13—and the pleasures of being a grandmother. She describes her three children, of whom she is proud. She even talks about the pictures she paints secretly in her hut: *I know my painting is really bad, but that's all right. I need to paint what I love, to relax.* In conversation with this Parisian lady, Daphne is only too happy to talk about her roots in Sarthe, her pride, and her family's artistic heritage—her novelist grandfather, her actor father, her painter sister, her son beginning a career in the cinema. The quality she most values? A sense of humour! Another? Intuition. And the journalist's final question: Why did she say yes to *Marie-France* when she has refused to speak to so many English magazines? A mischievous smile: because she hates them.

They pigeonhole women, only talk about little feminine preoccupations. A man can read Marie-France, *he can find something that interests him in it. Women's magazines in England are unreadable for men.* She is not a feminist but considers herself, quite simply, on the same level as men. Will there be a new novel soon? Daphne's blue eyes cloud over. She doesn't think she will write another novel. Stories, a biography, yes, probably. But who knows? Perhaps on some solitary walk, her fertile mind will be intrigued by an old mansion, a mysterious path, an enigma . . . Françoise Perret and her photographer leave with more than enough material for an article that Daphne is impatient to read.

As Daphne predicted, Tommy's retirement from the service of Prince Philip in May 1959 is an ordeal. Tommy struggles with his new status, feeling useless and elderly, and tells his godson Ken Spence that he worries he is a burden to Daphne, who is so strong and courageous. His wife never complains, always smiles; she seems to take everything in her stride. In private, however, Daphne is full of doubts: Is Tommy still seeing Covent Garden and Sixpence? Will he ever come out of his spiral of depression? He only ever looks happy with his grandchildren or on his boat, which he spends hours navigating.

Robert Hamer's film version of *The Scapegoat* is a flop, both critically and commercially. The *New York Times Film Review* regrets that "Daphne du Maurier's dazzlingly cunning puzzler is now a stately charade: handsome, curious and untingling." Apart from *Rebecca*, she has been unlucky, Daphne laments, when it comes to film adaptations of her books. She has not enjoyed any of the others. What will Hitchcock make of her short story "The Birds"? It is more than seven years since he bought the film rights. Given the coldness between them, she fears the worst.

But, in the summer of 1959, there are far worse things in Daphne's life than a bad film. One evening, she finds Tommy lying in bed in his room, his service revolver in hand. Ken Spence, his godson, had found him in the same posture a few months before in London and had talked to Daphne about it, but to see him like this, his face ravaged by suffering, holding the pistol, is a terrible shock for her.

This is the point of no return. *I just know I have to give, and give,* she writes to Oriel. *I've been right down in the depths of horror. I cannot write a long letter because at this moment part of Tommy's cure is for me to do everything I can for him, be with him.*[53] Doctors, nurses, antidepressants . . . Daphne makes sure that her husband has everything he needs. She knows she is not alone; she is surrounded by her children, her sisters, her friends.

How ironic that that issue of *Marie-France* should come out now, with her looking so serene under a headline that makes her shiver: "Obviously Happy." Françoise Perret describes her as "the most secret and most famous novelist of our age, who receives letters from all over the world," and sketches her in a few words: "Very slim, white hair cut short, face of a young girl, snub nose, small but determined chin. And blue eyes, bluer than any I have seen before." Daphne thinks she looks older than her fifty-two years in the photographs: her skin is lined, and her tightly permed hair makes her look like an old granny. But who cares! It is horrible to see these images of her looking so cheerful when she is going through hell. The magazine is filed away on a shelf and forgotten.

Now Tommy is at home full-time, on medication and still fragile, Daphne dreams of fleeing Menabilly for a breath of freedom. Rather a surprising reversal, as for sixteen years she has found it unbearable to be away from "Mena." The few trips she makes require organizing very precisely with Esther, the presence of a nurse, and the help of close friends who take turns looking after Daphne's husband while she is away. Thankfully, Tommy has decided to write an account of Queen Elizabeth's life, between her wedding and her ascension to the throne, with the cooperation of Buckingham Palace, so at least that will keep him busy for a while.

In the autumn of 1959, there is only one person who can save Daphne. A tormented poet, harmed by alcohol and fits of madness, solitary and misunderstood, overshadowed by his famous sisters, and dead at thirty-one.

Branwell Brontë.

❦

To follow him into his downward spiral, in order to escape her own, to understand and explain the nature of his decline. This is Daphne's aim when she heads back to Haworth, in Yorkshire, in December 1959. She is accompanied by Tessa, a good driver and ideal travelling companion. They have dealings with Mr. Mitchell, a fastidious man who runs the "Parsonage" museum, where the Brontë family once lived. *I nearly died from his endless "Tell-Hims"**[54] she writes to Oriel. But this is the price that must be paid when you want to narrate someone's life, going into the tiniest details, casting your nets wide, leaving no stone unturned. They also go to the Black Bull Inn, the three-hundred-year-old pub where Branwell first began drinking to excess. Daphne wants to write a real biography, rigorous, perfectly documented, that will reveal everything about the little-known Branwell, a book that at last will show his talent, a book that will stand the test of time. No one has ever written about him before. She will be the first. Daphne must travel frequently to London and Yorkshire for her research, the ideal excuse for getting away from "Mena" from time to time. John Symington, editor of works on the Brontës' youth, is thrilled at the prospect of helping the famous novelist to complete her project.

Daphne has already made quite a lot of progress when she learns through the press that a famous and respected biographer, Winifred Gérin, a specialist on the Brontë sisters, is also working on a book on Branwell. Panic and consternation. This is very bad news, according to Victor, because if Daphne's book on Branwell is published after Miss Gérin's it will effectively be stillborn. Daphne must pull out all the stops in order to finish it as soon as possible. Miss Gérin, already the author of a highly acclaimed biography on Anne Brontë, will be favoured by the press, and Daphne has no illusions about this. *My novels are what is known as popular, and sell very well*, she writes to John Symington, *but I am not a critic's favourite, indeed I am dismissed with a sneer as a bestseller.*

During the months that follow, Daphne works assiduously on her text. Each time she discovers that her rival is studying the same clues as her, she grows enraged. *Don't tell Miss G!*[55] she orders Symington as soon as she comes upon a new scent. She has never been in this kind of delicate situation before and begins to see the writing of this book as sort of fierce single-handed combat. And yet the fact remains that this competition galvanizes her: the book occupies her mind completely, allowing her to devote herself to Tommy in a more detached and patient way.

Finishing the book in March 1960, Daphne sheds a few tears as she rereads the final part, recounting the tragic end of the only Brontë son. She is proud of the completed work, of having been able to retranscribe the brilliant and ambidextrous teenager's youthful writings, unpublished tales of Angria and Glass Town, the imaginary worlds he created with Charlotte, Emily and Anne's response in the form of Gondal, as well as many poems and articles that she managed to unearth. Branwell was also a painter, but few of his canvases remain, apart from the best known, that of his three sisters Anne, Emily, and Charlotte, in which he painted himself and then painted over it, leaving only a vague silhouette. Daphne reveals his early addiction to alcohol and opium, his inability to deal with reality, his retreat into the world of imagination and fantasy. From his childhood, affected by the deaths of his elder sisters Elizabeth and Maria, subjected to the moralizing sermons of his father, the Reverend Brontë, Branwell forged his own personal hell that Daphne explores discerningly. Despite his prolific talent, he will never find success, discredited by his own family and outshone by his sisters. Every profession he attempts—portraitist, tutor, accountant—ends in failure. At twenty-eight, Branwell falls in love with a married woman fifteen years his senior, who also happens to be the wife of his boss, Mr. Robinson. The scandal has far-reaching consequences. But as Daphne suggests, might there not also have been a furtive, shameful episode with Edmund, the Robinsons' young son? Three years later, Branwell dies—of bronchitis, officially. His work will be forgotten, next to the immense literary success of his sisters. Daphne succeeds in bringing back to life this short, bespectacled young man with his thick, red hair and his aquiline nose. *The Infernal World of Branwell Brontë* will be published in October 1960, just ahead of Miss Gérin's, which is set for publication the following year. As she waits for her book to appear, Daphne congratulates herself: thanks to poor Branwell's torments, she has survived her first winter at Menabilly with the retired Tommy, something she wasn't sure she would manage. And she has an amusing adventure to look forward to: a trip to Italy with Kits, for three weeks in June. She is thrilled by the prospect.

Her joy is short-lived. On April 5, 1960, Daphne learns about the suicide of her cousin, and Angela's editor, Peter Llewelyn Davies, at sixty-three. Peter had seemed sullen and depressed for a few months before this, Daphne knew, devoting all his time to gathering and filing personal documents in a collection of letters that he ironically nicknamed The Morgue. His family had suffered a series of tragedies, with the deaths of his parents, both of cancer, then the loss of two of his brothers: George at the front and Michael, who drowned in mysterious circumstances in 1921. Daphne got along well with her cousin, ten years her senior; they would regularly meet for lunch in the stucco-and-mirrors décor of the Café Royal in Piccadilly, where they would talk about their parents, Gerald and Sylvia, brother and sister, and Kicky, their legendary grandfather, who died at sixty-one, whispering in French, *If this is death, it's not very cheerful.* Their conversations ceaselessly revisited the past and their childhoods. The day of his death, Peter had gone for a drink, alone, at the Royal Court Hotel, then went straight off to throw himself under a Tube train at Sloane Square. He did not leave any message for his wife and children. The next day's newspapers were full of headlines that Daphne found in dubious taste: "Peter Pan Killed by London Subway Train" and "Peter Pan's Death Leap." Poor Peter! He could no longer bear being asked about Barrie, his guardian, or about Peter Pan, who haunted his youth, just as he haunted Daphne's. For him, Barrie's play was *that terrible masterpiece*, which pursued him and his brothers throughout their lives. Barrie even admitted in 1928 that he had created Peter Pan by rubbing the five brothers together like sticks, the way early humans made fire. Each time the press mentioned George, Jack, Nico, or Michael, one of the Lost Boys, it was always with reference to that damned Peter Pan. George went to war in 1914, and it was "Peter Pan Joins the Army". Michael in 1919: "Peter Pan Fined for Speeding." Nico's wedding in 1926: "Peter Pan Gets Married." And when Peter set up his own publishing house: "Peter Pan Becomes a Publisher." Sickened, Daphne does not read any of the obituaries. Peter's suicide affects her very deeply. What drove him to throw himself under that train? Reading those moving letters, with all their mentions of death? Or simply the du Mauriers' black ribbon, handed on to Peter by his mother, Sylvia, the hereditary gift of melancholy and sorrow that ran through their veins? Two weeks later, Daphne looks visibly lined and grief-stricken as she inaugurates the blue plaque fixed to the house where George du Maurier lived, on Great Russell Street, in London: an event that should have been a celebration reduced to a brief ceremony, no press, no speech, in spite of the presence of Ellen Doubleday, who has flown over for the occasion.

The best cure for this sadness is Italian sunshine and Kits's irrepressible good humour. Venice and Rome in his company proves simultaneously exhausting and relaxing. Daphne's son has no interest in culture or tourism; what he likes best is driving his sports car around at top speed, shopping, and people-watching while sitting tranquilly on a café terrace, like his grandfather Gerald. Kits makes his mother weep with laughter with his imitations of Italian accents and "Witherspoons"*-style English tourists. Daphne returns to "Mena" reinvigorated, ready for the publication of her biography of Branwell Brontë. She notes that Nancy Mitford is publishing a novel in the same week, *Don't Tell Alfred*, the last volume of a highly successful trilogy, which discourages her, particularly as Victor is being unusually prudent, printing fewer than ten thousand copies of her biography. A disappointment for Daphne, who gave everything for that book. She could never rival the mastery and experience of Winifred Gérin, but her solid research and the finesse of her psychological approach are points in her favour. The book is well received, the reviews positive, but sales remain disappointing. One slight comfort: her friend Alfred Leslie Rowse, the eminent historian, believes it is her finest book.

❦❧

Dear Monsieur le Vicomte,

*I wanted to thank you for your great kindness in receiving me at the
Chateau de Chérigny last Monday, and in allowing my son to take
photographs of the old glass factory. It was a great pleasure for us to
see "Le Maurier," and to contemplate the same scenery and landscape
that our ancestors must have known so well more than two hundred
years ago.*

On April 22, 1961, Daphne writes to Viscount Foy, owner of the
Château de Chérigny, in Sarthe. She has just taken a trip with Kits in
France, a badly needed breath of fresh air. Her twenty-year-old son does
not speak a word of French, unlike Tessa, but this family pilgrimage
amuses him, and he takes dozens of photographs, including one of Le
Maurier farm, which Daphne will use as a Christmas card later that
year.

While she is still savouring this trip, Daphne is shaken by some unexpected news. With the death of old Dr. Rashleigh, "Mena" has been inherited by his nephew and heir, Philip. Until this point, Daphne had closed
her eyes to the end of the Menabilly lease in 1962, knowing that she has
been living in the manor for seventeen years as if it belonged to her. What
will she do if Philip Rashleigh, who is only in his thirties, wants to move
in earlier than expected? Leaving "Mena" is unthinkable, and yet she knows
she must prepare herself for it. To overcome her anguish, Daphne agrees
to a proposed book idea from her old friend Foy Quiller-Couch, who
suggests she complete *Castle Dor*, Foy's father's unfinished novel, an adaptation of the legend of Tristan and Iseult, which ended abruptly at chapter 17 when he died in 1944. This literary challenge is an honour, and
Daphne only hopes she is up to the task, in terms of the great Q's style and
prose. She is bewitched by this project, which is extremely time-
consuming, and even manages to rope in Tommy, as fascinated as she is,
to help her research it. Q's novel has its roots in the Cornish fable by the
medieval poet Béroul, a tragic love story set in the Castle Dor, a glorious

Iron Age fort, of which only a few ruins remain, just above Fowey. Equipped with old maps and binoculars, the Brownings go for long walks in the footsteps of Tristan and Iseult. Esther, the new housekeeper, watches them leave "Mena," thinking how elegant and classy they look, how slender and tanned and energetic. Tommy is interested in strategies of war, in battles, in troop advances on land and sea. His knowledge is of great help to Daphne, who is able in this way to rebuild the setting of another age. When the book is published in 1962, by J. M. Dent, Arthur Quiller-Couch's old editor, the reviews are kind, although the book is generally regarded as an exercise in style rather than a novel in its own right. Sales figures remain undisclosed. The only positive aspect Daphne is able to draw from this is the feeling that she has not betrayed Q. She has also grown closer to her husband, even if there are still painful moments, such as the evening in September 1961, described in a letter to Oriel: *I've had a frightful time with Moper again. Another frightful bout came on, so bad, I could hardly get him to bed.*[56]

Tommy has started drinking again. The only way out is hospitalization, a round of treatment, and then a nurse at home. Adding to this weight are the endless negotiations between Philip Rashleigh and Daphne's lawyer regarding the Menabilly lease. The Rashleigh heir has every intention of getting his family mansion back and Daphne realizes, to her chagrin, that her days at "Mena" are numbered. Her loved ones are more philosophical, quietly suggesting to her that the moment to find another house—smaller, more practical—has perhaps arrived. Daphne does not want to hear it. "Mena" is her muse, her inspiration, her passion. It is unimaginable for her to write anywhere else. She will fight tooth and nail to extend the lease, she will talk to the press about it, she will kick up a fuss. She refuses to be expelled without a fight. In a letter to Oriel, Daphne confides her secret method, the source of her well-being: she imagines that she is being mentally transported to Paris, to the traffic circle at the Champs-Élysées, that junction she loved so much, and that she is watching the faces of the passersby as she used to do at nineteen. But a new novel will be the key to her happiness, and at last it is to France that she looks for it.

Dear Mademoiselle,

I was enchanted to receive your very friendly letter, and to hear your news.

It is May 27, 1962. Daphne types a two-page letter in French to Mlle Marguerite Verrier, proprietor of the Les Glycines hotel-restaurant in Saint-Christophe-sur-le-Nais, in the Indre-et-Loire département. She had spent a few days with her sister and Noël there in 1955 and began a correspondence with Mlle Verrier, a woman her own age with a lively personality, who was interested in the research Daphne was carrying out to find her ancestors. As the old Underwood does not have any keys that would allow her to type French accents, she adds them by hand, in blue ballpoint. She politely asks Mlle Verrier for her help in obtaining further information about her family, in particular Mathurin Busson, born in 1720 in Coudrecieux, in Sarthe, and his wife, Madeleine Labbé, born in 1725 in Saint-Christophe-sur-le-Nais. These are the parents of Robert-Mathurin Busson, born at Le Maurier, in Chenu, on September 7, 1749.

> *I want to know so desperately* how *my Bussons lived,* Daphne writes to Oriel, *instead of being content to "Gondall"* them. I've been look-ing into my grandfather's* Peter Ibbetson *again, and it's queer how he had these same feelings about forebears that I have,–an almost ago-nized interest. I can't think how he did not go out to Sarthe and find out about them* truly, *instead of "Gondalling"* them, because he got them wrong, making them aristocrats instead of* bourgeois, *I s'pose a natural Victorian reluctance to be a bit "honky"*.[57]

The French literary agent Michel Hoffman has found Daphne a Parisian student to do further research for her—a Mlle Fargeaud—but Daphne knows how precious Mlle Verrier's aid could be, particularly as she is in situ at Saint-Christophe. She had been so welcoming, and Daphne had appreciated the comforts of the little hotel with its terrace under the wisterias, and the moving visit to the twelfth-century church, under whose vaults her forebears Mathurin Busson and Madeleine Labbé had walked ceremoniously, on their wedding, September 18, 1747.

Despite her very real worries about Menabilly, Daphne decides to begin *The Glass-Blowers*, her next novel. She is excited by the prospect of writing about her unusual great-great-grandfather, Robert-Mathurin Busson, the one who was born on the little Le Maurier farm, seven and a half miles from Saint-Christophe. She recalls perfectly this building with its pale walls and steep roof, surrounded by green fields, a stone's throw from the Château de Chérigny. Robert-Mathurin is the family's adventurer, the gambler, the black sheep. Like his father, Mathurin Busson, he becomes a glassblower and engraver of crystal, but Daphne knows from his letters to his sister, Anne-Sophie Busson, maiden name Duval, unearthed from Kicky's archives, that he was *a pretty boy, blond with blue eyes, with a turbulent life.*[58] A flamboyant, novel-like character, who first marries a Parisian woman, Mlle Catherine Fiat, and becomes the young manager of a glassworks in Loir-et-Cher. His excessive spending and his taste for luxury precipitate the company's bankruptcy, and he moves to Paris, where he opens an art and crystalware boutique near the Arcades du Palais-Royal, at 255 Rue Saint-Honoré. It is here that his first child, Jacques, is born and here too that he loses his wife, who dies in childbirth. But Robert-Mathurin's lifestyle is not moderated by his becoming a widower; on the contrary, he marries a second time, in 1789, as the revolution is rumbling in the background. His bride is Marie Bruère, from Dourdan. The boutique collapses beneath the weight of its debts, and the couple disappears soon after their wedding in order to escape their growing financial troubles. They go to London, where six children will be born between 1791 and 1800.

And this is the detail that so amuses Daphne: Robert-Mathurin Busson decides that it would be more distinguished, in this new English life, to be called Busson du Maurier, in secret tribute to the farm in Chenu where he was born. Of course, he leads people to believe that his family owned a château, a glassworks, and lots of land and that he lost it in the revolution. His children bear this new aristocratic-sounding surname, but only two of them will have a descendant: James, born in 1793, and Louis-Mathurin, born in 1797, Kicky's future father. Daphne makes other discoveries concerning her strange great-great-grandfather. In 1802, Robert-Mathurin decides to visit

France, briefly, but on the boat there he swaps his identity papers with a man who dies during the crossing. His wife, who has remained in London, thinks she is a widow, and the young children mourn their father for a long time, because he has simply invented a new life for himself, in Tours, where he founds a school and where he dies, in 1811. Now Daphne understands why Gerald's grandfather, Louis-Mathurin Busson du Maurier was convinced that his father was an aristocrat from Sarthe. A legend transmitted from Kicky to Gerald, along with the crystal tumbler, then from Gerald to his own daughters. Daphne remembers the distant stories of châteaux and aristocrats that her father used to tell her at Cumberland Terrace, when she was a little girl. And to think that their real surname is simply Busson!

Daphne constructs her novel around this irresponsible yet somehow endearing protagonist, Robert-Mathurin Busson. In this account, it is Robert's sister, Sophie Duval, who tells her young nephew Louis-Mathurin, the truth about his vanished father: that he was not an aristocrat who fled from the threat of the guillotine and took refuge in England. No, he was an ordinary man, from a family of artisans, ruined by debt and delusions of grandeur. It is not the tragic trajectory of the revolution that interests Daphne here—in spite of her precise, masterly descriptions of the Vendée uprising, the massacres of the Terror, the gratuitous acts of violence, the sufferings of the people—but the daily life of a family: *her* family, the Bussons. She feels convinced that she owes them so much, these Sarthe ancestors, this clan united by the love of family and land, by their respect for nature and tradition. And to that scatterbrained great-great-grandfather of hers, who built castles in the air, she probably owes her overflowing imagination, her youthful rebelliousness, and her love for France.

I think it's quite good, not wildly exciting or suspense-making, but rather nostalgic and mellow, she writes to Oriel upon finishing the book in June 1962. *I hate the idea of it being put into a garish yellow cover and boosted as the story of a Revolution, which only comes into the middle part. It's the story of a family, plain and simple, written with compassion.*[59] Passion and fever seem to have been removed from her writing—through a lack of "peg,"* perhaps? Is it possible that as she gets older those "pegs"* no longer have the capacity to overwhelm her mind with such tumultuous fervour? Sadness and resignation.

The Busson du Mauriers beat a retreat from Daphne's mind when Tommy announces that Elizabeth II will come to take tea at "Mena" on July 23, 1962. Action stations! This is even worse than the visit of P.P. twelve years earlier. The queen will come from the royal yacht, moored at Fowey, with her bodyguards, her chauffeurs, her entire retinue. *How* shall *we manage?* Daphne writes to Oriel. *It's ruining my summer! Piffy says I ought to do up the house, but really, one* can't![60] Every detail induces panic: to wear or not to wear a hat, which dress to choose (she no longer fits in the most elegant ones), and what to serve at this royal tea? Daphne loses her head, so it is Tommy who takes charge of everything, with military precision. Lady Browning's only task is to arrange flowers in the twenty-eight vases, and even that exhausts her.

The weather is good for the royal visit. The young queen, dazzling in white, descends from the Rolls-Royce outside the manor. The silverware shines, and an opulent feast is spread out on the dining room table, but though the queen does accept a cup of tea, she will not touch a single salmon and cucumber sandwich, to the disappointment of all. Angela, wonderfully chatty and adept at conversation, entertains the monarch, even making her laugh, while Daphne is paralyzed by nerves, just like the gauche second Mrs. de Winter. Thank goodness for Piffy: you can always count on her in difficult moments. Despite her ongoing lack of success, Angela is working on her eighth novel, *The Road to Leenane,* which takes place in Ireland, where she recently went with a friend. Angela radiates good humour and joie de vivre, despite a few minor health concerns. As for Jeanne, even the visit of the Queen of England is not enough to tempt her from home. Bird plays the recluse in her Dartmoor cottage with its thatched roof, where—between a few glasses of very good wine, the music of Bach, Mozart, and Chopin, a vegetable garden that she tends enthusiastically, five horses, seven dogs, and an indefinite number of cats, chickens, and rabbits—she devotes herself to her art, in the company of her partner, Noël. She moves her easel around the house, wherever inspiration takes her, and Noël has learned not to disturb her.

Some good news arrives: Philip Rashleigh finally agrees to let the Brownings stay at Menabilly for a few years longer, to Daphne's great relief. Even though Tommy tells her she is just delaying the inevitable, Daphne refuses to accept that she must, one day, leave her beloved home. The owner suggests they rent the little manor, Kilmarth, located on the grounds of Menabilly, with a view of the sea and St. Austell Bay. Tommy would be happy with this, but Daphne digs her heels in. Absolutely not! Not now!

Moper is enjoying a more peaceful period, in the summer of 1962. He continues to sail the *Jeanne d'Arc,* as well as a faster and more mobile boat, the *Echo.* He renews his interest in photography, taking out an old camera that he brought back from Asia. His three grandchildren entertain him, despite the ruckus they make. His favourite seems to be the youngest: Flavia's three-year-old son, Rupert. As for Daphne, her editor's announcement that the *Times Literary Supplement* is preparing a long profile on her for October both thrills and terrifies her. Daphne is still pained by the lack of critical recognition for her work, twenty-four years after *Rebecca.* The article, written anonymously, as is often the case in that newspaper, is something of a mixed bag: while the author finds remarkable qualities in *Rebecca* and *The Scapegoat,* he mercilessly slates Daphne's historical novels: "Miss du Maurier's historical sense is execrable." Victor is vexed, Tommy furious, but Daphne, surprisingly philosophical, is consoled by the article's positive conclusion: that it is time to stop underestimating her work. Critics who persist in demeaning her novels as "a glossy brand of entertaining nonsense"—to quote Ronald Bryden in last April's *Spectator* in his scathing article "Queen of the Wild Mullions"—are simply wrong.

But the harm is done. The label has stuck, to Daphne's dismay. Younger, more modern novelists like Iris Murdoch and Ivy Compton-Burnett are treated as serious authors, but not her. Perhaps she has become outdated, old-fashioned? She remembers an anecdote told her by her friend Clara Vyvyan, who was complaining about her books' modest sales figures, in spite of the critical acclaim they received. Her editor told her: *No one sells nowadays, not even Daphne du Maurier!*[61]

❧

When *The Glass-Blowers* appears in the spring of 1963, the press either ignores it or treats it as a dull historical romance. *Kirkus Reviews* considers it well below Daphne du Maurier's usual standards, and sales are poor, too.

Even the naturally optimistic Victor is disappointed. The best remedy for Daphne's disillusion is to go off to Italy with Tessa, who is herself going through a difficult period with her unfaithful, alcoholic husband. At nearly thirty, she is a mature, intelligent young woman, and Daphne enjoys this trip with her eldest daughter, knowing that Tommy is being well looked after by Esther, at Menabilly. Once again, it is Tessa who drives, as soon as they land at Rome airport, and Daphne who reads the map. They spend four days in the capital before heading for the wonders of Perugia: its large square, its palace, its cloisters, its cathedral. The city is full of rowdy students in costumes, an entertaining spectacle for Daphne, who loves sitting in cafés and watching them. Mother and daughter laugh together like young girls at the hotel, where Daphne discreetly mocks the English tourists, inventing fantastical stories to amuse Tessa. Then they go to Urbino and are fascinated by its medieval alleyways and impressive castle. If only this agreeable trip could give birth to a new book! Surely there is a story to be told about Urbino, its university, its ducal palace. . . . She takes a few notes: a professor, a family secret, a tragedy linked to the city's history, a murder, a mystery, two brothers who lose touch with each other . . . Daphne feels sure she is on to something, and she burns with the desire to write about Italy.

Back in England, Daphne sees Alfred Hitchcock's adaptation of her short story "The Birds," which received an ovation at the Cannes festival. The film was shot in the San Francisco area, at Bodega Bay, with Tippie Hedren, a blonde newcomer, in the central role. Hitchcock radically changed the plot, a fact that Daphne deplores even if she is impressed and frightened by the special effects. The viewer must wait over an hour to see the birds' first attack. Nevertheless, the film is an international success. Daphne, however, is irritated that her name is so rarely mentioned in interviews with the director. Hitchcock has adapted three of her stories in twenty-four years but has never paid tribute to her and has tended to minimize or even denigrate her work.

Daphne's morale is bucked up by the announcement of her son Kits's wedding. At twenty-two, he has fallen madly in love with an extra he met while shooting Carol Reed's latest film. Olive White is eighteen, the daughter of a plumber, the former Miss Ireland 1961, a model and TV presenter, and Kits finds her terribly "menacing."* *She is not a fool and reads Yeats!*[62] he writes to his mother. When she meets her son's fiancée at Menabilly in the summer of 1963, Daphne immediately feels reassured. Tall, blonde, serene, and charming, Olive is an instant hit with her future parents-in-law. She has never been to Cornwall before and is impressed by the house when she arrives at night, by the endless-seeming number of gates that must be opened and passed, the long driveway, and Sir Frederick and Lady Browning waiting for them on the threshold. Olive has read *Jamaica Inn* but still has no idea just how famous her fiancé's mother really is. The next morning, Olive discovers the garden, the path to the sea, and falls in love with Menabilly. She feels at ease with Daphne, who is cheerful and amusing and shares Kits's ironic, facetious sense of humour. The wedding is set for January 1964, in Dublin, Ireland. Daphne has a few concerns. Aren't they a little young to be getting married? Olive is Catholic and Irish, which seems an added complication, and Kits still does not have a secure job. But he is absolutely determined to marry his beauty queen, come what may.

In the run-up to the wedding, Daphne must deal with another crisis involving Tommy, who is still in thrall to alcohol. She tries to show herself patient and understanding, and Tommy, racked by guilt, confesses his drinking: he knows he shouldn't do it, but he can't help himself, it is beyond his control. And he is back in the downward spiral. This tension is eclipsed by the shock of President Kennedy's assassination, on November 22, 1963. Daphne and her husband sit in front of the television, too stunned to finish their dinner. *He was one of the few leaders for whom I had an enormous respect,* she writes to Oriel. *I can't tell you how it has moved me, and Moper too.*[63]

One December evening, Daphne waits for Tommy at Menabilly, glancing constantly at her watch. She has been worrying for hours now; her husband was supposed to return from a meeting with his army buddies, an event he had been dreading. The telephone rings, and as she picks up she has a bad feeling. It's the police. There has been an accident: Tommy lost control of his Alfa Romeo and two people were injured. Later, when he gets home, distraught and ashamed, escorted by a police officer, Tommy admits that he drank a few whiskies for Dutch courage before the meeting, unaware of just what a bad mix alcohol makes with antidepressants. The victims are not seriously hurt, but Tommy feels humiliated by his arrest and the trial that follows. Two days before Christmas, accompanied by Tessa, he appears in front of the judge at Truro and is found guilty of drunk driving. He must pay a fine of fifty pounds, as well as the victims' medical bills, and his driving licence is confiscated for six months. Mortified, Tommy hides out at home, refusing all invitations and giving up all his club memberships. He admits to his wife that the thought of going to their son's wedding frightens him more than the idea of returning to the Battle of the Somme in 1914 did. Daphne manages to reason with him, and they are both thrilled by the warm, spontaneous wedding celebration. Daphne tells Oriel all about it in a letter: *It was much more fun than the girls' weddings. I thought I might feel* triste,* *because of being so silly about Kits, but I didn't a scrap and felt thoroughly gay the whole time! The wedding itself was simple and nice, outside the crowds were incredible, like waiting for the Beatles, Olive being an ex Miss Ireland and on Irish TV, is of course well known.*[64] Even newspapers in America report on the wedding of the famous British novelist's son and an Irish beauty queen. At the reception, in Dublin's Gresham Hotel, Daphne and Tommy are swept away by the contagious good cheer of the other guests and the lusty renditions of traditional Irish songs.

After the excitement of the wedding, it is time to start writing again. Enough note-taking: she must dive into the book, her fifteenth novel. That figure amazes her. Fifteen, already? Urbino becomes her home away from home. She goes there every day in her imagination, while sitting in her hut. For hours, Daphne studies maps and postcards of the city. She knows this will almost certainly be the last novel she writes at Menabilly. At Easter, the young newlyweds come to spend a weekend with them and Daphne is blown away by the sight of her Kits as a husband, looking so happy. She is convinced he will make a wonderful father. Kits has never liked his wife's first name very much and thinks her middle name, Ursula, is even worse. During their honeymoon, he made fun of Olive with her curlers in her hair and her scarf tied over her forehead, giving her the appearance of having horns. According to Kits, she looks like Hacker, a delightful goat

---

* Sad.

in a children's TV series. So, no calling her Olive anymore. From now on, everyone names her Hacker, even Daphne and Tommy. Daphne makes good progress on the book: forty thousand words done already, a very good start. Daphne worries about inaccuracies regarding Urbino: *If ever it gets translated into Italian, I will be stoned,*[65] she writes to Oriel. Tommy seems better, but there remains a deep-lying sadness within him, which Oriel notices during a stay at "Mena." He has not touched a drop of alcohol since December and is devoting himself to finishing his new boat, *Yggy III.*

In June 1964, having practically finished her novel, Daphne, goes to Italy with Kits and Hacker and returns to Urbino. This is a happy trip, sunny and easygoing. She is relieved to discover that her descriptions of the city, which she nicknames Ruffano, were not inaccurate after all. The only source of vexation is her editor, Victor: that *ignorant old man*[66] has a tendency to consider her new novel a "thriller," whereas for her *The Flight of the Falcon* is much more than that. It is an Italian and political tragedy of two brothers turned enemies, separated for decades by the war, both persuaded that the other is dead, who see each other in Ruffano, their childhood home, amid conflict and blood. The story is told in the masculine voice of Eric Avon: it is one of the brothers who narrates the novel—Armino, the younger brother in the shadow of the older, more powerful and tortured brother who bears some resemblance to Svengali, Kicky's antihero. Their mother is a scandalous seductress defeated by cancer, reminiscent of the venomous Rebecca. Armino was hoping that, by returning to the city where he grew up, he would be able to rediscover his roots and find inner peace and was not expecting the climate of violence and terror that his brother, Aldo, has brought to this small university city haunted by an old, macabre legend. In this harsh allegorical novel that explores the destructive effects of excessive ambition, Daphne drew inspiration from the connections and invented rules of childhood. The book's publication is set for January 1965.

In the meantime, Daphne passes the summer peacefully at Menabilly, giving Oriel some advice on writing and spending time with her grandchildren. She adopts a new Westie, Morray, as a companion to the dog she already has, Bib. Tommy insists on visiting Kilmarth, the house offered them by the Rashleighs; it is near Polkerris, with a view of the bay. Daphne is forced to admit that it is a beautiful place, but—unlike her husband—she cannot see herself living here at all. Tod, still lively if somewhat deaf at eighty years old, has moved to London, an elegant apartment near Battersea Park. When the *Daily Express* suggests an article about her life as governess to the du Maurier children, Miss Waddell takes offence and replies that she has no intention of seeing her name displayed in the papers.

In September, Tommy's state of health suddenly deteriorates. During the summer, he'd suffered pain in his left foot, preventing him from enjoying his new boat, and he had been bedridden, in agony. In mid-September, Tommy is hospitalized in Plymouth; a blood clot is diagnosed, and he undergoes an operation. Ever since his glider accident in 1943, the flow of blood to his left leg has remained weak. After the operation, Daphne is alarmed by his waxy complexion and the fever that does not seem to diminish. He is still in pain, and the doctors explain to Daphne that the only solution is amputation. She firmly refuses. Her husband would never get over it. They must increase his morphine dose and pray that he gets used to the pain. When Tommy returns to "Mena," there is a wheelchair waiting for him. He reacts with great dignity and never complains. *He's very plucky. I help him dress and undress, he's not wandery or dopey, although awfully fatigued after bouts of pain,* she writes to Oriel. *I do get tired, but it's not the angry fatigue of the days when he drank, I have so much more sympathy now, and somehow it's less tiring. It's draining, yes, and I suffer every time I watch him suffer.*[67]

Tommy finds the strength to write a short note to Oriel in November 1964: *Thank you so much for the card and news, and was glad to hear you are having lovely weather. Here, thank goodness, it has been the mildest November ever, I should think, so I have been able to get out quite a lot in my electric chair. Apart from the old foot, Bing and I are flourishing, though the former had had a pretty trying time with a semi-invalid on her hands for three months. She has certainly been wonderful and very patient. We have got the whole outfit coming down for Christmas, which with my disabilities, will be a rather major operation, but still all very good fun.*[68]

Daphne's new novel is published in January 1965 by Gollancz and Doubleday. *The Flight of the Falcon* does not fare well with the critics. The *New Yorker* goes so far as to call it "this extraordinarily dull book." Daphne remains impervious to these articles. The novel vanishes without a trace, but she doesn't care because, in this gloomy January, all that matters to her is Tommy's health. Tessa, Flavia, and Kits, shocked by their father's condition at Christmas, had begged their mother to have him hospitalized again. This time, the doctors' verdict is irrevocable: Tommy's left foot must be amputated or he will lose his entire leg to gangrene. The operation takes place on January 14, 1965, in London. Tommy is sixty-eight.

While still recovering, Tommy is taken back to Menabilly by Daphne in early March. Two nurses have been hired to watch over him, Esther is at his beck and call, and his children are never far away. Daphne, exhausted, falls sick in turn, immobilized for two weeks by jaundice. Tommy catches bronchitis and grows weaker every day. *Why is it that a sudden doom descends on people in a flash?* she writes to Oriel. *I don't know when I shall be strong enough to cope. How I long for the spring.*[69]

Drained and emaciated, Daphne tries to gather what little energy she has in order to support Tommy, who is becoming ever sicklier now his bronchitis has turned into pneumonia. She manages to get out of bed and walk to his room, at the end of the corridor, to see him. Her handsome Boy is no more than a shadow of his former self, and tears spring to her eyes when she hears him speak. He is afraid of the coming night; he knows he won't sleep and he can't stand it anymore. She comforts him as best she can— tells him he'll fall asleep eventually—but she feels so fragile herself when she whispers these words to him. She knows, with infinite sadness, that Tommy will never be able to drive again, never go out in a boat again. Everything he liked doing best, everything he was so good at doing . . . it is all just a distant memory. She kisses him good night and leaves his room.

They wake her at dawn. Lady Browning must come immediately. It is still dark on this March morning when she grabs her bathrobe and follows the nurse down the long, red-carpeted corridor. She walks slowly, with dread in her heart. As soon as she sees her husband's face on the pillow, she knows.

Tommy is leaving them.

Part Five

Cornwall, 1969

Kilmarth

✦

I have exhausted Menabilly, I have squeezed it dry.
—Daphne du Maurier[1]

Kilmarth, Par
November 2013

D aphne du Maurier's last house is easier to reach than "Mena." It is not
hidden in the heart of a forest, but to the west of Menabilly, atop the
cliff that overlooks the little port of Polkerris and the bay of Par, by the
side of the road leading to the village of Twyardreath (pronounced *tower-
dreth*). Its name is Kilmarth, Cornish for "horses' ridge" or "Mark's retreat."
It is a manor house in grey slate, handsome and austere, protected by a high
gate.

Ned, one of Daphne's grandchildren, explained to me how much the
house had been altered and extended. It bears little resemblance to the
place he knew when he was a little boy, when his grandmother, Track, lived
there. Twenty years ago, the current owners, who are passionate gardeners,
had a swimming pool and a tennis court built there, as well as some water
pavilions that are now internationally renowned.

The new mistress of Kilmarth told me that living here is source of daily
happiness. Her friends even call the house the Kilmarth sanctuary. She
has not sensed Daphne's presence within these walls, but since she moved
there, twenty years before, one of her dachshunds never wanted to enter
Lady Browning's old bedroom. It was only when the floorboards were

covered with a carpet that the dog felt able to go into the room. Asked about this, Kits, Daphne's son, replied with his usual wit that it must be a dispute between the dachshund and the ghosts of his mother's Westies.

Kilmarth is the house on the water, turned towards the light and the open sea. The waves, omnipresent, seem to lap at the door, a constant reminder of the sea that Daphne loved so much and where she would swim every day, weather permitting. It was here, outside this manor house, that she took her daily walks, along cliffs thick with grass, gorse, and heather, followed by a trotting Westie. At Kilmarth, the house on the strand, Daphne communed with nature and the sea. The view over St. Austell Bay cannot have changed very much in the last twenty-five years. The brisk, salty wind blows the clouds through the sky, revealing the pale November sun. It is as if Daphne stood beside me, one of Tommy's old caps covering her white-haired head. I know she never missed a chance of bird-watching, that she could identify curlews, goldfinches, and yellowham-mers, that she used to watch out for cormorants and kingfishers. Climbing the steep slope that she nicknamed Thrombosis Hill, she would admire the trees, the Moorlands twisted by the power of the wind into the shapes of strange, disheveled witches, and the curious conifers with thorny branches, monkey puzzle trees, standing out proudly against the stormy sky.

My pilgrimage ends here.

July 1969. Leaving Menabilly. It has been four years since Tommy died, on March 14, 1965, four years during which she held on, four years of the Rashleighs' prevaricating. The agreement had been vague, imprecisely worded, and she took advantage of it: they couldn't demand she leave, she had just lost her husband, it would have been inhuman. But now, in June 1969, Daphne knows that she no longer has a choice. The renovation works at Kilmarth were finished long ago: everything is ready; the new house awaits her. The problem is that she cannot, does not want to, leave.

Over the past few weeks, most of the furniture has been moved, bit by bit, to Kilmarth, in the van belonging to her faithful handyman Mr. Pascoe. Daphne's children have helped her with this testing move, as have Esther, Oriel, and Tod, who is remarkably energetic for a woman in her eighties. But Daphne finds it impossible to choose a specific day for her departure; she cannot bear to say that *this* night will be her last at "Mena." While preparing to leave the nest, Daphne has spent hours in the large, empty living room, listening to the silence of the manor house, like a huge hollow shell, its walls containing the shadowy ghosts of her past. She saw herself again, forty years ago, a young girl fascinated by the abandoned mansion, face glued to the dusty windowpanes, then as a mother, triumphantly taking possession of the house in 1943, so proud and happy to be the mistress of Menabilly, the only one in her family to feel so bewitched by it; she thought of her marriage, weakened by the repercussions of the war and Tommy's painful return.

Daphne will never forget that gloomy March morning in 1965 when the nurse came to her room to fetch her. She had written so much about death, had constructed so many scenes in her books around it, but in that moment she found herself face-to-face with the dreadful reality of it, and it overwhelmed her. When she entered the room, Tommy had just enough strength to turn his face towards her. He was pale and barely recognizable, and at that very second death seized him. The last thing Tommy must have seen was his wife looking at him with her blue eyes. And then, panic. One of the nurses called the doctor, while the other one gave Tommy mouth-to-mouth resuscitation. Daphne tried, too, again and again, but she was aware, even while she was blowing between his cold lips, that it was no use, that Tommy's wide-open eyes, those beautiful green irises, had become glazed and lifeless. She held her dead husband in her arms and knew that her Boy was gone forever: the father of her three children, the man she had said "I do" to thirty-three years before, in the little chapel at Lanteglos. At last the doctor arrived, but it was too late. Daphne stood at the bedside, in silent horror, remembering her idiotic words of the night before, promising him he would fall asleep, and she wondered what would have happened if she'd stayed there all night to watch over him. Would it have changed anything? Might she have saved him? She should never have left him alone. She should never have gone to her own bed.

They'd had to call the children, right away, in spite of the early hour. Tessa had gone with her ten-year-old daughter to her new school in Berkshire: she was on the road, and Daphne had to leave a message for her with the headmistress. Daphne felt as if part of her brain was on automatic pilot, while the other part was numb, stunned. The automatic part asked the doctor to perform a postmortem to confirm the diagnosis of coronary thrombosis. The numb part, submerged by emotion, was already thinking about the obituary she would have to publish in the *Times*. She knew that Tommy wanted a simple, family-only ceremony, no mass, a cremation (which she would not attend), and no gifts or flowers—just donations to the Royal Air Force, his beloved "paras," his heroes, the glider pilots. On January 11, 1966, Daphne wrote to Mlle Verrier, the owner of the hotel Les Glycines, in Saint-Christophe-sur-le-Nais. She typed her letter in French. *Alas, I have had a terrible year. My dear husband died last March, after suffering with bronchitis and two operations. He suffered so much, and he was so brave. Now I am adjusting to my new circumstances, and my health is good. I am still here at Menabilly with the two dogs, who love me so faithfully. How is your little dog?*

Before leaving Menabilly for good, Daphne walked slowly through the empty rooms, stroked the bannister of the staircase with her hand. Everything had been packed up, but her life was still here: she could feel it, fluttering around, like a moth in search of the light. She remembered her final Christmas here, spent alone with Angela, her final birthday celebrated at "Mena" in May with Tod, Kits, and Hacker. She walked up the steps, caressed the walls, looked at her bedroom, where she once wrote with such frenzy and desire, where she dreamed, imagined, constructed imaginary worlds in her mind. In a distant future, perhaps one of Menabilly's inhabitants would pick up what she had left behind her there, those tiny particles of inspiration that clung to the walls like a secret magic spell.

Leaving "Mena." Walking out of the front door for the last time. Pretending that she was just going for a walk with her dogs on the beach, persuading herself that later she would return, whistling, and drink a cup of tea in the library while she read her mail or the newspaper. Closing the door, hearing its inimitable creak, feeling that thick, so-familiar handle in her palm. Not turning back, never turning back. Not looking at the façade, striding quickly away from those walls, within which she had spent twenty-six years of her life, those walls that had given birth to so many books, that had witnessed Tommy's last breath. It was here, she knew, that she had been happiest. To leave "Mena" . . . was to die, a little bit.

❧

How strange it is to think that this short driveway, this white gate, this square, unshaded house with its slate façade, is her home from now on. These few steps, this porch, these potted plants arranged by Tod, this entrance decorated with Tommy's bow and arrows and Gerald's baroque walking sticks, this really is where she lives now. The living room is to the right of the hallway, the dining room and library to the left. When all the doors are open, it gives the impression of being a long single orange-carpeted room, a bit like Menabilly, but more brightly lit. Daphne is proud of the neat, welcoming, modern kitchen, the domain of her dear Esther, given that her own culinary talents are still nonexistent. Last year, in October 1968, Esther lost her husband, Henry, to hepatitis, at only thirty-six, an event that upset Daphne, attached as she was to her able young housekeeper. Now Esther lives with her son in the neighbouring stables that have been converted into a cottage.

At Kilmarth, Daphne has had a separate wing renovated for her grandchildren, where they will be able to make as much noise as they like, unheard by their grandmother. In the large vaulted cellar, Daphne has created a small private room, a sort of personal chapel. She likes to go there, alone, to meditate. There is a rudimentary altar, a crucifix, some ecclesiastical relics, and each week Daphne puts out fresh roses. There is much work to be done in the garden: flowers to plant, brambles to remove. The hull of the *Yggy* is on the lawn and will be repainted next spring.

This is a big change for a sixty-two-year-old, and it is not easy to adapt. She misses her "routes"* and must find new ones. Daphne feels disorientated, wandering between the worn, old furniture from "Mena" that looks as lost as she is in this sunlit, brightly coloured décor, among these brand-new carpets and chintz curtains chosen by Tessa and Flavia. She likes to stroll around the lawn, the air full of butterflies, and watch the sun set from an old summer cabin built by her predecessors, including a lady from the previous century who apparently used to raise peacocks. But the place where she feels happiest is her bedroom, like the bow of a ship looking out on the sea through two large windows. Daphne has stood there every night, from her first evening, admiring "her" view, soothed by the immensity of blue spread out before her, by boats passing in the distance.

Daphne hears Esther making lunch downstairs, in the kitchen. What would she do without her? When Tommy died, Esther helped her reply to the hundreds of letters she received from all over the country. Maureen came to give a hand, too. The death of Lieutenant General Sir Frederick Browning was announced on the BBC, and there were numerous tributes. The queen and her husband sent a letter of condolence, as did General Eisenhower and Admiral Mountbatten. Messages of support came in a flood, from the Grenadier Guards, Tommy's former regiment, from the airborne troops that he founded, and from a mass of people unknown to Daphne who had been fond of her husband. She sees herself again, at "Mena," faced with these heaps of mail, simultaneously troubled and amazed by these expressions of sympathy. Some letters came as a surprise, like the one from Paddy Puxley, Christopher's wife, whom she had not seen since 1942, and an unexpectedly warm letter from Philip Rashleigh, heir to Menabilly. The only good news in that terribly sad spring, marked by the scattering of Tommy's ashes in the garden near her hut and some daffodils, a flower he loved, was the announcement that Hacker was pregnant. Now Frederick is nearly four, and his little brother, Robert, was born in 1967, another source of joy. Those little wheat-blond Brownings are Daphne's delight, and she was traumatized by the car accident they had last November near London, caused by a reckless driver, when their nanny was at the wheel. Thankfully, they all recovered.

Four years without Tommy already. But the next one, 1969, her fifth without him, will also be her first at Kilmarth. Perhaps the most difficult. She doesn't know yet. Her new guests will soon be here: Oriel is expected in a few days; she will sleep in the pink bedroom, in the four-poster bed that used to belong to Gerald. Tessa will come with her teenage children—Marie-Thérèse, known as Pooch, who is fourteen, and Paul, thirteen—but without her ex-husband: the divorce was finalized last year, in 1968. And then it will be Flavia's turn, accompanied by her ten-year-old son, Rupert, not forgetting the youngest grandchildren, Kits and Hacker's little blond boys. These guests will bring noise, life, animation, and goodness knows Daphne needs all of that.

At Kilmarth, when she goes for walks by the seaside, Daphne often thinks about the article she wrote on death and widowhood one year after Tommy passed away, which appeared in several newspapers and magazines, including the April 1966 issue of *Marie-France*. A few passages from it come to her mind as she walks. *I would say to those who mourn, and I can only speak from my own experience, look upon each day that comes as a challenge, a test of courage. The pain will come in waves, some days worse than others, for no apparent reason. Accept the pain. Do not suppress it. Never attempt to hide grief from yourself.*[2]

Tommy loved this house more than she did. He would have liked to grow old here, beside her, facing the sea. Daphne learned to tame her feelings of loneliness, helped by her daughters' tenderness and Kits's newfound maturity. Very quickly she decided she wanted to go forwards alone, not to depend on her children. But she remembers some difficult moments, when she looked through Tommy's belongings, his coat still hung on the chair, his hat in the entrance hall, his gloves, his walking stick, his sailing magazines. She found only one way to diminish her pain: taking possession of Tommy's things, touching them, appropriating them. She put on his shirts, sat at his desk, used his pens to reply to those letters of condolence. For a year, she wore nothing but black and white. But it was the evenings without Tommy that were the worst: she remembered the ritual of the herbal tea, the few lumps of sugar handed out to the dogs, the brief prayer that Tommy used to recite every night. She often found herself in tears, she who had so rarely cried in her life, even as a child.

When Daphne thinks about Tommy, as at this precise moment, the sun above Kilmarth shining in her eyes, the blue sea filling her field of vision, she likes to believe that he is content now, that he has found his parents again, his war buddies, that he is no longer suffering, that he is at peace.

⟡

And writing? All those people who, when her husband died in 1965, whispered their commiserations to her—*but you're not alone, you have your books*[3]—she felt like slapping them. As if she had a magic wand that would conjure up imaginary characters: the perfect antidote, or so they believed, to the desolation of grief. Before she could start writing again, she first had to get used to solitary life. Driving again, for example—she has a little red automatic DAF—gives her an extraordinary feeling of freedom. Thirty years since the last time she sat behind the wheel! Kits encouraged her to take driving lessons and she forced herself to go along with it, but once she got the hang of it again the adventure felt like a victory. She liked to visit Jeanne and Noël in Dartmoor, Angela at Ferryside, and to do the food shopping herself for the first time since her youth.

Menabilly seemed vast without her husband. Daphne accepted visitors, in order not to feel too alone. Ellen came in May, soon after Tommy's death. It was a joy to see her again, but Daphne couldn't help noticing that her once-beloved friend had become rather placid. And to think that this dignified seventy-something who now lived in Honolulu and politely sipped her Cointreau Blanc before dinner had, twenty years ago, been the dazzling centre of her universe! Mrs. Doubleday had really taken to the effervescent Esther, offering her a golden brooch set with a fragment of lava from Hawaii. Ellen felt sure that Daphne would be happy at Kilmarth, that she could turn it into a dream home. Daphne listened to her and took comfort in her words, but in truth, it was still too early to leave Menabilly. And too early to start writing again.

What a shock she got, in September 1965! Kits had taken some pictures of her, and then a professional photographer came from St. Ives for another session. When she saw the photographs, Daphne wrote to Oriel: *Poor Track looks just like an old peasant woman of ninety, far older and more wrinkled than Lady Vyvyan and I nearly cried when I saw them. I know I am lined, but I had not realized how badly!* Kits told her unceremoniously: *You must realize you do look a lot older than fifty-eight in real life.* And he was right. Was it Tommy's death that had aged her so suddenly? No, she had already noticed the wrinkles six years before, when she did the *Marie-France* photo shoot. *The only way to treat it is to think I'm a throwback to old glass-blowing provincial* aïeux,* *peasants wrinkled by forty and bent, in shawls, carrying pails of water to the cows!*[4]

Life after Tommy flowed along gently at Menabilly, in between visits from family and friends and the books she read. Daphne loved Simone de Beauvoir's *A Very Easy Death*, a sensitive book that reminded her of her own mother's passing away. She took her first post-Tommy trip in September 1965, visiting Venice with Jeanne. And she tasted happiness at the Hotel Monaco, in the company of her discreet, kindly sister. She was fascinated by the secret recesses of the Serenissima, the ballet of gondolas, and the palaces on the Grand Canal. But it seemed inconceivable that she could start writing another book, particularly after the poor sales figures of *The Flight of the Falcon,* which Victor told her had shifted barely twenty thousand copies. And now there was this new novelist everyone was talking about, a certain Mary Stewart, who was encroaching on her territory with novels full of dark suspense. Enough to discourage her from returning to work.

During the rainy Christmas of 1965, Daphne had an idea. Not really a novel, but a way of getting back into writing via an album conceived around her love of Cornwall. She would write texts illustrated by Kits's photographs (her son was now head of a small company they had founded together: Du

---

* Ancestors. (Daphne used the French word in her letter.)

Maurier Productions). The two of them had already worked on the script of a film commemorating the centenary of the Irish poet Yeats. After long negotiations, Daphne's publishers gave her the green light. This project allowed her to give free rein to her passion for Cornwall, describing how inspiration born on this rocky coastline had given birth to almost all her books. She also gave her (sometimes virulent) opinions on the negative effects of tourism, despoiling the beauty of the region's beaches, and her contempt for those who pollute the countryside with no respect for nature. In a letter to her Cornish writer friend Leo Walmsley, she wrote: *I get spasms all over when I walk down to Pridmouth, hoping for a quiet swim and find hordes of people playing transistors.*[5]

For three weeks, she and Kits roamed the region, going down to the Lizard peninsula in the south, following Mary Yellan's footsteps north through Bodmin Moor, not forgetting the excursions Daphne took with Tommy around the legend of Tristan and Iseult. In the evenings, they would sit by the fire at home, Kits with a beer, Daphne with a whisky, a map unfolded between them, to plan their next day's trip, and Daphne would tell Kits the tales and legends connected to each place. For her, this was the best possible way to get back in the saddle, in the company of the one person able to infect her with his love of life and make her laugh. Those day trips with Kits brought back childhood memories, a long-ago vacation at Mullion Cove when she was a little girl, a place that she found changed for the worse: packed beach, litter everywhere. She finished writing the book, a genuinely pleasurable experience, in August 1966, but Daphne suspected that it would be a long time before she would be able to write another novel.

As for Angela, she was publishing a book at that moment: her second autobiography, *Old Maids Remember,* and the few reviews she received were lenient. The *Western Mail* wrote: "Miss du Maurier has a strong personality and decided opinions. She enables us to answer her out loud, manages to spark a conversation instead of a monologue." Behind Angela's sparkling wit, though, lurked real emotion. *Daphne and I shared secrets and still do.* Daphne enjoyed reading these alphabetically ordered memoirs, with their superficial-seeming, lighthearted chapter titles: "A for Age," "B for Beauty," "H for Hotels," "J for Jealousy," "P for Parents," "S for Sisters," "T for Theatre," et cetera. *It is true I do not mind getting older. But I hate the word sixty.*[6]

❧

The summer storms at Kilmarth are even more spectacular than those at Menabilly. The wind howls around the house, the frothing waves smash against the cliffs, the thunder rocks the foundations, and lightning streaks over the raging sea. Daphne is not afraid: she has always loved seeing nature in the raw and stands at her window like a captain at the helm, her Westie at her feet.

On her bedside table lies the envelope she received this week, stamped with the royal seal. To her great surprise, Daphne was named Dame Commander by the queen for her services to literature, one of the highest British honours. On July 23, 1969, she is expected in London at a ceremony to receive her insignia from Elizabeth II. Family, friends, and readers applaud this consecration, but Daphne remains somewhat detached from it. First of all, that title, Dame, is laughable, and Dame Daphne even more so. Nico Llewelyn Davies, her cousin, admits to her that he almost choked on his boiled egg when he read the news in the paper, which makes her chuckle. Tommy and Gerald would have been so proud of her, as both Alec Guinness and Lord Mountbatten tell her in letters. Will she use this new title? Absolutely not. But, deep down, Daphne feels gratified. As she is by the critical welcome given to her latest novel, *The House on the Strand,* inspired by her new home, Kilmarth.

It all began in 1966, when Daphne visited the house with her architects to plan the renovation works. She was interested in the history of the old building that overlooked the sea and knew—through Mr. Thomas, of the Old Cornwall Society—that the foundations of Kilmarth dated back to the fourteenth century and that merchants used to live here in the Middle Ages, including a certain Roger Kylmerth, in 1327. She learned of the existence of an infamous old monastery located nearby, at Twyardreath, run by French monks of dubious morals. The memories held in those walls fascinated her, even if not quite so intensely as they had at Menabilly. The previous tenant was a fairly well-known professor, named Singer, and in the cellar where he carried out his scientific experiments, she found some macabre remains: animal embryos preserved in dusty jars, among them a calf with two heads and other oddities. The more she went to Kilmarth to oversee the renovations, the more strongly she scented a new novel intertwining past and present through this house, which, though it lacked Menabilly's magnetic mysteriousness, did intrigue her all the same. She didn't start work at once, though, preferring to let the book develop slowly in her head.

Tessa insisted on taking her mother on a trip in the spring of 1966, because Daphne had not left Menabilly since her vacation in Venice with Jeanne. They chose Greece, where Daphne had gone with her dear friend Clara Vyvyan in 1952. Tessa had to be patient and tender with her mother, because the thought of seeing so many people, so many strangers, on that boat panicked Daphne in advance, turning her back into the shy young girl she used to be. She feared she would quickly grow weary of people, but with Tessa's support—and aided by the fact that everyone aboard knew the famous novelist was among them but that her privacy must be respected— Daphne ended up enjoying herself. She met a couple she liked very much, Sir John and Lady Wolfenden, and even did some dancing, something she had not done for years and years. The highlights of the trip were the visits to places she had always wanted to see, such as Delos, and Daphne came home tanned and relaxed.

Some sad news awaited her at Menabilly in August 1966: the death of Fernande Yvon, at seventy-three. Ferdie had been at the American Hospital in Neuilly, near Paris, for months, bedridden with bouts of pleurisy and bronchitis. Tessa, who saw her regularly and felt a great affection for her, went to visit her the previous year. She had lost weight and her hair had turned grey. Ferdie had waited in vain for Daphne to pay her a visit; they had not seen each other in over a decade. At the announcement of her death, Daphne felt sad, but no more than that. It was as if Tommy's death had hardened her. She spent a few days thinking about Ferdie, her infatuation for her, the friendship that had lasted forty years. She remembered their complicity, their tenderness; she remembered Camposenea, La Bourboule, Trébeurden, "Les Chimères," but the page had been turned now. Fernande Yvon was gone from her life. When Daphne learned through the notaries in Mesnil-Saint-

Denis that she had inherited Mlle Yvon's furniture, Daphne gave it all to Tessa, in the name of the love that her eldest daughter had for France.

Another death marked Daphne's life with the same fleeting sadness—that of Victor Gollancz, on February 8, 1967, following a sudden illness. There too, a chapter ended after thirty-three years of her life. Her editor, though in many ways the architect of her huge success, had annoyed her in recent years, always insisting on flashy ways of publicizing her books, which she considered vulgar and detrimental to her literary reputation. All the same, she knew she was losing an important mentor and a loyal ally. She would never forget that letter, dated October 21, 1935, in which Victor wrote to her that he was *absolutely thrilled* by *Jamaica Inn*. Who could take the baton from Victor? Who would be able to understand her, this shy, complex novelist? Victor's daughter, Livia Gollancz, had taken over the reins of the publishing house after her father's death. It was she, in the summer of 1967, who published Daphne and Kits's book on Cornwall, a very personal work that, even though it had a print run of only seven thousand copies, was received favourably by press and readers alike, won over by this original hybrid of literature, travel, and history. Kits had decided, after this success, to make a film, financed by Du Maurier Productions, another chance to collaborate with his mother.

The House on the Strand was the last novel Daphne wrote at Menabilly, in her hut, between 1967 and 1968. It featured her future home, Kilmarth, probably in an attempt by her to come to terms with her new abode through the intermediary of writing. She threw herself into the book with the same appetite she had felt when writing *The Scapegoat,* ten years earlier. Again, it was her masculine alter ego, Eric Avon, who spoke in the first person, through Dick, a name she had already used in her second novel, *I'll Never Be Young Again.* As she admitted to Oriel, *I can think much better as an "I."*[7] At the start of the book, Dick Young, a biochemistry professor, moves alone into the Cornish home of his colleague the respected Magnus Lane, in order to carry out a few secret experiments as a voluntary guinea pig for a revolutionary new drug invented by his friend. The drug in question is an illegal substance that will allow its user to be transported into the past, the side effects of which remain unknown. During his first trial of the drug,

Dick finds himself in the Middle Ages. Is it a hallucination? Reality? Quickly addicted, Young cannot live without these spatio-temporal journeys that encroach on his everyday life. What he sees and understands of the fourteenth century takes on an outsized and disturbing importance in his mind.

While researching the book, Daphne went out to explore the pastures and farmland around Kilmarth in her little red car, armed with binoculars. *I am sure people think that I am a spy,* she wrote to Oriel. *It's so childish, really, and so like the games I used to play on Hampstead Heath, when I was a child!* On revient toujours à ses premiers amours.*[8]

Through studying maps and documents, Daphne realized how much the landscape had been transformed in recent centuries. The water level had varied, the courses of streams and rivers changed. To make her hero's wanderings plausible, she had to attain a perfect knowledge of the medieval topography and to call the villages and hamlets by their old names. Married to a stern, controlling American woman, Dick has trouble making her believe that he is simply working at Magnus's house. *He just can't stop,* Daphne explained to Oriel, *and his wife can't think what is the matter with him, and imagines he is drinking, or has some woman on the side.*[9]

Daphne made progress on her novel, feeling certain that what she was doing was genuinely original. Her research in the parish archives had provided her with precious documentation regarding families from the Middle Ages, with surnames that inspired her: the Champernounes, the Kylmerths, the Bodrugans, and the Carminowes. As she did with *The King's General,* Daphne merged history with fiction, with brilliant results. All the themes that most interested her were brought together here: psychology, scientific advances, the weight of history, and her grandfather Kicky's beloved "dreaming true." Sheila, her faithful editor, came to see her at Menabilly as Daphne was finishing the novel, in the early summer of 1968. Together, they visited the lands around Kilmarth, Daphne wearing her cap and holding her walking stick. Sheila was impressed by her vigour and the extent of her knowledge. The other unforgettable event of that summer was the famous ceremony in honour of Tommy, in Aldershot, Hampshire, by the Parachute Regiment. Daphne went, accompanied by Tessa, Kits, and Hacker.

---

* "We always return to our first loves."

Three parachutists landed precisely at Daphne's feet, and one of them presented her with a bronze statuette, of which she would remain very fond.

At the same time, Daphne was visited at "Mena" by her late editor's widow, Ruth Gollancz, a dignified and perceptive sixty-eight-year-old woman. The two women talked about grief. Daphne wrote to Oriel: *Ruth said she understood that thing of feeling out of things, she does find Victor's friends rather cliff* her. But she is nobly turning to new interests, and goes to lectures and classes, things she never did before, which is wise.*[10] Exactly what Daphne herself learned to do by leaving Menabilly.

᪐

Daphne at last gets her bearings at Kilmarth in August 1969. She described her handover to the Rashleighs in a letter to Oriel in April: *Philip Rashleigh and his mother came to lunch and I showed them all around Mena. Poor Philip, waine* and shaking with nerves, but the little mother rather sweet and frail. Very nice letter from them both afterwards. So it shows it is right to turn the other cheek.*[11] Now, however, passing the gates of "Mena" is like passing a gravestone, giving her a gloomy, oppressive feeling, and Daphne finds it a relief to get home to the light-filled welcome of Kilmarth.

The House on the Strand is published to great acclaim. *Good Housekeeping* magazine writes of Daphne: "She's a virtuoso, she can conjure up tragedy, horror, suspense, the ridiculous, the vain, the romantic." The *New York Times* goes even further: "*The House on the Strand* is prime du Maurier, she holds her characters close to reality, the past she creates is valid, and her skill in finessing the time shifts is enough to make one want to try a little of the brew himself." The English edition bears a cover illustration by Flavia Tower, which adds to Daphne's pride, and the book goes straight into the bestseller lists, another satisfaction.

From that first bright summer, Daphne has the impression that Kilmarth is embracing her, softly and compassionately. She begins to love this house. Will she be able to write here? And where will she write? There is no hut, and the little summer cabin will never be warm enough in winter. Difficult to find a spot where she will be able to sit and work when the urge returns. She doesn't think about this for the moment, however, welcoming her grandchildren in August and remarking ironically to Oriel that the "Zulus,"* the teenagers, do not know what to do with themselves. *They have their bikes here, there are plenty of buses at the top of the hill going to Fowey or Saint Austell, but all they ever do is lie on their beds and listen to pop music! A book is never opened, sailing bores them, walking bores them, so one is really rather defeated.*[12] In the late afternoon, once she is alone, Daphne reclines on an old blanket near the wall, at the bottom of the garden, towards the sea, and she is overcome by a feeling of peace and freedom. Watching a plane move across the blue sky, she feels completely happy for the first time in a long while.

She agrees to an interview in the English magazine *The Lady* and poses proudly in her new kitchen and in the garden. Each morning, she replies to all the letters she receives on her Adler typewriter. Esther helps her sometimes. Mail comes from all over the world, and Daphne reads and responds to each and every letter. Although she never does book signings or bookshop appearances, she enjoys this contact with her readers. Sometimes, her fans, as she calls them, come to Kilmarth to get a book signed. Esther opens the door to them, and Daphne signs the book inside the house, often without seeing them. It happened at "Mena," too: her bolder readers, ready to do anything to catch a glimpse of their favourite author, would regularly ring the doorbell. She smiles sometimes, thinking of how the Rashleighs must react, confronted with this flood of unexpected visitors bearing books.

While tidying up her papers after the move, Daphne comes across her private journal, that old black notebook she received as a Christmas present in 1920, and the others, all filled with her cramped handwriting. She takes the time to reread them. *So naïve,* she writes to Oriel, *and in the middle of it I had this awful thing for my cousin Geoffrey, aged thirty-six.*[13] All the same, reading this journal affects her much more than she admits. A lot of it is devoted to Fernande Yvon and those secret, intense moments they shared between 1925 and 1932. Daphne does not want her family, her friends, never mind her millions of readers, to find out about those pages. For now, she puts the journal away, promising herself she will find a solution to ensure it is not read by anyone for a long time to come.

The year 1970 begins. Daphne feels optimistic: *I like the sound of the 7 next to the 0.*[14] Tessa gets engaged to an elegant man in his forties with lively blue eyes, named David Montgomery, son of the famous "Monty," General Bernard Montgomery, an army comrade of Tommy's. Daphne finds him charming, if a little too chatty. Perhaps he is just trying to make a good impression on his future mother-in-law? Their wedding is set for the beginning of the year.

Daphne settles into her new "routes,"* with friends coming over for lunch, including the historian Alfred Leslie Rowse, a St. Austell neighbour. He has a soft spot for her, which provides her with a pleasant distraction. He invites her to his own house in return, but Daphne refuses to leave Kilmarth, prompting him to nickname her Madame Non-Non, a moniker that makes her laugh. She is as close as ever to her sisters and helps both of them financially. She talks to Angela, at Ferryside, every single day on the telephone. Jeanne she sees less often, but they remain in regular contact. She also watches over her aunt Billy, her mother's sister, who is aged and sick and has recently moved to the region. Daphne helps to find her a house and pays all her medical bills. Behind the wheel of her little red car, Daphne drives at such speeds that her son dubs her "the Niki Lauda of Cornwall." Her letters to Oriel retain their mordant wit, as with one recounting a morning she spent at the hairdresser's: *I tried on a curling, rather menacing* wig, and God, I looked such a fool! You see, it didn't go with one's age and it gave me quite a shock! And then, one of the girls came whisking through and saw me, and I felt such an ass. I bet she said to the others afterwards, "I saw Lady Browning trying on one of the wigs, I wonder if she wants to make herself look younger."*[15]

It rains constantly throughout January and February. When she is asked to contribute to an album celebrating Prince Philip's fiftieth birthday, Daphne agrees. Her text, "A Winter Afternoon, Kilmarth," describes a Cornish walk in terrible weather, with *massive clouds, driven by some demon force, reminding me of a rather too elaborate production of* Macbeth, before evoking her own outfit for braving the elements: *Dressed like Tolstoy in his declining years, fur cap with ear flaps, padded jerkin and rubber boots to the knee, I venture forth. Moray, my West Highland terrier, taking one look at the sky, backs swiftly into the porch, but brutally I urge him on.*[16]

Daphne enjoys writing a spirited, funny little essay like this, working on it for several days in a row. She portrays herself, facing the sea, watching the ships trapped in the bay by the raging storm, and tells how she lifted her arm, not in salute, but to protect her eyes from the hail. When she has finally battled through the gusting wind to reach her home, she is greeted by black, foul-smelling smoke. The fire in her hearth has died, and she must spend the rest of the evening wearing sunglasses to prevent her eyes from watering. Going up to her bedroom, followed by her dog, who is terrified by the screaming of the wind outside, Daphne senses that she is unlikely to have the most tranquil of nights. And indeed, as she starts to read the newspaper in bed, an ominous *drip . . . drip . . .* wets her pillow. *I look up to the ceiling, and perceive, all complacency gone, that a row of beads, like a very large rosary swinging from a nun's breast, is forming a chain immediately above my head and fast turning into bubbles.*[17] The only solution is to risk a hernia by dragging her bed over to a dry corner of the room, watched by the incredulous, half-asleep Moray. And all of this in front of the portrait of Tommy in his military beret, spryly smiling.

Daphne writes the text in the living room, as she has no separate office. Should she work here in the future? It's not ideal for writing a whole book, and the question is especially urgent as an idea has finally been "brewing"* within her since late March. She wants to write something set in Venice, which left a strong impression on her during her visit with Jeanne five years before. After the comic article, it is once again darkness that draws Daphne in—a terrible darkness to which she submits with rediscovered enthusiasm. *It's rather a nanny* story, very psychic,*[18] she tells Oriel. And so, sitting in the living room, looking out at sea, with a bouquet of dazzlingly yellow daffodils beside her, Daphne begins writing "Don't Look Now," the most terrifying short story she has ever written.

What keeps luring her into such black depths? The more morbid her work becomes, the more she pleasure she takes from it, just like when she was a young girl writing her first stories. With other people she puts on a show of carefree cheerfulness, smiling prettily, laughing infectiously, but in front of her typewriter she mines her inner darkness, the part of her that only ever comes out in her books. She has always made this choice, and she will stick to it. She would rather frighten her readers, give them the shivers, disturb their sleep, than produce something bland, easy, obvious, forgettable.

So she draws on the inspiration provided by the two old ladies in Menabilly's Southcott cottage, twenty years before, and turns them into sisters, strange witch-like women, one of whom is blind, with milky, horrifying eyes. She invents a couple who have been through a terrible tragedy, the loss of a young daughter to meningitis. And she sets the story in Venice, the hidden Venice, with its crumbling old façades, its damp cul-de-sacs, its black gondolas like coffins. John and Laura thought they could forget the cruel past by coming here, but a chance meeting with the sisters in a restaurant by the lagoon will plunge them into the worst of nightmares. The blind sister has psychic powers, and she manages to convince Laura that she "sees" their daughter. The story ends with a terrifying, spine-chilling climax.

And yet, while her mind is busy with the macabre and the violent, Daphne is also planning a trip to Crete with Kits and Hacker, set for just after her sixty-third birthday in May. She has time to go shopping, as she tells Oriel, for *a three-quarter length camel coat and a new shoulder-length bag* and to see an optician for a checkup: *Nothing wrong with my eyes, what a relief, didn't even need my glasses changing. It's so waine* going to the oculists, because they peer so closely into one's eyes, one dreads having bad breath.*[19]

The vacation in Crete is very welcome after a grey, rainy winter. In the fishing village of Agios Nikolaos, at the Minos Beach Hotel, she is recognized by two English fans—young Martyn and his aunt Bernice. The next day Daphne, Kits and Hacker go by boat to the island of Spinalonga. Back in Cornwall, she settles down to work again, imagining a short story set in the glorious sunny landscape that she has just left. The title: "Not After Midnight." Here again, the tale is rather dark, with a plot just as tragic as the one set in Venice. A lonely teacher, on vacation in Crete, is caught in the evil clutches of a shady American couple. The ambiguous denouement leaves her friends and her editor dissatisfied. Shouldn't she rework it? Doesn't matter: she is already working on another story, this time about a disastrous trip to Jerusalem made by a group of English tourists, where each one will face grim atonement. The most disturbing of her new stories is probably the one in which a young actress, after the sudden death of her father, is confronted with a particularly sordid truth. Tod, after reading this collection, exclaims: *My dear, I didn't like the first one at all,* most *unpleasant.*[20] Not that Daphne minds: she has once again successfully blended the subtle and the sinister, her trademark in the eyes of millions of readers.

On August 17, 1970, Kits and Hacker's third son is born—Edward, known as Ned. *I do love boys!*[21] Daphne admits to Oriel, and this joyous gaggle of lads—her grandsons, her godson Toby, and Esther's son—playing cricket on the lawn, begin to inspire her for a future book. Something amusing, for a change, a comic novel. Because it's true that Daphne is humorous in real life, even if many people don't realize it due to the horrifying nature of some of her books. Watching the boys make a racket, Daphne smiles, imagining a novel in the style of *The Parasites,* which she believes was widely misunderstood on its publication in 1949. She feels like taking that risk again, like changing her tune completely. She's had enough of readers who are still writing to her about *Rebecca,* thirty years after its publication. She wants to get rid of that damned Mrs. de Winter, once and for all, and let her take Maxim and his silly new wife and that horrible old Mrs. Danvers with her!

❧

Daphne chooses a large jumper with a pointed collar, in blue, her favourite colour. She went to the hairdresser yesterday, and her white hair looks glossy and perfectly styled. No foundation or lipstick, as she suspects the TV people will provide her with a makeup artist who will apply a cloud of powder to her face. She doesn't change her jewellery, wearing only her wedding ring, the blue-green cameo ring she wears on her right hand, a gold bracelet, and her watch. She is not going to transform herself into someone she's not, even if the BBC is coming to Kilmarth for the entire day to film the first TV interview of her career. She prefers to stay true to herself. The hook is the recent publication of her short stories, with another illustration by Flavia on the cover, which has been well received by critics and readers alike. In another coup for Daphne, the British film director Nicolas Roeg has bought the rights to "Don't Look Now." Donald Sutherland and Julie Christie have been given the principal roles and the film will be shot in Venice.

Esther has scoured the house from top to bottom, because Daphne has given the team the go-ahead, for the first time, to shoot the inside of her home. Kits encouraged his mother to agree to the interview, and she accepted, asking in return that the channel broadcasts Kits's film "Vanishing Cornwall", which had successfully run in London for six weeks. While she waits for the arrival of the journalist—Wilfred De'Ath, a young man of Kits's age, likable if rather pompous, whose finest hour was interviewing John Lennon, and with whom she already gave a radio interview a few years before—Daphne feels nervous, ill at ease. What a terrible idea, letting these strangers into her home. When she had been filmed at Menabilly, in the early forties, she had refused to let them inside. But now, she knows, everything is changing in the world of books. An author no longer sells on her name alone; she must be seen, her voice must be heard. How long ago it seems that she told her friend Foy that writers should be read but never seen or heard.

Daphne glances through the window and sees three cars arrive outside the gate. Thankfully, the weather is good, on this day in July 1971. Taking a deep breath, she goes out onto the front steps to greet Wilfred and his team, wondering why on earth there are so many of them. She must learn to forget the big man holding a camera on his shoulder, filming every movement she makes, as she shows them into the house, pointing out Gerald's walking sticks, Tommy's arrows, telling Wilfred, *I wanted it to look like Menabilly as much as possible.* In the living room, a glass of Dubonnet in hand, she tries to act naturally, to blot out the microphone, the lighting, and concentrate on the journalist's questions. *No, I'm not lonely, and the children are always ringing up. I'd be far lonelier if I had to live in London.* Her blue eyes are veiled with irony when Wilfred asks her if she thinks she will write many more books after the age of sixty-four, if she is not already past her peak. *Obviously, what one writes today isn't as fresh as it was when I was twenty, one goes through different phases, but I'm not aware of an awful decline or aching bones.* She will prove this a little later, when she leads Wilfred along the cliff top at an energetic trot with her Westie Moray. The young journalist lags behind and looks out of breath while she gambols lightly, walking stick in hand.

Every last nook and corner in Kilmarth is filmed: the staircase featuring the drawings of George du Maurier, Daphne's bedroom with "her" sea view, Tommy's teddy bears sitting on a shelf, the engravings of Mary Anne Clarke, her scandalous ancestor. The camera follows them into the little private chapel in the vaulted cellar of the old house, then into the archive room, where Daphne shows them the original manuscript of *Rebecca,* with its legendary opening sentence. Then Daphne is seen in front of her desk in the living room, face concentrated and unsmiling as she types, as if she were all alone in the world.

The interview seems to go on forever, but Daphne plays the game, remaining patient, replying with humour and kindness, occasionally bursting into laughter, lighting cigarette after cigarette. No one could imagine how it exhausts her to talk about her work, about her literary tastes from childhood (*Beatrix Potter, Stevenson, Katherine Mansfield, de Maupassant*), but also about her everyday life, her solitary dinner on a tray in front of the television, which she watches assiduously every night. Her voice remains melodious and gentle, not changing even when she deftly argues against the "romantic novelist" label the journalist applies to her. There is more laughter when he asks her if she is wounded by her lack of critical recognition: *It would be wonderful getting reviews saying you're Shakespeare, but I'm happy enough.* She remains guarded, even as she leans back on her cushions as if she's entertaining her best friends, one foot balanced nonchalantly on the sofa, cigarette stuck between her lips, like a sort of protection. She describes, with obvious awkwardness, her fascination for incest: *I don't mean bed incest, I mean this thing of sons looking for their mothers, daughters looking for their fathers. . . .* Her face relaxes when Wilfred asks her what job she would do now if she hadn't been a writer. Another exuberant burst of laughter. *Archaeologists, perhaps, digging, you see! If I'd had the brains, a doctor, or a chemist, to do with genetics, you see, family again.* Finally, they leave. It is time to savour a well-earned whisky, to collapse in front of the television, not to have to think about anything. Now she must wait for the show to be broadcast the following month, and Daphne knows that, when the moment comes, she will feel as if the whole of Great Britain is poking its nose into her bedroom.

For now, she is making good progress on a new, and very different, novel, with which she is rather pleased: the fantastical tale of an old, eccentric lady, inspired by Gladys Cooper—the du Maurier family's actress friend, to whom the book is dedicated—but also by Daphne herself. Mad (short for Madam) lives by the sea in a large house surrounded by a horde of adopted boys, bearing a startling resemblance not only to Barrie's Lost Boys but also to Daphne's own grandsons. She has given free rein to her inspiration, admitting to Oriel that she felt like *taking the mickey out of everything*,[22] her writing drifting into the realms of the absurd and the burlesque. The plot features England being unexpectedly invaded and annexed by the United States, then the fierce anti-American resistance born in the depths of this lost corner of Cornwall, led by the incorrigible grandmother and her tribe. It is a much more personal novel than it appears, and beneath the acerbic parody of a belligerent Peter Pan embodied by the indomitable Mad—whose clothes are a mix of Mao Tse-tung and Robin Hood—and Emma, her granddaughter, as a sensible, reasonable Wendy, the reader can sense Daphne's visceral attachment to Cornwall, shown in the real world by her joining the local independence movement, Mebyon Kernow, in 1969. Mad is an authentic du Maurier heroine: rebellious, audacious, in the lineage of Dona St. Columb and Honor Harris, only forty years older.

This is the first novel Daphne has written in her living room at Kilmarth. When the book, titled *Rule Britannia*, appears in January 1972, readers and critics are left baffled. What is du Maurier playing at? Her anti-Americanism appeared more discreetly through Stoll, the repulsive drunkard in "Not After Midnight," and Vita, the young scientist's persnickety wife in *The House on the Strand*, but why should she exhibit it so brazenly in this novel? Why has she suddenly turned so satirical, so political, so vulgar? The first word pronounced by Ben, the last adopted son, a little black boy three years old, is "Sh . . . sh . . . sh . . . shit!" In this dystopian novel, Daphne caricatures an England unwilling to become part of Europe, where prices soar and the government is so helpless and incompetent that it has to ally with the United States to form a new country, USUK, pronounced *you suck*, which doesn't leave much to the imagination regarding the author's standpoint on these fictional events. The reviews are awful, with *The Economist* reproaching Daphne for having isolated herself to the extent that she no longer has any idea what the modern world is like. The *Saturday Review of Arts* says it is "difficult to tell whether this novel is written with irony or genteel paranoia." One headline reads: "*Yankees Go Home*, Roars du Maurier." Her fans are disappointed, shocked, lost. Where has the magic of *Rebecca* and *My Cousin Rachel* gone?

Daphne accepts this negativity. Though widely misunderstood, this novel, *Rule Britannia*, enabled her to express her personal opinions. On the other hand, she is irritated by Tod's remark—*My dear, I don't like that character called Madam, she orders everyone about too much!*[23]—and by a letter from her friend Frank Price, who absolutely hates the book and tells her so in great detail: the plot is weak, the humour pale, the characters unconvincing, and the dialogue hollow. According to him, Daphne's editors did not have the courage to tell her just how bad the novel was. Moving on, Daphne enjoys a pleasant summer, swimming, walking, being with her family and friends. She meets Veronica Rashleigh, Philip's new wife, with whom she becomes friendly, and who allows her to walk around Menabilly whenever she likes. She goes on vacation in Dordogne for a few weeks with Kits and Hacker, her faithful travelling companions, her son behind the wheel, her daughter-in-law in the backseat, organizing the logistics of the trip. Daphne's only sadness that summer is not the poor reception given to *Rule Britannia,* which she is able to rise above, but the divorce of Flavia and Alastair, after fifteen years of marriage. Her trip to Provence comes as a breath of fresh air, *my old rusty French tripping from my tongue,*[24] and she tells Oriel about their stopover in Cap d'Ail at the sumptuous villa belonging to her old Camposenea friend Doodie, kitted out in a pink Chanel suit and high heels: *I doubt if she has ever worn trousers in her life!*[25] Doodie has become very posh and proper, serving them grilled fillets of trout, raspberries, and Vouvray wine. Later, Kits makes his mother laugh, as always, by saying that he thinks Doodie ought to organize orgies in her gloomy living room, with its décor straight from an Agatha Christie novel.

～❦～

She still has no ideas for a new novel. Daphne waits patiently, but nothing comes. She has to start work again before the start of winter, she must find something, make some progress. Another biography, perhaps? Maybe that would rehabilitate her after the unfavourable reaction to *Rule Britannia* the previous year, help win the critics back over to her side? Her last biography, on Branwell Brontë, came out twelve years ago, in 1960. Writing about another person would allow her to maintain her precious "routes,"* would give meaning to her life, keep her going. In a letter to Foy, she confesses: *One of the reasons I have a dog is that I have something to get up for, to take him walking.*[26] But, even more than her Westie, she knows that it is the prospect of a book to write that truly provides her days with a structure. Before, ideas used to come on their own; now, she must seek them out.

She starts to wonder about people whose lives would require her to embark on some long, fruitful research and ends up thinking about the Bacon brothers: Francis, the scientist and philosopher, born in London in 1561, and his elder and less illustrious sibling Anthony, born in 1558. Why the Bacons? Not much is known about their lives, certain aspects remain in the shadows, and this time, in contrast to the more psychological approach she attempted with Branwell Brontë, Daphne wants to build her book on solid research, in order to unearth new evidence and facts. Most pressingly, she must hire assistants who will meticulously search through all the documentation relating to the Bacon brothers at the London Library and Lambeth Place Library. Daphne closely examines everything she receives in the mail, dissecting the brothers' childhood, the deaths of their elder sisters, their relations with their demanding, erudite mother, their education at Cambridge. She is interested in Anthony, who spoke fluent French—*always menacing,* as she tells Oriel. Her assistants get their hands on documents that prove Anthony spent twelve years in France as a spy for the Elizabethan government. *I am now happily settled in for winter, surrounded by heavy-going books on Bacon and trying to make notes,*[27] she writes excitedly to Oriel in November 1972.

The following spring, while she continues to go through the discoveries concerning the Bacon brothers, Daphne invites Martyn Shallcross for lunch, the young man she met in Crete three years before, and with whom she has stayed in touch by mail. During the meal, served by Esther, the telephone rings several times. *I don't do personal appearances,* Daphne says into the receiver, rather irritably. *Why can't they get the vicar's wife or someone else, to open the fête?*[28] Now she has found the central theme of her book, Daphne gets down to work with a formidable energy that comes as a relief to her children and close friends. Her letters to Oriel testify to her fervour: *Surrounded with books from the London Library, and am getting more interested in Anthony than in Francis, even, and with secret spies in France.*[29] Her team of bloodhounds tracks down a significant family secret in the departmental archives of Tarn-et-Garonne. During the summer of 1586, Anthony Bacon was accused of sodomizing his young page, Isaac Burgades, and arrested in Montauban. In September 1586, Henri IV personally intervened, at the last minute, to save the young Englishman from execution—a story that never filtered back to England, his homeland, but which pursued him internally throughout his life. Daphne does not deny her subject's homosexuality but does refute the charges of cruelty and barbarism heaped on him. A shrewd observer of the world that surrounded him and an amateur poet, suffering with poor health and spiralling debts, Anthony remained one year longer in Montauban and Bordeaux, where he grew close to the philosopher Michel de Montaigne, before he was able to return to England. Another major breakthrough: Daphne's researchers succeed in locating, for the first time, Anthony Bacon's gravestone, in St. Olave's Church, on Hart Street, in London.

In early August 1973, Daphne receives a letter from her French publishers, Albin Michel. *Rule Britannia* is in the process of being translated—by Maurice-Bernard Endrèbe, who already translated *The House on the Strand*, following the death of Mme Butler in 1968. The translator would like to be given the references to various Wordsworth poems quoted by Daphne. It is Daphne herself who responds to this request on August 8, in French, cutting out the middleman of her French agent. *Thank you for your letter, and please excuse my poor French. Unfortunately, it will be quite difficult to find the exact verses of Wordsworth's poems, because I mixed them up, a few lines from one poem, a few from another. They are all taken from Miscellaneous Sonnets. My word! What a lot of work! You have my sympathies! P.S. In England and in the United States, no one seems to have understood that my novel* Rule Britannia *is FOR Great Britain's entry into Europe.*[30]

That same month, Daphne goes off in search of Anthony Bacon's traces in Aquitaine, along with Kits and Hacker. They go from Bordeaux to Agen, then to Montauban, up to the châteaux of the Loire, and, while in the region, pay a visit to Chérigny, where Kits takes a picture of his mother in front of the Le Maurier sign; Daphne particularly enjoys this part of her pilgrimage. Back at Kilmarth, Daphne gets down to work again, interrupting her flow of words only to attend a preview showing of Nicolas Roeg's version of "Don't Look Now" in London. For once, she is favourably impressed by the adaptation, which mirrors the intensity of her story, all the way to its dreadful climax in the confrontation of two worlds, the rational and the superstitious. The colour red recurs like an insidious refrain, and Venice is shown in its little-known autumnal aspect, sunk under rain and bereft of tourists, who all left with the warm sun.

When it is released, the film is a huge success, receiving rave reviews from critics. Daphne writes to Nicolas Roeg in October 1973: *Dear Mr Roeg, I must add my congratulations to the hundreds of letters and telephone calls you are surely receiving for the success of your film.* At the end of her note, she writes jokingly: *And please, one of these days, find another of my short stories to screen!*[31] The producers judged it prudent to show Daphne the American version, which did not include a torrid sex scene between Donald Sutherland and Julie Christie. *Kits says one sees EVERYTHING,* Daphne laments to Oriel. *A pity about the sexy bit, though, so unnecessary.*[32]

Winter arrives, bringing rain and grey skies, and Daphne's morale collapses. The writing of the biography does not give her the pleasure she was hoping for, and she is weakened by a bout of bronchitis. In 1974, she receives a copy of the book *A Bridge Too Far,* by Cornelius Ryan, a meticulous Irish journalist and author, known for his books on World War Two, *The Longest Day* and *The Last Battle*, published in 1959 and 1966 respectively. In 1967, two years after Tommy's death, Daphne had replied to the author's questions regarding Operation Market Garden. She had made clear that she knew nothing about that event at the time, that Tommy had barely mentioned it to her. She did say how badly affected her husband had been by the loss of his men. Reading the book, she notes that the author has quoted her accurately. What worries her most, however, is that a film of the book will be made by the British director Richard Attenborough. She, more than anyone, knows how far screenplays can diverge from the books they are based on. She writes to Attenborough, requesting that he send her the script when it is finished.

A series of deaths increases her sadness, beginning with the loss of Christopher Puxley to cancer, then, later in the year, of her aunt Billy, at ninety-three. When Daphne finally manages to finish her biography, Livia Gollancz informs her that it will not be published until September 1975, more than a year away. Daphne is perplexed. Does this mean that her publishers don't like the book? Otherwise, why delay its publication?

A grey summer does not help matters. It is too cold to go swimming. The only ray of light comes with the birth of Kits and Hacker's first daughter, Grace, in June 1974. Though she doesn't know exactly why, Daphne has the strange impression that this sadness is here to stay, that it won't be easy to get rid of. The du Maurier family's long black ribbon, which so affected Kicky and Gerald, is unfurling now between her fingers, wrapping itself around her wrists, as if to more fully imprison her.

༄༅

When her biography of the Bacon brothers, *Golden Lads,* is published in the autumn of 1975, the reviews are mostly favourable and only *Kirkus Reviews* judges the work "meandering" and "a shade dull." It doesn't sell much, but it does draw congratulations from Arthur Leslie Rowse, as well as some other well-known historians, impressed by the author's scrupulous research. Daphne now begins a new biography—of Francis Bacon alone, beginning after his brother Anthony's death in 1610. She believes there is still much to say about this man who was a writer, lawyer, philosopher, scientist, politician, and friend of William Shakespeare. Gollancz would have preferred a novel, and so would she, in truth, but fiction must wait a while longer. She has no ideas, no inspiration. Given that she still possesses all the documentation, it makes sense to continue writing about Francis, the younger brother, even if, deep down, the idea of this book does not really thrill her.

Every morning, Daphne replies to her letters before laboriously working on the Bacon biography. A fifteen-year-old reader named Julie, who dreams of being a writer, writes to her regularly. Daphne sends her a photograph of

Kilmarth, explaining how the house inspired her novel *The House on the Strand*, and wishing her good luck with her exams. In a following letter, she includes a signed photograph of herself on the beach at Par. She must also reply, and this is less amusing, to those irritating letters about *Rebecca*, which never seem to have stopped arriving, asking her to explain the ending and why she didn't give the second Mrs. de Winter a name. Even Agatha Christie, whom Daphne admires and with whom she exchanges a few letters, asks her this dreaded question.

The book about Francis Bacon, *The Winding Stair,* is published in January 1976. "Trivial pablum" is the brutal judgement of *Kirkus Reviews*, while the *Observer* is not much kinder. Thankfully, the *Sunday Times* reviews it positively, as does the *Yorkshire Post*. But this second biography does not have the power of the first one, and sales remain poor. Daphne suffers another humiliation when her French publisher, Albin Michel, suggests turning the two books into a single volume, a project that requires considerable cutting. Her German publisher wishes to condense the two books, too. This means the loss of more than a hundred pages, resulting in a book of 350 pages. Daphne has no choice. She writes to her agents to accept this proposal, but the cut pages leave her desolate.

It is in this gloomy context that Daphne starts dreaming up her next book. In 1977, the following year, she will turn seventy. Time for her to write her autobiography? Until now, she has always refused. But she is obsessed by her dearth of inspiration for another novel. What if *Rule Britannia* was her last work of fiction? She doesn't even dare think about it. Since *The House on the Strand*, the voice of Eric Avon has fallen silent. So often in the past, Daphne had relied on her masculine alter ego for inspiration. *I'm still passage-wandering re: work,*[33] she complains to Oriel. And so, as she has to write, she may as well write about her own life. To sate the appetite of the legion of Daphne du Maurier fans, Gollancz publishes a selection of her short stories, but none of them are new.

Writing about her life. What an idea! It is torture to dwell on her past, and Daphne doesn't know where to start. Wouldn't it be a terrible "tell-him"* to recount her life? What if she told it through the houses she had loved? She could begin with Cumberland Terrace, Cannon Hall, describe the inspiration she had drawn from Milton in her portrayal of Manderley, then Ferryside and Menabilly. She would talk about her first stories, how she wrote them, how she came to be published. Sheila, her editor, encourages her down this path, but Daphne is not convinced. Somehow, though, she sticks to her task during the icy winter that settles on Kilmarth, wrapped up in several jumpers, fur boots on her feet. She must look through her journal again, for the first time in six years. She does so with a certain amount of consternation, drawing on it for the construction of her account but toning down large parts of it. Now she knows what she must do with this journal: she will create an embargo on those pages; she'll talk to the husband of Tommy's former assistant, Bim Baker-Munton, about it, as he is in charge of her estate. There will be a fifty-year wait after her own death before anyone is allowed to read this private journal.

❦

In the spring of 1976, while she is still struggling over her memoirs, Daphne receives a first draft of the screenplay for *A Bridge Too Far* by Richard Attenborough. She is alarmed: just as she feared, Tommy is shown in an unflattering light, as a phlegmatic dandy bereft of charisma, who washes his hands of the consequences of the armed intervention. He will be played by Dirk Bogarde, an actor she considers unmanly and not at all like her late husband. The script takes liberties with the book, cutting out many of the key characters and leaving Tommy to take the blame for the carnage that resulted. Outraged, Daphne immediately calls Attenborough to voice her concerns. The director attempts to reassure her, but Daphne is not fooled. She waits anxiously for the film's release, scheduled for June 1977.

One morning in May 1976, she returns from the hairdresser's, turns on the radio and is shaken by the news she hears. Sir Carol Reed has died suddenly at his home in London. The day before, Daphne had written about him in her memoirs, describing their close relationship, their shared laughter and tenderness. She is stunned by this strange coincidence. Later, Kits tells her about the emotional ceremony at the church in Chelsea. Another death saddens her, too—that of her adored Westie, Moray. She even asks the doctor if it is normal for her to feel so devastated, even *gaga,* after the loss of her dog. In August, she spends several days with her sister Jeanne, in Dartmoor, and enjoys her intellectual discussions with Noël, Jeanne's poet partner. They cannot take their usual walks, however, because Britain has been hit by an unprecedented heat wave in that summer of 1976.

Daphne has made reasonable progress with her memoirs. Enough for her to think about taking a trip with Kits and Hacker to Scotland in October. *Well you never know, I might get inspired by old Scotch ancestors!*[34] she writes to Oriel. But, despite spending nine days in a wild, mountainous setting, between the Highlands and the lochs, the ruins of an old castle, inspiration does not come, as if the mechanism was somehow blocked. Back at Kilmarth, she is overcome by melancholy. It's those damned memoirs, Daphne feels sure. She's only written about a hundred pages, but it is such a struggle. To her mind, Angela's autobiography was so much better, full of humour and lucidity, whereas her own account seems dry, stiff, and grinds to a halt at the moment she marries Tommy. Impossible to go any further. She wrote about Geoffrey, of course, and about Fernande, too, but she didn't reveal everything. Her secrets remain secret. But the act of looking behind her, stirring up old memories, as her father did constantly, has tipped her over into depression. She cannot stop thinking about those distant reminiscences, about her childhood, her parents, her youth, all her friends who have passed away. She misses Tommy. Loneliness oppresses her. And winter only intensifies her torments, especially as she no longer has Moray to go for walks with her. Already she dreads the next year, when she will turn seventy. Her publishers want to organize a large party in May, to celebrate her birthday. She refuses: it's out of the question. However, she is going to have to agree to several interviews to publicize her autobiography in the spring of 1977. For the first time in her life, as her birthday draws closer, Daphne has a few health problems; her doctor diagnoses gallstones. She must follow a special diet, which makes her lose fifteen pounds, leaving her weak and sensitive to the cold. Even the arrival of two puppies, Mac and Kenzie, is not enough to put her back on an even keel.

It is in this fragile state that she submits once again to the arrival of a TV team at Kilmarth, though this time she is reassured by the fact that Kits is the director. The journalist, Cliff Michelmore, is someone she likes, a warm, well-known, and respected man. Kits is in charge of the choice of music, and he includes some of Daphne's favourite tunes, including Charles Trenet's "La Mer" and "Pavane pour une Infante Défunte" by Ravel. The show's title is *Let's Pretend: The Make-Believe World of Daphne du Maurier*. Supported by her son, Daphne forces herself to appear cheerful. She wears a pink woollen top and cardigan, a gold brooch, and beige trousers. She looks frail, in comparison with the 1971 interview, when she was full of energy, her figure rounder and her gait triumphant. But her voice remains lively. Kits begins the programme with her spirited voice, speaking over Charles Trenet's mellow singing as the screen shows the approach to Fowey from the sea. *I suppose I was born into a world of make-believe and imagination, I take after my father, Gerald, and my grandfather George. I was always pretending to be someone else and my father would say, "Don't take any notice; she's acting, she's always acting!"* Daphne sits in her living room for an hour and discusses her books, their film adaptations, and her youth. A few images show her at the helm of a little fishing boat in Fowey Bay. The tone of the conversation is light and pleasant. The only time her voice becomes firm, almost stern, is when she exclaims, *I am NOT a romantic novelist, and the only romantic novel I ever wrote, and I do admit it, was* Frenchman's Creek. She keeps smiling, albeit in a rather strained way, when her most famous novel is, inevitably, mentioned. *Apparently,* Rebecca *is the favourite of every reader of my books, I never knew quite why.* She stares wearily into space. *Rebecca, Rebecca,* always *Rebecca . . .*

Soon after this, Daphne agrees to an interview with a highly respected journalist from *The Guardian*, Alex Hamilton, a man in his forties who travels from London to Kilmarth in order to meet her. Over lunch, Hamilton notices that the novelist barely touches the delicious meal (*lamb, roast potatoes*) prepared by *pretty, dark-haired*[35] Esther, but that she has a second helping of lemon meringue. Her favourite object, placed on the dining room table, is the bronze statuette that the parachutists gave her in 1968, in memory of Tommy. Hamilton remarks that her voice seems younger than her appearance, and when she stands up to look after the dogs, he notes her lively, alert movements. She admits to him that she probably ought to stop calling her father Daddy, now that she is in her seventies. Why not simply Gerald?

The journalist brings up Daphne's two youthful crushes, as depicted in her memoirs: her cousin Geoffrey and the headmistress of her French boarding school, Fernande Yvon. Daphne visibly hesitates. What was her connection with Fernande? A little like a girl in search of a mother. She does not disapprove of physical relations between women, she is tolerant and always has been, but for her, it is merely a pale ersatz, a youthful pose. She admits she has never been a "sexy" person. Everything she repressed was used for writing her novels. Her most personal book? *The Parasites,* not one of her better-known novels. She was all three characters at once. Hamilton returns to the subject of her marriage: Was it difficult to reconcile her career as a writer with her husband's increasingly eminent positions? She smiles and says that when they first got married, Tommy would mock her excessive love for her family, that famous French blood of which she was always boasting. But he was proud of her novels, telling her each time, *I say, Duck, I'm on chapter fifteen, and it's really jolly good,* and yearning to give a good hiding to any journalists who gave her a bad review. There is only one thing she dreams about, she admits to Hamilton: being able to ask Tommy, up in heaven, if he found it unbearable, their marriage, with her writing in Fowey and him only there for the weekends, and *whether she'd bitched up his career. . . .*[36]

Daphne agrees to one last interview for BBC Radio 4's famous show *Desert Island Discs,* presented by Roy Plomley, where guests talk about their life through their favourite pieces of music. Plomley goes down to Kilmarth to record the show. Although Daphne's voice does not betray the fact, ringing out clear and self-confident and full of good humour, she finds it trying to reminisce about the music of her past. Each melody brings memories surging back, accompanied by a dreadful, gut-wrenching rush of nostalgia, as with the overture to the play of *Peter Pan,* which she cannot hear without tears welling in her eyes, without seeing her father on stage again. When Rachmaninoff's *Rhapsody on a Theme of Paganini* is played, it is Menabilly she sees, its mystery, its enchantment. Debussy's "Clair de Lune" brings to mind Christopher Puxley's long, slender fingers, while "Shall We Dance?" (from the musical comedy *The King and I*) conjures Gertie's pink crinoline. "Plaisir d'Amour" evokes Fernande's green eyes, and "You Were Meant for Me" (from *Broadway Melody*) the kisses of Carol Reed. *You're not writing anything at the moment?* asks Roy Plomley. *No, not at the moment, I'm too busy training my puppies.* Dame Daphne's laughter at this moment sounds a little forced.

Finally, the interviews are over. Daphne will never again talk about those memoirs, which she regrets writing. All they brought her was bitterness, and to make things worse, the book—titled *Growing Pains: The Shaping of a Writer*—is not well received by the press. "She is a far better novelist than journal-keeper," says the critic from *Kirkus Reviews.* Even her French publisher, Albin Michel, though generally keen on her recent works, refuses the book, after a negative reader's report written by Daphne's translator, Maurice-Bernard Endrèbe. *What a cruel disappointment,*[37] he writes to Mme Pasquier, assistant to Francis Esménard, who succeeded his father as the head of the publishing house. Daphne wonders if it has not been a fatal mistake, dipping her lips in the chalice of the past.

The phone call she receives, one morning in June 1977, from a journalist friend sends her into a fury. He attended a preview of Attenborough's film, and the Browning character played by Dirk Bogarde is disastrous for Tommy's reputation. In Cornelius Ryan's book, Tommy pronounced his famous phrase—that Arnhem would be *a bridge too far*—when giving his opinion to Montgomery during the first meeting to decide on the plan to seize the five bridges over the Rhine. But in the film, Dirk Bogarde speaks this line after the tragedy of Arnhem, with an insensitivity that Tommy's friends and colleagues consider despicable. When she read the script, Daphne had demanded, in her phone call to Attenborough, that he put this line back where it belonged chronologically, at the beginning. But her wishes had not been followed.

Indignant, Daphne writes to her friends in high places, asking them to boycott the film, which she refuses to see. She is not the only one to regret the cruel and unfair representation of her late husband. Other voices are raised, letters sent to the *Times,* and the controversy rages. Daphne herself writes in the *Times* on October 1977, and Brian Urquart, Tommy's former intelligence officer, writes to her personally to say how shocked he is at the appalling portrayal of Lieutenant General Browning in the film.

This film, which she would never watch, and the harm it does to her husband's reputation, becomes her obsession in late 1977. She can't stop brooding over it, and her friends and family are unable to reason with her or comfort her. After all those painful months turning back time to write her memoirs, this is the coup de grâce.

❧

Good morning, Lady Browning![38] Esther opens the door, then the curtains. It is an August morning in 1981 and the weather is beautiful. Daphne opens her eyes and sees the sunlight pouring into her bedroom. The smell of coffee fills the air. Esther goes downstairs, leaving her alone. For four years now, Daphne has been balanced precariously like a fragile tightrope walker, clinging to her "routes"* even though there is no book in the works. The typewriter remains silent: no more novels, and no letters either. It is Esther, now, who replies to Daphne's fan mail, with Daphne sometimes scrawling her signature or a few words at the foot of the page. She doesn't read much—a Jane Austen novel occasionally and the newspapers and magazines scattered all over the living room. It is the telephone that has become vital to her. The calls come at the same exact times, in accordance with Daphne's wishes. At nine in the morning, every day, Angela phones, from Ferryside. Oriel calls at 7:15 on Sunday evening. Each family member has his or her own time slot. These strict routines fill the void that her life has become since 1977. Her appetite has diminished, she has lost even more weight. She still takes the dogs for walks, but no longer with the same enthusiasm. Once a week, she tours the grounds of Menabilly. Her long winter evenings are filled by watching television. Nothing else.

She turned seventy-four in May. Nine years have passed since the publication of her last novel, *Rule Britannia*. Her mind is arid; not a single idea grows there. It is unbearable. Every writer's worst nightmare, the situation they all secretly fear, is now Daphne's reality. Daphne, who never lacked imagination; Daphne, who would lock herself in her hut with a novel all day long, as if the book were a lover, the very substance of her life. What remains of that secret passion, that fever? Hell. Her friends and family look at her compassionately, while other people watch with curiosity and pity. And all those imbeciles who try to give her ideas, as if that would help drag her from this pit! Even her friend Alfred Leslie Rowse has been at it, suggesting that she write a book about her dogs. Something seems to have died inside her. That flame that made her live, that urge which drove her on, it is gone. Forever.

Daphne stands in her room, looking out the window. Her breakfast, brought up by Esther, is still on her bed. Untouched. She should be outside with her dogs, enjoying the sunshine, the sea. But she no longer feels like it. She no longer feels like doing anything. On her bedside table are all those medications prescribed by her doctor, which she swallows obediently every day, those pills with their complicated names. The only one she can remember is Mogadon, the one that makes her sleep; the others are for her "nerves" or for her "melancholy." Since she started taking them, she has had dizzy spells, and she often has to lie down in the middle of the day. At night, even with Mogadon, it sometimes takes her a long time to fall asleep, and the waiting is unbearable.

A woman came to see her recently, a psychiatrist, a kind woman and a capable doctor, good at listening. But what could she do to help her regain her desire to write? And to think that, twenty years ago, Daphne had trotted out poems for her grandchildren, like those she wrote in a few minutes for Paul, a copy of which she recently found in a drawer.

> *Paul Zulu, an unlucky lad,*
> *Was sometimes happy, sometimes sad,*
> *He never knew—which made him vex't-*
> *What frightful thing would happen next.*
> *Chicken pox, jaundice, tonsils, 'flu,*
> *He had the Lot, and measles too.*
> *He swallowed pennies, burnt his bom,*
> *And fell into a goldfish pond.*
> *So many troubles, I declare,*
> *Would even make an angel swear.*[39]

Her grandchildren . . . She is only interested in the young ones now. The teenagers no longer amuse her.

What did she tell that psychiatrist? The two deaths that had deeply affected her: Frank Price in December 1977, just after the *Bridge Too Far* ordeal, and then her dear Ellen, in April 1978. And that trip to France in the autumn of 1979. It still makes her shudder now. Oriel had convinced Daphne to pay her a visit. As she packed her suitcase, Daphne had thought that her friend was right: it would do her good to go back to the country she loved so much, it would clear her mind. The journey she had to make terrified her, but she was too embarrassed to mention this to her friends and family, so she simply asked Oriel to pick her up at the airport. But when she landed at Roissy, her friend was not there. Panic took hold of her, and Daphne had to sit down, frightened, out of breath, heart pounding. A couple noticed her state of distress and offered to help her. Daphne was so upset, she couldn't speak. Her mouth was dry, she was close to fainting. At last Oriel appeared: the arrival boards had signalled the wrong gate, that was why she was late. It took Daphne a long time to calm down. The rest of her trip went well, however: Oriel took her to Chartres, Alençon, and Lisieux, in the footsteps of Saint Thérèse. She had regained her dark sense of humour and took obvious delight in speaking French. But behind the smiles, Oriel could tell, that tension never seemed to leave her.

And the death of her little red DAF, after fifteen years of good and loyal service . . . that had put her into such a state! No, Daphne did not want to hear anything about getting another vehicle. No matter how hard Kits tried to find one, the truth was that that model was no longer being made. In the end, she had to settle for a Mini Metro, which she considered unbearable. Just after this problem with the car, she had idiotically fallen down the stairs, last month, probably because her pills give her dizzy spells. She didn't break anything, but she spent three weeks in bed in the hospital at Fowey. When she came out, she felt numb, her limbs stiff, her morale low.

The sun shines in a cloudless sky, but Daphne doesn't see it. How can she survive, if she can no longer write? Her publisher brought out a new collection of short stories last year, but they were all old, things she wrote in her youth. They must have realized that she will never produce any more novels. She didn't tell them that, but they know. Livia Gollancz suggests publishing her notebook for *Rebecca*, the one she used during the trial, in 1947, as well as some articles Daphne wrote for the press, about ten years ago. She has to agree, for fear of running out of money, her biggest worry. She has given so much to the people around her: she helped her sister Jeanne buy her cottage, contributed to her grandchildren's school fees, and all three of her children have investments that she made on their behalf. What will she have left if she stops publishing books? So she says yes to Livia Gollancz. Are her readers fooled? Are they waiting for the new novel from the great Daphne du Maurier? The one that will never come?

Daphne watches the waves crash against the cliff. She opens the window, breathes in the salty sea air. That makes her feel better, for a few moments. But the pain returns, throbbing. A novelist who can no longer write is a being without life. One of the walking dead.

Daphne's gaze wanders over to the medications on her bedside table. In her last letter to Oriel, in January, she wrote, hypocritically: *Otherwise feel OK, and sleeping well, with Mogadon tablets.*[40]

It only takes a second. A few Mogadon pills in the hollow of her palm, which easily finds its way to her mouth. A mouthful of water, and it's over. She lies on the bed and waits. But instead of calming her, this action sends her into a panic. She feels like she's suffocating, gets to her feet, paces the room. She hears the front door bang, Esther's quick footsteps back from buying groceries. Daphne goes out to the top of the stairs, calls her housekeeper's name. She's done something stupid. They must call the doctor, right away. In her ears she hears the muffled thud of her heartbeat. Before her eyes, a thick fog blots out all light.

❦

Every evening, after her tea, she rolls the little rubber ball along the living room floor for her dogs. Again and again, she watches Mac and Kenzie rush over to bring it back to her. In the background, her favourite songs are playing on a tape made by Kits: "Stardust" by Nat King Cole, "How Loved You Are" by Peter Skellern, "Nice and Easy" by Frank Sinatra. The music does her good. Always those damned pills to take every morning, noon, and evening, and those damned nurses always there, watching her. She doesn't want to talk to them, has nothing to say to them. She hides behind her newspaper, turns the volume up on the television, pretends she's alone.

The fog is still there. It spreads around her, soft and oppressive. One night, she doesn't remember when, Esther invites a famous television presenter whom she likes, Val Doonican, to Kilmarth. He's passing through on his way to Fowey. Daphne never misses his appearances on TV. It makes her smile to see him in real life. Then she forgets. She forgets everything. Her memory is a jigsaw puzzle, with pieces missing. They vanished in the fog. It ate them, one by one, and slyly, it is now eating her, from inside. The only way to stop it, to defend herself against the encroaching fog, is to create new "routes."* Each morning she decides on her plan for the day, and sticks to it, come what may. Her schedule doesn't vary much. Every day, she goes for a walk on the beach at Par. On Mondays, she walks to Menabilly. The next day, she visits a neighbour, Mary Varcoe. On Saturdays, she goes to see Angela at Ferryside. All of this at the set time, accompanied by a nurse. If a TV programme finishes after 10:30, Daphne turns it off anyway. Who cares what happens next? Crosswords kill time, which is good. The sofa cushions have to be placed in a certain order. Often, Daphne gets angry. Nothing is going right. If her "routes"* are not respected by other people, if her meal is more than five minutes late, she screams, has a tantrum. Everything makes her furious. She is given more pills to calm her down, and the fog grows thicker. Sometimes she wants to fight against it. She hates it. It stops her remembering. It has destroyed everything, sucked it all up. But at other moments, she succumbs to the fog like a drug, so she can have peace, not have to speak anymore, not have to respond.

On good days, when Daphne feels in top form, she peppers Oriel with questions, eager to take control of her memories again. *Tell me, did I write Gone with the Wind, or was it someone else?*[41] Daphne notes down what she has forgotten on sheets of paper, trying desperately to remember. When she succeeds, a rare joy lights up her face. Her favourite moment, the only one that gives her any pleasure in these long, awful days, is the glass of whisky she is allowed each evening. No more cigarettes; she stopped smoking a while back. The fog lifts during that moment, her head feels less empty. She likes to evoke the past, little by little. One evening, Oriel asks her if she misses writing. Daphne shrugs, looking glum, and says that she doesn't miss anything anymore.

The only place where Daphne feels good is in her little basement chapel. She likes the smell of damp and mould down there. She kneels down, closes her eyes. God? Prayers? Not really, just the serenity of old walls, an unexplained and comforting mystic presence, as if someone is embracing her. Tenderness . . . it seems so long ago. She no longer knows how it feels. To give it, or to receive it. And love? Love is so distant. Passion, kisses, all that was in another life. When her family comes to visit her, it makes her happy, but not in the same, jolly way it used to. She remains taciturn in their company, leaves the table in the middle of a meal. Even Angela finds that conversations with Daphne lack liveliness now.

She approves of one of her nurses more than the others. Margaret. She enjoys conversations with her. With Margaret, she doesn't coldly order her to put another log on the fire or to make her bed. Margaret is from Yorkshire, and she is a fan of the Brontë sisters' novels. The fog has taken all Daphne's books, but not *Wuthering Heights,* which she is able to discuss in detail with the young nurse. One evening, after playing ball with the dogs, Margaret starts dancing to Nat King Cole's "A Nightingale Sang in Berkeley Square." Daphne admires her, astonished, then suddenly she gets to her feet, too, so thin and frail, and she begins to turn around, swept along by the music, a smile on her lips. She had forgotten what a pleasure it is to dance. She abandons herself to it now, happily, but a few days later she tells Margaret that she doesn't want to dance anymore. Ever.

The fog is voracious. It has gobbled up all her memories. Now it takes possession of time, stretching and condensing it at will, leaving her disorientated. The weeks and months blur together, as bland as one another.

Daphne abhors that blandness, but there is nothing she can do about it. The years slide past and she doesn't even see them, just wearily succumbs to the passing of time. Her dog Mac dies, and her sorrow deepens. With Esther, she goes to visit Tod, now ninety-five, in a nearby retirement home. Tod is thrilled to see her, but Daphne doesn't open her mouth. She stays only twenty minutes. Inside her, everything is turning dull. No matter how rigid the "routes"* that structure her days, Daphne is losing her taste for life. If this is what life is, she's had enough of it. No more appetite, no more urges, no more desire. No more books either, even if one last anthology of old short stories is published by Gollancz in July 1987. Her walks on the beach at Par grow shorter and shorter. For a long time, Daphne put on a brave face with Kits, managing to laugh with him, as she did before, but now, she can't pretend anymore. She's had enough of pretending. She wants the curtain to fall. She wants to bow out.

⁓❦⁓

Don't eat anymore. It's as simple as that. Hide her food without them knowing, in her napkin, in the pages of a book. Give bits of food to the dog, on the sly, all of this right under the noses of her nurses, Esther, her daughters. Chew it up, keep it in her mouth, then spit it back into her hand, into a handkerchief, into a cup, as soon as their backs are turned. No one suspects a thing. The fog has won. It encloses her in its impenetrable cloak, and Daphne can see nothing but that thick grey mist. The weight falls off her. She's just skin and bones now, wrapped up in layers because she is always cold. The nurses want to force-feed her, give her small snacks, but Daphne keeps her mouth firmly shut and shakes her head. They try to trick her, to threaten her: no more whisky for Lady Browning tonight if she doesn't finish her meal. But Daphne has made her secret decision. She will not eat anymore.

In the spring of 1989, aged eighty-one, Daphne stands on the bathroom scales and the nurses see that she weighs only eighty-four pounds. Her eyes have lost their sparkle; her smile has vanished. Does she know the effect she is having on her loved ones? Sometimes, from her bedroom, she will see Flavia's car, motionless on the path in front of Kilmarth's gates. Her daughter, hands gripping the wheel, petrified. What is she doing? Daphne doesn't realize that she is working up the courage to face the skeletal ghost that her mother has become. One morning, Margaret, the kind nurse, comes back. What is she doing there? Daphne does not know, either, that her friends and family called the nurse out of desperation, hoping that her presence would do some good to Lady Browning, whose emaciated appearance appalls everyone around her. Margaret does calm her down, but Daphne still won't eat.

On Sunday, April 16, Daphne asks Margaret to take her in the car to the beach at Pridmouth. This request comes as a surprise—Margaret knows how obsessive Daphne is about her rituals—but she obeys, in spite of the rain. Slowly, holding tightly to the young nurse's arm, wrapped up in a winter coat, Daphne walks down to the beach and looks out at sea for a long time, without a word, shivering in the cold wind and rain. She observes the waves, the remains of the *Romanie*, still there after fifty-nine years. Suddenly her voice rises up over the whisper of the waves, a remarkably strong voice coming from that feeble, fleshless body. She would like to go to Menabilly now, at once. Margaret can hardly believe it. On a Sunday? Menabilly is her Monday outing. But Lady Browning is so determined that she doesn't dare refuse her. Slowly, they walk back to the car, then Margaret drives along the long, winding driveway that leads to the manor house. Still leaning on Margaret's arm, Daphne walks across the lawn outside the house, then to the place where they scattered Tommy's ashes. Her face is impassive. Impossible to tell what she's thinking, what she's feeling. The rain has stopped and a ray of sunlight caresses the façade of "Mena." Margaret feels Daphne's hand trembling under her sleeve. Back at Kilmarth, Daphne does not speak again, except to make a phone call to Oriel, as she does every Sunday evening, at 7:15 pm precisely. The conversation lasts a little longer than usual, and Daphne's voice sounds assured, almost normal. When will Oriel come to see her? In ten days, her friend promises.

The next day, Monday April 17, there is another unexpected demand from Daphne: she wants to go see Angela at Ferryside, right away, whereas this is normally something she does on Saturdays. Margaret complies, troubled. The steep staircase at Ferryside is difficult to climb. Daphne takes it slowly, carefully, still with that same extreme determination. A kiss on her sister's cheek, a few words, and the visit is over. In the middle of the afternoon, Daphne calls Oriel again. Her friend is startled to hear from her. They have talked only on Sunday evenings for years now. Oriel asks her if everything is all right. *Yes, I just wanted to speak to you.* Oriel senses that something unprecedented is happening and tries to reassure her by repeating that she will be there soon. Daphne nods, then pronounces this strange phrase: *Are you writing? You must, it's the only way!* And before saying goodbye, Daphne whispers, *I went down to the chapel today, and I said a prayer for you.*[42]

On Tuesday April 18, around 10:00 pm, Daphne climbs slowly upstairs to her bedroom. Margaret helps her get ready for bed, then withdraws. Lying in her bed, Daphne closes her eyes, listens to the distant murmur of the sea, the sea she so often described in her books, and which is singing her to sleep now. The night stretches out in front of her, long and dreaded, despite the Mogadon that makes her feel sluggish. And yet she has done it, what she wanted to do, these past few days: she has said goodbye to the places she loved, to her dear sister. Eyes shut, Daphne sees herself again at "Mena," walking from room to room, and the woman who is reflected in the windows, in the mirrors, is herself at forty, the mistress of Menabilly, self-assured, swaggering, the writer who has inspired the whole world, who has sold millions of books, invisible but famous, the writer who will be eternal, because of one novel in particular. On Sunday, when Daphne went to the beach, in the drizzle, it was Rebecca she saw in front of her, black hair blowing in the wind, dressed in her trench coat, a handkerchief embroidered with the intertwined initials *R de W* stuffed in the bottom of her pocket, its fabric stained with red lipstick, perfumed by her azalea scent. When Daphne had gone in the car with Margaret up the long driveway to "Mena" it was once again Rebecca who opened the gates of Manderley to them, with that triumphant smile that Maxim, her husband, so feared. Rebecca is the one to blame for all those critics who haven't taken her seriously for the last fifty years, because she sold too many books, because they saw her as a storyteller rather than a writer. It is Rebecca's fault that she was labelled with all those adjectives she hated: "romantic," "Gothic," "sentimental." One would think they had never read any of her books, that they knew nothing about the darkness of her fictional world. But can she really hold it against that paper heroine who brought her so many readers, such glory? Perhaps the time has come for her to make her peace with Rebecca de Winter.

Through her closed eyelids, Daphne discerns the grounds of Menabilly in the spring, when the rhododendrons dazzle the surrounding greenery with their incandescence. The children are playing on the lawn, Tod is ringing the bell for lunch, and Tommy, at ease, cigarette between his lips, is looking up at the swallows flying above the treetops. It is good to see herself as a young woman again, beautiful, smiling, to feel the sunlight on her skin, to inhale the wooded smells of Menabilly's grounds. The dreamer is all-powerful; her gaze is a coloured kaleidoscope that snubs the present: that poor body stretched out on the sheets, that clinging fog that has been suffocating her for the last ten years. The long black ribbon comes loose, releasing her bound hands. The images rush past: her hut, her typewriter, her own fingers moving rapidly over the keys, the blank page filling with words. It is impossible to imprison a dreamer, because a dreamer can walk through walls, unlock doors, cast aside the weight of the years. The dreamer can do anything—Kicky whispered it to her. The dreamer is free.

Quotes upon the Death of
Daphne du Maurier

Dame Daphne du Maurier, author of *Rebecca* and *Jamaica Inn,* died in her sleep at her home in Cornwall, aged 81.

—*Daily Telegraph,* April 20, 1989

The death of a grand dame of popular literature.

—*Figaro,* April 20, 1989

The gentle romantic dies at the age of 81.

—*Daily Mail,* April 20, 1989

Rebecca is the profound and fascinating study of an obsessive personality, of sexual dominance, of human identity and the liberation of the hidden self.

—*The Independent,* April 21, 1989

Dame Daphne wrote 29 books, mainly historical romances.

—*Daily Telegraph,* April 20, 1989

Skilful purveyor of romance and melodrama.

—*The Times,* April 20, 1989

Read all over the world after the 1938 publication of *Rebecca,* whose enormous success (30 million copies!) put her in the same league as Agatha Christie and Barbara Cartland, the queens of, respectively, suspense and romance.

—*France-Soir,* April 20 1989

Daphne du Maurier, string of bestsellers.

—*Financial Times,* April 20, 1989

Daphne du Maurier, 81, Author of Many Gothic Romances, Dies

—*New York Times,* April 20, 1989

Daphne du Maurier did not understand why she was seen as a romantic novelist. (. . .) Her prose wasn't exactly purple, anyway. In fact, her prose didn't really matter. What mattered was her sense of adventure and atmosphere.

—*Libération,* April 20, 1989

Miss du Maurier for most of her life, fought an unsuccessful battle to keep her from being branded a Grand Dame of romance.

—*Los Angeles Times,* April 20, 1989

Acknowledgments

This book would never have been written had not Gérard de Cortanze suggested it to me, more than ten years ago. I would like to thank him for his obstinacy and his patience. My thanks to my French editor, Héloïse d'Ormesson, and to Francis Esménard, at Albin Michel. My thanks to Daphne du Maurier's three children, Tessa Montgomery, Flavia Leng, and Kits Browning. My thanks to Ned Browning, her grandson. For their feedback, I would like to thank Arnaud Guillon, Julia Harris-Voss, Sarah Hirsch, Nicolas Jolly, Didier Le Fur, Laure du Pavillon, Catherine Rambaud, Chantal Remy, and Stella de Rosnay.

On the tracks of Daphne in Meudon, Boulogne, and Neuilly, I would like to thank Julien Le Magueresse, from the Hauts-de-Seine Departmental Archives, and Stéphanie Le Toux, from the Archives Deparment in Meudon, as well as Thérèse-Marie Brachet, from the Documentation Centre of the Art and History Museum in Meudon. For their precious help concerning the genealogy of the Busson du Maurier family, my thanks to Anne Hall, Philippe Larus, Lionel and Monique Royer. My thanks to Xavier Lachazette for his works on the novelist. In Fowey, my thanks to Ann and David Willmore, from the Bookends bookstore, Lynn Goold, from the Daphne du Maurier Literary Centre, and Alex and Martin, from the Old Quay House Hotel. My thanks also to: Felicity Blunt, Bruno Corty, Claire Desserey, Laila Embelton, Emma Harding, Christine Faunch, Christianne Lim, Anouk Neuhoff, Géraldine Meignan, Esther Rowe, Audrey Siourd, Philippe de Spoelberch, Isabella Thomas-Varouxakis, Christiana and

Arnaud Troubetzkoy. A special thank-you to my translator, Sam Taylor, who worked on this edition in English. It's not easy translating a bilingual author and he handled it brilliantly. Thank you to my new UK publisher Clare Drysdale for her enthusiasm.

Last but not least, my thanks to Nicolas for his serenity during the writing of this book, even when I sprayed Daphne's perfume around (*Vent Vert* by Balmain) in an attempt to help bring her back to life. He now knows the du Maurier code as well as I do.

Glossary

The DuMaurier Code

list of code words

Brewing: thinking up a novel

Cairo: intercourse

Crumb: good, wonderful

Dago: effeminate

Doing a Miss Clarke: overdoing it

Gondal: the world of the imaginary

Hard chair: to be offended

Honky: vulgar

Menace: an attractive person

Nanny: scary

Pegs: inspirations for characters

Robert: menstruation

Routes: habits

Royal: well brought up

See-me: vain

Shilling: disappointment

Spinning: sexual preliminaries

Tell-him: boring

To cliff: to ignore

Venetian: lesbian

Waine: embarrassing

Wax: make love

Witherspoons: boring people

NICKNAMES

Bing, Track, or Tray: Daphne du Maurier

Bird: Jeanne du Maurier

Ferdie: Fernande Yvon

Hacker: Olive Browning

Kicky: George du Maurier

Kits: Christian Browning

Lady Mo: Muriel du Maurier

Mena: Menabilly

Moper: Tommy Boy Browning

Piffy: Angela du Maurier

The Zulus: the children of Tessa and her first husband, Peter de Zulueta

NOTES

EPIGRAPH

1. Daphne du Maurier, *Myself When Young: The Shaping of a Writer* (London: Virago Modern Classics, 2004), 144.

PART ONE

1. Daphne du Maurier, *Myself When Young: The Shaping of a Writer* (London: Virago Modern Classics, 2004), 64.

2. Margaret Forster, *Daphne du Maurier,* (London: Chatto & Windus, 1993), 16.

3. Daphne du Maurier, *Gerald: A Portrait* (London: Virago Modern Classics, 2004), 108.

4. du Maurier, *Myself When Young,* 51.

5. Ibid., 52.

6. Ibid., 62.

7. Daphne du Maurier, *The Rebecca Notebooks and Other Memories* (London: Virago Modern Classics, 2005), 80–81.

8. du Maurier, *Myself When Young,* 17.

PART TWO

1. Daphne du Maurier, *Myself When Young: The Shaping of a Writer* (London: Virago Modern Classics, 2004), 140.

2. Margaret Forster, *Daphne du Maurier* (London: Chatto & Windus, 1993), 27.

3. du Maurier, *Myself When Young,* 85.

4. Ibid., 82.

5. Ibid., 86–87.

6. Ibid., 95–96.

7. Ibid., 100.

8. Ibid., 99.

PART THREE

1. Daphne du Maurier, *Myself When Young: The Shaping of a Writer* (London: Virago Modern Classics, 2004), 103.

2. Ibid., 110.

3. Ibid., 116.

4. Ibid., 117.

5. Ibid., 121.

6. Ibid., 130.

7. Ibid., 131.

8. Ibid., 135.

9. Angela du Maurier, *It's Only the Sister* (London: Peter Davies, 1951), 141.

10. du Maurier, *Myself When Young,* 142.

11. Ibid., 147.

12. Ibid., 149.

13. Ibid.

14. Ibid., 150.

15. Ibid., 159–60.

16. Ibid., 163.

17. Ibid., 186–87.

18. Ibid., 191.

19. Ibid., 192.

20. Ibid., 193.

21. Ibid.

22. Ibid., 194.

23. Ibid., 195.

24. Helen Taylor (ed.), *The Daphne du Maurier Companion* (London: Virago Press, 2007), 36–37.

25. Margaret Forster, *Daphne du Maurier* (London: Chatto & Windus, 1993), 105.

26. Ibid., 126.

27. du Maurier, *It's Only the Sister,* 196.

28. Daphne du Maurier, *The Rebecca Notebooks and Other Memories* (London: Virago Modern Classics, 2005), 5.

29. Forster, *Daphne du Maurier,* 135.

30. Ibid.

31. Ibid., 139.

32. Padraic Flanagan, "Interview of Kits Browning," *The Daily Telegraph,* April 15, 2014.

33. Forster, *Daphne du Maurier*, 145.

34. Ibid., 144.

35. du Maurier, *It's Only the Sister*, 208–9.

36. Ibid., 209–10.

37. Letter from Robert Esménard, IMEC (Institut de la Mémoire de l'Edition Contemporaine, France).

38. Forster, *Daphne du Maurier*, 147.

39. du Maurier, *It's Only the Sister*, 215–16.

40. Ibid., 217–18.

41. Ibid., 222–23.

42. Forster, *Daphne du Maurier*, 162.

PART FOUR

1. Margaret Forster, *Daphne du Maurier* (London: Chatto & Windus, 1993), 188.

2. Flavia Leng, *Daphne du Maurier: A Daughter's Memoir* (London: Mainstream, 2007), 60.

3. Letters from Tommy to Daphne, private collection, Tessa Montgomery.

4. Forster, *Daphne du Maurier*, 393.

5. Letter from Robert Esménard, IMEC (Institut de la Mémoire de l'Edition Contemporaine, France).

6. Leng, *Daphne du Maurier*, 79.

7. Forster, *Daphne du Maurier*, 194.

8. Angela du Maurier, *It's Only the Sister* (London: Peter Davies, 1951), 96.

9. Leng, *Daphne du Maurier*, 96.

10. Ibid., 121.

11. Forster, *Daphne du Maurier,* 221.

12. Ibid., 222.

13. Ibid., 223.

14. Leng, *Daphne du Maurier,* 148.

15. Ibid., 150.

16. Ibid.

17. Ibid., 151.

18. Forster, *Daphne du Maurier,* 234.

19. Ibid., 230.

20. Martyn Shallcross, *The Private World of Daphne du Maurier* (London: Robson Books, 1998), 136.

21. Leng, *Daphne du Maurier,* 166.

22. Letter from Tessa to Daphne, private collection, Tessa Montgomery.

23. Forster, *Daphne du Maurier,* 252.

24. Leng, *Daphne du Maurier,* 187.

25. Ibid., 188.

26. Ibid.

27. Letter from Tessa to Daphne, private collection, Tessa Montgomery.

28. Oriel Malet, *Letters from Menabilly* (London: Orion Books, 1993), 3.

29. Ibid., 20.

30. Ibid., 29.

31. Forster, *Daphne du Maurier*, 262.

32. Details of Albin Michel translation, IMEC (Institut de la Mémoire de l'Edition Contemporaine, France).

33. Malet, *Letters from Menabilly*, 29.

34. Ibid., 36.

35. Ibid., 36.

36. Forster, *Daphne du Maurier*, 272.

37. Malet, *Letters from Menabilly*, 39.

38. Ibid., 33.

39. Forster, *Daphne du Maurier*, 272.

40. Ibid., 274.

41. Letter from Michel Hoffman, 1954, IMEC (Institut de la Mémoire de l'Edition Contemporaine, France).

42. Forster, *Daphne du Maurier*, 283.

43. Malet, *Letters from Menabilly*, 68.

44. Ibid., 75.

45. Letter from Michel Hoffman, IMEC (Institut de la Mémoire de l'Edition Contemporaine, France).

46. Forster, *Daphne du Maurier*, 420–21.

47. Ibid., 424.

48. Malet, *Letters from Menabilly*, 100.

49. Ibid., 99–100.

50. Ibid., 102.

51. Ibid., 106.

52. Forster, *Daphne du Maurier,* 303.

53. Malet, *Letters from Menabilly,* 117.

54. Ibid., 118.

55. Forster, *Daphne du Maurier,* 308.

56. Malet, *Letters from Menabilly,* 128–29.

57. Ibid., 131.

58. Anne Hall, *Au pays des souffleurs de verre* (Vendôme: Editions du Cherche-Lune, 2010), 170.

59. Malet, *Letters from Menabilly,* 136.

60. Ibid., 136.

61. Ibid., 138.

62. Ibid., 142.

63. Ibid., 164.

64. Ibid., 166.

65. Ibid., 173

66. Ibid., 176.

67. Ibid., 181.

68. Ibid., 183.

69. Ibid., 184.

PART FIVE

1. Margaret Forster, *Daphne du Maurier* (London: Chatto & Windus, 1993), 318.

2. Daphne du Maurier, *The Rebecca Notebooks and Other Memories* (London: Virago Modern Classics, 2005), 130.

3. Oriel Malet, *Letters from Menabilly* (London: Orion Books, 1993), 185.

4. Ibid., 194.

5. Hilary Macaskill, *Daphne du Maurier at Home* (London: Frances Lincoln, 2013), 114.

6. Angela du Maurier, *Old Maids Remember* (London: Peter Davies, 1966), 157, 1.

7. Malet, *Letters from Menabilly*, 219.

8. Ibid., 214.

9. Ibid., 215.

10. Ibid., 224.

11. Ibid., 229.

12. Ibid., 233.

13. Ibid., 234.

14. Ibid., 237.

15. Ibid., 239.

16. Daphne du Maurier, *The Rebecca Notebooks and Other Memories,* 152–53.

17. Ibid., 164–65.

18. Malet, *Letters from Menabilly*, 243.

19. Ibid., 244.

20. Ibid., 257.

21. Ibid., 244.

22. Forster, *Daphne du Maurier*, 382.

23. Malet, *Letters from Menabilly*, 261.

24. Ibid., 260.

25. Ibid.

26. Forster, *Daphne du Maurier,* 386.

27. Malet, *Letters from Menabilly,* 262.

28. Martyn Shallcross, *The Private World of Daphne du Maurier* (London: Robson Books, 1998), 11.

29. Malet, *Letters from Menabilly,* 262.

30. Letter from Daphne du Maurier to her French publisher Albin Michel, IMEC (Institut de la Mémoire de l'Edition Contemporaine, France).

31. Shallcross, *The Private World of Daphne du Maurier,* 179–80.

32. Malet, *Letters from Menabilly,* 266, 269.

33. Ibid., 277.

34. Ibid., 282.

35. Alex Hamilton, *Writing Talk,* (Leicestershire: Matador, 2012), 152.

36. Ibid., 156.

37. Report by Maurice-Bernard Endrèbe to Albin Michel, IMEC (Institut de la Mémoire de l'Edition Contemporaine, France).

38. Interview with Esther Rowe, November 2014.

39. Private collection, Tessa Montgomery.

40. Malet, *Letters from Menabilly,* 292.

41. Ibid., 293.

42. Ibid., 295.

Sources

My sources are Daphne du Maurier's memoirs, her correspondence, and her author file at the IMEC (the French Institute for Contemporary Publishing Archives).

Her sister Angela du Maurier's memoirs were indispensable to me, as were her daughter Flavia Leng's, as well as all three works by her biographers, Margaret Forster, Jane Dunn, and Judith Cook.

Auerbach, Nina. *Daphne du Maurier, Haunted Heiress.* Philadelphia: University of Pennsylvania, 2000.

Birkin, Andrew. *J. M. Barrie and the Lost Boys.* London: Constable, 1979.

Cook, Judith. *Daphne: A Portrait of Daphne du Maurier.* London: Corgi, 1992.

Doe, Helen. *From Facts to Fiction: The Men and Women of Polruan Who Inspired Daphne du Maurier's First Novel.* Oxon: Parchement (Banbury), 1997.

Dudgeon, Piers. *Captivated.* London: Vintage, 2009.

Du Maurier, Angela. *It's Only the Sister.* London: Peter Davies, 1951.

———. *Old Maids Remember.* London: Peter Davies, 1966.

Du Maurier, Daphne. *Enchanted Cornwall.* London: Penguin Books, 1981.

———. *Myself When Young: The Shaping of a Writer.* London: Victor Gollancz, 1977.

———. *The Rebecca Notebook and Other Memories.* London: Victor Gollancz, 1981.

Dunn, Jane. *Daphne du Maurier and Her Sisters: The hidden lives of Piffy, Bird and Bing.* London: Harper Press, 2013.

Forster, Margaret. *Daphne du Maurier.* London: Chatto and Windus, 1993.

Hall, Anne. *Au pays des souffleurs de verre.* Vendôme: Éditions du Cherche-Lune, 2010.

Hamilton, Alex. *Writing Talk.* Kibworth: Matador, 2012. (See p. 151 in particular.)

Harris, Martin. *The Official Guide to Daphne du Maurier in Cornwall.* Paignton: Creative Media, 2011.

Hawthorne, Bret. *Daphne du Maurier's Cornwall.* Wellington: Halsgrove, 2010.

Kelly, Richard. *Daphne du Maurier.* Boston: Twayne, 1987.

Lachazette, Xavier. *Toit et moi, les maisons réelles ou rêvées de Daphné du Maurier.* Le Mans: Université du Maine, 2009.

Leng, Flavia. *Daphne du Maurier: A Daughter's Memoir.* Edinburgh: Mainstream, 1994.

Macaskill, Hilary. *Daphne du Maurier at Home.* London: Frances Lincoln, 2013.

Malet, Oriel. *Jam Today, Two Girls in Paris.* London: Victor Gollancz, 1957.
———. *Letters from Menabilly.* London: Weidenfeld and Nicholson, 1993.

Mead, Richard. *General "Boy": The Life of Lieutenant General Sir Frederick Browning.* Barnsley: Pen and Sword, 2011.

Picardie, Justine. *Daphne.* London: Bloomsbury, 2008.

Robert, Pierre. *L'Ascendance française de Daphné du Maurier.* Tours: Centre généalogique de Touraine, 1993.

Royer, Lionel, and Anne Hall. *L'Ascendance française et anglaise de Daphné du Maurier,* Saint–Christophe-sur-le-Nais: Histoire et Patrimoine conference, September 28, 2007.

Shallcross, Martyn. *The Private World of Daphne du Maurier.* London: Robson Books, 1991.

Taylor, Helen (ed.). *The Daphne du Maurier Companion.* London: Virago Press, 2007.

Welch, Noël. *A Personal View.* Axminster: Samphire Books, 2012.

Williams, Michael. *The Three du Maurier Sisters.* Clifton-upon-Teme: Polperro Heritage Press, 2012.

Works by Daphne du Maurier

The Loving Spirit, novel (London: Heinemann, 1931)

I'll Never Be Young Again, novel (London: Heinemann, 1932)

The Progress of Julius, novel (London: Heinemann, 1933)

Gerald: A Portrait, nonfiction (London: Gollancz, 1934)

Jamaica Inn, novel (London: Gollancz, 1936)

The du Mauriers, nonfiction (London: Gollancz, 1937)

Rebecca, novel (London: Gollancz, 1938)

Come Wind, Come Weather, short stories (London: Heinemann, 1940)

Frenchman's Creek, novel (London: Gollancz, 1941)

Hungry Hill, novel (London: Gollancz, 1943)

The Years Between, play (London: Gollancz, 1945)

The King's General, novel (London: Gollancz, 1946)

September Tide, play (London: Gollancz, 1949)

The Parasites, novel (London: Gollancz, 1949)

My Cousin Rachel, novel (London: Gollancz, 1951

The Birds and Other Stories, short stories (London: Gollancz, 1952)

Mary Anne, novel (London: Gollancz, 1954)

The Scapegoat, novel (London: Gollancz, 1957)

The Breaking Point, short stories (London: Gollancz, 1959)

The Infernal World of Branwell Brontë, biography (London: Gollancz, 1960)

Castle Dor (with A. Quiller-Couch), novel (London: J. M. Dent, 1962)

The Glass-Blowers, novel (London: Gollancz, 1963)

The Flight of the Falcon, novel (London: Gollancz, 1965)

Vanishing Cornwall (London: Gollancz, 1967)

The House on the Strand, novel (London: Gollancz, 1969)

Not After Midnight, short stories (London: Gollancz, 1971)

Rule Britannia, novel (London: Gollancz, 1972)

Golden Lads: Anthony Bacon, Francis and Their Friends, biography (London: Gollancz, 1975)

The Winding Stair: Francis Bacon, His Rise and Fall, biography (London: Gollancz, 1976)

Echoes from the Macabre, short stories (London: Gollancz, 1976)

Growing Pains: The Shaping of a Writer, nonfiction (London: Gollancz, 1977)

The Rendezvous and Other Stories, short stories (London: Gollancz, 1980)

The Rebecca Notebook and Other Memories, nonfiction (London: Gollancz, 1981)

Classics from the Macabre, short stories (London: Gollancz, 1987)

The Doll, short stories (London: Virago Press, 2011)

FRENCH FAMILY TREE

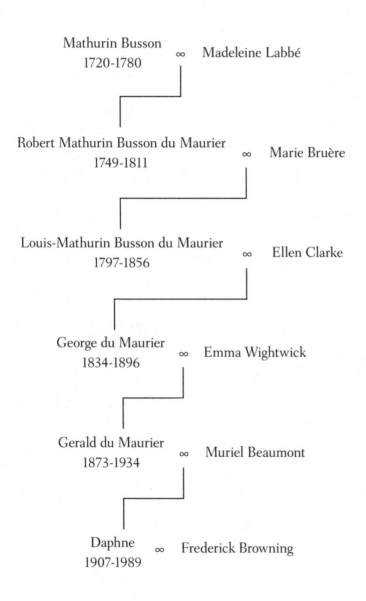

Mathurin Busson
1720-1780 ∞ Madeleine Labbé

Robert Mathurin Busson du Maurier
1749-1811 ∞ Marie Bruère

Louis-Mathurin Busson du Maurier
1797-1856 ∞ Ellen Clarke

George du Maurier
1834-1896 ∞ Emma Wightwick

Gerald du Maurier
1873-1934 ∞ Muriel Beaumont

Daphne ∞ Frederick Browning
1907-1989

FOWEY

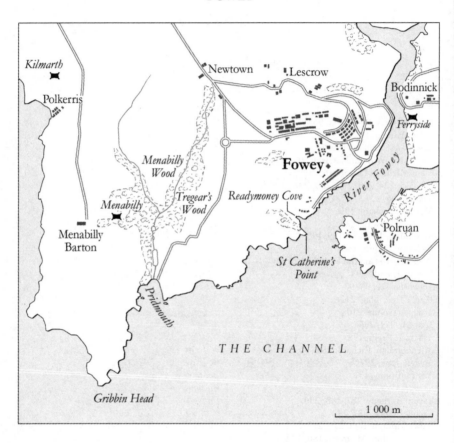

Kilmarth

Polkerris

Newtown

Lescrow

Bodinnick

Ferryside

Menabilly
Wood

Fowey

Tregear's
Wood

Readymoney Cove

River Fowey

Menabilly

Polruan

Menabilly
Barton

St Catherine's
Point

Pridmouth

THE CHANNEL

Gribbin Head

1 000 m

INDEX